Lecture Notes in Information Systems and Organisation

Volume 30

Lecture Notes in Information Systems and Organization—LNISO—is a series of scientific books that explore the current scenario of information systems, in particular IS and organization. The focus on the relationship between IT, IS and organization is the common thread of this collection, which aspires to provide scholars across the world with a point of reference and comparison in the study and research of information systems and organization. LNISO is the publication forum for the community of scholars investigating behavioral and design aspects of IS and organization. The series offers an integrated publication platform for high-quality conferences, symposia and workshops in this field. Materials are published upon a strictly controlled double blind peer review evaluation made by selected reviewers. LNISO is abstracted/indexed in Scopus

More information about this series at http://www.springer.com/series/11237

Youcef Baghdadi · Antoine Harfouche
Editors

ICT for a Better Life and a Better World

The Impact of Information
and Communication Technologies
on Organizations and Society

 Springer

Editors
Youcef Baghdadi
Department of Computer Science
Sultan Qaboos University
Muscat, Oman

Antoine Harfouche
Business Department
Paris Nanterre University
Nanterre, France

ISSN 2195-4968   ISSN 2195-4976   (electronic)
Lecture Notes in Information Systems and Organisation
ISBN 978-3-030-10736-9   ISBN 978-3-030-10737-6   (eBook)
https://doi.org/10.1007/978-3-030-10737-6

Library of Congress Control Number: 2018965456

This Springer imprint is published by the registered company Springer Nature Switzerland AG
The registered company address is: Gewerbestrasse 11, 6330 Cham, Switzerland

Preface

The third ICTO conference (ICTO2017) took place in Paris on March 16th and 17th, 2017. Like the previous editions (ICTO2016 and ICTO2015), this edition focused on the impact of Information and Communication Technologies (ICTs) on organizations and society, specifically how can such technologies improve our life and our world to make them better.

This conference was concerned with these technologies, shedding light on how they were, how they are, and how they will be understood, adopted, adapted, and used within organizations and more generally, within the society as a whole.

The main concerns were how actors understand the potential of ICTs to support organizational activities and hence how they adopt and adapt these technologies to achieve their goals.

The conference called for papers in different areas of the organization's strategy through new business models, competitive strategies, knowledge management, etc. Specific areas dealt with are newer technologies for a better life, innovation for e-government, and technologies enhancing enterprise modeling. These issues can be addressed both in private and public sector either at national or international level, mainly through technology innovations. The conference was also concentered on how an organization impacts society through sustainable development and social responsibility, and how ICTs use social media networks in the process of value co-creation.

The conference invited submissions in all areas of ICTs and organizations especially innovative, interesting and rigorously developed conceptual and empirical contributions, and also encouraged multi- or interdisciplinary research.

The conference received 86 submissions in all areas of ICTs and information systems and accepted 60 papers from 20 countries: France, Italy, UK, Canada, USA, Austria, Japan, Greece, Slovakia, Singapore, Malaysia, Algeria, Morocco, Tunisia, Lebanon, Oman, United Arab Emirates, Saudi Arabia, Cameroon, and Nigeria.

Several innovative and rigorously developed contributions raised interesting debates at the conference.

This book includes 26 chapters that have been selected through a double-blind review process, as the best and most interesting ICTO2017 submissions.

The 26 chapters have been clustered around three parts: (1) Newer Technologies for Better Life and World, (2) Innovation for e-Government, and (3) Technologies Influencing Enterprise Modeling.

Newer Technologies for Better Life and World: In this part, nine chapters show how newer technologies improve the life of the individuals, organizations, and societies.

1. Chapter "The Power of Web 2.0 Storytelling to Overcome Knowledge Sharing Barriers" by C. Meret, M. Iannotta, and M. Gatti seeks to explore the importance of Web 2.0 storytelling for overcoming barriers to knowledge sharing.
2. Chapter "A Pervasive IoT Scheme to Vehicle Overspeed Detection and Reporting Using MQTT Protocol" by E. Nasr, E. Kfoury, and D. Khoury conveys an innovative, pervasive, effective, and adaptable IoT system to detect and report vehicle overspeed as well as issuing tickets and fines.
3. Chapter "Building Inclusive Digital Societies Through the Use of Open Source Technologies" by P. Turkama contributes to the adaptation of open-source technologies through a study that shows the needs of industry to evolve toward increased customer orientation.
4. Chapter "ICT in a Collaborative Network to Improve Quality of Life: A Case of Fruit and Vegetables Re-use" by S. Bonomi, F. Ricciardi, and C. Rossignoli highlights how ICT plays a pivotal role in enabling the growth of new organizational forms, which creates value at the territorial level, triggers positive changes in social and economic environment, and improves the quality of life of people involved.
5. Chapter "Identifying Disguised Objectives of IT Deployment Through Action Research" by P. B. Saba, M. Saba, and A. Harfouche delivers the results of a 4-year action research project conducted at a leading French federation of agriculture cooperatives. The study reveals that identifying contagion mechanisms at the very preliminary phases of implementation may be strategic for a successful IT deployment, despite the tool's imperfections.
6. Chapter "Using QFD Method for Assessing Higher Education Programs: An Examination of Key Stakeholders' Visions" by N. Raissi identifies which indicators are more suitable to measure professional skills and ensure training conform to employer's requirements. The performed study in this chapter relied on the reflective evaluation of education quality in universities by employers, students, and graduates with professional experience by applying the technique of quality function deployment (QFD).
7. Chapter "The Effect of ICT Usage on Employees' Satisfaction: A Job Characteristics Perspective" by T. Torre and D. Sarti investigates employees' job satisfaction, examining the relationship with 33 job-related variables and considering the impact of the use of Information and Communication

Technologies (ICTs) at work. The study performed in this chapter finds that ICT usage plays a controversial role.

8. Chapter "Artificial Intelligence a Disruptive Innovation in Higher Education Accreditation Programs: Expert Systems and AACSB" by C. Chedrawi and P. Howayeck proposes a model for the implementation of AI through expert systems (ES) within the AACSB accreditation programs. The chapter tried to answer two main questions: whether AI can be implemented through ES and how such systems can reshape the AACSB accreditation process. It concludes that in fact, ES will reshape such process while ensuring more reliable and efficient results and reducing time, cost, and errors.

9. Chapter "Interactive Scheduling Decision Support System a Case Study for Fertilizer Production on Supply Chain" by A. Azzamouri, I. Essaadi, S. Elfirdoussi, and V. Giard presents an architecture of an interactive scheduling decision support system (ISDSS), allowing users to find the optimal solution for fertilizer production on parallel heterogeneous processors. The approach proposed in this chapter takes into account different production process constraints such as launch time, delivery date, preventive maintenance, and the impact of scheduling on supply chain management.

Innovation for e-Government: In this part, nine chapters address some key challenges in e-government, specifically in developing countries.

10. Chapter "The E-Banking and the Adoption of Innovations from the Perspective of the Transactions Cost Theory: Case of the Largest Commercial Banks in Lebanon" by C. Chedrawi, B. Harb, and M. Saleh studies the effects of the adoption of innovations on transactions costs and shows the key role played by ICT in organizations, especially at the cost level. Using a qualitative approach, the study reveals the complexity of this concept, particularly regarding the integration strategies of the latest technological innovations within the banking sector, which appear to be essential for the development and the continuity of the sector at the national and regional levels.

11. Chapter "Economic Effect by Open Data in Local Government of Japan" by T. Noda, A. Yoshida, and M. Honda aims at establishing a point of view and methods for the estimation of the economic effect through the utilization of open data. The authors conducted a questionnaire survey on local governments in Japan. The result of the survey shows that open data in local governments in Japan is still in an earlier stage and it should be difficult to produce the economic effect within the area. But, it also shows the possibility of estimating the economic effect of the utilization of open data quantitatively.

12. Chapter "Innovation, New Public Management and Digital Era Government, Towards a Better Public Sector Performance Through ICT: The Case of the Lebanese Ministry of Environment" by N. M. Boustani and C. Chedrawi examines the existing literature and theory regarding innovation while focusing on the new public management, the new era government, ICT, and innovation theories. Using a qualitative approach, this chapter reveals the actions currently

undertaken by the Lebanese government to innovate in public services using ICT that can set the scene for a better public sector performance.

13. Chapter "Choosing Valuation Models in the UAE" by K. Aljifri and H. I. Ahmad aims to empirically examine the valuation models used by UAE investment analysts. A questionnaire and interviews were used to answer the research questions. Thirty-five investment analysts answered the questionnaire. The results reveal that discounted cash flow and P/E ratios are the most preferred valuation methods used by these analysts.

14. Chapter "Empowering Farmers in India Through E-Government Services" by J. Nair and B. N. Balaji Singh adopts a case-study research methodology to analyze consumer considerations through a process workflow model in an e-government program, initiated for farmers through an agricultural extension center. The study is conducted in Karnataka, a southern state in India. The study proposes an enhanced ICT-based process workflow model at Raitha Samparka Kendras (RSK).

15. Chapter "E-Society Realities in Sub-Saharan Africa: The Case of Cote d'Ivoire" by Z. R. Ahouman and Z. Rongting studies the formation of the e-society in sub-Saharan Africa by querying some scientific publications or other qualitative data to see, as most of the illiterate and poor citizens are concentrated in this area. The study revealed two modes under which the e-society operates, namely: government-type organizations (e-government, e-commerce, e-education, e-health, and e-agriculture) and private-type organizations (private communities or platforms, working groups and academics exchanges, and social networks).

16. Chapter "Disclosure and Communication of the Corporate Social Responsibility (CSR) in Morocco: The Case of a Bank" by W. Tahri and A. El Khamlichi aims at clarifying the CSR concept, its practices along with their evolution in time in the Moroccan context. The objective of this study is the evaluation of the bank's engagement in the sustainable development in reference to the seven principles of ISO 26000. The methodology consists of a thematic analysis using Nvivo and annual reports of a Moroccan bank during the period of 2007–2015.

17. Chapter "Does Persuasive E-commerce Website Influence Users' Acceptance and Online Buying Behaviour? The Findings of the Largest E-commerce Website in Malaysia" by N. A. Abdul Hamid, C. H. Cheun, N. H. Abdullah, M. F. Ahmad and Y. Ngadiman discusses the assessment of persuasive design to one of the famous e-commerce Web site in Malaysia. The assessment is adapted from original persuasive system design (PSD) model in combination with the technology acceptance model for the user acceptance and Web site usage level.

18. Chapter "Exploring Factors Affecting the Adoption of HRIS in SMEs in a Developing Country: Evidence from Cameroon" by A. Noutsa Fobang, S. Fosso Wamba and J. R. Kala Kamdjoug integrates the unified theory of acceptance and use of technology (UTAUT) model. The authors have collected the primary data through a survey by administrating structured questionnaire to the employees (HR department) of a number of organizations. They found that

performance expectancy and internal social influence have a significant effect on the intention to adopt HRIS.

Technologies Influencing Enterprise Modeling: In this part, eight chapters address issues such as how newer technologies affect enterprise modeling.

19. Chapter "Big Data at the Service of Universities: Towards a Change in the Organizational Structure and the Decision-Making Processes" by D. Sidani and M. Sayegh shows, through a qualitative study conducted in six universities, how the adoption of big data will transform the organizational structure and the decision-making processes within the universities of Lebanon.

20. Chapter "Online Consumer Reviews in the Hotel Sector: Why and How to Answer?" by T. Pekarskaia Dauxert aims to analyze the practices of the online review management by hotels. The results show differences existing in the online review responding practices: from a simple monitoring without response to a regular policy of response to all reviews.

21. Chapter "Evaluating the Performance of IT Governance in Service-Oriented Enterprises" by M. Alaeddini and S. A. Hashemi focuses on the necessary reforms in the traditional IT governance methods in a service-oriented enterprise to propose an evaluation framework for assessing IT governance in such service-oriented enterprises.

22. Chapter "New Market Creation for Technological Breakthroughs: Commercial Drones and the Disruption of the Emergency Market" by F. Carli, M. E. Manzotti, and H. Savoini provides an in-depth picture of commercial drones as a breakthrough innovation and to gather whether they are to disrupt the emergency market among the several new applications currently being incepted for their technology.

23. Chapter "Enterprise Architecture: A Pillar in an Integrated Framework to Measure the Internal Control Effectiveness in the Oil & Gas Sector" by M. Akoum and V. Blum proposes to use the methods put forward by this practice to gain operational insight into the oil and gas industry. The authors used the Zachman Framework as one of the four pillars of an integrated framework to measure the internal control effectiveness of petroleum companies. Following the evidence-based management (EBM) methodology, they created a new tool by applying the methodical thinking of EA on COSO's internal control framework. The outcome is an integrated framework named Internal Control Effectiveness Measurement Framework (ICEMF).

24. Chapter "Ontology for Enterprise Interactions: Extended and Virtual Enterprises" by F. Al Hadidi and Y. Baghdadi proposes an ontology to share a common understanding of two types of enterprise collaborations. The proposed ontology is meant to share the semantics of the two types of collaborations, in order to rationally decide their implementing technologies.

25. Chapter "Technological Innovation: The Pathway to Entrepreneurs' Economic Advancement" by W. Palmer explores the meaning of human experiences relating to entrepreneurs in New York City who have not adopted the adequate

innovative technology. The research was based on Kaplan and Warren's entrepreneurship management theory.

26. Chapter "How Communities Affect the Technology Acceptance Model in the Retail Sector" by D. Pederzoli analyzes how groups of consumers create value during the shopping process and help one other to manage relations with technologies and overcome the perceived threats of the shopping and user experience.

Muscat, Oman   Youcef Baghdadi
Nanterre, France   Antoine Harfouche
September 2018

Acknowledgements

We would like to express our gratitude to the president of Paris Nanterre University for hosting ICTO2017 and allowing us to use the facilities of the university.

ICTO 2017 would never have seen the day and gather this quality researcher without the huge efforts of the tireless and extremely patient Prof. Antoine Harfouche, the general organization chair, to whom we extend here our warm thanks.

We extend our gratitude to Prof. Teresina Torre, Università di Genova, Italy, Prof. Béatrioce Bellini, Paris Nanterre University, France, and Prof. Mokhtar Amami, Royal Military College of Canada, the Conference Co-Chairs, and the ICTO2017 keynote speakers: Prof. Georges Aoun, Prof. Karl S. Koong, Prof. Antoine L. Harfouche, Prof. Paolo Spagnoletti, and Prof. Maurizio Cavallari.

A special thanks to Prof. Marco De Marco, who received the ICTO Golden Medal for his lifetime achievement during the ICTO2015 conference.

Last but not least, we want to thank the 144 members of the scientific committee and reviewers who generously gave of their time and knowledge, especially: Abbas Tarhini, Abdallah Nassereddine, Adriana Schiopoiu Burlea, Ahmed Ahmedin, Alberto Romolini, Alice Robbin, Amal Dabbous, Amevi Acakpovi, Angelika Kokkinaki, Anne-Céline Ginoux, Antonio Daood, Balasaraswathi Ranganathan, Batoul Khalifa, Bellini Béatrice, Bernard Quinio, Bessem Boubaker, Busisiwe Alant, Cândida Silva, Cecilia Rossignoli, Charbel Chedrawy, Daniele Pederzoli, Daria Plotkina, Dina Sidani, Elie Nasr, Emna Gana-Oueslati, Francesca Ricciardi, Francesco Bellini, Georges Aoun, Hafiz Imtiaz Ahmad, Hamzah Elrehail, Houda Guermazi, Imed Ben Nasr, Imene Belboula, Jamil Arida, Jessy Nair, Kalinka Kaloyanova, Karina Sokolova, Karine Aoun, Kamel Merdaoui, Kenneth Deans, Kwame Simpe Ofori, Laurice Alexandre, Lhoussaine Ouabouch, Luís Alves, Łukasz Tomczyk, Manal Abdel Samad, Manel Hamouda, May Sayegh, Michael Dzigbordi Dzandu, Milan Kubiatko, Mokrane Ali, Moufida Sadok, Mustafa Coşkun, Nabil Georges Badr, Nada Mallah Boustani, Nadia Tebourbi, Nadine Dubruc, Nasri Messarra, Nikos Vasilakis, Nizar Raissi, Nor Hazana Abdullah,

Osama Isaac, Patrignani Norberto, Pauline de Pechpeyrou, Rina Tsio, Roeland Aernoudts, Roope Jaakonmäki, Sana Rouis, Sarah Mokaddem, Sarah Richard, Maria Menshikova, Shabina Shaikh, Slim Turki, Soraya Ezzeddine, Syed Mohsin Saif, Tariq Shahzad, Tatiana Dauxert, Teresina Torre, Thierry Delecolle, Verica Milutinović, Véronique Blum, Wael Jabr, Walid Abou-Khalil, Yasir Hamid, and Youcef Baghdadi.

Muscat, Oman   Youcef Baghdadi
Nanterre, France   Antoine Harfouche
September 2018

Contents

Part I   Newer Technologies for Better Life and World

**The Power of Web 2.0 Storytelling to Overcome Knowledge
Sharing Barriers** 3
Chiara Meret, Michela Iannotta and Mauro Gatti

**A Pervasive IoT Scheme to Vehicle Overspeed Detection
and Reporting Using MQTT Protocol** 19
Elie Nasr, Elie Kfoury and David Khoury

**Building Inclusive Digital Societies Through the Use of Open
Source Technologies** 35
Petra Turkama

**ICT in a Collaborative Network to Improve Quality of Life:
A Case of Fruit and Vegetables Re-use** 51
Sabrina Bonomi, Francesca Ricciardi and Cecilia Rossignoli

**Identifying Disguised Objectives of IT Deployment Through
Action Research** 69
Peter Bou Saba, Mario Saba and Antoine Harfouche

**Using QFD Method for Assessing Higher Education Programs:
An Examination of Key Stakeholders' Visions** 83
Nizar Raissi

**The Effect of ICT Usage on Employees' Satisfaction:
A Job Characteristics Perspective** 99
Teresina Torre and Daria Sarti

**Artificial Intelligence a Disruptive Innovation in Higher Education
Accreditation Programs: Expert Systems and AACSB** 115
Charbel Chedrawi and Pierrette Howayeck

**Interactive Scheduling Decision Support System a Case Study
for Fertilizer Production on Supply Chain** 131
Ahlam Azzamouri, Imane Essaadi, Selwa Elfirdoussi and Vincent Giard

Part II Innovation for e-Government

**The E-Banking and the Adoption of Innovations from the Perspective
of the Transactions Cost Theory: Case of the Largest Commercial
Banks in Lebanon** 149
Charbel Chedrawi, Bissane Harb and Mariam Saleh

Economic Effect by Open Data in Local Government of Japan 165
Tetsuo Noda, Akio Yoshida and Masami Honda

**Innovation, New Public Management and Digital Era Government,
Towards a Better Public Sector Performance Through ICT:
The Case of the Lebanese Ministry of Environment** 175
Nada Mallah Boustani and Charbel Chedrawi

Choosing Valuation Models in the UAE 191
Khaled Aljifri and Hafiz Imtiaz Ahmad

Empowering Farmers in India Through E-Government Services 205
J. Nair and B. N. Balaji Singh

**E-Society Realities in Sub-Saharan Africa: The Case
of Cote d'Ivoire** 221
Z. R. Ahouman and Z. Rongting

**Disclosure and Communication of the Corporate Social
Responsibility (CSR) in Morocco: The Case of a Bank** 247
Wadi Tahri and Abdelbari El Khamlichi

**Does Persuasive E-commerce Website Influence Users' Acceptance
and Online Buying Behaviour? The Findings of the Largest
E-commerce Website in Malaysia** 263
N. A. Abdul Hamid, C. H. Cheun, N. H. Abdullah, M. F. Ahmad
and Y. Ngadiman

**Exploring Factors Affecting the Adoption of HRIS in SMEs
in a Developing Country: Evidence from Cameroon** 281
A. Noutsa Fobang, S. Fosso Wamba and J. R. Kala Kamdjoug

Part III   Technologies Influencing Enterprise Modeling

Big Data at the Service of Universities: Towards a Change in the Organizational Structure and the Decision-Making Processes 299
Dina Sidani and May Sayegh

Online Consumer Reviews in the Hotel Sector: Why and How to Answer? 313
T. Pekarskaia Dauxert

Evaluating the Performance of IT Governance in Service-Oriented Enterprises 323
Morteza Alaeddini and Seyed Alireza Hashemi

New Market Creation for Technological Breakthroughs: Commercial Drones and the Disruption of the Emergency Market 335
Federico Carli, Maria Elena Manzotti and Hugo Savoini

Enterprise Architecture: A Pillar in an Integrated Framework to Measure the Internal Control Effectiveness in the Oil & Gas Sector 347
Mohamed Akoum and Véronique Blum

Ontology for Enterprise Interactions: Extended and Virtual Enterprises 365
F. Al Hadidi and Y. Baghdadi

Technological Innovation: The Pathway to Entrepreneurs' Economic Advancement 381
Wesley Palmer

How Communities Affect the Technology Acceptance Model in the Retail Sector 395
Daniele Pederzoli

Part I
Newer Technologies for Better Life and World

The Power of Web 2.0 Storytelling to Overcome Knowledge Sharing Barriers

Chiara Meret, Michela Iannotta and Mauro Gatti

Abstract Through a narrative review of the literature, this paper seeks to explore the importance of Web 2.0 Storytelling for overcoming barriers to knowledge sharing. While storytelling has been traditionally addressed as a valuable lever for many knowledge sharing issues, recently Web 2.0 technologies are becoming essential in enabling employees to participate in knowledge creation and sharing. However, the link between Web 2.0 Storytelling and barriers to knowledge sharing behavior remains quite unexplored in the extant literature. By filling this gap, we pose the first pillars to explain this connection. Overall, our conceptual framework reveals that, since knowledge resides in people, the extensive use of ICT tools may be not sufficient to capture the organizational advantages of sharing, if the human dimension is neglected. The twofold nature of Web 2.0 storytelling emerges as a powerful tool to manage the most important barriers to knowledge sharing. Such evidence may have meaningful implications.

Keywords Knowledge sharing · Web 2.0 Storytelling · Knowledge sharing barriers

1 Introduction

Knowledge Management is entering an era in which it is expected that everyone, starting from employees, is able and has the desire to significantly contribute to the creation and management of knowledge. Companies have to manage critical

C. Meret (✉) · M. Iannotta · M. Gatti
Department of Management, Sapienza University of Rome,
Via del Castro Laurenziano 9, 00161 Rome, Italy
e-mail: chiara.meret@uniroma1.it

M. Iannotta
e-mail: michela.iannotta@uniroma1.it

M. Gatti
e-mail: mauro.gatti@uniroma1.it

© Springer Nature Switzerland AG 2019
Y. Baghdadi and A. Harfouche (eds.), *ICT for a Better Life and a Better World*,
Lecture Notes in Information Systems and Organisation 30,
https://doi.org/10.1007/978-3-030-10737-6_1

knowledge (both tacit and explicit) promoting the involvement and collaboration of staff at all levels. This is made possible by a new way of thinking the Knowledge Management, which is essentially based on a fundamental innovation: the so-called Web 2.0 [1]. Technological developments and internationalization have made virtual communication a central part of everyday life. Social networking tools are essential in making easier for employees to participate in the creation, sharing and diffusion of knowledge. This system encourages continuous learning and facilitates the processes for the movement of organizational knowledge, by building a network of relationships.

Despite the significant contribution of Web 2.0 technologies, a number of barriers to knowledge sharing still hinder the flow of knowledge among people, including colleagues. This is mainly due to the fact that individuals bring their own principles, beliefs, values and habits into their workplace and Knowledge Management cannot prevail over the related criticalities without implementing solutions to overcome behavior-related barriers. Indeed, the effectiveness of sharing behaviors depends on multiple dimensions at individual, organizational and technological level [2]. According to Sparrow [3], making knowledge visible so that it can be better accessed, discussed, valued or generally managed is a hard work.

In line with these considerations, the narrative dimension has to be considered as a strategic variable in order to manage a context-specific knowledge complexity [4–6]. With this in mind, organizational storytelling means the strategic use of storytelling through which companies are able to translate into words, sounds, images and/or video events that can affect people, the way they work, social relationships and the organization itself [6–8]. Nowadays, Digital Storytelling has raised its potential, by digital technology standards, as an instrument for reflection, empowerment and learning. It relies on digital stories, based on multimedia features such as images, video, text and audio [9]. Conceived as a dynamic improvement of Digital Storytelling, Web 2.0 Storytelling is particularly said to produce a network of connections via social networking, blogging, and other platforms, transcending the traditional linear flow of Digital Storytelling. This new environment for storytelling offers both readers' and co-writers' points of entry, which enhance distributed discussion, based on the user-generated content: each reader has the possibility to directly add contents in the story platform by editing a wiki page, commenting on the post, and so on [9].

This state of the art suggests that Web 2.0 Storytelling may represent a powerful tool to manage the barriers that constrain knowledge sharing. Interestingly, it combines the ability of new technologies to open multiple forms of communication with the power of stories to elicit emotional connections, shared values and trust in organizational environments. From a theoretical perspective, this means that there is a chance to overcome the recurring debate about whether "sharing practices should be people-driven or technology-driven" [2: 20]. Despite the importance of these arguments for the managerial audience, the relationship between Web 2.0 Storytelling and knowledge sharing barriers represents a missing link in the extant research and it still requires a deepened investigation. Consequently, two substantive research questions arise: (1) Why and How Web 2.0 Storytelling can contribute to overcome the most common barriers to knowledge sharing? (2) In doing so, can it be considered an alternative route to the trade-off between people and technology in knowledge sharing research? In order explore these issues, we present a narrative review of the literature aimed at explaining how Web 2.0 Storytelling acts as an antidote to common syndromes related to non-sharing behaviors. The resulting conceptual framework is discussed by highlighting the complementarity, rather than the trade-off, between the human and technological dimensions of knowledge sharing. Overall, this can be considered the first step for further inquiries in this field.

The paper is structured as follows: the next section describes the research approach we adopted to address our research inquiry. The third section presents an in-depth description of the main topics we derived from a first-step analysis of the literature. The fourth section explains the powerful role of Web 2.0 Storytelling to overcome the previously identified barriers to knowledge sharing. Conclusions, limitations and further insights are presented in the final section.

2 Research Approach

With the aim of better understanding how Web 2.0 Storytelling can contribute to overcome the main barriers to knowledge sharing, this paper adopts a qualitative approach by presenting a narrative review of the literature. This research strategy is particularly suitable when emergent issues are explored, because it allows for taking account of both practitioner and scientific articles. In this way, the review is not limited to, albeit it is mainly focused on, academic literature, but it aims to capture some insights deriving from professional and managerial writing, as well.

First, we collected several contributions directly and indirectly linked to the role that Web 2.0 Storytelling may have in overcoming knowledge sharing barriers. In detail, the process of reviewing was conducted by combining three main fields of the literature: Knowledge Management, Information Technology (IT), and Storytelling literature. Afterwards, the three authors were assigned to select and analyse a number of papers related to each of these mainstreams. The underlying selection criterion of the articles was the focus on knowledge sharing. Therefore, both abstracts and keywords of papers were checked to this scope. In order to identify recurring themes, this analysis was performed separately by the three authors, who summarized the main contents within a standardized format.

Through this first-step analysis, we derived four main topics fitting our purpose: (1) a clear relationship between the use of Web 2.0 technologies and knowledge sharing; (2) a clear influence of storytelling tools on knowledge sharing behaviors; (3) the existence of four main barriers to knowledge sharing; and (4) a recent trend in the application of ICT tools in storytelling initiatives. The next section is dedicated to discussing these subjects.

Finally, these emergent themes were jointly discussed by the authors with the aim of explaining the role of Web 2.0 Storytelling for overcoming each of the identified barriers to knowledge sharing. The resulting conceptual framework is presented in the fourth section.

3 Literature Review

3.1 Knowledge Sharing

Because of the amount of potential benefits of knowledge sharing, many organizations have invested considerable money into Knowledge Management initiatives and systems in order to enhance motivation to knowledge sharing. As suggested by Reid [10], it creates opportunities to maximize the ability for organizations to produce solutions and efficiencies that generate competitive advantage.

Finding the effective ways, conditions and incentives for sharing has been one of the major issues of organizations and Knowledge Management research [11, 12]. Due to the latest technology, organizations are able to collect, store and share both internal and external knowledge [13]. According to Berggren et al. [14], we can distinguish between knowledge sharing and knowledge transfer, since the former can be defined as a multidirectional flow between two or more units. In literature, the social exchange theory [15] emphasizes this interpersonal reciprocity. Consequently, technology can only be treated as a knowledge management instrument to connect people.

Moreover, knowledge sharing within organizations depends on the nature of the knowledge being shared. When considering the difference between tacit and explicit knowledge, the process of sharing differs significantly, because tacit knowledge is the unarticulated part of knowledge residing in individual's mind [16, 17]. In this way, extant literature mostly considered the sharing process a difficult task which mainly involves only people-to-people interactions. Differently, explicit knowledge sharing has been associated to the use of ICT tools, such as Data Warehouses, repositories, Lotus Notes, telecommunications networks and Intranets, with the advantages of time-saving and overcoming geographical boundaries [18]. However, Davenport and Prusak [18] also understate the role of technology without central human support. In fact, the knowledge sharing process within organizations occurs both through formal and informal ways. Formal ways are more linked to explicit knowledge and can include the routines and practices to archive knowledge in databases, as well as conferences, seminars, brochures, guidelines and training programs [13, 18]. Informal ways of sharing knowledge can be coffee breaks during conferences or seminars, "coffee corners" volunteer interchanges [18]. From an individual perspective, Bartol and Srivastava [19] offer four major approaches for sharing knowledge in organizations: (1) contribution of knowledge to organizational databases; (2) sharing knowledge through formal interactions between groups or across teams; (3) sharing knowledge through informal interactions among individuals; (4) and sharing knowledge within voluntary forums and/or CoPs of employees around topics of interest. In addition to the more traditional tools, organizations face the latest internal social media platforms technology or Enterprise Social Networks (ESN).

Finally, according to Connelly and Kelloway [20] and Lin and Lee [21], organizations can successfully promote a knowledge sharing culture not only by directly incorporating knowledge in their business strategy, but also by looking at (and influencing) employee attitudes and behaviors to promote consistent knowledge sharing. In fact, knowledge sharing is very often conditioned by some barriers that depend on individuals themselves.

3.2 Barriers to Knowledge Sharing

Organizations can face different barriers to knowledge sharing, including the possibilities that employees are not willing to share information, in order to protect their jobs, or when they hesitate to contribute and share their knowledge because of lack of trust or fear of criticism [1, 12, 17, 22, 23]. Accordingly, barriers to knowledge sharing can be addressed to multiple causes, such as organizational knowledge management system, organizational culture, organizational technological attributes, and so on. An exhaustive list of barriers is proposed in Riege's work [2], where they are classified into three clusters, often closely intertwined: individual, organizational, and technological barriers. Among the others, the presence of fear, the lack of contact time, interaction and social networks, the low awareness of the value of possessed knowledge to others, and the lack of trust, represent the most common barriers at individual level. From an organizational point of view, the abovementioned author underlines the shortage of formal and informal spaces to share and reflect, the role corporate culture, the presence of hierarchical structures and inappropriate physical work environment as some of the barriers that most hinder the sharing of knowledge. Finally, Riege [2] questions the role of technology as facilitator in knowledge sharing processes, by highlighting the importance to implement technologies fitting both individual and organizational needs.

An interesting key to interpret the main knowledge sharing barriers is offered by Collison [24], when he examines "syndromes" of non-sharing behaviours, namely: (1) the Tall Poppy syndrome; (2) the Shrinking Violet syndrome; (3) the On the Web syndrome; and (4) the Communities of Practically Everything syndrome. We will briefly explain each of them.

The Tall Poppy syndrome consists in a condition where individuals are afraid to share good practices for fear of being judged by their peers quickly: fear of judgment and criticism of others holds them. The Shrinking Violet syndrome regards the thought of not having anything actually interesting to say. According to Collison [24: 16], it's often the business units who live with a sense of isolation that develop innovative practices that should be shared more widely. This isolation may be cultural—a new acquisition perhaps, or geographical—particularly business units in antisocial time zones. The On the Web syndrome is the extreme vision of elimination of face-to-face conversation with the consolidation of a thrust coding phenomenon, which does not allow for identifying the author who shares knowledge. In line with these reflections, Collison [24: 17] refers to Mehrabian's work [25], when he outlines that "in any communication, roughly 7% percent of the message is in the words, 38% is in the tone of the voice and the remaining 55% of the message is communicated in body language. If this suggestion bears out, then we lose 93% of the message—the context—when we reduce it from someone telling a story to a simple textual document". Accordingly, old and simple ICT tools within organizations are now insufficient to reclaim the missing 93%. Lastly, the Communities of Practically Everything syndrome is linked to the extensive use of CoPs to answer to every problem the organization faces, when participants are not effectively aware of the reasons they need to use them and whether they are relevant to the business or not. CoPs are incorrectly perceived as a panacea and they are left untended until they stop enabling the flow of learning and knowledge and start becoming a liability.

3.3   Storytelling for Knowledge Sharing

Simultaneously, Knowledge Management is becoming more and more collaborative, since it is expected that everyone, starting from employees, is able and has the desire to significantly contribute to the creation and management of knowledge. In order to understand this organizational phenomenon, the narrative dimension becomes a strategic variable [4–6].

In line with these considerations, storytelling is emerging as an effective tool for enhancing and consolidating knowledge [26, 27]. Under an organizational profile, storytelling means the strategic use of stories through which people inside and outside the organization can translate into words, sounds and images, affecting events [7, 28]. In fact, storytelling can be used to describe complex issues, explain events, interpret changes, present different perspectives, communicate experiences and, as a result, make connections [27].

Different research suggest that the use of narrative methods in sharing experiences is effective for building trust, transferring tacit knowledge, facilitating and generating emotional connections [26, 27], enabling people to listen to others' approaches to problems [4, 27]. In addition, Organizational Neuroscience confirms that communicating information using narrative makes an emotional connection by those who listen, watch, or read, much easier [29–31].

According to the literature, Klitmøller and Lauring [32] outline main difficulties in managing effective communication, in relation to knowledge sharing, within virtual teams, due to lack of channel richness and to possible delayed feedback in some communication technologies. At the same time, Hayward [33] underlines the potentiality of "rich media" in overcoming criticalities linked to differences between verbal and non-verbal signs of support or disagreement with a speaker's message [32]. These elements drive to a change in the stories themselves. They can now be "open-ended, branching, hyperlinked, cross-media, participatory, exploratory, and unpredictable" [34: 40]. The oldest powerful and effective digital collaboration tools are Wikis, which first appeared in the mid-1990s as Web pages that users can edit directly in the browser with the possibility to collaborate on stories through wikis as a form of document hosting. This process can elicit creativity, as well as building relationships.

When we introduce the concept of "rich media" [33], we include visual literacy by adding the power of images to influence others. Images are not only able to communicate information, but also to share moods, persuading audience's emotions.

Starting from the extant literature, we outline the widespread practice of using the two terms of "Digital Storytelling" and "Web 2.0 Storytelling" in an interchangeable and indistinct way. However, we define Digital Storytelling as a narrative made with digital tools with the aim of organizing content selected by the web into a coherent system, governed by a narrative structure, in order to get a story made up of many elements in different formats (video, audio, images, text, maps) [35–37]. According to Alexander and Levine [34], Digital Storytelling is a narrated personal story in which people share way of overcoming obstacles, achieving dreams or describing a critical event. Other authors, such as Cao et al. [35] assume Web2.0 as an application field of Digital Storytelling, understood as way of for creating stories with help of digital media (pictures, video or text), where more than a person is involved in the creation process of the story. Against this linear meaning, Alexander and Levine [34] underline the difference between Digital Storytelling and Web 2.0, considering the latter as an evolution of the former. Moreover, with the participatory media afforded through the new Web 2.0 technologies, one's stories can be shared with an audience of thousands [9]. In addition, Macaskill and Owen [38] define Web 2.0 as different web-based platforms in which authors are also users, since they can gain access, contribute, describe, harvest, tag, annotate and bookmark Web mediated contents in various digital formats. Virtual social interactions, shared collaborative and communication tools provided by Social Media, allow people to make use of storytelling with these new generation Web 2.0 technologies [39].

Despite the urgency of considering this issue, only few studies have tried to systematize the existing relationship between Digital Storytelling and knowledge sharing. Most of them have tried to investigate the impact of social media tools to enable tacit knowledge sharing [12, 26, 39–42]. Other recent studies analyse Digital Storytelling, in relation to knowledge sharing behaviour (KSB), compared to the tacit sphere of knowledge. However, we highlight a gap in the literature, both academic and managerial, with reference to the relationship between Web 2.0 Storytelling, as an evolution of Digital Storytelling, and barriers to the sharing of knowledge.

4 The Power of Web 2.0 Storytelling to Overcome Knowledge Sharing Barriers

The analysis of recurring themes in the reviewed topics drove us to the identification of the potentialities of social media tools in encouraging, supporting, and enabling the knowledge sharing behavior among people [9, 12, 43]. On the other hand, the narrative dimension of Web 2.0 Storytelling seems to reinforce the process of knowledge sharing by triggering individual implicit attitudes. This state of affairs suggests that Web 2.0 Storytelling might be a powerful lever to overcome the identified barriers of knowledge sharing. In fact, Web 2.0 technologies substantially contribute to encourage knowledge sharing, at the same time enhancing both tools and channels in which it can flow. Nevertheless, the technological dimension alone is not enough, because knowledge is something that resides in people. If combined with technologies 2.0, the narrative dimension can make a further step in the process of knowledge sharing: it can help to overcome the barriers that may limit the sharing of knowledge, by acting on both implicit and explicit attitudes of people.

The following paragraphs analyze the role of Web 2.0 Storytelling with regard to the most common barriers to knowledge sharing. For the purpose of this study, we make reference to the non-sharing behaviors "syndromes" provided by Collison [24], while highlighting the importance of Web 2.0 Storytelling in terms of "antidotes" to treat them.

4.1 Trust Who Tells You a Story!

According to Collison [24], the "Tall Poppy Syndrome" concerns the fear of judgment and criticism of others that make individuals afraid to share good practices. In other words, employees hesitate to contribute and share their knowledge because of lack of trust, fear of criticism, or of misleading peers, for instance not being sure that their contributions are important, or completely accurate, or relevant to a specific discussion [12, 22]. This kind of fear is also due to the uncertainty about the intent of colleagues or senior management, to the extent that employees perceive sharing knowledge as a potential reduction of their job security [44]. As reported by Riege [24: 24], "lower and middle level employees often hoard their knowledge intentionally, expecting that their supervisors may not promote them if they appeared to be more knowledgeable than them". As a consequence, hierarchy, position-based status and formal power also have a role in constraining the sharing of individual knowledge [24]. To that regard, we propose a first antidote that Web 2.0 storytelling may offer employees for overcome this syndrome.

The use of narrative methods in sharing experiences resulted to be effective for building trust, sharing knowledge, facilitating and generating emotional connections [26]. From such perspective, Web 2.0 Storytelling essentially holds a collaborative nature. When stories flow through Web 2.0 platforms, they have a manifold effect. The use of stories for sharing knowledge within organization both "represents and invites the construction of meaning" [9: 44]. Moreover, a story makes sense according to experiences of the audience. These aspects show how story-telling generates a close interconnection between those who share their knowledge and those who receive it. In addition, stories are more powerful when they evolve from personal experiences and ideas in relation to the context of knowledge sharing [26, 41]. As noted by Dorsey et al. [45], rather than traditional and hierarchical mechanisms, organizations need a new combination of processes to encourage knowledge sharing as a horizontal phenomenon. According to the author, knowledge-based approaches reveal to be unsuccessful without effective collaboration.

At the same time, the Web 2.0 environment reinforces peer-to-peer communication by connecting users to users in an interactive way [40, 46], and it harnesses a collective participation and collaboration of participants in content generation [40, 47]. Through Web 2.0 Storytelling, knowledge sharing becomes the content to be collectively generated. In this process, storytelling contributes to the creation of shared values and trust among employees [48], because trust itself derives from a narrative process [49]. According to Kalid and Mahmood [27], the use of stories to share knowledge allows people to listen to others' approaches to problems and facilitates to build trust, and to generate emotional connections. In addition, Web 2.0 technologies reduce perceived risks, uncertainties, and fear of judgment associated to knowledge sharing [40]. According to some authors, this is due to the presence of swift trust, typical of temporary groups [40, 49, 50]. Therefore, trust allows individuals to justify their decision to contribute [49, 51, 52, 53] and allows individuals to freely exchange information and share knowledge that is critical to the success of collaboration.

4.2 Learn from Those Who Tell a Story!

The second type of barrier is labeled as the "Shrinking Violet Syndrome" [24]. This syndrome regards the condition of people that believe to not having anything really interesting to say; this may be also due to a sense of isolation [24]. However, when knowledge is considered a "public good", knowledge sharing is encouraged by a sort of moral obligation and community interest, rather than by self-interest [54]. Related to this aspect, another barrier that can contribute to this "silent behavior" is the poorness of verbal or written communication skills, as well as interpersonal skills of employees [2, 55]. According to Shirky [43: 48], "our electronic networks are enabling novel forms of collective actions, enabling the creation of collaborative groups that are larger and more distributed than at any other time in history. The scope of work that can be done by non-institutional groups is a profound challenge to the status quo". Recently, O'Dell and Hubert [56] argue that social networking tools are reinvigorating knowledge management, making it easier for employees participating in the creation of knowledge. At the same time, under an organizational profile storytelling is practically used for sharing experiences of corporate life through testimonies offered by the employees in order to spread knowledge, and create and strengthen a common identity and a sense of belonging [6].

Therefore, the second antidote provided by Web 2.0 Storytelling may be the possibility for employees of learning from those who tell a story, thus becoming aware of the importance of their own knowledge to complete that (collective) story. Interestingly, the Web 2.0 environment enables interactive observation of the others: through observing practices, people are encouraged to adopt certain skills and imitate behaviors [40]. Furthermore, the use of pictures, drawings and videos can elicit people discussions and knowledge sharing behaviors [57]. In line with these considerations, Alexander and Levine [34] argue that distributed discussion offers many points of entry, both for readers and for co-writers. In this way, the new environment of Web 2.0 storytelling generates synergistic effect, including conversations that occur across people [34]. In fact, long-term impact of web 2.0 storytelling is inextricably tied to individuals' access to multiple viewers/listeners trough the web [9]. Taken together, these arguments suggest that Web 2.0 Storytelling may significantly reduce the sense of isolation, and let people become aware of their knowledge.

4.3 Restore Emotional Links by Telling a Story!

When speaking about the "On the Web Syndrome", Collison [24] refers to the lack of face-to-face conversations, which results in the inability of identifying the author who shares knowledge. This barrier is sometimes caused by technology itself, and somehow it is related to a broader issue of the role of technology as facilitator in knowledge sharing processes. In fact, academics frequently question whether sharing practices should be "people-driven" or "technology-driven" [2: 20]. This debate often assumes knowledge sharing practices in terms of a trade-off between individuals and technology. However, the recent development of Web 2.0 technologies has contributed to get an alternative route to such perspective.

When referring to Mehrabian's work [25], it has been demonstrated that in any communication, organizations might lose 93% of the message represented by the tone of the voice and the body language. While traditional ICT tools fail to overcome this barrier, Web 2.0 Storytelling seems to be able to overcome it by reclaiming the missing 93% of the message. In fact, the combination of images, voice and videos can stimulate a variety of associations and emotional responses [9]. This is confirmed by organizational neuroscientists, when they observe that narrative communication creates strong emotional connections between those who listen, watch, or read [29–31]. Overall, with Web 2.0 Storytelling tools each contribution is made visible and valuable, and stories are full of voiced and bodily meaning. As a result, Web 2.0 Storytelling contributes to enhance intrinsic motivations to share personal knowledge, by leveraging visual, vocal, and emotional links. Furthermore, the potentiality of Web 2.0 in making a story as a participatory process by directly linking co-authors, allows the activation of virtual social interactions and shared collaborative behaviours [39]. In this way, the hyperlinked and participatory environment of Web 2.0 Storytelling, not only accelerates the flow of knowledge, but also enriches it with new contents, due to the presence of many-to-many conversations.

4.4 Take Part in Telling a Story!

As noted by Collison [24], the "Communities of Practically Everything Syndrome" concerns the extensive use of CoPs as a panacea to every problem the organizations face. According to the author, communities of practice are becoming incorrectly used, thus limiting the flow of knowledge sharing and learning. This means that they are downgraded to mere liabilities. Web 2.0 Storytelling might overturn this path, and re-evaluate them as active assets of the knowledge sharing process. Accordingly, this new environment for storytelling offers both readers' and co-writers' points of entry, which enhance distributed discussion, hyperlinked stories based on the user-generated content, in which each reader has the possibility to directly add contents in the story platform by editing a wiki page, commenting on the post, and so on [9, 34].

In line with Mason and Rannie [58], this shift is made possible by: (1) an active engagement in the construction of users' knowledge, rather than a passive and absorbing behavior; (2) a continuous refresh of users' contents; and (3) a collaborative work. In a synergic perspective, this means that Web 2.0 storytelling allows everyone to take part in telling a story through the complementary power of the abovementioned antidotes. More exhaustively, the re-establishment of trust, awareness and emotions may combine into a more effective sharing behavior, where knowledge is not conceived as an individual property and CoPs are not a mere formal sum of personal knowledge. In this way, employees are more engaged in a real common purpose, which poses the sharing of knowledge neither as a formal task, nor as a compelled expectation, but as a voluntary and emotional process where employees are aware writers and active storytellers of a social tale.

5 Conclusions, Limitations and Future Research

Nowadays, technological developments and internationalization are driving organizations to the strategic use of knowledge as a critical resource of competitive advantage. The raising of new ICT powerful tools to foster a systemic approach to knowledge sharing, combined to new methodological approaches, such as the one we deal with in our paper, open the way to new analytical frontiers of knowledge management and its strategic importance for organizations.

Our research inquiry represents an exploratory effort that has its roots in the broader debate about the trade-off between the importance of individuals and the role of technology in knowledge sharing practices. The intent is to delve into the chance of finding an alternative route to bring together both the human and the technological dimension of knowledge sharing. To that aim, we propose Web 2.0 Storytelling as a valuable tool that fit our purpose. In detail, this study reveals how Web 2.0 Storytelling not only reclaims the human dimension of knowledge sharing, but also takes a part in enhancing both implicit and explicit attitudes of people. Moreover, according to the extant literature and in line with business results, informal ways of communicating between people are considered the most effective instruments to share peer-to-peer knowledge. In this way, Web 2.0 Storytelling represents an antidote to several syndromes of non-sharing behaviors and it may lead to overcome most of the traditional barriers that limit knowledge sharing in organizations.

By posing the first pillars to investigate the role of Web 2.0 Storytelling in Knowledge Management, this work contributes to the existing literature by revealing an interesting new research area. From a theoretical perspective, our analysis combines the technological dimension of Web 2.0 with the narrative dimension of storytelling in order to investigate "complementary" approaches to reduce knowledge sharing barriers. Our conceptual framework suggests that technologies can help to re-establish trust, awareness, emotions, and actual participation in order to support knowledge sharing in organization. This means moving knowledge sharing debates to a synergic, rather than alternative, view of individuals and technology, and focusing on the role that organizations have in better integrating them. Moreover, this work also poses some advances in the field of tacit knowledge sharing. To that regard, tacit knowledge has been traditionally linked to face-to-face interaction, while we stress the people-to-people nature of interaction within Web 2.0 Storytelling environment. Such evidence may have meaningful implications for the enhancement of what Spender [59: 52] defines "collective", or "social tacit knowledge". By allowing everyone to be storytellers, Web 2.0 Storytelling may play a key role in overcoming the individualism of knowledge holders and making them as part of a wider social, collective, and shared story.

From a managerial perspective, we offer some insights with reference to the new available tools for Knowledge Management. In fact, since knowledge is something that resides in people, the extensive use of ICT tools may be not sufficient to capture the organizational advantages of knowledge sharing, if the human dimension is neglected. Accordingly, Web 2.0 Storytelling is said to produce this network of both human and technological connections via social networking, blogging, and other platforms.

Considering the explorative nature of this work, further research will be devoted to validating our preliminary insights, and to empirically test our conceptual framework. A first intent is to realize a more systematic review of the literature that supports the theoretical implications of our conceptual model. Some other possibilities concern future investigations that analyze barriers to knowledge sharing in combination with barriers to the utilization of knowledge. Related to this aspect, another important issue to be deepened would be the role of swift trust as a bridge between sharing and utilization behavior. Finally, it would be useful and conduct case studies aimed at highlighting emergent trends in business experiences of Web 2.0 Storytelling.

References

1. Sultan, N.: Knowledge management in the age of cloud computing and Web 2.0: experiencing the power of disruptive innovations. Int. J. Inf. Manage. **33**, 160–165 (2013). (Elsevier Ltd.)
2. Riege, A.: Three-dozen knowledge-sharing barriers managers must consider. J. Knowl. Manage. **9**(3), 18–35 (2005)
3. Sparrow, J.: Knowledge in Organizations: Access to Thinking at Work. Sage, London (1988)
4. Czarniawska, B.: Narrating the Organization: Dramas of Institutional Identity. The University of Chicago Press, Chicago and London (1997)
5. Musacchio Adorisio, A.L.: Raccontare la banca: la banca racconta, pp. 16–26. Storytelling e ricerca narrativa nelle organizzazioni. Sviluppo & Organizzazione, Maggio/Giugno/Luglio (2011)
6. Cesareo, L., Giordani, F., Iannotta, M.: Le learning histories come strumento di knowledge transfer: un comparative case study. In: Conference: XIV Workshop dei Docenti e Ricercatori di Organizzazione Aziendale (WOA) (2013)
7. Fontana, A.: Lo Storytelling per la comunicazione d'impresa. In: Barone, M., Fontana A. (eds.) Prospettive per la comunicazione interna e il benessere organizzativo. Appartenere, integrarsi e comunicare nell'organizzazione che cambia. Franco Angeli, Milano (2005)
8. Gill, R.: Using storytelling to maintain employee loyalty during change. Int. J. Bus. Soc. Sci. **2**(15), 23–32 (2011)
9. Rossiter, M., Garcia, P.: Digital storytelling: a new player on the narrative field. New Dir. Adult Continuing Educ. 37–48 (2010). https://doi.org/10.1002/ace.370
10. Reid, F.: Creating a knowledge sharing culture among diverse business units. Employ. Relat. Today **30**(3), 43–49 (2003)
11. Allen, J.P.: How Web 2.0 communities solve the knowledge sharing problem. In: IEEE international Symposium on Technology and Society, Fredericton (2008)
12. Panahi, S., Watson, J., Patridge, H.: Towards tacit knowledge sharing over social web tools. J. Knowl. Manage. **17**(3), 379–397 (2013)
13. Wang, S., Noe, R.A.: Knowledge sharing: a review and directions for future research. Hum. Resour. Manage. **20**, 115–131 (2010)
14. Berggren, C., Bergek, A., Bengtsson, L., Hobday, M., Söderlund, J.: Knowledge Integration and Innovation: Critical Challenges Facing International Technology-Based-Firms. Oxford University Press, London (2011)
15. Levin, D.Z., Cross, R.: The strength of weak ties you can trust: the mediating role of trust in effective knowledge transfer. Manage. Sci. **50**(11), 1477–1490 (2004)
16. Nonaka, I.A.: Dynamic theory of organizational knowledge creation. Organ. Sci. **5**(1), 14–37 (1994)
17. Hislop, D.: Knowledge Management in Organizations. A Critical Introduction, vol. 2. Oxford University Press, Oxford (2009)
18. Davenport, T., Prusak, L.: Working Knowledge: How Organizations Manage What They Know. Harvard Business School Press, Bostan (1998)
19. Bartol, K., Srivastava, A.: Encouraging knowledge sharing: the role of organizational reward systems. J. Leadersh. Organ. Stud. **19**(1), 64–76 (2002)
20. Connelly, C.E., Kelloway, E.K.: Predictors of employees' perceptions of knowledge sharing culture. Leadersh. Organ. Dev. J. **24**(5), 294–301 (2003)

21. Lin, H.F., Lee, G.G.: Perceptions of senior managers toward knowledge-sharing behaviour. Manage. Decis. **42**(1), 108–125 (2004)
22. Ardchvili, A., Page, V., Wentling, T.: Motivation and barriers to participation in virtual knowledge-sharing communities of practice. J. Knowl. Manage. **7**(1), 6477 (2003)
23. Kaplan, J.M.: The cloud's answer to the knowledge management challenge. E-Commerce Times, http://www.ecommercetimes.com/story/The-Clouds-Answer-to-the-KnowledgeManagement-Challenge-70363.html?wlc=1278951103 (2010)
24. Collison, C.: Avoiding the typical barriers to effective KM. Seven syndromes to look out for in your organization. Knowl. Manage. Rev. **9**(4), 16–19 (2006)
25. Mehrabian, A.: Silent Messages: Implicit Communication of Emotions and Attitudes. Wadsworth, Belmont, CA (1981)
26. Singh, B.N., Chandra, A., Al-Haddad, K.: Digital implementation of an advanced static VAR compensator for voltage profile improvement, power factor correction and balancing of unbalanced reactive loads. Electr. Power Energy Res. **54**(2), 101–111 (2000)
27. Kalid, K.S., Mahmood, A.K.: The development of a storytelling framework to support knowledge management process. J. Theor. Appl. Inf. Technol. **90**(1), 12–22 (2016)
28. Fontana, A.: Storytelling management. Narratologia, organizzazioni e economie del simbolico. Sviluppo & Organizzazione, 220 (2007)
29. Damasio, A.R.: L'errore di Cartesio. Emozione, ragione e cervello umano, Adelphi (1995)
30. Becker, W.J., Menges, J.I.: Biological implicit measures in HRM and OB: a question of how not if. Hum. Res. Manage. Rev. **23**(3), 219–228 (2013). https://doi.org/10.1016/j.hrmr.2012.12.003
31. Boyatzis, R.E.: When pulling to the negative emotional attractor is too much or not enough to inspire and sustain outstanding leadership. In: Burke, R.J., Cooper, C.L. (eds.) The Fulfilling Workplace: The Organization's Role in Achieving Individual and Organizational Health, pp. 139–150. Routledge, London and New York (2013)
32. Klitmøller, A., Lauring, J.: When global virtual teams share knowledge: media richness, cultural difference and language commonality. J. World Bus. **48**, 398–406 (2013)
33. Hayward, P.: A comparison of face-to-face and virtual software development teams. Team Perform. Manage. **8**, 39–48 (2002)
34. Alexander, B., Levine, A.: Web 20 storytelling: emergence of a new genre. EDUCAUSE Rev. **43**(6), 40–56 (2008)
35. Cao, Y., Klamma, R., Martini, A.: Collaborative storytelling in the Web2.0. In: Klamma, R., Sharda, N., Fernández-Manjón, B., Kosch, H., Spaniol, M. (eds.) Proceedings of the First International Workshop on Story-Telling and Educational Games (STEG'08) at ECTEL 0, CEUR-WS.org. (2008)
36. Robin, B.R.: Digital storytelling: a powerful technology tool for the 21st century classroom. Theory Pract. **47**(3), 220–228 (2008)
37. Snelson, C., Sheffield, A.: Digital storytelling in a Web 2.0 world. In: Proceedings of the Technology, Colleges & Community Worldwide Online Conference, pp. 159–167 (2009)
38. Macaskill, W., Owen, D.: Web 2.0 to go. In: Proceedings of LIANZA Conference (2006)
39. Zammit, P.J., Gao, J., Evans, R.: A framework to capture and share knowledge using storytelling and video sharing in global product development. In: IFIP International Federation for Information Processing. Springer International Publishing, pp. 259–268 (2016)
40. Panahi, S., Watson, J. Patridge, H.: Social media and tacit knowledge sharing: developing a conceptual model. In: World Academy of Science, Engineering and Technology (WASET), pp. 1095–1102 (2012)
41. White, G., Classen, S.: Using storytelling to elicit tacit knowledge from SMEs. J. Knowl. Manage. **16**(6), 950–962 (2012)
42. Avery, A.: Just do it! Web 2.0 and the breaking of the tacit dimension for knowledge acquisition. In: SAIS 2016 Proceedings of the Southern Association for Information Systems Conference, Paper 1, http://aisel.aisnet.org/sais2016/1 (2016)
43. Shirky, C.: Here Comes Everybody: The Power of Organizing Without Organizations. Penguin Books, England (2008)

44. Lelic, S.: Creating a knowledge-sharing culture. Knowl. Manage. **4**(5), 6–9 (2001)
45. Dorsey, D.W., Campbell, G.E., Foster, L.L., Miles, D.E.: Assessing knowledge structures: relations with experience and posttraining performance. Hum. Perform. **12**(1), 3157 (1999)
46. Mayfield, A.: What is social media? http://www.icrossing.co.uk/fileadmin/uploads/eBooks/ What_is_Social_Media_iCrossing_ebook.pdf (2008)
47. O'reilly, T.: What is web 2.0: design patterns and business models for the next generation of software. Commun. Strat. **65**, 17–37 (2005)
48. Auvinen, T., Aaltio, I., Blomqvist, K.: Constructing leadership by storytelling—the meaning of trust and narratives. Leadersh. Organ. Dev. J. **34**(6), 496514 (2013)
49. Fisher, W.R.: Human Communication as a Narration: Toward a Philosophy of Reason, Value, and Action. University of South Carolina Press, Columbia, SC (1987)
50. Lionel, P.R., Alan, R.D., Yu-Ting, C.H.: Individual swift trust and knowledge-based trust in face-to-face and virtual team members. J. Manage. Inf. Syst. **26**(2), 241–279 (2009)
51. Meyerson, D., Weick, K.E., Kramer, R.M.: Swift trust and temporary groups. In: Kramer, R. M., Tyler, T.R. (eds.) Trust in Organizations: Frontiers of Theory and Research, pp. 166–195. Sage Publication, London (1996)
52. Brewer, M.B.: Ethnocentrism and its role in interpersonal trust. In: Brewer, M.B., Collins, B. E. (eds.) Scientific Inquiry and the Social Sciences, pp. 214–231. Jossey-Bass, San Francisco (1981)
53. Kramer, R.M.: Trust and distrust in organizations: emerging perspectives, enduring questions. Annu. Rev. Psychol. **50**(1), 569–598 (1999)
54. McLure Wasko, M., Faraj, S.: It is what one does: why people participate and help others in electronic communities of practice. J. Strateg. Inf. Syst. **9**(1–3), 155–173 (2000)
55. Hendriks, P.: Why share knowledge? The influence of ICT on the motivation for knowledge sharing. Knowl. Process Manage. **6**(2), 91–100 (1999)
56. O'Dell, C., Hubert, C.: The new edge in knowledge: how knowledge management is changing the way we do business. Knowl. Manage. Res. Pract. **10**, 99–101 (2011)
57. Eraut, M.: Non-formal learning and tacit knowledge in professional work. Br. J. Educ. Psychol. **70**, 113–136 (2000)
58. Mason, R., Rennie, F.: Using Web 2.0 for learning in the community. Internet High. Educ. **10**, 196–203 (2007)
59. Spender, J.C.: Making knowledge the basis of a dynamic theory of the firm. Strateg. Manage. J. **17**, 45–62 (1996)

A Pervasive IoT Scheme to Vehicle Overspeed Detection and Reporting Using MQTT Protocol

Elie Nasr, Elie Kfoury and David Khoury

Abstract One particular concern that Public Safety Organization (PSO) must account for is the excess of speed of vehicles in motion. The high speed is typically responsible for a significant proportion of the mortality and morbidity that result from road crashes. Various ineffective proposed methods and solutions have been implemented to control speed limits; for instance, Speed Detection Camera System (SDCS), Radio Detection and Ranging (RADAR), Light Detection and Ranging (LIDAR). This paper conveys an innovative, pervasive, effective and adaptable Internet of Things (IoT) system to detect and report vehicle overspeed as well as issuing tickets and fines. Our aggregated prototype is composed of five components: IoT vehicle on-board unit, Message Queuing Telemetry Transport (MQTT) broker, application logic server, data storage, and monitoring engine. A software simulation has been implemented and tested as a proof of concept. This novel technique is restricted only for governmental use since it surrogates the contemporary afore-mentioned speed detection systems paving the way toward a smarter and sustainable solution, and thus ensuring public safety.

Keywords PSO · WHO · Vehicle · Overspeed · IoT · Radar · MQTT · Ticket

E. Nasr (✉) · E. Kfoury · D. Khoury
Department of Information and Communications Technology,
American University of Science and Technology, Beirut, Lebanon
e-mail: enasr@aust.edu.lb

E. Kfoury
e-mail: ekfoury@aust.edu.lb

D. Khoury
e-mail: dkhoury@aust.edu.lb

© Springer Nature Switzerland AG 2019
Y. Baghdadi and A. Harfouche (eds.), *ICT for a Better Life and a Better World*,
Lecture Notes in Information Systems and Organisation 30,
https://doi.org/10.1007/978-3-030-10737-6_2

19

1 Introduction

Many reasons lead to fatal road crashes that occur disproportionally and are stretched from road state, car situation, weather condition, driver alertness to speed which remains a major safety concern on the nations' roadways. Vehicle high speed is considered a crucial factor that typically leads to a significant increase in the morbidity and mortality rate. Moreover, governments and PSOs invest enormous amount of money and human resources to provide efficient traffic surveillance systems which control the excess of speed and hence enforcing traffic speed laws. The (WHO) organization states that road traffic crashes are predicted to become the 7th leading cause of death by 2030. An adult pedestrian's risk of dying is less than 20% if struck by a car at 50 km/h and almost 60% if hit at 80 km/h [1]. A 30 km/h speed zones can reduce the risk of a crash and are recommended in areas where vulnerable road users are common like residential and schools areas. According to the Association for Safe International Road Travel (ASIRT), nearly 1.3 million people die in road crashes each year, on average 3287 deaths a day. Road crashes resulting from high speed cost $518 billion globally, constituting 1–2% of individual countries' annual Gross domestic product (GDP) [2].

Many speed devices are currently available: The RADAR, the LIDAR, and the Speed Detection Camera System (SDCS). However, the use of these speed control devices has not resulted in definitive conclusions about their effectiveness as stated in the next section.

Based on the above aforesaid facts, an ample and doable solution for high speed detection becomes a must. Hence, the research question rises up: "How can we provide an innovative, faultless, and effective scheme for over-speed detection?"

To combat the speeding problem, we propose an effective and innovative IoT scheme which depends on the following components: a software component, for instance, an application that relies on the MQTT lightweight protocol to report instantly the speed of the vehicle, and to issue a ticket when over-speed threshold value is defeated; an on-board unit integrated into the vehicles which is responsible for broadcasting the vehicle geo-location information as well as its speed to a processing server; a processing server to retrieve and calculate the speed limit taking into account several factors: state of the road, traffic congestion, weather conditions and the like.

The main contributions of this paper are: (a) Developing a new smart IoT solution which helps governmental authorities in supervising vehicle over-speed. (b) Issuing and collecting car tickets autonomously. (c) Implementing a cost efficient and accurate solution for overspeed road control. (d) Collecting geographical data which can be fed into a data mining engine to extract roads conditions. (e) Providing traffic descriptive statistics reports for some critical areas.

This paper starts with descriptive and inferential statistics about road traffic crashes, high death rates, prorated cost as well as its influence on the individual countries' annual GDP. Sections 2, 3, and 4, describe the related work, the proposed scheme, the design and implementation respectively. Sections 5, 6, and 7 expose results, performance, and conclusions and future work.

2 Related Work

This section discusses and studies the traditional radar systems, their requirements, functionalities and their intrinsic drawbacks.

2.1 RADAR (Radio Detection and Ranging)

There are two types of radar that are commonly used in almost all countries by law enforcement personnel to measure the speed of moving objects. Their functionalities are based on Doppler shifts to measure the speed of vehicle. Fixed high way radar: It calculates vehicle's speed by means of sensors and capturing still images. This type of radar is considered extremely expensive. Its cost ranges from $20,000 to $30,000 [3].

Mobile inner town radars or radar guns: This device may be hand-held or vehicle mounted. It calculates vehicle's speed by means of sensors, and it needs an operator to capture the images.

Various limitations of the radar system are perceived and not limited to: (a) User training and certifications are required, (b) Installation and deployment requires planning and mathematical consideration for better field of view, (c) Radar can take up to 2 s to lock on and hence, cannot detect two excessive speeders simultaneously, (d) Large targets close to radar can saturate or hide other smaller objects; therefore, the radar fails to locate the vehicle, (e) Radar-triggered cameras are imperfect and can result in tickets being generated for false readings, (f) Human intervention is required. They have no mechanism of sending the captured images. The authorities have to make periodic stops to collect the films.

2.2 LIDAR (Light Detection and Ranging)

The Lidar system relies on the principles of time-of-flight of two or more short wave length laser pulses. Sweep for instance, is a $250 Lidar with range of only 40 m [4]. If we calculate the number of Lidars in a country, their cost will be very high.

Some of the disadvantages are: (a) Particles (dust, water) in air can limit range, (b) Rounded surfaces, the color black, blue, and violet are poor reflectors, (c) Alignment can cause severe error, (d) Extreme sunlight can be damaging.

Other technologies can be used to avoid and defeat radar and Lidar systems:

- Laser detectors and radar detectors. They detect if the speed is being monitored and warn the driver.
- Laser jammers and radar jammers. They jam the laser and the radar signal and return a scrambled signal so as the radar speed camera cannot process [5].

2.3 SDCS (Speed Detection Camera System)

SDCS is a camera that uses image processing to detect traffic regulation violations. It can be mounted beside or over a road or installed in an enforcement vehicle.

Some of the perceived drawbacks are: (a) SDCS method requires large database for storing video, therefore the cost of this method is higher than of the RADAR and LIDAR, (b) In December, 2012, Speed Camera Contractor Xerox Corporation admitted that cameras they had deployed in Baltimore city were producing erroneous speed readings, and that 1 out of every 20 citations issued at some locations were due to errors, (c) One issue is the potential conflict of interest when private contractors are paid a commission based on the number of tickets they are able to issue.

The purpose of the speed camera program is to improve safety by reducing unsafe speed and must be persuasively and evidently communicated to the public. As a matter of facts, signs announcing the possible presence of speed cameras should be obviously posted throughout the enforcement area. To do otherwise, the suspicion that those cameras are being used mainly for revenue purposes rather than safety reasons [6].

Based on the above discussion, these traditional speed devices need to be replaced by an automated system having better precise outputs, less expensive, and exclude human factor.

3 The Proposed Scheme

This section outlines our proposed system at a high level scope. The system is composed of the following phases: (a) Service's registration and IoT device integration, (b) Speed and geo-location reporting, (c) Overspeed detection and tickets' issuing.

3.1 Service's Registration and IoT Device Integration

The IoT device must be integrated into every vehicle through the on-board Diagnostic (OBDII) plugin standard. After installation, this device automatically acquires the VIN (Vehicle Identity Number) and maps it to its Universal Unique Identifier (UUID). The combination of the VIN and the UUID ensures authentication and genuineness and thus, prevents device's counterfeiting. The first time the device is plugged in into the moving object, its mapping record is then posted to the server's database for registration and consequently, for post-matching. Since the database is managed by the government, then there exist a mapping among the three attributes VIN, plate number, and the vehicle's owner. If the IoT device has been plugged out intentionally or unintentionally then the server can detect the action as described technically in Sect. 4.3 and consequently, the government applies the appropriate measures.

3.2 Speed and Geo-location Reporting

The IoT device reports repeatedly the speed of the car including its geo-location for a configurable time interval. In order to use the full potential of IoT paradigm, the device reports the data to the main server using the lightweight protocol MQTT over the mobile network. MQTT is an open-source protocol for passing messages between multiple clients through a central broker. The MQTT architecture is broker based, and uses long-lived outgoing TCP connection to the broker. MQTT can be used for two way communications over unreliable networks. It is also compatible with lower consumption devices [7]. In our system, each MQTT message is composed of the vehicle's speed, its geo-location, its VIN, and the date & time. In case the TCP connection is disrupted then all MQTT messages are stored temporarily on a secondary storage device. When the IoT device is reconnected, the stored messages are republished again to the server. This ensures service availability at any time.

3.3 Over-Speed Detection and Tickets' Issuing

To be able to issue over-speed ticket, there should be a mechanism to map the vehicle's geo-location to the exact street name or number. Many such services are available in the cloud through well-defined Application Programming Interface (API). But due to the high number of expected transactions published constantly to the server, a bandwidth problem might arise. Therefore, a dedicated server is developed to perform reverse geo-location offline.

Two alternative models have been proposed for over-speed detection: the static model and the adaptable model. The first is implemented by comparing the current vehicle's speed and its associated attributes to a speed record located into a database server provided by the government. The second is achieved through an adaptable solution based on weather forecast, and a universal standard adopted by many states and cities for establishing regulatory speed zones.

With respect to tickets' issuing, if the system detects overspeed then a vehicle record representing a ticket is added to a governmental database dedicated for that purpose (see Sect. 4.3.1 for ticket's attributes). Consequently, the governmental database server maps the vehicle's VIN to its plate number and determines the fine that has to be paid by the car owner (owner of plate number).

Having described the system at a high level scope, the following section illustrates the system's design and describes its implementation in details.

4   Design and Implementation

4.1   System Architecture

Below is the system architecture of the conceptual model that exposes the model, the behavior, and the views of our proposed system in a sequence.

Figure 1 shows the consecutive steps of the different components of the system and how they interact with each other:

1. The speed control server which is considered as an MQTT client subscribes to the MQTT-Broker server to receive the messages published by all the moving vehicles.
2. The vehicle publishes its identity (VIN) as well as the speed, the GPS coordinates, and the time stamp.
3. Since the speed control server is already subscribed to the same published topic[1] (see Fig. 2) of the vehicle; therefore, it receives the published information.
4. The speed control server is constantly performing reverse geo-location to map the received coordinates against the street name/number and hence, it detects the speed limit.
5. In case of over-speed detection, a ticket is issued spontaneously and stored in a database.

---

[1]A topic in MQTT technology represents the key that identifies the information channel to which payload data is published.

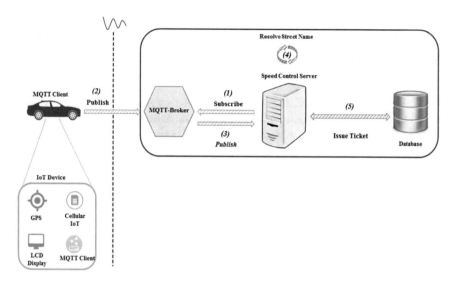

Fig. 1 System architecture

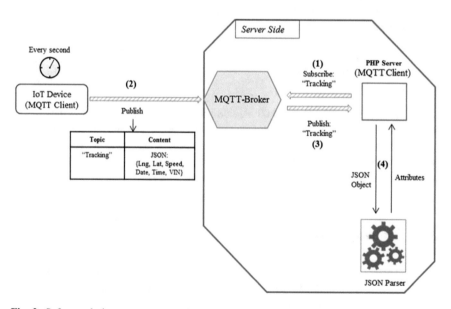

Fig. 2 Software design

4.2   Device Components

4.2.1   Cellular IoT

Our IoT device uses the cellular 3G module through a Subscriber Identity Module (SIM) card to establish all kind of wireless communications from and to the server.

It is required to implement cellular IoT 3rd Generation Partnership Project (3GPP) technologies: Extended coverage Global System for Mobile communication (ECGSM), Long Term Evolution (LTE), Long Term Evolution Machine to Machine LTE-M, and the new radio access technology Narrowband IoT (NB-IoT) specifically tailored to form an attractive solution for emerging low power wide area (LPWA) applications [8].

4.2.2   Global Positioning System (GPS)

The GPS navigation is a component that accurately calculates geographical location by receiving information from GPS satellites [9]. The GPS device is used to send to server the exact vehicle location (longitude and latitude).

4.2.3   MQTT Client

MQTT client API is installed on the device to enable the "publish/subscribe" model to the MQTT broker located on the server side as shown in Fig. 2. Each vehicle's published message includes a topic and its corresponding payload. The topic designates the routing information for the broker. Clients that subscribe to a specific topic receive the message pertaining to the topic's key.

4.3   Software Design

Figure 2 depicts the software design of the system. On the server side, Mosquitto™ which is an open source MQTT message broker is adopted as the system's broker. It is responsible to distribute the messages related to a topic to all its subscribers.

In our software design, the vehicle equipped with the IoT device publishes to the topic "Tracking" a JSON object (the topic's payload) containing the following parameters:

a. Longitude: East-West geo coordinate of a point on the earth's surface.
b. Latitude: North-South geo coordinate of a point on the earth's surface.

c. Speed: Using the GPS's internal clock, the speed is calculated by measuring the time the vehicle needs to traverse between two points. As an alternative to GPS, the vehicle speed can also be obtained through the OBDII interface.
d. Date and Time: The National Marine Electronics Association (NMEA) data generated from the GPS is converted to readable format to extract the current date and time.
e. VIN: A unique combination of 17 letters and digits to identify a vehicle.

One of the subscribers to the MQTT broker is the speed control server which uses the Mosquitto-PHP library to become an MQTT client. Once the control server receives a message, it parses it retrieve every attributes separately.

Our software design is based on two alternatives: The first is the static model which relies on offline reverse geocoding for speed limit detection. The second is the adaptable model in which the speed limit parameter is detected dynamically as described in Sect. 4.3.2. This method is based on the continuous weather forecast and the 85% percentile theorem.

4.3.1　Static Model

The static model is illustrated in Fig. 3 as shown below:

1. The PHP server sends the longitude and latitude parameters to a java application through PHP-JAVA-Bridge.
2. KD-Tree [10], as shown in Fig. 4, for nearest neighbor lookup algorithm is implemented in Java to perform offline reverse geocoding. The Java application accepts as input the longitude and the latitude, and then compares them against a database provided by the government containing all country's street names and their corresponding speed limit.

Fig. 3　Static pattern

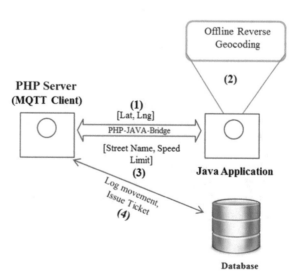

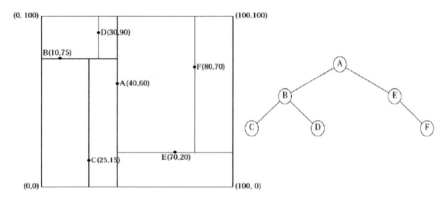

Fig. 4 Spatial indexes—KD tree

3. The street name and the speed limit are returned to the PHP server for processing.
4. The PHP server extracts the speed from the JSON object and checks if it exceeds the speed limit. A ticket is issued and stored into the database in case of over-speed detection.

The ticket record's attributes are: VIN, speed limit, longitude and latitude, exceeded speed, date and time.

4.3.2 Adaptable Model

In the adaptable model, the speed limit is considered as variant parameter and is calculated according to two factors: 85th percentile theorem of vehicles speed, continuous weather forecast.

85th percentile: The speed that 85% of vehicles do not exceed. Figure 5 shows this theorem. Since the system is collecting all vehicles' velocities as well as their locations, then, the 85th percentile theorem can be used to determine the new speed limit. Every T seconds/minutes (configured per country), the speed control server calculates the new speed limit per cluster and updates the database accordingly. A cluster as shown in Fig. 6 is a segment defined by the country in a highway. The dynamic clustering system for highways is still an area under research.

The use of the 85th percentile speed concept is based on the theory that the large majority of drivers: (1) Are reasonable and prudent, (2) do not want to have a crash, (3) desire to reach their destination in the shortest possible time.

A speed at or below which 85% of people drive at any given location under good weather and visibility conditions may be considered as the maximum safe speed for that location [11].

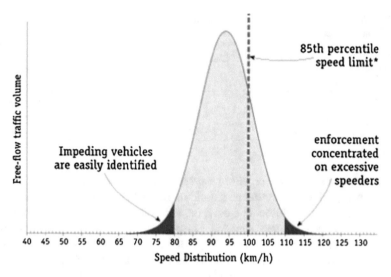

Fig. 5 Adaptable pattern (*Source* http://michigandistilled.org)

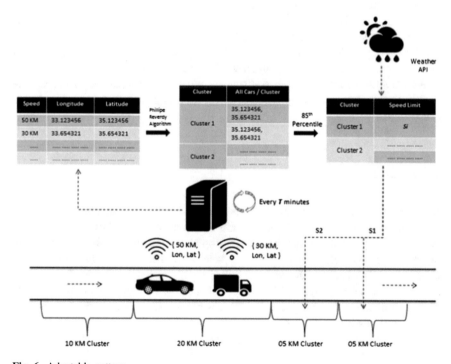

Fig. 6 Adaptable pattern

Table 1 Speed limit reduction rates according to weather conditions (*Source* U.S. Department of Transportation: Road Weather Management Program)

Weather conditions	Freeway traffic flow reductions			
	Average speed (%)	Free-flow speed (%)	Volume (%)	Capacity (%)
Light rain/snow	3–13	2–13	5–10	4–11
Heavy rain	3–16	6–17	14	10–30
Heavy snow	5–40	5–64	30–44	12–27

How to determine if a car lies within a specific cluster? To determine whether a car lies within a specific road cluster an algorithm proposed by Philippe Reverdy is used. By considering a road cluster as a polygon, this algorithm computes the sum of the angles made between the test point and each pair of points making up the polygon. If this sum is 2π then the point is an interior point (vehicle lies within the cluster), if it is 0 then the point is an exterior point (vehicle lies outside the cluster) [12].

Weather conditions: Another variable used in the adaptable model is the current weather conditions. The vast majority of most weather-related crashes happen on wet pavement and during rainfall: 73% on wet pavement and 46% during rainfall [13]. In this system, we relied on "Highway Capacity Manual 2000" Chapter "New Market Creation for Technological Breakthroughs: Commercial Drones and the Disruption of the Emergency Market" as the source for changing the speed according to the weather as shown in Table 1. Table 1 summarizes the reduction rates.

As a matter of fact, the server contacts the Weather Underground API to acquire the weather forecast of the current cluster and consequently, it reduces the speeds accordingly.

5 Results

In this section we focus on showing the results of only the adaptable model since the static model relies on fixed speed limits and does not depend on dynamic speed detection. To validate the results, we developed an Android mobile application to determine the vehicles' speed within a selected cluster of 06 km between two Lebanese towns namely, Jounieh and Jbeil as illustrated in Fig. 7. This mobile application was distributed to 150 drivers using a link on a file server. We used the mobile application knowing that it is infeasible to manufacture 150 IoT devices considering this method is still under research.

Table 2 exhibits the 150 average speeds calculated by the server. The mobile app publishes the speed to the server every one second; consequently, the server calculates the average speed per car every T seconds (preconfigured per country).

For better graph visualization, we calculated the frequencies of the speeds by dividing them into class intervals of width of 05 km/h each as shown in Table 3.

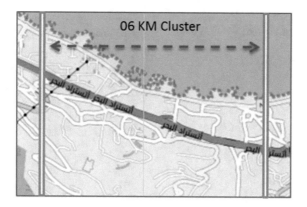

Fig. 7 Jounieh-Jbeil Highway Cluster (Lebanon)

Table 2 Speed collected from the mobile applications distributed to 150 drivers

Speed in Km/h collected from 150 vehicles														
55	85	75	65	95	50	75	40	70	55	73	85	85	85	70
40	40	95	95	85	60	100	70	100	40	100	90	100	100	35
80	65	85	55	40	35	85	75	80	35	80	75	100	95	35
80	90	90	50	80	35	40	50	55	40	40	35	95	35	65
35	72	70	75	65	35	40	45	50	90	40	95	35	55	65
85	80	80	95	85	35	60	80	90	80	70	70	65	60	55
90	40	40	50	95	80	80	35	35	65	60	85	90	45	85
65	75	95	65	60	85	90	45	45	60	50	55	35	65	60
90	90	35	100	70	60	80	35	80	35	77	45	85	95	95
40	70	55	35	50	75	40	60	35	80	60	95	55	80	100

Table 3 Frequency table of speeds per class

35–39	40–44	45–49	50–54	55–59	60–64	65–69	70–74	75–79	80–84	85–89	90–94	95–100
19	14	5	7	9	10	10	5	8	15	13	10	20

Applying the 85th percentile theorem stated in Sect. 4.3.2 on the frequency shown in Table 3, the resulting speed limit showed 90.0 km/h. The exact result is illustrated in Fig. 8.

The server correlates the maximum speed limits to the current corresponding weather condition, applies the speed reduction rate as depicted in Table 1, and deduces the final maximum speed limit.

As a result, our IoT device considers 90 km/h as the speed limit and an embedded customized panel displays the maximum allowed speed limit.

Fig. 8 Jounieh-Jbeil
Highway Cluster (Lebanon)

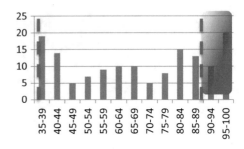

6 Performance

This IoT device could have been implemented using the HTTP protocol instead of MQTT. But since HTTP is a stateless protocol in which each client request is treated as an independent transaction that is unrelated to any previous request, many additional technical requirements are then needed to maintain session awareness between the client and the server; therefore, more system resources and networks capabilities are required. That would lead to poor system performance, memory leaks, and power drain.

Unlike HTTP, the adopted MQTT is a bidirectional IoT protocol which maintains stateful session awareness. What differentiates MQTT is its lightweight overhead; it requires minimal bandwidth and less power consumption. Thus it helps minimize the resource requirements for the IoT device and ensures reliability and some degree of assurance of delivery with grades of service.

The table below shows a comparative test of a certain number of messages sent and received over HTTPS (HTTP secure) or MQTT and the battery power consumption per message in 3G and WiFi has been recorded.

This test had been conducted by using a smartphone running Android 2.2, and was simulated by sending 1024 messages, of one byte each, to and from the mobile device. Results shown in Table 4 offered tremendous advantages of the MQTT protocol over the HTTP [14].

Table 4 The following table compares messages per hour, and battery usage per message, between HTTP and MQTT networks

		3G		WiFi	
		HTTPS	MQTT	HTTPS	MQTT
Receive	Msgs/hour	1708	160,278	3628	263,314
	% battery/msg	0.01709	0.00010	0.00095	0.00002
	Msgs (note losses)	240/1024	1024/1024	524/1024	1024/1024
Send	Msgs/hour	1926	21,685	5229	23,184
	% battery/msg	0.00975	0.00082	0.00104	0.00016

7 Conclusions and Future Work

In this paper, we proposed and implemented an innovative IoT system which may help the community reducing the death rates resulting from high speed vehicles crashes. It is worth mentioning that the use of this IoT system is restricted for governmental use only due to some privacy concerns related to the drivers' identity and vehicles' tracking. Two models were successfully implemented to detect the speed limit and verified in real environment.

This autonomous system also assists governments in issuing car tickets, collecting fines, controlling the speed limit, and reporting road conditions without human interaction. The results showed that this system is robust and efficient due to the adoption of the MQTT lightweight IoT protocol. Results also showed that system helps the government in: (a) Practicing full control on traffic monitoring and enforce speed laws in all roads and not only highways. (b) Issuing real time tickets without any human interaction. (c) Dismissing traditional devices like RADAR, LIDAR, and SDCS, and thus saving remarkable amount of money. (d) Generating daily records related to the traffic state, to the number of issued tickets in all over the country or in a specific area. These records are stored instantaneously into a dedicated database and can be later fed into a data mining engine for future statistical analysis. (e) Producing daily monetary reports related to fine amount. (f) Customizing the overspeed threshold value conferring to each country's speeding policy and procedures. (g) Reducing the number of policemen in the road. (h) Decreasing the maintenance cost compared to traditional systems. (i) Adopting inexpensive solution to traffic control and traffic issuing. (j) Reducing the number of accidents and lessening the mortality and morbidity rate.

As future work, our intention is to update/upgrade/enhance this system to become an aggregated unit and to embed it into every vehicle during the manufacturing phase. Also, future dynamic road clustering allocation problem is one of our key factors to solve.

References

1. World Health Organization. http://www.who.int
2. ASIRT, Annual Global Road Crash Statistics. https://asirt.org/initiatives/informing-road-users/road-safety-facts/road-crash-statistics
3. Bole, A., Wall, A., Norris, A.: Radar and ARPA Manual, 3rd edn (2013)
4. Weitkamp, C.: Lidar: Range-Resolved Optical Remote Sensing of the Atmosphere (2005)
5. How Laser Jammers Work. http://www.laserjammer.net/2012/how-laser-jammers-work/
6. Bhatkar, S., Shivalkar, M., Tandale, B., Joshi, P.: Survey of various methods used for speed calculation of a vehicle. Int. J. Recent Innov. Trends Comput. Commun. 3(3), 1558–1561 (2015)
7. Friess, P.: Internet of Things: Converging Technologies for Smart Environments and Integrated Ecosystems (2013)

8. Ericsson: Cellular networks for massive IoT. https://www.ericsson.com/assets/local/publications/white-papers/wp_iot.pdf (2016)
9. Leick, A.: GPS Satellite Surveying, 2nd edn (1995)
10. Al-Jabbouli, A.: Data Clustering Using the Bees Algorithm and the Kd-Tree Structure (2011)
11. Texas Department, Procedures for Establishing Speed Zones Manual. http://onlinemanuals.txdot.gov
12. Paul Bourke, Determining if a point lies on the interior of a polygon. http://masters.donntu.org/2009/fvti/hodus/library/article2/article2.html
13. Road Weather Management—FHWA Office of Operations. https://ops.fhwa.dot.gov/weather/
14. IBM. Enabling the Internet of Things. https://www.ibm.com/developerworks/community/blogs/c565c720-fe84-4f63-873f-607d87787327/entry/tc_overview?lang=en

Building Inclusive Digital Societies Through the Use of Open Source Technologies

Abstract Digital convergence offers many new opportunities, but also poses architectural and structural issues. One of the most critical obstacles is the 'vertical silos model' that shapes much of today's Internet. The accumulation of money, power and influence create further concern. We propose the use of open source technologies as a partial solution for the identified challenge. These technologies enable scalability of innovations and drive distribution wealth. Open source technologies have been studied extensively from technical view point, but less from adaptation side. Our research took customer view in technology sourcing. Data was collected in a survey and interviews with 120 companies in Europe. The enquiry revealed that open source technology adaptations were limited due to the uncertainties related to sustainability of communities, SLAs and regulations. The study implied that the industry needs to evolve toward increased customer orientation. The study contributes to adaptation of open source technologies.

Keywords Internet evolution · Open source software · Innovation

1 Introduction

Internet has evolved significantly during the past few decades. Over the past decade, a flourishing number of concepts and architectural shifts have appeared such as the Internet of Things (IoT), Big Data Cloud Computing, and Software-Defined Networking. The gradual evolution in Internet development brings forward large societal and economic opportunities for reducing various costs for societies, creating efficiencies, increasing the service for the citizens in a vast number of areas, and fostering sustainable economic growth with notable productivity gains. Although these convergent forces offer the potential to create new business models

P. Turkama (✉)
School of Business, Center for Knowledge and Innovation Research,
Aalto University, PO Box 11000, 00076 Aalto, Finland
e-mail: petra.turkama@aalto.fi

© Springer Nature Switzerland AG 2019
Y. Baghdadi and A. Harfouche (eds.), *ICT for a Better Life and a Better World*,
Lecture Notes in Information Systems and Organisation 30,
https://doi.org/10.1007/978-3-030-10737-6_3

and system designs, they also pose key architectural and structural issues that must be addressed for businesses to benefit, as well as societal and value laden questions that we must address in order to make the future internet serve people and societies as expected.

The main Internet challenges include security for the data collected to cloud from interconnected machines in an Internet of Things (IoT) setting. Increasing the number of connected devices increases the opportunity to exploit security vulnerabilities, as do poorly designed devices, which can expose user data to theft by leaving data streams inadequately protected. In some cases such as implanted, Internet-enabled medical devices and hackable cars people's health and safety can be put at risk. The homogeneity of devices magnifies the potential impact of any single security vulnerability by the sheer number of devices that all have the same characteristics.

Privacy concerns are elevated through integrating data collecting devices into our environments without us consciously using them. However, privacy concerns extend beyond collection of people's personal data. Tracking devices for phones, cars and smart televisions record with voice recognition or vision features can continuously listen to conversations or watch for activity and selectively transmit that data to a cloud service for processing. The collection of this information exposes legal and regulatory challenges facing data protection and privacy law. Legal systems struggle to keep up with the technology developments.

The lack of standardized processes can limit the potential scalability of Internet-enabled innovations and limit reaching its' full potential. Without standardized processes to guide manufacturers, developers design proprietary solutions that can operate in disruptive ways on the Internet domain without full regard to their impact. If poorly designed and configured, such Internet solutions can have negative consequences for the networking resources they connect to and to the broader Internet development. The concept of standardized processes should be expanded to cover not only technologies and interfaces where architectural deficiencies appear, but also operational procedures and data management models to ensure trust.

Legal issues with Internet and IoT devices currently include cross-border data flows; conflicts between law enforcement surveillance and civil rights; data retention and destruction policies; mediating the tension between data ownership and open access; and legal liability for unintended uses, security breaches or privacy lapses. The present situation is not a given state of affairs and there are international business and economic developments already modifying it. Furthermore, the expectations and values of today's digi-natives don't necessarily resonate with the monopolistic and institutionalized approaches, but rather demand support for more distributed, fast moving and dynamic collaborations and interactions. One example of this phenomenon is the interest toward blockchains—the connection of vertical silos horizontally without a platform owner.

One of the most critical obstacles is the 'vertical silos model' that shapes much of today's Internet service offering. Products and services are increasingly developed on closely-controlled and increasingly vertically integrated technology platforms, which are controlled by a few major US enterprises. This is a serious impediment for the global co-creation of products and services in the spirit of open innovation, effectively hindering the scalability of Internet-enabled services and new concepts beyond a limited scope of investment criteria, as well as creating concerns regarding the accumulation of money, power and influence.

Internet of the future will trigger the disruption and transformation of the existing value chains. The changes will be faster first in the fields of telecommunications, traffic, healthcare and education, and will reach also sectors such as agriculture and public governance.

Furthermore, digital development paths should reflect our commonly shared values and objectives for *inclusiveness, openness, regional development and successful collaboration of public sector and industries, as well as cross-industry collaboration and enhanced SME empowerment.* Development is being viewed from a general, technology-neutral perspective legal lens, which seeks to prevent unfair or deceptive practices against consumers. From this new human-centric perspective, the Internet should offer *more at the service of people and society.* It should provide better services, more intelligence, higher involvement and participation—to better embrace the *social and ethical* values that we enjoy in our societies, and contribute to building equal and stable societies. Figure 1 describes a human-centric internet structure, where each technical layer is constructed with the focus on utility and added value for humans as users. It takes into account our shared values and social structures, and ensures business sustainability with mechanisms for value creation and capture for all involved parties. This approach likens the approach of purpose economy.

Fig. 1 Human-centric view on future internet development

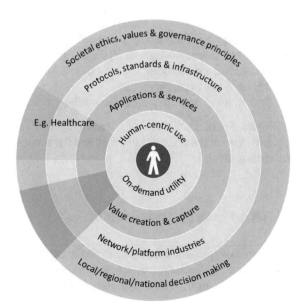

Fig. 2 Internet development
landscape

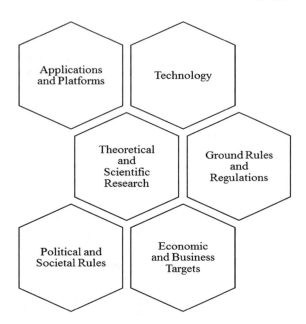

Internet has proven to be a powerful game changer in many vital functions of society and business. In order to fully utilize the opportunities of Next Generation Internet, it is necessary to include the fundamental principles of society and business in the research. This inclusion should consider:

- Agreed values, processes and rules should guide the development and application of technology and it's applications
- Society and regulation should be able to faster adapt to the development of technology enabling totally novel structures and practices
- Economic sustainability and business logic should drive technology evolution
- Theoretical and scientific research should be brought out of the labs and blended with real life experimentation
- Scalability of concept should drive selection with the convergence of industries

Figure 2 visualizes the inter-connectivity between the technical internet development, the related rules and policies, and the economic and societal objectives and developments.

2   Open Source Technologies

OSS technologies have been considered as the major driver for scalability of innovations [1]. Technical concerns in different industry sectors and usage areas have been reported increasingly assimilated, and thus the same general enabling technologies and solutions can be used in a variety of application areas. Only open, standardized interfaces enable scale efficiencies, drive vertical innovation co-creation, and deliver novel customer value. As such OSS technologies can be considered as an enabler for sustainable business practices for the express purposes of leveraging human and non-human resources for the benefits of all the stakeholders of the society, as stated in the objectives of the conference.

Open source providers such as OpenStack and Hadoop provide clones for the leading commercial solutions with the same functionality. Feature parity analyses have reported that alternative open source solutions cover the cloud offering extensively in the infrastructure layer, while platform and software layers still have some gaps in the offering [2]. Despite the fast maturing of the technologies, their commercial adaptation remains limited. The main limitations include technical barriers like interoperability, application programming interface (API) compatibility and integration challenges. There are also numerous non-technical challenges like business continuity, reliability and continued support of technologies. Customers are uncomfortable with the lack of clear service level agreements (SLA) and visibility to the future roadmaps. This is particularly true in cloud computing environments where customers expect convenience and turnkey solutions with masked complexity. The solutions are purchased as standardized, modular components 'as-a-service'.

OSS cloud platforms have been studied extensively from technical and developers' point of view. Much of the research focuses on contributors' incentives, service providers' business logic and technical assessments. There are no studies on customers' acceptance of OSS technologies in cloud context, or the broader impacts on society as a driver for more equal, transparent and sustainable future for internet. Our research tapped into this less studied area with an objective to understand cloud customers' relationship value drivers leading to vendor selection, and their implication to the evolution of cloud industry. We assumed service science oriented approach to understanding the customer value in cloud supplier relationships. After an extensive literature review, an online survey with 120 major European companies was conducted, and findings were complemented with interviews with the CTOs of 55 major companies. The collected data was analyzed with an acknowledged framework in order to get a holistic view of the customers' preferences.

OSS development started to gain momentum in the 1990s. The phenomenon builds on voluntary communities and software developers making their source code available free-of-charge to end users and improvers in cumulative context, sometimes subject to license restrictions [3]. The area that was first considered as a hobbyist activity or academic exercise has turned into significant commercial field with participation and support of the world's largest commercial software companies (e.g., Facebook, Google) that are spending billions on open source, with over 50% of OSS communities today being backed up by large companies, or even owned and controlled by them [4, 5]. In order to understand the scale, one of the first movers in the area, Linux statistics state that in 2015 there are 566,665 users and 159,985 machines registered to Linux only, and the estimate for the total number of Linux users exceeds 82 million (Linuxcounter site).

In terms of predictions, Gartner expects that 99% of Global 2000 companies will incorporate open source into their operations by 2016, and IDC predicts that by 2018, 60% of IT solutions originally developed as proprietary, closed solutions, will become open-sourced [6]. To complement these predictions, Sect. 2.1 briefly discusses the business models and communities governing OSS solutions, while Sect. 2.2 provides an in-depth discussion about the pros and cons of using OSS for Cloud Computing.

2.1 Open Source Business Models and Communities

Open source business models rely on approximation and complementarity to other resources like human capital or proprietary products and services. This can include supply of support personnel, user toolkits, coordination functions or virtual communities [7, 8]. OSS communities enjoy from network externalities in the same manner as proprietary software [9], which incentivizes building large developer communities. Large communities with industrial support also benefit from perceived credibility and community of choice for top contributors and users. Despite that, most OSS communities remain small with less than 50 contributors [10] although small OSS communities can be very viable in niche areas, as open source software design is modular [11]. Due to its complexity and broad impact, the phenomenon of OSS has been studied extensively by multiple research communities ranging from legal scholars, economists, sociologists, anthropologists to computer scientists. In addition to countless technical studies and reports, the research seeks to explain the developers' motives, rewarding mechanism, signaling and societal impact, as well as IPR questions and business models [10, 12, 13]. Our research focuses on the less studied phenomenon of OSS adaptation in cloud computing context from the customer point of view. The objective is, on the one hand, to better understand the different drivers cloud customers have for service and service provider selection, and on the other hand, to support OSS providers to plan their services and business models accordingly.

2.2 Cloud Computing Characteristics

The key features of cloud computing are resource pooling, rapid elasticity, on-demand service and guaranteed availability. The customers only pay for the services they use, and can plug and play with different services. When it comes to open source software, these features can be somewhat compromised. The main challenges from customers' viewpoint are:

(i) Reliability: the lack of documentation, inability to negotiate contracts and support [14];

(ii) Standardization: market is still missing dominant standards for open interfaces, which has led to challenges with interoperability and versioning [15, 16];

(iii) Usability: the challenge refers to integration to heritage systems and interoperability with supply network partners' systems.

These challenges are accounted for the developer profiles and valuations. Most of the OSS contributors are IT professionals [12] and rather focus on technologically virtuous technologies for sophisticated users than serving the masses [16]. The developers prefer to work independently with technical challenges, whereas most cloud computing services consists of mature technologies. Developers are also selective with the communities they contribute to, which leads to challenges with sustainability [17, 18]. Given this situation, customer business concerns are left with less attention.

3   Customer Relationship Value Drivers

Cloud computing is essentially an IT procurement model where the on demand technologies are delivered as-a-service. This highlights the importance of customer-service provider relationship and dialogue for joint value creation and mutual benefit. Given this, we adopt a customer relationship value approach to investigating the customers' perception of value in these encounters in an effort to support OSS providers to better target their offering to mass customers. Value to the customer has several dimensions ranging from utility value to social value, and further functional customer experience, i.e. the ease of access, adaptation, development, and use of platform technologies. Section 3.1 provides a general overview of the customer perceived value model, while Sect. 3.2 focuses on the customer value perception of OSS in cloud computing environments.

Customer value proposition must provide distinctive, measurable, and sustainable value [19]. Viewing cloud computing from the service science perspective highlights the role of cloud as an orchestration device of value co-creation processes. Supplier must be able to support customers, not only in those processes that are most relevant for customer's businesses, but also in all stages of customer interaction, even during stages that do not directly contribute to the balance sheet such as in sales [20]. Cloud computing service relationship integrates supplier, customer and end-users tangible assets (i.e. technology, people) and intangible assets (i.e. value propositions, shared information) [20]. The key idea is that the underlying technology is invisible for the end-users, clients and developers. The service oriented view supports companies in identifying new horizontal value creation opportunities and business models [21].

3.1   Customer Value Principles

Service providers' ultimate objective is to add value to customers' business, processes and operations. The customer perceived value is defined as value that customer receives in return of investment, which in many cases deviates from the suppliers' intended value creation. In case of services, the value is created in co-creation with the customer [22]. Therefore the supplier relationship value is of greater importance than the customer delivered value. Customer value has been categorised by Smith and Colgate [23] as follows:

1. Functional value: the attributes that help create value, i.e. cost, quality, reliability, security, and performance [1];
2. Cost/sacrifice value: comparable overall life cycle value [24];
3. Relationship value: the overall customer experience, i.e. product quality, service support, delivery performance, supplier know-how, time-to-market, personal interaction, price, and process costs [25];
4. Co-creation value: the capabilities that enable designing or modifying service or source code [26];
5. Brand value: the social value in peer group [19];

The four most common challenges in creating customer value are insufficient wealth, access, skill, and time [27]. The scholars urge for more customer research to validate the points of value creation, to determine new dimensions of value, and to assess the relative importance of each dimension of value from a customer's perspective. The relationship value driver framework introduced by Ulaga's [25] maps customers' perceived value in service relationships. The authors identified 8 dimensions of value, which correspond to the ones introduced in Fig. 1 (each dimension having sub-categories describing elements of perceived value).

We selected Ulaga's framework for analysing customers' perception of open source cloud software. The different elements of customer reported valuations were mapped under the eight categories in order to have an overall view of customers' drivers in selecting cloud computing services. This would support our understanding of opportunities and limitations of OSS in cloud computing from customers' perspective. The framework applies well to an open source context, because most consumers or end-customers of commercial OSS are businesses [28]. The limitations of the framework relate to little attention given to external environment and context where the value creation takes place. Figure 3 lists the eight dimensions of Ulaga's framework.

In this framework, product quality is defined as the extent to which the supplier's product meets the customer's specifications. Service Support refers to the provisioning of the right information, at the right time, as requested by customer. This is related to *Personal Interaction*, which refers to proximity, ease of collaboration and personalized relationship. *Service Delivery* is measured by accuracy, experience and consolidating the supply base, and delivering integrated systems as opposed to single parts. *Supplier know-How* involves resources, skills, and strength in

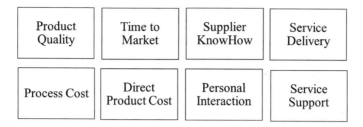

Fig. 3 Ulaga (2003): 8 dimensions of customer relationship value drivers

long-term relationships. The aspects in this facet include the supplier's extant knowledge of the supply market, improving existing products, and assisting in developing new products. *Time-To-Market* is measured by design capability, prototype and development efforts. *Direct Product Cost* is the price at time of purchase, as opposite to process and life cycle costs. *Process Costs* include the costs associated with process improvements and other transformation processes.

3.2 Customer Value Perception of Open Source Cloud Software

The literature on customer value creation in OSS is still very new and few authors have addressed the creation of value in the OSS development model, with the exception of West (2007) [3] and Morgan and Finnegan (2008) [1]. The nature of OSS allows users to co-create value by actively participating in the development process, audit the software and change vendors with low switching cost. Therefore, customer value perceptions in OSS will differ from proprietary software. The commoditization of OSS allows suppliers to provide undifferentiated software at a lower price point, thereby increasing the customer perception of value added [26, 29]. The level of formal control that a firm has over its open source resources impacts the extent to which a firm can capture value from OSS [30].

Cloud computing has changed the way open source technologies are distributed. Much of OSS is available on a SaaS basis, which makes it convenient for customers without the need to deploy software on their own servers. Many of open source projects, in turn, take place in cloud, or focus on developing infrastructure and management software that makes cloud computing possible. These tools are used by public cloud computing providers and by organizations that want to set up private or hybrid clouds. These tools and the enhanced collaboration opportunities increase customer relationship value and make cloud based OSS technologies more appealing for customers than the traditional open source technologies. The concept of open source also conveys a collaborative approach to innovation. This provides customers increased perception of value and opportunities for innovation. OSS can be combined with complementary assets such as support, customization, integration, or upgrades [29] in hybrid set ups. This will impact the process value of the technologies and provide opportunities for developing sponsored open source projects, where specialists develop OSS modules to their needs.

Adaptation of open source cloud software creates opportunities, but also risks related to intellectual property infringement. Cloud based delivery has created newer cloud-driven restrictive open-source licenses (e.g., AGPL) that have changed the traditional open-source compliance mechanisms. The subsequent development of remedial open-source licenses can impact users' data management policies and risk infringement. Open source communities have tools for detecting software components with license obligations that are provided as a service.

4   Methodology

Our research project studied customers' value drivers in cloud environments with a special focus on OSS technologies. The project is built on the assumption that the use cases for cloud computing have converged, and IoT and M2M visions drive the development of the future Webs, namely the Web 3.0 (also known as the *Semantic Web*) and the Web 4.0 (also known as the *Meta Web*). Consumers' interests are increasingly in applications and services, thus requiring a completely transparent and heterogeneous network. We further investigated how open source cloud technologies impact the evolution and maturing of cloud computing industry, and differentiation of various ecosystem actors' roles as the industry matures. In order to verify this assumption, we investigated the customers' value drivers for adapting cloud services and selecting vendors. Data collection was done predominantly in Finland, which is the number one cloud computing adaptor in Europe, and avid supporter of the OSS movement, represents mature and specialized cloud computing environment. Finnish customers also have specific demands due to regulations, data proximity and language, which make it an ideal environment for analyzing the opportunities for regional provider roles.

Data regarding customer preferences, perceived adaptation opportunities, implementation barriers and valuations was collected from leading Finnish companies in form of online survey and interviews. The survey reached 122 respondents from various industries in Finland, including 34 responses from companies offering cloud computing services. The collected data was complemented with 52 interviews with leading Finnish companies Chief Technology or Information Officers. Data collection was done in April-July 2015.

The collected data was analyzed applying Ulaga's relationship model in order to categorize and organize the findings in logical order. In our computation, we organized the interview questions under the 8 relationship value categories introduced in Fig. 1. The findings were then analyzed in order to describe their implications and contribution to the research community and practitioners. This analysis is presented in the next section.

5 Results

The survey collected 122 respondents from different fields of business, including energy, forestry, finance, ICT, logistics, media and public sector. 75% of the respondents represented large organizations (over 150 employees). 58% of the companies operated internationally, while the rest solely on national markets. 33 of the respondents represented cloud service user-providers and 89 organizations were cloud service users. Section 5.1 presents the trends identified from the survey for adopting cloud services, while Sect. 5.2 focuses on identifying the relationship value drivers.

5.1 Trends for Adopting Cloud Services

The multi-sided view to the service use and user preferences provided a holistic view of the situation. The most commonly used services were standard communication services like email, website and blogs. Other commonly used services were business support services like enterprise resource planning systems, customer relationship management software, as well as human resources and finance and control services and data storage.

As emphasized, the main drivers for using cloud computing included flexibility and scalability of IT resources, which were reported as the major driver by over 40% of the respondents. With this, capital expenditure to IT was reduced and overall cost reduced. Improvements were sought through improved business processes and modernization of user interfaces and systems. The results also highlighted the interesting feature in cloud adaptation statistics. While the cloud user base is wide, the extent to which services are used is overall very small, less than 5% of IT budget for over 90% of the organizations. All respondents reported plans to increase use of cloud services in the future.

The main criterion for selecting cloud service providers was the fit for business needs. Regional, EU based providers were considered too add business value through knowledge on the local legislation, culture and norms. Price, operability and service level were rated second in importance, followed by data center location and reputation of the vendor. Local language support was not among the main criteria as could have been expected. The communicated barriers for using cloud services highlighted the earlier identified concerns related to control over own data. Privacy, confidentiality and access to own data caused concern, amplified by the fear of regulatory changes. Experienced user also reported difficulties with service integration to existing systems and hardware, which undermined the initial objectives to reduce investment in in-house ICT competency.

As previously mentioned, the survey results were complemented by a set of 55 interviews with the major Finnish companies. The interviews elaborated on the survey questions, and raised the question of open source cloud technology and platform use. The companies used both international cloud service providers like Microsoft, Fujitsu and Amazon, but also regional providers like Nordic Cloud and Appelsiini. Preference was for national or EU based suppliers due to language, specific knowledge, politics and proximity. Challenges were caused by the lack of suitable regional providers, or gaps in their offering and incompatibility with SLAs and companies' objectives.

5.2   Relationship Value Drivers

The interviews revealed that the companies were reluctant to adapt OSS due to the uncertainty related to their sustainability, usability, customer support and future regulations. There were also concerns with the usability of the systems, and risks of running parallel systems for different purposes, with need for training users to the interfaces. Somewhat surprisingly, the expected issues related to privacy and securiies were not listed among the main barriers for the use of open source technologies. Energy efficiency and related standards were raised several times in discussion. The interviewees reported supplier reputation as among the main selection criteria, along with the data center location. Even for companies not operating with the public sector, the geographical location of the data center was a major risk management issue in terms of changing regulations and security. Regional and EU supplier would be given preference, providing there were enough alternative suppliers. The respondents also mentioned energy efficiency and sustainability related concerns weighting in decision making.

The interviews included explicit questions related to the use of open source cloud software. None of the respondents had preference for OSS, even some of them used OSS in small scale. The reasons for the aversion mirrored the earlier reported concerns with business continuity, support capabilities and required efforts for integration to in-house heritage systems. Customers valued regional suppliers with contextual knowledge, geographical proximity and customized support services. In the analysis reliability and support were the major criteria for supplier selection. Several respondents reported using regional small-scale providers form their own administrative services delivery, while they preferred reputable international players as channel partners for distributing own services and applications. Service pricing was considered moderate to fair across all respondents.

The collected data was next analyzed using the Ulaga's 2003 relationship value framework. In our operationalization the survey question were grouped to the most suitable categories. Time to market dimension was dismissed since this was not in the scope of the questionnaire. In this computation, cost is raised as the main driver for selecting cloud services. Other major drivers are product quality, service support and process cost. Business drivers impact strongly the cloud service selection, along with total cost (direct cost and operational costs). Time to market was not

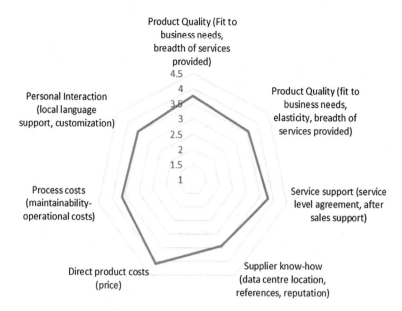

Fig. 4 Customer value drivers in cloud computing services

considered as a major driver since the objectives with cloud adaptation were mostly cost related. Figure 4 summarizes the findings of the study in a spider diagram. The diagram illustrates the customer relationship priorities and price, service support and product fit to business needs. Lesser attention was given for personal interaction and process costs.

The results supported earlier results on customers' valuation of both product and service attributes in cloud computing service context. Customers consider the total cost of ownership resulting from initial service purchase, integration to heritage systems, and continuous operations support and maintenance when making selections on applied technologies and vendors. The importance of service support is highlighted in cloud context, where the solutions are sourced as a service. The results also showed that the major customer value drivers were the service quality, support and supplier know-how, referring to the suppliers' knowledge of their context and specific requirements. All informants were satisfied with the price levels for the service. With significant improvements to current situations, cost was not considered a major driver in vendor selection. Cloud customers preferred local or EU based service providers with knowledge of local culture, customs and regulations. Also data centre location and instant support were considered among the main vendor selection criteria. OSS were considered cumbersome due to required in-house integration, requirements for user training and concerns regarding future availability and updates to the software.

The findings highlighted new opportunities for niche players and smaller regional actors, and overrode the dominant thinking on the economies of scale driven cost advantages and savings as major drivers for the selection of cloud vendors. The increased emphasis on support capabilities and need for differentiated service roles was further highlighted with large organizations moving to cloud in incremental steps. OSS providers have their niche in cloud markets, and could improve their position significantly through increased customer focus.

6 Discussion

This paper discussed the less studied area of customer perception of open source technologies. It reviewed related literature and conducted an empirical enquiry in order to further understand the value drivers in software procurement context. Increased awareness of customer preferences helps designing service models that respond to customer needs, and drive adaptation of open standards and pave away for Internet of Things, open interfaces, and interoperability, and consequently scalable innovations, distributed systems and new business opportunities for SMEs.

Open source technologies have potential to accelerate the much discussed industrialization of services, and drive open innovation in virtual venues. Our enquiry on customer value drivers and OSS technologies was limited both in terms of scope and sample, but served to draw attention to this critical trajectory in the evolution of open source software markets. With the global characteristics of internet services, the authors believe that the results can be considered valid also on broader context. However, more research would be needed on the opportunities of OSS technologies and customer dynamics with these user-developer communities specifically in open source context, and their impacts on markets, regulations and business models, as well as society as a whole.

7 Conclusion

Our research revealed a mismatch between open source cloud providers intended, and customers' perceived relationship value. While OSS providers aim to deliver superior software to respond to the customers' needs, the customers perceive non-technical relationship values as important as the technical features. This leads to loss of business opportunities for OSS providers, as companies prefer to fulfil their need with suitable service with no additional integration or further development.

As to summarize, OSS providers typically conceptualize their offering as an infrastructure or software. The value is considered to accumulate with the service functionalities and regular new releases. This is also the dominant view in technology-oriented research. However, marketing and service science approaches adopt broader understanding of customer value, and conceptualize software as services, or even further, value co-creation venues. In this respect, we conceptualise open source software as a service system, where value is created downstream, originated from the customers' requirements and added value. Service providers position themselves to this customer value network with their own value offering. Obviously, both engineering and service-oriented views are needed, and they are complementary.

The main contribution of the paper is the recommendation that with increased customer focus and understanding of adaptation barriers, OSS companies can fulfil the role of transformers of the future of internet business evolution, moving away from the proprietary technology platform based value creation now controlled by the likes of IOS and Android, contributing to more equal, accessible and interoperable web for the benefit of societies, environment and citizens.

References

1. Morgan, L., Finnegan, P.: Deciding on open innovation. An exploration of how firms create and capture value with open source software. In: Gonzalo, L. (ed.) Open IT-Based Innovation: Moving Towards Cooperative IT Transfer and Knowledge Diffusion, pp. 228–247 (2008)
2. Heljanko, K., Hussnain, A.: State of the Art Survey of Open Source Cloud Platform Components. Tekes Publications, Helsinki (2015)
3. Lerner, J., Tirole, J.: The Economics of Technology Sharing: Open Source and Beyond. NBER Working Paper 10956 (2004)
4. Schweik, C.M., English, R., Haire, S.: Factors leading to success or abandonment of open source commons: an empirical analysis of Sourceforge.net projects. In: The Free and Open Source Software for Geospatial Conference, Cape Town (2008)
5. Capra, E., Francalanci, C., Merlo, F., Lamastra, C.R.: A survey on firms' participation in open source community projects. In: IFIP International Federation for Information Processing, pp. 225–236. UNESCO, Laxenburg (2009)
6. Hughes, A.: IDC Reveals Worldwide Internet of Things Predictions for 2015. https://www.idc.com/getdoc.jsp?containerId=prUS25291514 (2015)
7. West, J., Gallagher, S.: Key Challenges of Open Innovation: Lessons from Open Source Software. San Jose State College of Business Mimeo (2004)
8. West, J., O'Mahoney, S.: Contrasting community building in sponsored and community founded open source projects. In: IEEE Proceedings of the 38th Annual Hawaii International Conference on System Sciences. IEEE Computer Society Press, Los Alamitos (2005)
9. Varian, H.R., Shapiro, C.: Linux Adoption in the Public Sector: An Economic Analysis. University of California Haas School of Business, Mimeo (2003)
10. Ghosh, R., Glott, R., Kriger, B., Robles, G.: Free/Libre and Open Source Software: Survey and Study. University of Maastricht Institute of Infonomics and Berlecon Research GmbH Mimeo (2002)
11. Maurer S., Scotchmer, M.: Open source software: the new intellectual property paradigm. In: Economics and Information Systems, vol. 1, pp. 285–322. Whinston, Amsterdam (2006)
12. Lakhani, K., Wolf, R.: Why hackers do what they do: understanding motivation and effort in free/open source software projects. In: Feller, J., Fitzgerald, B., Hissam, S., Lakhani, K. (eds.) Perspectives in Free and Open Source Software. MIT, Cambridge and London (2005)
13. Von Krogh, G., Haefliger, S., Spaeth, S., Wallin, M.: Open source software: what we know (and do not know) about motivations to contribute. In: The DRUID Conference, Copenhagen, Denmark (2008)

14. Mockus, A., Fielding, R.T., Herbsleb, J.D.: Two case studies of open source software development: Apache and Mozilla. ACM Trans. Softw. Eng. Methodol. **11**, 309–346 (2002)
15. Gruber, M., Henkel, J.: New ventures based on open innovation—an empirical analysis of start-up firms in embedded Linux. Int. J. Technol. Manage. **33**(4) (20006)
16. Lerner, J., Tirole, J.: Some simple economics of open source. J. Ind. Econ. **52**, 197 (2002)
17. Shah, S.K.: Motivation, governance, and the viability of hybrid forms in open source software development. Manage. Sci. **52**, 1000 (2006)
18. Fang, Y., Neufeld, D.: Understanding sustained participation in open source software projects. J. Manage. Inf. Syst. **25**, 9–50 (2009)
19. Anderson, J.C., Narus, J.A., Van Rossum, W.: Customer value propositions in business markets. Harvard Bus. Rev. **84**, 1–4 (2006). (Harvard)
20. Grönroos, C.: Service logic revisited: who creates value? And who co-creates? Eur. Bus. Rev. **20**(4), 298–314 (2008)
21. Haynie, M.: Enterprise cloud services: deriving business value from Cloud Computing. Micro Focus Technical Report, http://techrepublic.com (2009)
22. Gustafsson, A., Kristensson, P., Witell, L.: Customer co-creation in service innovation: a matter of communication? J. Serv. Manage. **23**(Iss: 3), 311–327 (2012)
23. Smith, J.B., Colgate, M.: Customer value creation: a practical framework. J. Mark. Theory Pract. **15**(1), Taylor Francis online (2007)
24. Zeithaml, V.A.: Consumer perceptions of price, quality, and value: a means-end model and synthesis of evidence. J. Mark. **52**(3), 2–22 (1988). (American Marketing Association)
25. Ulaga, W.: Capturing value creation in business relationships: a customer perspective. Ind. Mark. Manage. **32**, 677–693 (2003)
26. O'Cass, A., Ngo, L.V.: Examining the firm's value creation process: a managerial perspective of the firm's value offering strategy and performance. Br. J. Manage. **22**(4), 646–671 (2011)
27. Johnson, M, Christensen, C., Kagermann, H.: Reinventing your business model. Harvard Business Review, Harvard (2008)
28. Shanker, A.: A customer value creation framework for businesses that generate revenue with open source software. Technol. Innov. Manage. Rev. **3** (2012)
29. West, J.: Value capture and value networks in open source vendor strategies, system sciences. In: HICSS 2007. IEEE Proceedings of the 40th Hawaii International Conference on System Sciences (HICSS 2007). IEEE Computer Society Press, Los Angeles (2007)
30. Bonnacorsi, A., Rossi, C.: Licensing schemes in the production and distribution of open source software: an empirical investigation. Sant' Ana School for Advanced Studies Institute for Informatics and Telematics Mimeo (2003)

ICT in a Collaborative Network to Improve Quality of Life: A Case of Fruit and Vegetables Re-use

Sabrina Bonomi, Francesca Ricciardi and Cecilia Rossignoli

Abstract Negative externalities of economic development impact on the numerous areas and deteriorate quality of their resident's life. Systems address these dramatic challenges through collaborative innovation of organizations, which, enabled by new technologies, create or capture attractive opportunities. The aim of this paper is to highlight how Information and Communication Technology (ICT) plays a pivotal role in enabling the growth of new organizational forms, which create value at the territorial level, trigger positive changes in social and economic environment and improve the quality of life of people involved. Literature review considers the multiple perspectives of Institutional Entrepreneurship, Social Entrepreneurship, Socio-Ecological Systems and Socio-Technical Systems that until now were separate. This study highlights instead that their integration provides a satisfying explanation of the phenomena observed, and well explain different motivations of the examined organizations. ICT-based organizations, point out interesting opportunities for all organizations, public institutions, companies and social enterprises. In particular, the paper analyses a case of reutilization of fruit and vegetables surplus in the third Italian Agricultural centre. This action reduces production of waste and pollution, fights poverty and improves health, ultimately creating social inclusion.

Keywords Network organizations · Social entrepreneurship · Institutional work · Information systems · Collaborative innovation · Better life

S. Bonomi (✉)
eCampus University, via Isimbardi 10, 22060 Novedrate, CO, Italy
e-mail: sabrina.bonomi@uniecampus.it

F. Ricciardi · C. Rossignoli
University of Verona, via dell'Artigliere 8, 37139 Verona, Italy
e-mail: francesca.ricciardi@unito.it

C. Rossignoli
e-mail: cecilia.rossignoli@univr.it

© Springer Nature Switzerland AG 2019
Y. Baghdadi and A. Harfouche (eds.), *ICT for a Better Life and a Better World*,
Lecture Notes in Information Systems and Organisation 30,
https://doi.org/10.1007/978-3-030-10737-6_4

1   Introduction

The so-called grand challenges, which imply sustainability issues, are raising growing attention on the part of the scholarly world [1], also in a field, that of organization and management studies, that traditionally targets firms, and their performance, as main scope of inquiry. Negative externalities of economic development, such as pollution, waste production, overpopulation, traffic, poverty and social exclusion of fragile people, have many implications and the quality of their citizens' life gets worse. Systems address these dramatic challenges through collaborative innovation of organizations, which, enabled by new technologies, can take a range of interesting opportunities. For this reason, the global community is focused on the opportunities offered by technology in order to address emerging social and environmental challenges.

The aim of this paper is to understand if and how the Information and Communication Technology (ICT) can play a pivotal role in generating new organizational collaborative forms (CO), which create value in their territorial areas, trigger positive changes in social and economic environment and improve the quality of life of people involved. These organizations, based on ICT, open up interesting opportunities for both institutional entrepreneurs and a new generation of social entrepreneurs. Several branches of research represent these opportunities: Institutional Entrepreneurship, Social Entrepreneurship, Socio-Ecological Systems (SES) and Socio-Technical Systems (STS) that until now were isolated. We think that only a joint interpretation of these theories offers a satisfactory explanation of the phenomena observed. This overlapping interpretation also well illustrates, in researchers' opinion, the different motivations of the organizations analysed. The paper suggests that the CO can be the engine for sustainability and resilience of local systems. This perspective should lead to a world in which economic development and prosperity are combined with greater social and ecological sustainability, a better quality of life for everybody and a greater resilience of social systems, such as local communities. In other words, a "better world" must be built, and this requires significant changes in practices, in shared values, in the roles and rules enabled by high technologies.

This work presents, as an example of this interpretation, a case of fruit and vegetables re-use, specifically the reutilization of surplus generated in a fruit and vegetable markets and agricultural producer organizations because of unsold, deterioration, other economic reasons or Community rules, in favour of non-profit organizations (NPOs) that assist socially disadvantaged people. This will convert the negative externalities, caused by the disposal of surpluses once become waste, primarily pollution, in value creation to donor companies, for beneficiaries (NPOs), for public institutions and for socially disadvantaged people. Papargyropoulou et al. [2] suggest to focus efforts on reducing food waste, in situations where the food, although no commercial value, for its nutritional properties still has economic and social value, through re-use, for example, or recycling or recovering.

This paper, therefore, aim to show the importance of CO, like the one acting in the case, which, by means of ICT, create and manage collaborative networks that improve people's lives and the environment in which they operate.

2 Theoretical Background

2.1 Institutional Entrepreneurship

Within the perspective of institutional theory, entrepreneurs recognize the decline of institutions, and they design new structures to implement institutional changes. Therefore, they are able to challenge existing rules and practices and institutionalize those who support them [3]. Entrepreneurs, to be regarded as institutional entrepreneurs, should have two characteristics: (1) initiate divergent changes [4], i.e. the changes that break the institutional framework; (2) actively participate in the implementation of these changes [5], actively mobilizing and managing resources.

Institutional theory also identifies several mechanisms, tactics and strategies used by institutional entrepreneurs to implement changes: cooperation and collective action [6]; political tactics and practices [7], framing [8], resources and strategies employed. The institutional entrepreneurship studies emphasize the role of cooperation and collective action [6]. Therefore, institutional entrepreneurs were also called "actors with social skills", in reference to their ability to motivate other actors to co-operation by providing a common identity [9]. Under this perspective, these entrepreneurs should support a collective identity and find new ways to connect and combine the different interests of the groups [9]. Institutional entrepreneurs operate to find common solutions to collective problems, also working in collaboration with other actors, leveraging the benefits that result from convergent interests and relying on collective action to influence the macro-level institutions [10]. More recently, theorists started to consider the dilemmas of collective action such as free riding and the distribution of public goods [11]. For example, Wijen and Ansari [12] blend the knowledge of the institutions and develop a framework to explain the "collective institutional entrepreneurship". This is the process of overcoming the collective action dilemmas, which enables the interaction between actors to create or transform institutions. Institutional entrepreneurs' ability to drive change requires the cooperation of many other actors. Many institutional changes are complex social processes involving different interests and perspectives; they require collective action that integrates the mutual interests of several groups of actors [13].

Collective institutional entrepreneurship [14] is a process that moves on from collective inaction through collaboration between various actors for the creation of new institutions or transformation of existing ones. This process includes a "collaborative leadership" [15], a form of leadership emanating not only driving actors but also by providing integrated structures and processes within a partnership [16].

It also requires an institutional work and some practices that go beyond those of institutional entrepreneurs [17] that include proactive actions of many individuals and organizations aiming to create, sustain or disrupt the institutions. Since the collective interests do not always produce collective action [18], it is necessary to provide collective resources to support the issue [19], and also to motivate the individual whose interests may lie in the non-cooperation. To promote collective change, collective institutional entrepreneurs should explore the best combination of tools to involve institutional actors. They can, firstly, attract actors through ethical impulses and explore common ground to generate critical mass; secondarily, they have to mobilize actors through appropriate incentives, timely; finally, they have to encourage agreements that others perceive as correct and develop the necessary skills to support and implement change.

2.2   Social Entrepreneurship

Most definitions of social entrepreneurship refer to the ability to mobilize resources to solve social problems [20] through creation of social value. The most suitable definition of social entrepreneur, according to the different actors involved in the project, is that provided by Light [21] which states: "A social entrepreneur is an individual, group, network, organization, or alliance of organizations that seeks sustainable, large-scale change through pattern-breaking ideas in what or how governments, non-profits, and businesses do to address significant social problems." Social entrepreneurs leverage three types of key resources to achieve some fruitful opportunities. They are relational, cultural and institutional resources. The meaning of relational resources is of social capital and social skills [9], that include abilities to generate social networking or interpersonal situations [22], to create social interrelationships, networks connected by formal and informal social strengthened bonds, and to access to communication channels and networks [23]. Relational resources give many opportunities for both to exchange information, leveraging interpersonal relationships, and to fulfil goals. Cultural resources mean rules, values, roles, languages, behaviours, and expressions of a community. Usually they are considered and studied like an internal resource of organizations [24].

Institutional resources concern political, legal and institutional infrastructures. Robinson [23] concisely explained the "institutional barriers", like the cultural ones, as problems that come from the incomprehension of those resources. Therefore, the most important thing is social entrepreneur's ability to create resources to fill an institutional gap, more than ability to use the existing institutional resources. Entrepreneurs, who can recognize as weak institutional frameworks, may facilitate the development of their businesses and give an advantage on achieving long-term sustainability. Both forms of entrepreneurs, institutional and social, initiate change processes, solve problems of change, and address the challenge of resistance to change.

2.3   *Institutional Systems Studies*

E. Ostrom said that the promotion of change should take place by the efforts of mutual collaboration and creativity and reflection of the people, rather than by government intervention [25]. This would ensure a greater collective value gain. The idea of a co-evolution bottom-up of institution and technologies come from two complementary theories, SES and STS. The SES theory explains the management of resources, by observing the specific interactions between natural environment and social system as well as institutional and technological structures [26]. Technology focuses on innovation processes, addressing the co-evolution of technologies and institutions, but while ignoring environmental impacts [27]. STS studies, instead, derive from Trist's investigations. He argues that technology can change institutions, structures of power and rules of cooperation [28]. On the other hand, however, the same institutions affect technologies, and they explain inertia and stability, but also dynamism and innovation [29]. Humans are surrounded by several technological tools, which reflect their perceptions, behaviours, relationships, and habits in addition to material artefacts. Indeed, "the rules that drive societies are not just shared in social groups and carries inside actors' heads, but can also be embedded in artefacts and practice" [27]. Therefore, rules and beliefs can be absorbed into artefacts and practices; these change with more difficult because a lot of costs can't be recovered. SES and STS studies encourage new ways to understand institutional change [30]. In addition, they provide the scientific basis to explain how institutions interact with resources and technologies on which the community relies, and how these interactions determine sustainability, resilience and strength and adaptability [31]. The latest discoveries of SES and STS theories highlighted some factors that facilitate processes of technical and institutional redesign. Consequently, sustainability and resilience of the system increases. Organizational implications are represented by a bottom-up poly-centrism of institutional activism [26]. A cross-fertilization of the SES and STS studies with institutional entrepreneurship makes these studies extremely interesting and promising.

3   Method

The research question proposed by this study is to understand if and how ICT can play a crucial role enabling the emergence of new organizational forms, the COs, that create value at regional level, trigger positive changes in social and economic environment and improve the quality of life of people involved and thus, in general, create a better world.

A qualitative research approach is the most suited to handle this type of enquiry [32], because this study revolves around a "how" question, and also because scientific research on this topic is still in a pioneering phase, as shown in the previous section. More specifically, a longitudinal, in-depth case study seems particularly suited to address the research question [33].

The case-study was selected because it is suitable for illuminating and extending relationships and logic among constructs [34] and because of the privileged access to the relevant information. One of the authors of this study, in fact, has been involved in key roles (idea developer and project manager) in an important social entrepreneurship initiative from 2007 to 2014. During these years, the researcher was actively engaged in social entrepreneurship activities, including the development and experimentation of new possible business models; the development of a network of partners and beneficiaries; the development of ICT-enabled processes and solutions; and the development of educational [35] and institutional work to support the successful adoption and replication of the proposed solutions. The researcher had regular contact with all the stakeholders of the initiative, and participated to almost all the relevant meetings for the development of the relating projects; she took careful notes and kept a diary of her relevant conversations, experiences and impressions. She used the diary also to regularly draw cognitive maps of the evolving situation and of the perceived threats, opportunities, needs and success factors. She monitored and wrote reports on the activities of the social entrepreneurship organization and on the impacts of these activities. She systematically studied the legal framework influencing the activities and participated in the analyses that led to the implementation of the ICT solutions. In real time, she regularly collected all the relevant documents regarding these activities. This direct involvement ended in 2014. After 2014, the authors of this study conducted further field research through 10 semi-structured interviews (about 40 min each) and the collection of reports and contents on the press. The interviewees represent the whole range of the stakeholders of this initiative; the data collection phase was concluded in 2015; overall, it covers nine years of real-time research, providing a very rich body of material for the analysis phase. The researchers, through group work and discussion on this body of materials, selected the most interesting and relevant contents and, when necessary, transcribed these contents with a word processor, in order to have a homogeneous archive for the analysis.

4 The Veronamercato's Case: Social Entrepreneurship to Re-use Surplus of Fruit and Vegetables to Give a Better Quality Life

4.1 Food Waste and Collaborative Network

Fight food waste is an issue for public institutions that involves several areas, social and health, environmental and economic. A FAO's study [36] showed that the amount of food wasted in industrialized countries (222 million tons) is equal to the available food production in sub-Saharan Africa (230 million tons). The parallel increase of people who belong to the poverty slot or in marginal conditions and discomfort, put the institutions at the forefront of social health. In fact, they must reconcile benefits and the growing scarceness of available economic resources.

In fruit and vegetable sector, many wastes are physiological at all stages of the supply chain. Causes of waste are various: natural disaster can hit from planting to harvest; storage can increase the risk of perishability, packaging can be broken during distribution process, value decreases during marketing caused by the time of the day and so on. A lot of fruit and vegetables could be recovered, for example by purifying and sell the saved parts, but the labour cost for these operations does not justify the activity. These products, indeed, like all consumption goods, have a low profitability. NPOs, i.e. voluntary associations, social enterprises, and cooperatives, may be pivotal in food waste reduction, through the recovery of surplus and unsold products to assist poor people. The first benefit is a savings of purchase of food; NPOs can use this money to improve existing or add new services, providing in any case a better social and health care. Another benefit is the improvement of quality of nutrition of assisted people and therefore of public health. Consumption of fruits and vegetables, in fact, is minimal in disadvantaged people, due to its high purchase cost. Furthermore, donations by charities usually consist in pasta, rice or other long-storage products that do not, however, provide vitamins or mineral salts. But the World Health Organization (WHO) identifies in the consumption of at least 5 daily servings of fruits and vegetables an important part of healthy and balanced diet, also useful for the prevention of chronic diseases, particularly cardiovascular, diabetes and some types of cancer. Organizations, recovering fruits and vegetables, would receive the necessary quantity depending on of the patients' number, thus achieving concrete action against food waste along the entire supply chain.

However, even win-win projects like this, show critical issues that could have negative consequences for all involved if they are not properly managed.

The recovery process requires some organizational changes to enterprises, through various investments. People have to be trained on the correct method, about the appropriate procedures and on the precise selection of vegetables that are intended for the project. This requires time-consuming actions for staff, which represents a cost for companies that must be offset by benefits from project. Enterprises have also to do financial investments to modify software. Finally, the concerns of bad storage of food could lead unpredictable consequences in addition to worsening enterprises' reputation rather than improve it.

The difficulties of non-profit sector originate from organizational inefficiencies or structural simplicity. To do the activities requested by the project, indeed, it is necessary a good logistic organization; associations have to invest in equipment, such as lorries, blast chillers or refrigerating rooms, very important for the correct conservation of food. They also have to compile the correct documentation and guarantee the food traceability. These actions aren't usual for this kind of organizations.

Public Administration (PA) uses economic incentives, such as ticket lunch, voucher or gift grocery shopping, to help poor people; this kind of help is not personalized, based on standard rules that often fail and can not promote social inclusion.

The management of the project as a collaborative network allows addressing the critical issues, through various actions. For example, non-profit organizations may integrate disadvantage people in separating the surplus in waste and edible and prepare this latest for distribution to other assisted people, helping donors. PA could engage with procedures and their validation, could supervise and inspect the process to protect assisted people. The supervisor, an association of social promotion (APS), can report quantitative and qualitative data. Lastly, practices of profit and non-profit organization can be a laboratory from which PAs could extrapolate innovative ideas to achieve in their territories. They can also create specific training or educational path aiming to the employment of assisted people within these organizations.

4.2   The Case of Veronamercato S.p.A.

Veronamercato S.p.A (VM) is a joint-stock company founded in 1989 by a majority of public sources (75% Municipality of Verona) and some private. Veronamercato S.p.A built the Agricultural Centre of Verona (the third in Italy) and owns and manages it directly [37]. VM is a virtuous example in social and environmental sphere thanks to the best Italian award in recycling (90%), to the energy saving caused by modern technologies (i.e. the photovoltaic system on the roof of the market guarantee the energetic self-sufficiency) and to the recovery of about a thousand tonnes of unsold fruit and vegetables donated to NPOs accredited. For many years wholesalers occasionally donated to NPOs, depending on their personal sensitivity. Sometimes donations were ineffective and inefficient because of high costs of food storage in warehouses and often of the generation of waste at the NPO. Moreover, the logistic process of recovery and distribution of fruit and vegetables, without any traceability neither control, sometimes allowed opportunistic behaviours. This is the reason why VM participated in R.e.b.u.s. project (the acronym means "Recovery of Surplus of unsold goods in solidarity"), implementing an ad hoc project for fruit and vegetables. The network organization created by an APS allows donating the surplus directly, immediately but systematically, to NPOs those assist socially disadvantaged people. In this way, the food, which otherwise would have been wasted, becomes an important social and economic resource.

The project is an example of value co-creation. The test began in late November 2008 after mapping organizations already working. Focusing on fruit and vegetables, that are essential for a healthy diet, the project seeks to respond to the WHO's recommendation. Disadvantaged people are far from consuming at least five portions. Many charitable organizations, in fact, collect food to donate people who cannot buy it, but exclude fresh products because they require to be quickly allocated. In the VM case, instead, this is possible, thanks to the collaboration of about seventy organizations [37], coordinated by the APS through an ICT. In researchers' opinion, this an interesting case of CO, a collaborative network organization that uses new technologies to improve sustainability, resilience and quality of life of territorial system. Thanks to innovative strategies, the CO:

- transforms a negative externality (waste, in this case) in commons (better quality of life and public health);
- creates and refines a set of rules that helps to make better use of the commons;
- plays a pivotal role in the daily management of commons;
- triggers institutional changes in a wide sphere, including institutional, community expectations, practices of enterprises and of non-profit organizations.

The aims of the VM network, and R.e.b.u.s in wider terms are intertwined with each other. Their aim is both to reduce waste at the source, throughout the food chain, and to reduce malnutrition of disadvantaged people. Therefore, VM project extends the product life cycle, avoiding it becomes waste; at the same time, it fulfils a social need by helping to improve the environment (fewer emissions, less inserting into landfill) and public health. This is possible thanks to a systematic and organized activity, managed by ICT, which achieve full compliance with the health, fiscal and administrative rules, by procedures, coordination tables, memoranda of understanding and agreements, and traceability documentation in the recovery process (i.e. DDT, loading and unloading tables). Transparency avoids health risks or opportunistic behaviours. Reports are structured among all kind of organizations: VM and AMIA, manager of the waste authority, are companies; Municipality and the Province of Verona, and Hygiene Food Nutrition Service (SIAN) of the Prevention and Health Department of Local Health Department (ASL 20), are public institutions; beneficiary associations are NPOs. This allowed achieving the objectives of the project in an effective and efficient way, and to strengthening inter-organizational relations.

The project has been approved by regulations through insertion in municipal decision on the environmental hygiene tariff (TIA; TARI at the present). In fact, companies involved in R.e.b.u.s. project take advantage of a percentage discount on the waste tax, proportional to the waste reduction; for VM, corresponds to about 70000 euros per year. The proceeding started in 2006, in agreement with the city administration. The discount was calculated on the amount certified by the APS through ICT. This non-budgeted savings stimulated donations. A part of discount can be transferred to provide for economic sustainability of the project. Since 2010, VM transferred one-third of its discount; financial autonomy has given the APS the chance to create jobs.

Data analysis and structure of the project show that this topic significantly involves organizations, cohesive in an integrated management strategy for reducing food waste and production of organic waste. The relationship of collaborative network is constantly evolving. In 2008, an agreement between the APS and VM was signed for deployment and the start of the regulatory procedures, managed by the APS with the technical support of the operators of the VM S.p.A.

Since 2013, when the agreement renewed, organizations are working in a synergistic way to resolve issues raised in previous years, such as the regularization of documents of non-profit organizations and their correct emission by wholesalers. Donors, in fact, encountered some difficulties in completing documents and in the establishment and standardization of the procedure. The agreement provides that only NPOs participating in the project with certain requirements, can ask for accreditation and thus could qualify for the recovery of goods, filling in the forms inserted on VM's website. Standardization of procedures and processes allowed the model to be replicated in different areas (i.e. Bergamo's Ortomercato; Padua's and Vicenza's market are evaluating), although each of them has its own peculiarities.

Only the involvement of all three kinds of organizations, bound by stable and mutual relationships in a circular subsidiarity, allows to achieve the goals efficiently and effectively as well as ensure sustainability and continual improvement of the project.

The VM project has a flexible structure, without fixed costs for the management of warehouses and logistics facilities, because the recovery, thanks to ICT, takes place per day by the NPOs those access via identification card. Distribution takes place in spatial proximity logic; therefore, there is a reduction of environmental impacts, including those caused by transport. Free food, provided by the network built and managed by APS, allows NPOs to offer better nutrition of poor people thanks to the wide variety of available fruit and vegetables. In this phase of recovery and transport, NPOs can promote the social inclusion of people assisted, taking them both to collection and transport and for selection and distribution of fruit and vegetables. The food collected is however released immediately, without storage. Thanks to the just-in-time logistics realized by its information system, network does not need a warehouse and consequently presents very low coordination costs and risks. Network operates through ICT, thanks to full-time and part-time employees and volunteers of APS who perform a fundamental part of the job: database upgrade, monitoring and reporting. The APS collaborates with Veronamercato and PA in control and verification of procedures, and in establishment of documents for administrative and fiscal transparency of donors. The APS also supports non-profit organizations in accordance with Regulation ensuring precision. It finds new donors and beneficiaries. Finally, APS processes results, in order to communicate to stakeholders, and supervises the entire process.

4.3   The Role of ICT

The CO initially used a general computer program, easy to use and affordable for all (Excel), to improve the coordination of the network of organizations in a just-in-time logic. This IT tool aims to create a database of organizations to classify their necessities, give them procedures and improve their knowledge, therefore each line was associated to a data profile; the purpose was also to have a more rapid consultation and to collect quantitative information and archive documents for traceability and certification of the process of recovery (i.e. DDT, authorizations, identification card etc.). ICT were able to solve some emergencies (e.g. a beneficiary that cannot recover goods, can be replaced in real time) and avoid warehousing. Then CO used ICT to collect qualitative data (interviews, satisfaction questionnaires, analysis of recovered food etc.) and a dedicated software was created; it became a way to share information and enhance the coordination of the activity and finally the IT become the essence, the boundaryless organizational structure of the network.

Information systems play an important role in the project because ICT promotes both efficiency and sustainability. Furthermore, ICT helps to increase the credibility of the project. Without ICT, the network of collaborative relations shouldn't be created or managed well, because it wouldn't be possible to provide partners with real-time information on food available for recovery. Even discount on the waste tax wouldn't be paid, because only an IT solution is able to provide the PA transparent monitoring and certified data. Specifically, thanks to ICT, VM takes care of: improve quality of products, ensure continuity in the supply chain of donations to non-profit organizations, improve organization of the recovery system, formalize procedures and fiscal aspects, ensure hygienic quality and maintain traceability of the products.

VM also collaborated to produce informative material for an educational project for teachers and children in primary and secondary schools on issues related to VM and R.e.b.u.s. project [35]. APS deals instead of the reporting management, guaranteeing fiscal and administrative transparency, product traceability, verification and direct check of the use of assets by the associations beneficiaries. APS prepares forms and procedures for beneficiary associations and monitors their compliance, develops and provides necessary data to compile statistics and fiscal assessments required, meets periodically inspectors of VM to inform wholesalers, promote their participation as donors and in compliance with the procedures, ensures consistent alignment, monitoring critical issues that arise and identifying decisive solutions.

4.4 The Effects on Quality of Life

It is started a study in order to evaluate, if possible, positive impacts on the physical well-being through a distribution of questionnaires to associations and assisted and monitoring their state of health, in collaboration with SIAN. In 2015, in fact, the amount of recovered fresh produce has reached an unprecedented record, amounting to 1,220,599 kilograms, 331,113 kg of fruit and 889,486 of vegetables; the increase, compared to 2014, is about 33% and a value of approximately

Table 1 The recovery at Veronamercato: a comparison of 2013/2014/2015 years

Year	kg	Increment percentage
2011	347,249	
2012	438,885	+26.4%
2013	787,246	+79%
2014	915,469	+16%
2015	1,220,599	+33%

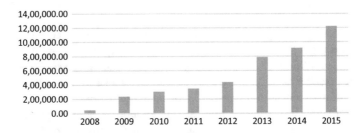

Fig. 1 Food collected at Veronamercato, from the beginning of the project (2008) to 2015

1,478,145 euros[1] With the involvement of all the wholesalers of VM S.p.A., the amount of fruits and vegetables recoverable in Verona would be reasonably about 1,445 tons only from the VM, as shown in Table 1.

Fruit and vegetables collection at VM aims to guarantee the access to fresh food to everybody and a correct diet to disadvantage people. "VM S.p.A—told us the public relation manager—liked this project since the beginning and participated in the network in order to start the recovery at the Agricultural Centre, becoming one of the key actors of the project. Thanks to the results of collaboration with APS, we made great strides: from 4,744 kg donated in 2008, in 2015 it was collected 1,220,599 kg of fruit and vegetables (see Fig. 1). The involved non-profit organizations are 16, and they take care of about 3000 people in marginality and discomfort; 61 wholesalers donate daily".

VM – the president continued – does a concrete action of corporate social responsibility; on the basis of the incentive annually obtained, VM give a contribution to the APS, to support a project that we like very much, ensuring a job role and giving continuity to the coordination at the same vegetable market. The logic of reducing waste is extended even to the overall management of the recycling process. In fact, VM is directly connected with beneficiaries and this collaboration eliminates the intermediate steps and, consequently, their costs and impacts, to a complete waste reduction.

---

[1]This value was calculated based on the average retail price indicated in the report of Macfrut "Macfrut Consumers Trend" in collaboration with CSO (Fruit and Vegetables Services Centre) on GFK data Italian and marked down 30%.

"The food recovery - the director said - is based on specific sanitary procedures, developed in collaboration with the ASL20 of Verona; each donation is traced via particular documents to protect firstly consumers' health, especially those in marginal and discomfort situation, assisted by the beneficiaries of our donations (NPOs). Secondarily, we want to guarantee transparency, honesty and legality, for a better quality of life for all people involved. This circular model of waste management is based on an integrated ecological approach constituted on a social perspective". "In addition to the fruit and vegetables collection and donation – concluded the public relation manager - we started an educational project with the purpose of working in a preventive logic. We realize workshops and activities for schools as well as public events in order to attract interests about fighting food waste and healthy food and good nutrition".

VM Network was founded in March 2013 to become more competitive at national and international level, aiming in particular to Eastern European countries. The coordinator of the network, currently composed by 57 companies of wholesalers, is a wholesaler of VM too; in the interview, he highlights the crucial role, played by several wholesalers, in donate unsold vegetables: "Within the Agri-food Centre there were a lot of products not more marketable because their aesthetic characteristics worsened due to the continuous movements along the supply chain. Products lost their commercial value but didn't lose their organoleptic qualities, which remained intact. Here it is considered to adhere to R.e.b.u.s. project, given that we don't give waste but a product perfectly comestible. (...) Before participation, products were thrown out. Now, thanks to donations, costs are reduced, and we fulfil a social need meeting the expectations that the community can put in company. There is a greater focus on products when it became clear that the economic advantages of enterprises could be combined with common goods or the community's social needs. The collaborative network is essential to achieve the goals of the project: "VM provides the product but the collaboration of NPOs is necessary; they pick fruit and vegetables; they distribute them to needy families. The collaborative network among PA, enterprises and NPOs achieves the maximum output. Collaborative network ensures mutual controls and supervision between the different actors, and only this mutual control prevents any economic speculations on recovered products". And, again: "Network is trying to develop new knowledge through mutual collaboration. The exchange of ideas generates and implements new solutions. Organizational culture changed, thanks to the activities of several operators. For example, they pay more attention to unsold products, realized that this project is not only a tax benefits, but also a moral behaviour. There are also benefit directly coming from use of ICT: it simplifies management and logistic; it clears spaces for fresh products (...) We know that this is above all a cultural and educational challenge, therefore we also activated on the promotion to healthy and sustainable lifestyles in younger generations. The goal of the educational project is mainly to sensitize young people to the consumption of fruits and vegetables according to the principle of the five daily portions of five different colours (red, yellow/orange, green, blue/purple, and white)". A council member of VM said: "The most important nutritionists in the world recognize the role of the five colours

in the protection of health and in the defence from the most common diseases. (…)
The growth of the culture of a healthy diet is one of the primary purposes of VM,
which is responsible to invest resources in education of the most sensitive parts of
the population, as the new generations"." VM is the only market, in Italy, that has
all the certifications of Quality, Health and Safety and Environment, which reflect
the quality of fruit and vegetables and allowed to improve reliability and safety of
donated products.

5 Discussions and Conclusion

The described case study shows that ICT can be an instrument, through which a CO
can coordinate inter-organizational relationships and trigger positive changes in the
social and economic context. These changes need an institutional legitimacy
through specific rules, and ICT favourite that. "The project has great value for
enrichment of quality of diets and, consequently, for public health, but especially
because this is achieved with all respect of laws, that has been studied by our
department"—says the executive of SIAN—"When people work together, they
trigger mechanisms that promote adoption of healthy behaviour. Human health
depends on healthy food systems." In researchers' opinion, this case has a lot of
connection with the theoretic constructs presented. We studied institutional
entrepreneurship literature and this theory well explains one actor's (VM) activities
analysed in the project. The actions of the second player (APS) are based on the
second current of thought described, the social entrepreneurship. Social entrepreneurs are able to mobilize resources to solve significant problems through social
innovations. Their initiatives are located in a cultural and institutional context; thus,
it is necessary to consider the wide range of limitations that potentially enabling or
constraining the success of the implemented social initiatives.

Inter-organizational networks are studied because they represent the concrete
operation of VM network. It is a system made up of actors and technologies that
leverage on institutions and ICT in order to protect the fragile resources of the
whole system. Collaborative networks are presented because the cooperation
between the three kinds of organizations involved in VM case (PA, enterprises and
NPOs) is based on typical ethical principles: trust, ethics solidarity, altruism,
reciprocity and reputation. The interdependence relationships among several
organizations imply also flexible problem solving and spontaneous knowledge
sharing. These important factors ensure the stability of the network. The identification of a common interest and a collective result allows the control of the collaborative network activities, creating a flat and flexible organizational structure.
The coordination of the CO, through ICT, allows a knowledge transfer and learning
in order to achieve the shared objectives and to obtain satisfactory results for all
people involved, according to win-win logic. Resources sharing involves not only
material, but also intellectual resources, such as knowledge and information, that
improve through simple and pervasive technologies. Enterprises begun to take on

social problems at territorial system level, searching for new organizational forms that allow taking advantage from opportunities offered by ICT. In other words, changes in practices, shared values and rules enhance sustainability and resilience of social systems. The use of increasingly innovative technologies improves quality of life for individuals and achieve uniform and equitable prosperity for all.

Data analysis and articulation of the VM project, both are in exponential growth, shows that the topic involves significantly organizations in an integrated management strategy that reduces waste and stimulates the consumption of fruit and vegetables to enrich diets, and improve health and quality of life.

In brief, VM acts as an institutional entrepreneur, APS as a CO, and the role of ICT is very important: ICT can automatically transform and improve the action of recovery of food; ICT stimulate the involvement of public, profit and non-profit organizations, that are bounded by stable and mutual relationships; this connection through ICT allows achieving objectives efficiently and effectively in just-in-time logic and ensuring the transparency, legality and sustainability (certifying the recovered food in order to obtain tax reduction) of the project.

Relationships, in the VM case, are regulated by protocols, groups of strategic co-planning and negotiations and ICT permit to coordinate their actions. Consequently, there is knowledge sharing, exchange of ideas, and organizational practices that ensure mutual support. The combination of the different resources and technologies creates inter organizational synergies among the several actors involved that have a positive impact on the intangible capital. These relationships advantage all stakeholders and allow them to fight critical issues, reinforce the social and economic environment, and reduce environmental impacts. The positive impacts of the project are numerous: economic, social, environmental and healthy; ICT can be an instrument to measure and show results to all the stakeholders. Interactions among organizations consolidate the best practices, compliance with sanitary regulations, administrative transparency, traceability of process and mutual support.

In the end, ICT, thanks to standardization of procedures, processes and rules, facilitate the repeatability of the VM model in others territories.

References

1. Crutzen, P.J.: Geology of mankind. Nature **415**(1), 23 (2002)
2. Papargyropoulou, E., Lozano, R., Steinberger, J.K., Wright, N., Bin Ujang, Z.: The food waste hierarchy as a framework for the management of food surplus and food waste. J. Clean. Prod. **76**, 106–115 (2014)
3. Garud, R., Jain, S., Kumaraswamy, A.: Institutional entrepreneurship in the sponsorship of common technological standards: the case of Sun Microsystems and Java. Acad. Manag. J. **45** (1), 196–214 (2002)
4. Battilana, J.: Agency and institutions: the enabling role of individuals' social position. Organization **13**(5), 653–676 (2006)

5. Battilana, J., D'Aunno, T.: Institutional work and the paradox of embedded agency. Institutional work: actors and agency in institutional studies of organizations, pp. 31–58 (2009)
6. Lawrence, T.B., Hardy, C., Phillips, N.: Institutional effects of interorganizational collaboration: the emergence of proto-institutions. Acad. Manag. J. **45**(1), 281–290 (2002)
7. Maguire, S., Hardy, C., Lawrence, T.B.: Institutional entrepreneurship in emerging fields: HIV/AIDS treatment advocacy in Canada. Acad. Manag. J. **47**(5), 657–679 (2004)
8. Zilber, T.B.: Institutionalization as an interplay between actions, meanings, and actors: the case of a rape crisis center in Israel. Acad. Manage. J. **45**(1), 234 (2002)
9. Fligstein, N.: Social skill and institutional theory. Am. Behav. Sci. **40**(4), 397–405 (1997)
10. Tolbert, P.S., Zucker, L.G.: The Institutionalization of Institutional Theory. Studying Organization. Theory & Method. London, Thousand Oaks, New Delhi, pp. 169–184 (1999)
11. Olson, M.: The Logic of Collective Action: Public Goods and the Theory of Groups. Cambridge, MA (1965)
12. Wijen, F., Ansari, S.: Overcoming inaction through collective institutional entrepreneurship: Insights from regime theory. Organ. Stud. **28**(7), 1079–1100 (2007)
13. Marwell, G., Oliver, P.: The Critical Mass in Collective Action. Cambridge Un Press (1993)
14. Möllering, G.: Collective institutional entrepreneurship? The recursive interplay of action networks and institutions in market constitution. In: Institutional Embeddedness of Markets Conference. Max Planck Institute, Cologne (2007)
15. Chrislip, D.D., Larson, C.E.: Collaborative Leadership: How Citizens and Civic Leaders Can Make a Difference, vol. 24. Jossey-Bass Inc Pub (1994)
16. Huxham, C., Vangen, S.: Leadership in the shaping and implementation of collaboration agendas: How things happen in a (not quite) joined-up world. Acad. Manag. J. **43**(6), 1159–1175 (2000)
17. Lawrence, T.B., Suddaby, R.: Institutions and Institutional Work. The SAGE Handbook of Organization Studies, 215 (2006)
18. Heckathorn, D.: The dynamics and dilemmas of collective action. Am. Sociol. Rev. 250–277 (1996)
19. Westlley, F., Vredenburg, H.: Interorganizational collaboration and the preservation of global biodiversity. Organ. Sci. **8**(4), 381–403 (1997)
20. Zahra, S.A., Gedajlovic, E., Neubaum, D.O., Shulman, J.M.: A typology of social entrepreneurs: motives, search processes and ethical challenges. J. Bus. Ventur. **24**(5), 519–532 (2009)
21. Light, P.C.: Reshaping social entrepreneurship. Stanf. Soc. Innov. Rev. **4**(3), 47–51 (2006)
22. Rossi, P.H.: Research strategies in measuring peer group influence. In: College Peer Groups. Aldine, Chicago, pp. 190–214 (1966)
23. Robinson, J.: Navigating social and institutional barriers to markets: how social entrepreneurs identify and evaluate opportunities. In: Social Entrepreneurship, pp. 95–120. Palgrave Macmillan, UK (2006)
24. Barney, J.B.: Looking inside for competitive advantage. Acad. Manage. Exec. **9**(4), 49–61 (1995)
25. Ostrom, E.: Beyond markets and states: polycentric governance of complex economic systems. Trans. Corp. Rev. **2**(2), 1–12 (2010)
26. Brondizio, E.S., Ostrom, E., Young, O.R.: Connectivity and the governance of multilevel social-ecological systems: the role of social capital. Annu. Rev. Environ. Resour. **34**, 253–278 (2009).
27. Geels, F.W.: From sectorial systems of innovation to socio-technical systems: insights about dynamics and change from sociology and institutional theory. Res. Policy **33**(6), 897–920 (2004)
28. Trist, E.: The evolution of socio-technical systems. Occasional paper, 2 (1981)
29. Smith, H.E.: Exclusion versus governance: two strategies for delineating property rights. J. legal Stud. **31**(S2), S453–S487 (2002)

30. Young, O.R., Demko, G.J., Ramakrishna, K.: Global Environmental Change and International Governance. Dartmouth Publishing Group (1996)
31. Folke, C.: Resilience: the emergence of a perspective for social–ecological systems analyses. Glob. Environ. Change **16**(3), 253–267 (2006)
32. Bryman, A., Bell, E.: Business Research Methods. Oxford University Press (2011)
33. Pettigrew, A.: Longitudinal field research on change: theory and practice. Organ. Sci. **1**(3), 267–292 (1990)
34. Eisenhardt, K.M., Graebner, M.E.: Theory building from cases: opportunities and challenges. Acad. Manag. J. **50**(1), 25–32 (2007)
35. Bonomi, S., Moggi, S., Ricciardi, F.: Innovation for sustainable development by educating the local community. The case of an Italian project of food waste prevention. In: International Conference on Exploring Services Science, pp. 705–716. Springer, Berlin
36. FAO—UN: Global Food Losses and Food Waste—Extent, Causes and Prevention. UN Food and Agriculture Organization, Rome (2011)
37. http://www.Veronamercato.it

Identifying Disguised Objectives of IT Deployment Through Action Research

Peter Bou Saba, Mario Saba and Antoine Harfouche

Abstract Little research in IS has examined the contagion mechanisms of conflicts during IT deployment between organizational members in a network. A focus on an organizational network's contagion mechanisms is important to anticipate potential contagious conflicts that may lead to the failure of a mutual IT project. The paper delivers the results of a 4-year action research project conducted at a leading French federation of agriculture cooperatives. The study reveals that identifying contagion mechanisms at the very preliminary phases of implementation may be strategic for a successful IT deployment, despite the tools' imperfections. Destabilizing "automatic" conflict contagion between cooperatives have led to engaging contagious survival mechanisms, limiting conflict contagion and accelerating the tool's adoption. For IS managers and practitioners, considering conflict contagion in the translation process, one can work to more actively contain and resolve conflicts before they have a chance to affect the rest of the members.

Keywords Conflict contagion · Organizational network · Agricultural cooperatives · Actor network theory

P. B. Saba
EDHEC Business School—Efficient Innovation, Paris, France
e-mail: saba.p@aol.com

M. Saba (✉)
Cesar Ritz Colleges Switzerland—Washington State University Carson
College of Business, Switzerland International Center, Brig, Switzerland
e-mail: m-saba@outlook.com

A. Harfouche
EDHEC Business School, Lille, France
e-mail: harfoant@yahoo.com

© Springer Nature Switzerland AG 2019
Y. Baghdadi and A. Harfouche (eds.), *ICT for a Better Life and a Better World*,
Lecture Notes in Information Systems and Organisation 30,
https://doi.org/10.1007/978-3-030-10737-6_5

1 Introduction

Research in social psychology has proposed theories and methodologies to manage conflicts occurring between employees [1] or understand conflict contagion between teams. However, little research in information systems (IS) has examined the contagion mechanisms of such conflicts during IT implementation, between organizational members in a network. On an organizational network scale, very limited research has tackled the conflict contagion mechanism through which organizations (members) in the network influence each other. In such networks, the latter behaviors do not occur as conflicts in which all members are totally and equally involved [2]. A focus on the network's contagion mechanisms is thus important to anticipate potential contagion phenomenon that may lead to the failure or success of a mutual IT project. Aside from the stated above, and this time on a sociological scale related to the actor network theoretical approach [3], the sociology of translation may disambiguate the link between IT implementation and conflict contagion. The rest of the article is structured as follows. A literature review presents the concept of contagion, user conflicts and conflict contagion, as well as the actor network theory. The case study delivers the results of a 4 year action research project conducted at the Regional Federation of Agricultural Cooperation in southern France (FRCA LR). First, the IT project witnessed several technical imperfections as well as conflict behaviors and socio-political conflicts during implementation by few cooperatives, despite having initially accepted the IT initiative. Second, through the actor network approach, the translation operation included the latter identified conflict contagion mechanisms leading to the successful implementation of the IT tool called COOPERFIC.

For IS researchers, by looking at factors that could lead to conflict contagion in a network of organizations, we may better understand why, when and how conflicts evolve to affect new network members. From a managerial perspective, considering conflict contagion in the translation process, managers can work to more actively contain and resolve conflicts before they have a risk to affect the rest of the members.

2 Theoretical Background

While an abundance of research in psychology and IS has examined how intragroup conflicts affect the project and group performance [2, 4–8], less research in IS has explored the contagion dynamics underlying inter-organizational conflicts.

2.1 Contagion

The concept of contagion is richly found in the social psychology literature through the phenomenon of social contagion [9–14]. Social contagion research can be broken down into two major areas: (1) research work exploring emotional contagion, and (2) studies investigating behavioral contagion (see Table 1).

In the organizational behavior literature, Humphrey et al. [38] suggest that emotions are present in the workplace. Additionally, leaders (emitters of emotions) at work, as well as followers (receivers of emotions), can trigger behavioral stimuli. On the other hand, Tee [39] argues that researchers in psychology should differentiate the primitive, tacit, implicit contagion processes, driven primarily by subconscious, automatic motor mimicry, from the more explicit processes which can be regulated in human interactions [58]. This is consistent with the multilevel model of contagion effects in organizations (see Table 2).

Table 1 Behavioral contagion types

Area	Principle	Authors
Hysterical contagion	The spread by contact of symptoms and experiences usually associated with clinical hysteria in the absence of a biological contagion	Pfefferbaum and Pfefferbaum [15]; Showalter [16]; Colligan and Murphy [17]; Houran and Lange [18]; Kerckhoff and Back [19]
Deliberate self-harm (DSH) contagion	Suicide rates and other examples of DSH vary proportionally according to the intensity and content of exposure	Marsden [12]; Higgins and Range [20]; Phillips [14];
Aggression contagion	Aggression transfer between transitory and unpredictable angry individuals, where media exposure has an impact of infection rates	Phillips [21]; Goethals and Perlstein [22]; Wheeler and Caggiula [23]; Bandura et al. [24]
Rule violation contagion	Rule violation contagions have been identified in teenage smoking, speeding, substance abuse, delinquency, youth sex and criminality	Ennett et al. [25]; Jones and Jones [26]; Connolly and Aberg [4]; Rodgers and Rowe [27]
Consumer behavior contagion	The spread of consumer fashions and fads through populations in a manner more indicative of an influenza epidemic than rational behavior	Rogers [28]; Bass et al. [29]; Rapoport [30]; Rashevsky [31, 32]
Financial contagion	The behavior of stock markets which lurch from state to state because of selling panics and buying frenzies that sweep across the globe	Lux [33]; Temzelides [34]; Orlean [35]
Conflict contagion	Conflicts transmitted to other individuals, groups, or countries, through behavioral actions, leading others to behave in a conflictual manner	Jehn et al. [2]; Philips and Loyd [36]; Yang and Mossholder [37]

Table 2 Multilevel behavioral contagion

Level	Principle	Authors
Level 1: Within persons	Behavioral contagion relies on two-key underlying mechanisms, mimicry and synchrony, as well as, emotional experience and feedback	Tee [39]; Arizmendi [40]; McIntosh [41]; Chartrand and Bargh [42]; Trout and Rosenfeld [43]
Level 2: Between persons	Individual differences moderate the extent to which individuals are receptive of, positive and negative affect, leading to contagion	Tee [39]; Tee et al. [44]; Judge et al. [48]; Eid and Diener [45]; Bolger and Schilling [46]; Watson and Clark [47]
Level 3: Interpersonal/ interactional	Leaders' behavior can influence follower behavior through contagion processes. Mood contagion processes occur in two stages, starting by leaders, and propagated among followers at the group level	Tee [39]; Sy and [48]; Johnson [49]; Awamleh and Gardner [50]; Conger and Kanungo [51]; Bass [52]
Level 4: Groups and teams' collective emotions	Behavioral contagion processes impact overall team cooperation and conflict tendencies. Recurring behavioral contagion processes led to convergence of behaviors between individuals	Tee [39]; Seger et al. [53]; Anderson et al. [54]; Barsade [9]; Kelly and Barsade [10]; Totterdell [55]
Level 5: Organizations	The spread of behaviors is linked to infectious diseases, influencing the experience of large numbers of individuals	Tee [39]; Hong et al. [56]; Hill et al. [57]; Dasborough et al. [58]; Fowler and Christakis [59]; Ashkanasy and Nicholson [60]

While the role of behaviors in social psychology is widely recognized, and although conflict behaviors are contagious between individuals [39], teams of individuals [9], or inside organizations [56], information systems research streams seem to lack knowledge on whether conflict behaviors are transmitted between multiple organizations in a network.

2.2 Conflict Contagion

Research considering conflicts as a behavioral form to express resistance [8, 61] are about the object on which resistance is occurring as well as the respective perceived threats [62]. Conflict is a disagreement of persons or group of persons that perceive a situation as being incompatible with their own interests [63]. At the group level, conflicts could be task-oriented where issues arise between groups because of differences between professional assignments to be realized [64, 65]. In this research, we draw from the literatures in psychology on intragroup conflicts [5, 6], group composition and coalition formation [66] and emotional contagion [9] to describe the progression and evolution of a conflict between organizations over

Table 3 Forms of conflicts

Conflict form	Description	Authors
Conflicts about the IT system	Conflicts about the design of the IT itself, including its functionalities. These conflicts are associated to technology acceptance	Davis et al. [70]; Venkatesh and Davis [71]
Conflicts about the task that employees must fulfil	Conflicts caused by the way firms' processes must be changed or adapted to fit with the new IT process requirements	Markus et al. [72]; Besson and Rowe [73]; Lim et al. [74]
Conflicts due to cultural principles	Psychologically based conflicts referring to employees' ideologies by which they share beliefs and make sense of their words	Trice and Beyer [75]; Stewart and Gosain [76]
Conflicts due to a loss of power	Conflicts associated with the way how hierarchical authorities and management are likely to be reformed after IT implementation	Markus, [77]; Davis et al. [70]; Besson and Rowe [73]; Avgerou and McGrath [78]

time, from involving just a few members to drawing in the whole network. In this article, we assume that actions such as engaging in process control, forcing, confronting, accommodating, compromising, problem solving, and avoiding are also engaged in the context of a network of organizations, between several firms, members of the latter network [8]. Accordingly, we formulate our first research proposition.

Proposition 1 *Conflict behaviors expressed by an organization toward an IT initiative infect other organizations in the same network involved in the latter IT project.*

The conflict contagion process is most likely to occur because of interdependence between individuals [67, 68]. Therefore, an issue that affects a few members is likely to affect all team members and network members over time, because of coalition formation and behavioral contagion [2, 67, 69] (see Table 3).

Additionally, persons or organizations involved in the initial conflict may also proactively recruit other persons to form coalitions [79].

2.3 The Actor Network Theory

The actor network theory provides a framework to understand the implementation of innovation projects in the field of information systems. The word "actor" refers not only to humans, but also to any object that may have a role in the establishment of a network helping the implementation of an IT project [80]. Considering innovation as unpredictable and uncertain, the actor network theory considers sociological factors that would influence IT implementation initiatives. From a theoretical point of view, we are assuming that the success or failure of an IT project could be explained by the actor network theory. This would help us observe the IS design process while considering the positions of all the actors, in favor or against the implementation of this tool, in a specific business environment. Accordingly, the actor network theory is based on human/objects interactions that are the bases for networks' creation. These interactions can be seen through 'the model of translation' defined by Callon and Latour as the negotiations, acts of persuasion, calculations, violence behaviors, expressed by an actor who acts on behalf of another actor [80]. According to Callon [81, 82] and Akrich et al. [83, 84], the translation process is done in four steps: (1) Problematization, which is defining the nature of the problem in a specific situation by an actor and the following establishment of dependency; (2) Interessement, which is engaging other actors into the roles that were proposed for them in the actor's program to resolve the latter problem; (3) Enrolment, which is the definition of the roles that were assigned to other actors during interessement; and (4) Mobilization, which is ensuring that the spokespersons for relevant collective entities are properly representative of these. Despite the importance of the actor network approach in our study, considered alone, it would be insufficient to tackle our research proposition. Yet, in the context of contagion, it would be interesting to include an additional dimension into the translation process, which is conflict contagion.

Proposition 2 *Destabilizing "automatic" conflict contagion between cooperatives engages contagious survival mechanisms, limiting conflict contagion and augmenting the number of the tool's adopters.*

3   Case Description

The Regional Federation of Agricultural Cooperation in the Languedoc-Roussillon (FRCA LR) was founded in 2006, representing a network of more than 300 territorial agriculture cooperatives, based in southern France. Its purpose is to promote the cooperatives' activities to professional organizations, governmental departments, local authorities and national and European authorities. At a time when agriculture is on a very important turning point of its history, and when cooperatives of the Languedoc-Roussillon region in southern France increasingly engage with alliance and merger operations, it became essential to the FRCA LR to develop a collective intelligence IT tool, and provide it to the member cooperatives. The tool has three main objectives: (1) Providing managers of the latter agricultural cooperatives with a dashboard of key indicators (economic, social, commercial, and environmental), specific to each sector; (2) Allowing managers to know their positions in comparison with other cooperatives in the regions, and benchmark with the regional average of cooperatives of the same status and the same sector; and (3) Building and implementing a comprehensive online administrative directory of agricultural cooperatives to promote relationships between leaders of agricultural cooperatives, while at the same time follow the development of the regional agricultural cooperative perimeter.

4 Method

The research design of Susman and Evered [85] is one of the most action research method used in social sciences [86]. The method relies on a cyclical process in five steps: (1) diagnosing; (2) action planning; (3) action taking; (4) evaluating; and (5) specifying learning (see Tables 4 and 5). Our research field seams to follow a problem-solving approach than a research dominant approach. Therefore, in this article, we will use an action research (AR) method to analyze the selected case study based on two cycles.

Action research has been employed to conduct empirical research within the IS discipline because it has a practical value to both researchers and employees [87]. Since our research question is difficult to answer in a quantitative manner, qualitative analysis was deemed particularly appropriate for examining conflict contagion mechanisms between organizations. Problem identification calls for action AR acts as a liberating agent of change, and is [83, 88–90]: (1) Cyclic: as iterative steps recur in a longitudinal time frame (4 years, in our case), generating knowledge to engage further actions; (2) Participative: as employees and researchers collaborate in partnership as co-researchers, and where stakeholders are full participants in the research process or where practitioners serve both as subject and researcher, one

Table 4 Methodology

	First cycle (28 months)	Second cycle (20 months)
Diagnosing	*Objective*: Explore the existing COOPERFIC tool to understand its technical characteristics, and clarify conflicts towards the first version, expressed by several opposing organizations in the network	*Objective*: Enquire about possible conflict contagion effects between cooperatives in the network. Find a consensus to deploy COOPERFIC on a large scale
	Sources: Existing documentation on the COOPERFIC project; 19 in-depth interviews with key actors at the FRCA LR; Informal communications; literature	*Sources*: 14 in-depth interviews; Direct day-to-day observations; Academic literature; 29 informal meetings and discussions with managers at both opposing and advocate cooperatives
	Data analysis: During several sessions with managers and key employees, direct observations, verbal and nonverbal communications were noted	
Action planning	Identifying both task-oriented and socio-political oriented conflicts; Analyzing the cooperatives' cultures; Process analysis for the new version of the tool	Observing conflict contagion mechanisms toward COOPERFIC between the cooperatives. Launching the translation process in accordance with the actor network theory

Table 5 Results

	First cycle (28 months)	Second cycle (20 months)
Action taking	The purpose is to rapidly adapt the tool's characteristics taking into account the wishes/tasks of the 'tool's opponent' organizations then implement the new version on a large scale in the network; 'Go decision' concerning the tool's implementation	An 'induction session' organized with key cooperatives (tool-opposing and advocate organizational members) to "talk" and "interact" about the tool between other subjects
Evaluating	Task-oriented conflicts were evaluated during the 'change session'. Socio-political oriented conflicts were evaluated during unofficial individual conversations. 15 of the opposing cooperatives had to evaluate if their main expectations were satisfied by the tool	Beyond the purposes for which COOPERFIC was designed, the very same tool has started to play an additional role between cooperatives, "inducing" and causing interactions that did not exist before the tool's implementation
Specifying learnings	A task-oriented conflict appeared to hide a socio-political conflict: managers of opposing cooperatives stated that they cannot trust their confidential information would be safely protected in the tool's imperfect database. Hence, they decided to reject the tool. However, during unofficial interviews, few of the opposing managers stated that they do not trust the management of the FRCA LR and prefer to "follow" the decision of the many opposing cooperatives that decided to reject the tool. Accordingly, opposing cooperatives had hidden the "mistrust" motive (socio-political conflict) for rejecting COOPERFIC and decided to express conflicts on the tool's low database security (task-oriented conflicts) only. Only 39 cooperatives have adopted the tool at the end of Cycle 1	Following the COOPERFIC implementation, the tool was the mean through which advocate cooperatives were able to interact with other members of the network. Consequently, advocate cooperatives were able to orally share key information on the market's conditions as well as on the overall agricultural cooperative business and economic challenges. Consequently, tool-opposing cooperatives showed a great interest in the "interaction" session, and asked to do the same session the following month. This experience showed us that implementing the tool has led to a disturbance of the historic network of agriculture cooperatives in the LR region. "Automatic" conflict contagion between the cooperatives in particular, have woken hidden re-stabilization processes and engaged contagious survival mechanisms. At the end of Cycle 2, the number of cooperatives that adopted COOPERFIC was doubled, gathering 89 cooperatives

refers to participative action research; (3) Qualitative: operating more through verbal conversations than by numbers; (4) Reflective: because critical feedback on the process is essential to each cycle, and is used in designing subsequent steps and actions; and (5) Responsive: as it reacts and adapts flexibly to the findings from each previous cycle. Lastly, AR considers that it is useless to study a real-world problem without working to propose a solution [91]. Additionally, the creation and observation of interactions seems to be adapted to our field because we can expect that the fundamental properties of the natural environment are that everyone agrees with this tool, while at the same time it could be expected that many reject the tool for many reasons, including technical, social, cultural and political ones. Our epistemological posture is interpretative. Hence, the researchers were requested to gather information through unstructured and unofficial interviews, observations, field notes, meetings, focus groups, and documentary analysis. The following section expands on these results and provides a discussion on their implications.

5 Results

Table 5 summarizes the results of the two cycles with respect to the research design of Susman and Evered [85].

Proposition 1 examined whether conflict behaviors expressed by an organization toward an IT initiative infect other organizations in the same network involved in the latter IT project. As stated in Table 5, we have observed contagious mechanisms: 'neutral' cooperatives have become automatically involved in their network peers' conflicts. Accordingly, out of 300 cooperatives, only 39 decided to adopt the tool whereas opposing cooperatives rejected it, under the same guise of possible data-security gaps in the tool. Thus, Proposition 1 was strongly supported at the network level, through cooperatives manifesting the same task-oriented conflicts (database security) to hide socio-political ones (mistrust in the management of FRCA LR). On the other hand, Proposition 2 aimed to test whether destabilizing the existing way-of-doing of the network through the translation process, have a positive impact on IT success despite IT technical imperfections. As shown in Table 5, the COOPERFIC tool has shifted from being "the subject/purpose" into being "the mean" through which tool-advocate cooperatives were able to communicate with their peers in the network, which was not possible. Furthermore, considering the tool as a mean of communication and not an objective by itself, has led to augmenting and accelerating the tool's adoption through reverse-contagion, despite its technical imperfections. Consequently, the number of cooperatives that adopted COOPERFIC was doubled, gathering 89 cooperatives. Therefore, Proposition 2 was also strongly supported—the translation process—engaging interactions between cooperatives, has led to breaking down prior communication barriers between actors, where the tool by itself was no longer the principle objective. Instead, mobilizing the different actors of the network and making them interact has led to oral and traditional information exchange, which made the tool-opposing cooperatives realize that they strongly depend on information to survive. Consequently, more than 100 cooperatives agreed to participate in "interaction" sessions on a monthly basis, and 89 of them asked to adopt the tool.

6 Conclusion

Contagion theories seek to explain networks as conduits for "infectious" attitudes generally perceived as negative behaviors. These theories focus on the different aspects of the social construction process. Contact is provided by communication networks in contagion theories. These communication networks serve as a mechanism that exposes organizations to information, attitudinal messages and the behaviors of others. Because of this exposure it increases the likelihood that network members will develop beliefs, assumptions, and attitudes similar to those of their networks. Contagion theories seek the relation between organizational members and their networks. The organizational members' knowledge, attitudes, and behavior are related to the information, attitudes, and behavior of others in the network to which they are linked. Our research is based on a single case study, and therefore we cannot claim any generalization of the results, as we could have if we had used several case studies or sample quantitative analysis. Further research should be done in order to examine findings in other professional and organizational contexts to provide a deeper understanding of IT conflict contagion between members of an organizational network. However, we highlight in-depth research versus cross-sectional data collection, to analyze the dynamic nature of conflict contagion between agricultural cooperatives. For IS managers, one should not to take as granted and solely-sufficient, task-oriented resistance behaviors expressed by users, but understand instead whole resistance causes related to IT deployments, through unusual means of conflict identification. Moreover, identifying potential conflict contagion effects turns out to be necessary to the change management style to adopt. In our case, the number of cooperatives that adopted COOPERFIC has doubled because we have provoked tacit interactions between the actors. For instance, key oral information on market feedback have favored the adoption decision of COOPERFIC by cooperatives that have first decided to reject the tool automatically, having been influenced/contaminated by the vast IT opposing majority. For IS practitioners, this article suggests a greater attention to issues related to tacit/automatic conflict contagion effects between "organizational leaders" and "organizational followers", but also issues related to tacit socio-political motives/conflicts. For academics, our results enrich the literature in information systems on IT conflict behaviors. Beyond the way IT projects are designed, developed and presented in terms of objectives, they can endorse value conflicts between cultural principles of cooperatives or network of cooperatives and the perceived underlying strategic objectives assigned to IT implementation. Such a holistic way of managing IT projects can be a way to grasp the systemic dimension of the organizational information system they are part of. The underlying message of this paper for researchers and practitioners is to consider potential IT conflict contagion effects as a key process embedded into IS management. We encourage IS researchers to pursue investigations on the resistance legacy of IT projects and to figure out how IS projects management could be enriched to prevent or anticipate the latter contagion effects.

References

1. Greer, L.L., Jehn, K.A.: The pivotal role of emotion in intragroup process conflict. Res. Manag. Groups Teams **10**, 23–45 (2007)
2. Jehn, K., Rispens, S., Jonsen, K., Greer, L.: Conflict contagion: a temporal perspective on the development of conflict within teams. Int. J. Conflict Manag. **24**(4), 352–373 (2013)
3. Latour, B.: The powers of association. power, action and belief. A new sociology of knowledge?. Soc. Rev. Monogr. **32**, 264–280 (1986)
4. Connolly, T., Aberg, L.: Some contagion models of speeding. Accid. Anal. Prev. **25**(1), 57–66 (1993)
5. De Dreu, C., Weingart, L.: Task versus relationship conflict, team performance, and team member satisfaction: a meta analysis. J. Appl. Psychol. **88**(4), 741–749 (2003)
6. De Wit, F., Greer, L., Jehn, K.: The paradox of intragroup conflict: a meta analysis. J. Appl. Psychol. **97**(2), 360–390 (2012)
7. Lapointe, L., Beaudry, A.: Identifying IT user mindsets: acceptance, resistance and ambivalence. In: HICSS, 2014, 47th Hawaii International Conference on System Sciences (HICSS), pp. 4619–4628 (2014)
8. Meissonier, R., Houzé, E.: Toward an 'IT Conflict Resistance Theory': action research during IT pre implementation. Eur. J. Inf. Syst. **19**(5), 540–561 (2010)
9. Barsade, S.: The ripple effect: emotional contagion and its influence on group behavior. Adm. Sci. Q. **47**(4), 6–44 (2002)
10. Kelly, J.R., Barsade, S.G.: Mood and emotion in small groups and work teams. Organ. Behav. Hum. Decis. Process. **86**, 99–130 (2001)
11. Pugh, S.D.: Service with a smile: Emotional contagion in the service encounter. Acad. Manag. J. **44**(5), 1018–1027 (2001)
12. Marsden, P.S.: Operationalising memetics suicide, the Werther effect, and the work of David P. Phillips. In: Proceedings of the 15th International Congress on Cybernetics, Namur, Belgium (1998)
13. Levy, D.A., Nail, P.R.: Contagion: a theoretical and empirical review and reconceptualization. Genet. Soc. Gen. Psychol. Monogr. **119**, 233–284 (1993)
14. Phillips, W.A.: On the distinction between sensory storage and short term visual memory. Percept. Psychophys. **16**, 283–290 (1974)
15. Pfefferbaum, B., Pfefferbaum, R.L: Contagion in stress: an infectious disease model for posttraumatic stress in children. Child Adolesc. Psychiatr. Clin. N. Am. **7**(1), 1–83 (1998)
16. Showalter, E.: Hystories. Columbia University Press, NY (1997)
17. Colligan, M.J., Pennebaker, J., Murphy, L.R.: Mass Psychogenic Illness. Routledge, NY (1982)
18. Houran, J., Lange, R.: Hauntings and poltergeist like episodes as a confluence of conventional phenomena: a general hypothesis. Percept. and Mot. Skill **83**(2), 1307–1316 (1996)
19. Kerckhoff, A.C., Back, K.W.: The June Bug: A Study in Hysterical Contagion. Appleton Century Crofts, NY (1968)
20. Higgins, L., Range, L.M.: Does information that a suicide victim was psychiatrically disturbed reduce the likelihood of contagion? J. Appl. Soc. Psychol. **26**(9), 781–785 (1996)
21. Phillips, D.P.: The impact of mass media violence on U.S. homicides. Am. Soc. Rev. **48**, 560–568 (1983)
22. Goethals, G.R., Perlstein, A.L.: Level of instigation and model similarity as determinants of aggressive behavior. Aggressive Behav. **4**, 115–124 (1978)
23. Wheeler, L., Caggiula, A.R.: The contagion of aggression. J. Exp. Soc. Psychol. **2**, 1–10 (1966)
24. Bandura, A., Ross, D., Ross, S.: Imitations of aggressive film mediated models. J. Abnorm. Soc. Psychol. **66**, 3–11 (1963)

25. Ennett, S.T., Flewelling, R.L., Lindrooth, R.C., Norton, E.C.: School and neighborhood characteristics associated with school rates of alcohol, cigarette, and marijuana use. J. Health Soc. Behav. **38**(1), 55–71 (1997)
26. Jones, M.B., Jones, D.R.: Preferred pathways of behavioural contagion. J. Psychiatr. Res. **29** (3), 193–209 (1995)
27. Rodgers, J.L., Rowe, D.C.: Social contagion and adolescent sexual behavior, a developmental EMOSA model. Psychol. Rev. **100**(3), 479–510 (1993)
28. Rogers, E.M.: The Diffusion of Innovations, 4th edn. The Free Press, New York (1995)
29. Bass, F.M., Mahajan, V., Muller, E.: New product diffusion models in marketing: a review and directions for research. J. Mark. **54**(1), 1–26 (1990)
30. Rapoport, A.: Mathematical Models in the Social and Behavioral Sciences. Wiley, NY (1983)
31. Rashevsky, N.: Mathematical Biophysics. University of Chicago Press, Chicago (1939)
32. Rashevsky, N.: Mathematical Biology of Social Behavior. University of Chicago Press, Chicago (1951)
33. Lux, T.: The socio dynamics of speculative markets: interacting agents, chaos, and the fat tails of return distribution. J. Econ. Behav. Organ. **33**(2), 143–165 (1998)
34. Temzelides, T.: Evolution, coordination, and banking panics. J. Monetary Econ. **40**(1), 163–183 (1997)
35. Orlean, A.: Contagion of opinion in financial markets. Revue Economique **43**(4), 685–698 (1992)
36. Phillips, K.W., Loyd, D.L.: When surface and deep level diversity collide: the effects on dissenting group members. Organ. Behav. and Hum. Decis. Process. **99**, 143–160 (2006)
37. Yang, J., Mossholder, K.W.: Decoupling task and relationship conflict, the role of intragroup emotional processing. J. Organ. Behav. **25**, 589–605 (2004)
38. Humphrey, R.H., Burch, G.F., Adams, L.L.: The benefits of merging leadership research and emotions research. Front. Psychol. **7**, 10–22 (2016)
39. Tee, E.Y.J.: The emotional link: leadership and the role of implicit and explicit emotional contagion processes across multiple organizational levels. Leadersh. Q. **26**, 654–670 (2015)
40. Arizmendi, T.G.: Linking mechanisms: emotional contagion, empathy, and imagery. Psychoanal. Psychol. **28**, 405–419 (2011)
41. McIntosh, D.N.: Spontaneous facial mimicry, liking and emotional contagion. Pol. Psychol. Bull. **37**, 31–42 (2006)
42. Chartrand, T.L., Bargh, J.A.: The chameleon effect: the perception behavior link and social interaction. J. Pers. Soc. Psychol. **76**, 893–910 (1999)
43. Trout, D.L., Rosenfeld, H.M.: The effect of postural lean and body congruence on the judgment of psychotherapeutic rapport. J. Nonverbal Behav. **4**, 176–190 (1980)
44. Tee, E.Y.J., Ashkanasy, N.M., Paulsen, N.: The influence of follower mood on leader mood and task performance: an affective, follower centric perspective of leadership. Leadersh. Q. **24**, 496–515 (2013)
45. Eid, M., Diener, E.: Intra individual variability in affect: reliability, validity, and personality correlates. J. Pers. Soc. Psychol. **76**, 662–676 (1999)
46. Bolger, N., Schilling, E.A.: Personality and the problems of everyday life: The role of neuroticism in exposure and reactivity to daily stressors. J. Pers. **59**, 355–386 (1991)
47. Watson, D., Clark, L.A.: Negative affectivity: the disposition to experience aversive emotional states. Psychol. Bull. **96**, 465–490 (1984)
48. Sy, T., Choi, J.N.: Contagious leaders and followers: exploring multistage mood contagion in a leader activation and member propagation (LAMP) model. Organ. Behav. Hum. Decis. Process. **122**, 127–140 (2013)
49. Johnson, S.K.: I second that emotion: Effects of emotional contagion and affect at work on leader and follower outcomes. Leadersh. Q. **19**, 1–19 (2008)
50. Awamleh, R., Gardner, W.L.: Perceptions of leader charisma and effectiveness: The effects of vision content, delivery, and organizational performance. Leadersh. Q. **10**, 345–373 (1999)
51. Conger, J.A., Kanungo, R.N.: Charismatic Leadership in Organisations. Sage, California (1998)

52. Bass, B.M.: Leadership and Performance Beyond Expectations. Free Press, New York (1985)
53. Seger, C.R., Smith, E.R., Mackie, D.M.: Subtle activation of a social categorization triggers group level emotions. J. Exp. Soc. Psychol. **45**, 460–467 (2009)
54. Anderson, C., Keltner, D., John, O.P.: Emotional convergence between people over time. J. Pers. Soc. Psychol. **84**, 1054–1068 (2003)
55. Totterdell, P.: Catching moods and hitting runs: mood linkage and subjective performance in professional sports teams. J. Pers. Soc. Psychol. **85**, 848–859 (2000)
56. Hong, Y., Liao, H., Hu, J., Jiang, K.: Missing link in the service profit chain: A meta analytic review of the antecedents, consequences, and moderators of service climate. J. Appl. Psychol. **98**, 237–267 (2013)
57. Hill, A.L., Rand, D.G., Nowak, M.A., Christakis, N.A.: Emotions as infectious diseases in a large social network: the SISa model. Proc. R. Soc. **277**, 3827–3853 (2010)
58. Dasborough, M.T., Ashkanasy, N.M., Tee, E.Y.J., Tse, H.H.M.: What goes around comes around: how mesolevel negative emotional contagion can ultimately determine organisational attitudes toward leaders. Leadersh. Q. **20**, 571–585 (2009)
59. Fowler, J.H., Christakis, N.A.: Dynamic spread of happiness over a large social network: longitudinal analysis over 20 years of the Framingham Heart Study. Br. Med. J. 3–37 (2008)
60. Ashkanasy, N.M., Nicholson, G.J.: Climate of fear in organizational settings: construct definition, measurement and test of theory. Aust. J. Psychol. **55**, 24–49 (2003)
61. Ajzen, I., Fishbein, M.: Understanding attitudes and predicting social behavior. Prentice Hall, Englewood Cliffs, NJ (1980)
62. Lapointe, L., Rivard, S.: A multilevel model of resistance to information technology implementation. MIS Q. **29**(3), 461–491 (2005)
63. Robbins, S.P.: Managing Organizational Conflict. Prentice Hall, Englewood Cliffs, NJ (1974)
64. Jehn, K., Bendersky, C.: Intragroup conflict in organizations: a contingency perspective on the conflict outcome relationship. Res. Organ. Behav. **25**, 187–242 (2003)
65. Walton, R.E., Dutton, J.M., Cafferty, T.P.: Organizational context and interdepartmental conflict. Adm. Sci. Q. **14**(4), 522–543 (1969)
66. Li, J., Hambrick, D.: Factional groups: a new vantage on demographic fault lines, conflict, and disintegration in work teams. Acad. Manag. J. **48**(5), 794–813 (2005)
67. Lewin, K., Lewin, G.: Resolving social conflicts. Harper, New York (1948)
68. Langfred, C.: The paradox of self management: individual and group autonomy in work groups. J. Organ. Behav. **21**(5), 563–585 (2000)
69. Hackman, R.J.: The design of work teams. In: Lorsch, J.W. (ed.) Handbook of Organizational Behavior, pp. 315–342. Prentice Hall, Englewood Cliffs, NJ (1987)
70. Davis, F., Bagozzi, R., Warshaw, P.: User acceptance of computer technology: a comparison of two theoretical models. Manag. Sci. **35**(8), 982–1003 (1989)
71. Venkatesh, V., Davis, F.: A theoretical extension of the technology acceptance model: four longitudinal field studies. Manag. Sci. **46**(2), 186–204 (2000)
72. Markus, M., Axline, S., Petrie, D., Tanis, C.: Learning from adopters' experiences with ERP: problems encountered and success achieved. J. Inf. Technol. **15**(4), 245–265 (2000)
73. Besson, P., Rowe, F.: ERP project dynamics and enacted dialogue. SIGMIS Database **32**(4), 47 (2001)
74. Lim, E., Pan, S., Tan, C.: Managing user acceptance towards enterprise resource planning (ERP) systems, an understanding the dissonance between user expectations and managerial policies. Eur. J. Inf. Syst. **14**(2), 135–149 (2005)
75. Trice, H.M., Beyer, J.M.: The Cultures Work Organ. Prentice Hall, Englewood Cliffs, NJ (1993)
76. Stewart, K.J., Gosain, S.: The impact of ideology on effectiveness in open source software development teams. MIS Q. **30**(2), 291–314 (2006)
77. Markus, M.: Power, politics, and MIS implementation. Commun. ACM **26**(6), 430–444 (1983)
78. Avgerou, C., Mcgrath, K.: Power, rationality, and the art of living through sociotechnical change. MIS Q. **31**(2), 295–315 (2007)

79. Smith, K.K.: The movement of conflict in organizations: the joint dynamics of splitting and triangulation. Adm. Sci. Q. **34**, 1–20 (1989)
80. Callon, M., Latour B.: Unscrewing the big Leviathan: how actors macrostructure reality and how sociologists help them to do so. In: Advances in Social Theory and Methodology: Toward an Integration of Micro and Macro-Sociologies, Boston, pp. 227–303 (1981)
81. Callon, M.: Éléments pour une sociologie de la traduction. La domestication descoquilles SaintJacques et ses marins pêcheurs dans la baie de SaintBrieuc. L'année Sociologique **36**, 168–208 (1986)
82. Callon, M.: Réseaux technicoéconomiques et irréversibilités. Figures de l'irréversibilité en économie 195–230 (1991)
83. Akrich, M., Callon, M., Latour B.: A quoi tient le succès des innovations. Premier épisode: l'art de l'intéressement. Annales des Mines 14–29 (1988a)
84. Akrich, M., Callon, M., Latour, B.: A quoi tient le succès des innovations. Deuxième épisode: l'art de choisir les bons portes paroles. Annales des Mines 4–17 (1988b)
85. Susman, G.I., Evered, R.D.: An assessment of the scientific merits of action research. Adm. Sci. Q. **23**, 582–603 (1978)
86. Davison, R.M., Martinsons, M.G., Kock, N.: Principles of canonical action research. Inf. Syst. J. **14**(1), 65–86 (2004)
87. Davison, R.: An instrument for measuring meeting success. Inf. Manage. **32**(4), 163–176 (1997)
88. Baskerville, R.L.: Investigating information systems with action research. Commun. AIS **2**(3), Article 19 (1999)
89. Dick, B.: A beginner's guide to action research. http://www.scu.edu.au/schools/gcm/ar/arp/guide.html (1995)
90. Du Poy, E., Gitlin, L.N.: Introduction to Research: Understanding and Applying Multiple Strategies, 2nd edn. Mosby Inc., St Louis (1998)
91. Lindgren, R., Henfridsson, O., Schultze, U.: Design principles for competence management systems: a synthesis of an action research study. MIS Q. **28**(3), 435–472 (2004)

Using QFD Method for Assessing Higher Education Programs: An Examination of Key Stakeholders' Visions

Nizar Raissi

Abstract The purpose of this paper is to identify which indicators are more suitable to measure professional skills and that ensure training conform to employer's requirements. The study relied on reflective evaluation of education quality in universities by employers, students and graduates with professional experience applying the technique of Quality Function Deployment (QFD). Therefore, the analysis of survey results founded on a sample of 31 companies, 717 students and 104 graduates reveals a strong correlation between achieving the objectives of operability, efficiency and integration of graduates and the commitment degree of universities to implement relevant and valid assessments that promote the development of skills needed by labour market. Moreover, employers believe that the skills assessed are not those required by the labour market. Results also show that graduates consider evaluation system as irrelevant because it is not objective and does not allow everyone to have the same chances of success.

Keywords Human resources · Quality function deployment · Training · Labour market

1 Introduction

The need for continuous development of skills and knowledge covered by training in higher education, which is centrally located in a wide and diverse set of procurement practices and amplification of "performance" as individual and organizational. The skills acquired in initial training, whatever the level and quality, are no longer a sufficient guarantee to be and remain effective. The training allows students to update their knowledge and integrate new concepts and trends in knowledge. Training is not a goal in itself but a knowledge acquisition process that appreciates

N. Raissi (✉)
Finance Department, College of Islamic Economics and Finance,
Umm al Qura University, Makkah, Saudi Arabia
e-mail: naraissi@uqu.edu.sa; raissinizar1510@gmail.com

© Springer Nature Switzerland AG 2019   83
Y. Baghdadi and A. Harfouche (eds.), *ICT for a Better Life and a Better World*,
Lecture Notes in Information Systems and Organisation 30,
https://doi.org/10.1007/978-3-030-10737-6_6

its impact on individual and organizational. Therefore, the effectiveness of training actions is the major concern of human resources managers [1, 2]. Many business models, decision and standards are being justified by the need to improve quality in higher education which is a multidimensional concept, in that it covers all the functions and activities of higher education establishment (training programs, research, staffing, infrastructure …). Thus, the main objective is the improvement of internal and external yields and the quality of training within the institution. This will generate more performance indicators such as better capitalization of knowledge and learning and graduates employability with a higher rate of what exist in fact. But, these goals are somewhat difficult to reach because of various constraints and lack of technical and scientific process for designing courses that meet the needs of the labour market [3]. Indeed, the content of these sectors begin typically from supply rather than the demand, the manager collect human skills (scientific, educational, technical, and others) and the material resources available to the institution and trying with these ingredients to create consistent training. With this approach the risk is high to repeat the same failures and to integrate unsuitable graduates to labour market resulting from such training establishment that does not meet the expectations of potential recruiters. We have tried, at this level, to make an analogy with the industrial sector which is constantly confronted to our research in this part. In fact, when designing or re-designing a product, the designer is not sure that the product will arose a commercial success. To minimize the company risk different techniques have emerged, attempting to integrate customer expectations throughout different phases of product creation. Then, the most widely approach used to achieve our objective is the QFD technique.

2   Literature Review and Research Problem Background

The quality management in higher education is difficult to set up because "quality" has different meanings for different stakeholders; of which there are both internal and external parties who may have conflicting definitions of quality. External stakeholders are concerned with quality assurance procedures. While internal stakeholders are not only focused on quality assurance, but also on "the quality improvement that aims to an overall increase of the real quality of teaching and learning, often through innovative practices" [4, 5]. Moreover, Deming [6] shows that quality is difficult to manage in higher education because of the complex nature of education output. The education was seen as a system or "a network of interdependent components that work together to try to reach the goal of system". The system consists by inputs, transformation processes and outputs. Sahney et al. [7] declared that in education there are human resources contribution, material and financial which undergoing processes, including teaching, learning, research, administration and transformation of knowledge. Thus, to answer to the question: "How to manage quality in a higher education institution"? Several models from industry were adopted in higher education such as Total Quality Management

(TQM). The TQM is defined as "the process of integration of all activities, functions and processes within an organization to achieve continuous improvement in
cost, quality, function, and delivery of goods and services for customer satisfaction"
[6]. It refers to the application of quality principles at global processes and all
management functions to ensure total customer satisfaction. Therefore, TQM has
the potential to include the perspectives of the quality of both internal and external
stakeholders in an integrated manner. In consequence, it enables a holistic approach
to quality management that ensures quality and it facilitates change and innovation
[8]. According to the work of Harris [9], there are three generic approaches of TQM
in higher education:

- The first approach explains the customer orientation, where the notion of student
  services is favoured by staff training and development, which promotes student
  choice and autonomy.
- The second approach targets the employees and cares about the value and
  increases the contribution of all staff to the efficient functioning of institution, it
  is also concerned with establishing policies and priorities. This implies a more
  horizontal management structure and acceptance of action responsibility of
  defined workgroups.
- The third approach focuses on service agreements position and seeks to ensure
  compliance with the specification of certain measurable key points of educational processes. The assessment assignments by teachers in a specific time
  frame for example.

The application of the TQM in higher education was the research goal of several
authors who proposed a system of safeguards to accommodate many stakeholders
with diverse and changing roles of students in the educational process [10]. Their
safeguards system focuses on three customer groups: students, teachers who rely on
the prerequisites courses and third, the organizations that employ university graduates.
A safeguards system provides an institution with a competitive advantage by enabling
it to materialize the education quality for students and their parents. On the other side,
when Osseo-Asare and Longbottom [11] applied TQM model in educational institutions, it appears a motivation criteria, which affect performance and help organizations to achieve organizational excellence. These criteria are leadership, policy and
strategy, human resources management, resources, partnerships and processes. They
also suggest criteria of results such as customer satisfaction, employee satisfaction,
impact on society and key performance results to measure the effectiveness of TQM
implementation. Azizi [12] selected nine TQM techniques taking into account the
requirements of ISO TS 16949: 2002, the Japanese management mode and six criteria
of quality satisfaction. The nine TQM techniques include: five basic techniques
(Advanced Product Quality Planning: APQP, Production Part Approval Process:
PPAP, Statistical Process Control: SPC, Measurement System Analysis: MSA and
Failure Mode and Effects Analysis: FMEA), two techniques of optimized production
according to Toyota Production System (Sort (Seiri), Straighten (Seiton), Shine
(Seiso), Standardize (Seiketsu), Sustain (Shitsuke): 5S and Improvement: Kaizen) and

two other techniques of design and planning (Quality Function Deployment: QFD; Management and Planning: MP). Furthermore, various techniques and approaches have been proposed to describe the total quality management and in this paper we focus on the QFD technique as a measuring instrument of quality assurance in education.

3   Theoretical Framework and Research Hypotheses

3.1   The Quality Function Deployment (QFD) Technique

According to Liang-Hsuan and Cheng-Nien [13], the QFD is an approach invented by Yoji Akao in 1960; its purpose is to help engineers to take into consideration the products quality as soon as possible in the design process. Akao [14] defined the QFD as "an approach that offers specific methods to ensure quality at every stage of the product development process, beginning with the design. In other words, it is a method for introducing quality from the design stage, in order to satisfy the customer and translating customer requirements into design objectives and key points that will be needed to ensure quality in production". Thus, the QFD is an approach allows converting appropriately the customer expectations to product specifications or service and its process. It is a specific tool to ensure quality at every stage of the product development process. Monica et al. [15] explain how using QFD method in e-Learning systems evaluation and they reveal that it considers the customer as the key player and it begins from the design stage of product or service production process. The central idea is to integrate the customer's request in designer language, in order to design and produce a product that precisely meets request and without unnecessary costs. The QFD is often known as the "House of Quality" which is the graphical basic tool of the method. It takes its name from its typical form of the correlation matrix between customer expectations and product attributes. This matrix consists of several zones:

- WHAT: it contains the customer's expressed needs and hence the requirements to be met by the product. Each WHAT is noted from 1 to 5 according to its customer importance (sometimes the notation used as a percentage).
- WHY: it identifies the current market and allows locating the product in the market target (competitors, customers ...).
- WHAT versus WHY: it allows locating needs according to the market. This is the marketing part of matrix.
- HOW: it represents the solutions that satisfy customer expectations.
- WHAT versus HOW: it quantifies the satisfaction brings by a solution to meet a customer's expectation. It is a subjective rating scale that uses the 1–5–9 (or 1–3–9) to record weak, moderate and strong relations, respectively, between the WHAT and the HOW. Depending on the importance of relationships, then we calculate the evolution of each HOW to multiplying WHAT note per relationship coefficient.

- HOW MUCH: This area contains the evaluation criteria of HOW.
- HOW versus HOW: This area helps to qualify the correlations between the various solutions provided to satisfy the customer, and thus update the contradictions that may arise between these solutions.
- The last zone plays a role in the development of specifications and quantification of requirements. Indeed the party HOW MUCH versus HOW encrypts HOW and allows an assessment of the importance of these: therefore, this step makes quantifying product requirements and solutions.

In summary, the QFD matrix allows both to define the specifications of a product (the HOW) from the expectations of the customer (WHAT), to compare the product with its competitors and show the optimal solution to setup by the company. The goal of QFD is not to complete matrix, but to improve the quality of products designed using this approach [16]. The QFD matrix shows the support that formalizes the process. Thus, when we filling correctly all the elements of this matrix, we are obliged to validate successively all the steps that lead to success. ReVelle et al. [17] define the steps of QFD approach as:

- Identify customer expectations: they are often imprecise and expressed in a qualitative way.
- Define WHAT converting expectations to precise specifications on the finished product and prioritize the WHAT.
- Define the technical characteristics of produced pieces (the HOW) necessary to secure the final specifications.
- To determine the relationship between the WHAT and the HOW in the QFD matrix using a weighting 1, 3, 9 (or 1, 5, 9) for weak, medium and strong relationships.
- To determine the correlations between the HOW in the QFD matrix. We must identify all the positive and negative relationships (contradictory).
- Define the target values to achieve for HOW.
- Calculate the scales of the HOW from scales of WHAT and the matrix relations.
- Check and finalize the QFD matrix.
- Karanjekar et al. [18] consider that the quality house is the first phase of QFD process which has four phases. Each of the four phases in a QFD process uses a matrix to convert customer requirements from the initial planning stages through to production control.
- Phase 1, product planning: this phase is to convert customer needs into technical specifications of the product or service.
- Phase 2, product design: this phase consists of defining the components characteristics from the technical specifications of the product or service.
- Phase 3 planning process: starting from the set of components characteristics, we can define the key parameters process.
- Phase 4, process control: It consists to determine the process control features from key process parameters. We speak about the determination of work and control indications from process data.

According to Ahmed [19], the implementation of QFD method can cause a variety of advantages (Benefits) and some limits, but these limits must be avoided by adopting a right process role. Also, the QFD allows to:

- Show a very useful communication support of company, allowing extreme formalization of its expertise (How Know).
- Focus all product development activities on customer needs rather than on technology skills.
- Reduce significantly the time of products launch.
- Contribute to the improvement of customer satisfaction.
- Improve the quality of production processes.

We can found some limitations or Drawbacks of the method such that:

- The need of working group.
- The short-term results are not always obvious.
- The method is based on the study of customer perceptions. Its effectiveness depends on the study quality.
- The needs and customer requirements can change quickly.

3.2 Research Hypotheses

To confirm our purpose, we choose to concentrate our study on two research hypotheses which help to explore the main problematic in order to explain the relationship between education quality and tools used to assessing higher education system. Many studies have revealed that QFD is the most applicable technique for identifying the quality design, customer needs (WHATs) and customer satisfaction (HOWs/technical specifications), and they find a model which integrate process of employers' requirements into design of education program [15, 18, 20]. Billing [21] declares that exist many implications for the teaching of key skills in higher education. He proved the role of practices skills and their effect on programs quality. He confirmed that Training in insightful thinking is only effective for transfer, while abstract principles and rules are joined with applied examples. He recommended using meta-cognitive strategies in learning to ensure high quality transfer. Thus, based on these previous studies, we will present the first research hypothesis in the following:

Hypothesis H1: The Employers believe that the skills assessed are not those required by the labour market.

Moreover, many studies prove that combined professional experience and employer involvement in degree course design and knowledge transfer have positive effects on the capability of alumni to secure employment in 'graduate-level' jobs [22–36]. Also, the results confirmed that the future training strategies emphasis to collect recommendations and requirements from employers about the gap perceived in the employability skills of newly recruited graduates. Hence the following hypothesis is advanced:

Hypothesis H2: The Graduates consider that the evaluation system is irrelevant because it is not objective and does not allow everyone to have the same chances of success.

4 Methodology

4.1 Background

We propose an approach which consists to design teaching program to satisfy recruiters' needs in terms of skills using the basic concepts of the QFD method. We are called to present the product and the customer; Tunisian university graduates represent the product and we will consider customer as potential recruiters.

4.2 Sample

To identify the customers' expectations a questionnaire was distributed to a sample of 31 companies, 717 students and 104 graduates, which enabled us to identify the desired skills or expectations of future recruiters of university graduates in the education fields of Management and Information Technology (IT). These skills were fixed by studying the jobs corresponding to existing business sectors in the Tunisian University and using a reference that includes the skills required for each job. These skills are grouped into three categories: scientific and technical, managerial and cognitive. For management fields (Financial Accounting Techniques: FAT, Web Marketing: WMKG, Bank and Insurance: BI and Management: MNG) each domain has the scientific and technical expertise of its own, while those of IT sectors (Computer Networks Technology: CNT, E-Service: ESER, and Information System: IS) have been grouped together because these fields share acquired skills.

4.3 Analysis Procedures

4.3.1 Definition of WHATs

The "WHATs" represent the expectations of potential recruiters, the required quality or customer requirements. The "WHATs" may be defined through more than one activity such as the determining of customers' needs and their grouping and arrangement; assessing priorities to different customer requirements, etc. The analysis of questionnaire results allowed us to fixing customer requirements or "WHATs" which are the skills that have a high priority. These skills are:

Table 1 The scientific and technical skills

IT department	Bank and insurance department	Management department	Technical accounting and Financial department	Web marketing department
Systems Design and development of information systems Manage graphics tools Manage the security standards and procedures Programming languages Ability to manage IT equipment User interface	Assess customer needs Analyse the risks Know the sales techniques Manage customer contracts	Ability to plan, organize, manage and control Negotiation Listening Lead and manage a team Spirit of communication Analytical mind Manage daily conflicts	Manage accounting techniques Insurance Payroll management Manage tax bases Inventory management Issue invoices Manage accounting transactions	Implement marketing plan Manage business strategies CRM techniques Negotiation Manage online sales techniques Manage internet

- Managerial skills: planning, teamwork, customer relations, conduct project, animation team, management and team motivation.
- Cognitive skills: discipline, dynamism, analytical mind, organization, team spirit and openness, rigor.

The scientific and technical skills, as shown in Table 1.

Then, we will assign priority indices and the magnitudes of customer requirements weight (WHATs). This is done using the results of the questionnaire: according to the rank assigned by recruiters in each qualification.

4.3.2 Definition of HOWs

The "HOWs" are identified by a multidisciplinary work team towards the criteria of graduates which directly affecting the expectations expressed by potential recruiters (WHATs). They are appointed by TSs (Technical Specifications). The "HOWs" or technical specifications were fixed with two heads departments and the director of the institution (The QFD team). The critical customer attributes were divided into 2 groups: those corresponding to managerial and cognitive skills and those corresponding to the scientific and technical skills.

The technical specifications related to managerial and cognitive skills

The technical specifications related to managerial and cognitive skills are: reading room, number of reviews, books..., room internet access, educational database, research lab, language lab, dynamic platform, online activities, student forum, online course, clubs (cultural, sports,...), project graduation internships, ethical materials, projects, presentations and case study.

Table 2 The technical specifications related to scientific and technical skills

Teaching methods	Content of courses	Types of courses	Nature of courses
Role playing game	Focused on the learner	Scientists	Tutorials
Simulation	Access on activities	Communication	Practical work
Seminars	Interactive	Ethics	Lectures
Presentations	Multimedia	Specific courses for craft	
Case studies			
Projects			
Course materials			
Team work			
Formative			
Evaluation			
Factory tours			

The technical specifications related to scientific and technical skills

The technical specifications that correspond to the scientific and technical skills are grouped into four groups, as shown in Table 2.

4.3.3 Construction of Matrices

Develop the correlation matrix between the "WHATs" and "HOWs" means determining how a technical attribute assigns a client attribute or more. Once the "WHATs" and "HOWs" are fixed, we can build quality houses or correlation matrices. These matrices were distributed to QFD group in order to determine correlations between "WHATs" and "HOWs" (R_{ij}), using weighting; often used: 0, 1, 3, and 9 which correspond respectively to the lack of correlation, low (weak), medium (moderate), and high (extreme) correlation.

4.3.4 The Calculation of "HOWs" Weight

Once the matrices recovered of QFD group, we calculated weights of "HOWs" using the following equation:

$$D_j = \sum_{i=1}^{n} A_i R_{ij} \quad \forall j, \quad j = 1, \ldots, m.$$

where

D_j = index of technical or absolute importance of jth technical attribute (TA_j); j = 1, 2,..., n
A_i = the degree of importance of ith customer attribute (CA_i); i = 1, 2,..., m
R_{ij} = index of correlation represented the relation between CA_i and TA_j

n = number of technical attributes
m = number of customer attributes.

This relationship allows identifying the interdependencies between TAs, that is to say: what are the criteria in conflict, and those that promote the achievement of others?

5 Results

The threshold corresponding to the mean of each matrix will help us determine the attributes that must strengthen. For matrices of cognitive and managerial skills the threshold is 6.25% as they share the same technical attributes and for other matrices (which also share the same technical attributes) the threshold is 4.76%. The matrices and their results will be presented in next subsection.

5.1 Matrix of Cognitive Skills

The attributes which characterized cognitive skills and that have exceeded the threshold of 6.25% are listed as following: Number of reviews and Books, Educational database, Research Lab, Clubs (cultural, sports …), Ethical Materials, Projects, and Presentations. These attributes are strongly linked with the creation and improvement of cognitive skills for students. By giving more importance to these attributes, universities can satisfy the needs of employers. Therefore, the universities offer several technical specifications which respond to cognitive qualities that are developed and mobilized at the workplace. The findings show that customer needs (WHATs) represented by discipline, dynamism, analytical mind, organization, team spirit and openness, and rigor have extreme impact with cognitive skills offered by universities as Number of reviews and Books, Educational database, Research Lab, Clubs (cultural, sports …), Ethical Materials, Projects, and Presentations.

5.2 Matrix of Managerial Skills

The specifications which characterized Managerial skills and that have exceeded the threshold of 6.25% are Research Lab, Dynamic Platform, Online Activities, Student Forum, Online course, Clubs (cultural, sports …), Project Graduation Internships, Projects, and Presentations. Then, to improve the Managerial Skills of students, the university should enhance and involve the attributes previously cited. Furthermore, the findings explain the needs of employers (WHATs) by the following list:

Planning, Teamwork, Customer relations, Conduct project, Animation team, Management and team innovation. The correspondence between customers' needs (WHATs) and technical specifications (HOWs) reveals significant effects on managerial skills with extreme impact.

5.3   Matrices of Technical and Scientific Skills

The analysis of technical and scientific skills through 5 educational fields: Computer science, Financial Accounting Techniques, Management, Bank and Insurance, and Web Marketing shows that exist a variety of findings. Also, each program has a specified customer needs and technical specifications. Importantly, we showed that the relative importance of general versus work-specific cog-nitive abilities varies systematically between specialities.

5.3.1   Matrix of Computer Science Field

The results of this matrix show that university must give more importance to these technical specifications (HOWs): Seminars, Case studies, Projects, Factory Tours, Multimedia (contained courses), Scientists (Scientific courses), Specific courses for craft, and Practical work. The employer's needs represented by 7 computer science skills which are required by labour market as: operating systems, design and development of information system, manage graphics tools, manage the security standards and procedures, programming language, ability to manage IT equipment, and user interface. Also, the matrix of computer science field indicates that a technical specification (HOWs) discloses a strong impact with employer's needs (WHATs). The teaching methods defined by seminars, case studies, projects, and factory tours. The content of courses determined by multimedia (contained cour-ses). The types of courses designated by Scientists (Scientific courses), and Specific courses for craft. Finally, the technical attribute nature of courses that defined by practical work.

5.3.2   Matrix of Financial Accounting Techniques Field

Regarding this field, the results show that university must improve these technical specifications (HOWs): Seminars, Case studies, Projects, Course materials, Factory Tours, Focused on the learner, Access on activities, Communication courses, and Ethics courses. Also, similar to our analyses for technical specifications (HOWs), the employers needs show a several labour market requirements presented as fol-low: manage accounting techniques, insurance, payroll management, manage tax bases, inventory management, issue invoices, and manage accounting transactions. To illustrate the relative importance of customer needs, the findings indicate that in

FAT field the importance rating of manage accounting techniques has got 30% and manage tax bases with 26%. All both courses have extreme importance to respond to the needs of labour market in this domain.

5.3.3 Matrix of Management Field

The attributes which university must improve are recognized in matrix of managerial field as role playing game, presentations, case studies, course materials, focused on the learner (content of courses), multimedia, communication, ethics, specific courses for craft, and lectures. As already discussed, the determinants of customer needs (WHATs) in regards to management field are listed as the ability to plan, organize, manage and control, negotiation, listening, lead and manage a team, spirit of communication, analytical mind, and manage daily conflicts. These results indicate that ability to plan, organize, manage and control is the most required by employers in labour market with 62% of importance rating. In addition, the labour market gives high interest to the 4 key functions of management as needs of organisation.

5.3.4 Matrix of Bank and Insurance Field

To improve the scientific and technical skills of students for this field, university must deal with these attributes: Simulation, Presentations, Case studies, Access on activities, Interactive courses, Communication courses, Ethics courses, and Practical work. The employers consider that the most important requirements in Bank and Insurance field are 4 key criteria: assess customer needs, analyse of risks, know the sales techniques, and manage customer contracts. According to matrix of bank and insurance field, it is clear that the first labour market needs defined by assess customer needs with 60% of importance. This result prove that employers gives interest to customer satisfaction and search the best way to improve quality assurance through the evaluation of clients' needs and claims. Also, to respond to this need labour market recommends universities to develop their courses and programs in Bank and insurance to be conforming to employer's needs.

5.3.5 Matrix of Web Marketing Field

The results of this matrix show that university must deal with these attributes: seminars, presentations, case studies, projects, factory tours, access on activities, and multimedia. The technical specifications offered by university should give extreme importance to seminars, factory tours and access on activities. According to findings, it is clear that the web marketing as IT field focus on practice skills more than theoretical. Furthermore, the employer's expectations indicate that alumni be able to implement marketing plan, manage business strategies, manage CRM techniques, negotiate, manage online sales techniques, and manage internet. Also, the two most required criteria are to implement marketing plan and manage business strategies with successively importance rating 33 and 22%. In addition, the seven House of Quality (HOQ) allowed us to determine the technical attributes that should be strengthen to make the students training in the university adapted to labour market requirements.

6   Discussion of Research Findings

We have in previous parts sought to reveal a new measure for education evaluation in universities. The analyses of results presented in our research reflect the views, judgments and assessments of graduates from higher education. The representativeness of studied sample allows that we can generalize the results. It emerged as a result the training content are more theoretical than practical. Also, according to graduates, even the theoretical concepts transmitted are insufficient and unsatisfactory. This means that many theories are not taught and what is taught is not usually updated. The university curriculum focuses on developing in students the only ability to understand and remember. The needs of students are not included in the programs. Then, the hypothesis 1 which argued that employers believe that the skills assessed are not those required by the labour market was confirmed. These findings are coherent with previous studies [15, 18, 20, 21]. According to graduates' vision, the evaluation system has not an educational vocation. The evaluation focuses on the capabilities of students to reproduce the course. The students marks and degrees are not always objective and they are not those who deserve are the only ones succeed. Also, the results confirmed the hypothesis which argued that graduates consider evaluation system irrelevant because it is not objective and does not allow everyone to have the same chances of success. This result is consistent with several researches [22, 30–32, 35, 36]. After analysis of House of Quality for many fields through QFD technique used to assess programs in universities, the results provide that in cognitive skills, employer's emphasis to discipline, dynamism and analytical mind. For managerial skills, they interested to planning and team work. For computer science field (IT), they concentrated to operating systems, design and development of IS, programming language, and ability to manage IT equipment. For financial accounting techniques field, the labour market focuses to manage accounting techniques, and manage tax bases. For management field, the interesting is focused to ability to plan, organize, manage and control. For Bank and Insurance field, the motivation is about assess customer needs. Finally, for Web Marketing field, the companies interested to implement marketing plan and manage business strategies. These results are consistent with studies of [15, 18, 20]. In our research, we present the main shortcomings, weaknesses and deficiencies in the courses content and in the evaluation system at universities. Additionally, the results of research explain alongside other aspects of training, the low capability of universities to achieve operational objectives, efficiency and graduates integration.

7 Conclusions, Limitations and Further Research

The obvious conclusion is that the two main assignments entrusted to university are: in the one hand, to developing effective operational competences; and in the other hand, to produce a training which the economy needs. In reality and on basis to our results, the both objectives are far from being realized. To resolve gaps and weaknesses that have emerged, we believe that a global reform of the university is required. This reform should be preceded by a series of evaluative research as the one we present in our research, but involving other categories of actors and covering all aspects of the training process. We believe that the key word is the «evaluation». Consequently, the implementation of universities observatory as a structure that would be responsible for collecting data for all elements of university education and suggest a strategy for change and continuous improvement in higher education is recommended. In our research, the collection of information available on the university and its training was done by the graduates, students and companies. Also, the opinions, views and feelings expressed by the three interviewed categories were taken into account. In addition, this study interest researcher, but especially to scientists in field of quality assurance in education. Our aim is to show the researchers community how they can benefit from studies the assessment techniques of programs in universities. Therefore, we devise further development and application of this work to accelerate discoveries concerning education assessment's impact on quality of employees in labour market. The difficulties encountered throughout this research are summarized in the data collection phase with students and companies. We suggest as perspectives the automation of the process and the approach that we proposed and deployed at the universities observatories and to be generalized and projected to other academic fields and domains.

References

1. Bennett, D.C.: Assessing quality in higher education. Liberal Educ. **87**(2), 40–46 (2001)
2. Raissi, N.: Pre-certification requirements of integrated management system and its consequences on human resource behavior: an empirical investigation of Tunisian industry. Eur. J. Econ. Finan. Adm. Sci. **74**, 52–84 (2015)
3. Wong, Y.Y.: Academic analytics: a meta-analysis of its applications in higher education. Int. J. of Serv. Stand. **11**(2), 176–192 (2016)
4. McKay, J., Kember, D.: Quality assurance systems and educational development. Part 1: the limitations of quality control. Qual. Assur. Educ. **7**(1), 25–29 (1999)
5. Raissi, N., Trabelsi, S., Ibrahim, H.: The impact of new public management performance of Tunisian universities. J. Bus. Manage. Res. **5**, 112–124 (2014)
6. Deming, W.E.: The New Economics for Industry, Government and Education, 2nd edn. Center for Advanced Engineering Study, Massachusetts Institute for Technology, Cambridge, MA (1994)
7. Sahney, S., Banwet, D.K., Karunes, S.: Conceptualising total quality management in higher education. TQM Mag. **16**(2), 145–159 (2004)

8. Raissi, N., Chaher, M.: The relationship between ISO certification and companies performance: Case of certified Tunisian companies. J. Bus. Manage. Res. **6**, 131–150 (2014)
9. Harris, R.W.: Alien or ally? TQM, academic quality and the new public management. Qual. Assur. Educ. **2**(3), 33–39 (1994)
10. Lawrence, J.J., McCollough, M.A.: A conceptual framework for guaranteeing higher education. Quality Assurance in Education. **9**(3), 139–152 (2001)
11. Osseo-Asare Jr., E.A., Longbottom, D.: The need for education and training in the use of the EFQM model for quality management in UK higher education institutions. Qual. Assur. Educ. **10**(1), 26–36 (2002)
12. Azizi, A.: Satisfactory prediction of performance of total quality management critical techniques. In: 13th Asia Pacific Management Conference, pp. 332–337. Melbourne, Australia (2007)
13. Liang-Hsuan, C., Cheng-Nien, C.: Normalisation models for prioritising design requirements for quality function deployment processes. Int. J. Prod. Res. **52**(2), 299–313 (2014)
14. Akao, Y.: Quality Function Deployment: Integrating Customer Requirements into Product Design. Productivity Press, Cambridge (1990)
15. Monica, L., Andreea, C.I., Eduard, E.: QFD—Method for eLearning systems evaluation. In: 2nd World Conference on Educational Technology Research, vol. 83, pp. 357–361. Procedia —Social and Behavioral Sciences (2013)
16. Chen, S.H., Yang, C.C.: Applications of Web-QFD and E-Delphi method in the higher education system. Hum. Syst. Manage. **23**, 245–256 (2004)
17. ReVelle, B.J., Moran, W.J., Cox, A.C.: The QFD Handbook. Wiley, New York (1998)
18. Karanjekar, S.B., Lakhe, R.R., Deshpande, V.S.: A QFD framework for translating customer requirements into key operational activities in technical education sector. Int. J. Eng. Res. Technol. (IJERT) **2**(10), 712–718 (2013)
19. Ahmed, S.: QFD application to improve management education at KIMEP. Issues Inf. Syst. **7** (1), 193–198 (2006)
20. Boussada, H., De Ketele, J.M.: L'évaluation de la qualité de la formation et du système d'évaluation universitaire: Le point de vue des diplômés. Avaliação, Campinas; Sorocaba, SP **13**(1), 39–61 (2008)
21. Billing, D.: Teaching for transfer of core/key skills in higher education: cognitive skills. High. Educ. **53**(4), 483–516 (2007). https://doi.org/10.1007/s10734-005-5628-5
22. Brooks, R., Youngson, P.L.: Undergraduate work placements: an analysis of the effects on career progression. Stud. High. Educ. **41**(9), 1563–1578 (2016)
23. Cavanagh, J., Burston, M., Southcombe, A., Bartram, T.: Contributing to a graduate-centred understanding of work readiness: an exploratory study of Australian undergraduate students' perceptions of their employability. Int. J. Manage. Educ. **13**, 278–288 (2015)
24. Collet, C., Hine, D., Du Plessis, K.: Employability skills: perspectives from a knowledge-intensive industry. Education + Training **57**(5), 532–559 (2015)
25. Eden, S.: Out of the comfort zone: enhancing work-based learning about employability through student reflection on work placements. J. Geogr. High. Educ. **38**(2), 266–276 (2014)
26. Farenga, S.A., Quinlan, K.M.: Classifying university employability strategies: three case studies and implications for practice and research. J. Educ. Work **29**(7), 767–787 (2016)
27. Greenbank, P.: Career decision-making: 'I don't think twice, but it'll be all right'. Res. Post-Compulsory Educ. **19**(2), 177–193 (2014)
28. Heckman, J.J., Stixrud, J., Urzua, S.: The effects of cognitive and noncognitive abilities on labor market outcomes and social behavior. J. Labor Econ. **24**(3), 411–482 (2006). https://doi. org/10.3386/w12006
29. Humburg, M., Van Der Velden, R.: Skills and the graduate recruitment process: Evidence from two discrete choice experiments. Econ. Educ. Rev. **49**, 24–41 (2015)
30. Lim, N-C.: Towards an integrated academic assessment: closing employers' expectations? Education + Training **57**(2), 148–169 (2015)

31. Monteiro, S., Almeida, L., Aracil, A.G.: Graduates' perceptions of competencies and preparation for labour market transition. High. Educ. Skills Work-Based Learn. **6**(2), 208–220 (2016)
32. O'Leary, S.: Graduates' experiences of, and attitudes towards, the inclusion of employability-related support in undergraduate degree programmes; trends and variations by subject discipline and gender. J. Educ. Work **30**(1), 84–105 (2017)
33. Pitan, O.S.: Employability development opportunities (EDOs) as measures of students' enhanced employability. High. Educ. Skills Work-Based Learn. **6**(3), 288–304 (2016)
34. Serrano, G., Llamazares, F., Otamendi. F.: Measurement and sustainability of the qualifications frameworks in the european higher education area through an employment survey on access to the labour market. Sustainability. **7**, 13777–13812 (2015)
35. Spence, S., Hyams-Ssekasi, D.: Developing business students' employability skills through working in partnership with a local business to deliver an undergraduate mentoring programme. High. Educ. Skills Work-Based Learn. **5**(3), 299–314 (2015)
36. Taylor, A.R., Hooley, T.: Evaluating the impact of career management skills module and internship programme within a university business school. Br. J. Guidance Couns. **42**(5), 487–499 (2014)

The Effect of ICT Usage on Employees' Satisfaction: A Job Characteristics Perspective

Teresina Torre and Daria Sarti

Abstract The paper investigates employees' job satisfaction, examining the relationship with 33 some job related variables and considering the impact of the use of Information and communication technologies (ICTs) at work. One job demand that is workload and one job resource that is work-life balance are included. On the basis of our analysis, carried out on a sample of 33,265 employees in Europe (data source: European Working Conditions Survey 2010, last at disposal), we conclude that ICT usage plays a controversial role. Indeed, on the one hand, we prove that ICT usage might weaken the negative relationship between workload and individual job satisfaction. On the other hand, while we hypothesize that ICT might increase the strength of the positive relationship between work-life balance and job satisfaction, the results demonstrate the opposite. Managerial implications are finally considered to underline how important a 'good' management of the ITCs is to improve of job satisfaction.

Keywords Job satisfaction · Workload · Work-life balance · Information and communication technologies · ICT usage

1 Introduction

Many forces are compelling modern firms to rethink continuously their relationships with clients and employees. The increasing competition and connected complexity of the market 'constraints' drive organizations to look for new solutions

T. Torre (✉)
Department of Economics and Business Studies,
University of Genova, Genoa, Italy
e-mail: teresina.torre@economia.unige.it

D. Sarti
Department of Economics and Management,
University of Florence, Florence, Italy
e-mail: daria.sarti@unifi.it

© Springer Nature Switzerland AG 2019
Y. Baghdadi and A. Harfouche (eds.), *ICT for a Better Life and a Better World*,
Lecture Notes in Information Systems and Organisation 30,
https://doi.org/10.1007/978-3-030-10737-6_7

for the products and services they provide. In this context, the fundamental role of human resources has been demonstrated [1] and many studies are concerned with the identification of the conditions that predict and favor employees' positive attitudes necessary to get quality work from them [2]. Job satisfaction is a pivotal variable used in the organizational behavior domain [2]. It represents an important element that influences employees' attitudes [3].

According to scholars, job satisfaction can be defined as an affective orientation towards the role a person occupies [4] Armstrong [5] also suggests that job satisfaction refers to the aptitude and the sentiments an individual has about his/her work. Coherently, job satisfaction is presented as a psychological measure of the degree to which the employee is satisfied and happy with his/her job [6], with fellow workers, supervision, company policy and support, pay, and also with promotion and advancement [7].

Many studies deepen job satisfactions implications. For example, Dawal et al. [6] show that employees generally work harder and perform better when they are satisfied with their jobs. On the other hand, it is demonstrated that if job satisfaction is low, an individual's work commitment is influenced negatively and his/her intention to withdraw either from the job or the organization increases [8]. The idea that job satisfaction may or may not lead directly to customer satisfaction has been discussed. For example, authors suggest that in service firms this linkage is evident [9]. The relationship between job satisfaction and job performance is also much debated [10, 11].

Scholars have also shown a broad interest on the determinants of positive attitudes at work. In such circumstances, this paper aims at investigating the antecedents of individuals' job satisfaction. Through the theoretical framework of Conservation of Resources theory (COR) and the Job Demand-Resources (JD-R) model, our analysis will focus on two specific determinants of job satisfaction. These, according to our opinion, might play an important role in predicting job satisfaction itself. The first is workload and it is expressed in negative terms. The other is and work-life balance and it is defined in positive terms.

The model of analysis also considers the improvement of ICT practices at work, because the two chosen elements are highly related to ICT practices at work. More exactly, we wish to investigate the moderating role of ICT usage in the relationship between job satisfaction and workload, on the one hand, and work-life balance, on the other hand. Indeed, this issue can offer interesting stimuli to better understand the role of ICT usages in employees' work conditions, being evident the increasing presence of technologies.

As Kiesler et al. [12] prophetically suggested 'computers are transforming work and, in some cases, lives' (1123). If several studies have already been conducted with attention to the implications of this evolution, research is still needed to deepen the relevance of ICT usage in the work organization, which could influence employee attitudes [13, 14] and prevent their perceived techno stress [15] and tele pressure [16, 17].

In order to pursue our goal, the paper has been organized in the following manner. In the second paragraph, we offer the theoretical background and introduce our hypotheses. In the third, we present the analysis and the most relevant results. Finally, some preliminary suggestions in relation to the research question and its managerial implications are introduced and considerations useful for future research activities proposed.

2 Theoretical Background

This paragraph will introduce the theoretical context in which the elements at the heart of this paper have just been analyzed and which represents the basis for this study. In greater detail, at the beginning the relationship between job satisfaction and job demands and resources is introduced. Later, attention is focused on the connection between ICT use and job satisfaction.

2.1 Job Satisfaction and Its Antecedents

Job design has long been recognized as one of the key determinants to predict critical psychological states of employees at the individual level. In their well-known work, Hackman and Oldham [18] identify some core job characteristics —in detail: skill variety, task identity, task significance, autonomy and feedback— as the critical determinants to affect positive outcomes, such as: work motivation, work performance and job satisfaction and to prevent negative outcomes, such as: absenteeism and turnover, burnout and absences [19, 20].

In general, it is widely recognized that organizational conditions fulfil a positive role in predicting employees' behaviors at work [21, 22] and, in particular, their job satisfaction [23].

Many theories suggest that organizational conditions—also referred to as job resources—can have positive effects on employee outcomes. For example, according to the Job Demands-Resources perspective [24] resources may influence individuals' attitudes at work. According to authors, job demands are those aspects of a job- that require sustained physical and/or mental effort. These are therefore, associated with certain physiological and/or psychological costs [24, 25]. Instead, job resources are features of a job that: (1) help one to achieve organizational goals or accomplish personal tasks, (2) reduce the impact of job demands and their corresponding costs, and (3) stimulate personal growth, and development [24].

Consistent with COR [26], basic human motivation is directed toward the creation, maintenance and accumulation of resources. At the same time, it was demonstrated that when employees experience a positive balance in terms of job resources, they go beyond actual goal accomplishment, performing extra-role behaviors [27]. The COR theory is consistent with the assumptions of the JD-R theory, which states that a lack of job resources may preclude a real accomplishment. This, in turn, may result in failure and frustration [24, 27]. Relationships have indeed been found between human service burnout and poor job resources, such as low job control [28] and skill underutilization [29].

According to the COR, it has been demonstrated that while job demands are positively linked with negative attitudes at work, on the other side job resources are negatively correlated with those. A number of studies have identified role stressors —that are a specific kind of job demands—as the primary antecedents of burnout [30, 31] and the intention to quit [32]. Further, it was demonstrated that job demands, which are considered as 'hindrance job demands', may have a negative effect on positive outcomes [33].

In the same theoretical domain, many studies have highlighted the evidence that an increase in job resources predicts work engagement [19, 20]. It has also been proved that an increase in job resources may help one cope with demanding jobs [34]. This reduces exhaustion and, in turn, increases work engagement. Indeed, it has been demonstrated that while relationships between resources and positive outcomes from employees are consistently positive, relationships between demands and individuals' positive attitudes are highly dependent on the nature of the demand. Hence, "demands that employees tend to appraise as hindrances were negatively associated with engagement, and demands that employees tend to appraise as challenges were positively associated with engagement" [33, 35: 834].

In their meta-analysis, Podsakoff et al. [36] showed that role stressors, which include work demands and time pressure, explain 37% of the variance in job satisfaction. Further, Eatough et al. [37] demonstrate in another meta-analysis that role stressors, including role ambiguity and role conflict, negatively predict job satisfaction. Studying a sample of 271 nurses operating in Greek hospitals, Trivellas et al. [38] examine the degree to which job stressors influence job satisfaction. They find that conflict, heavy workload and a lack of job autonomy are negatively associated with job satisfaction dimensions. Also, the results of a recent study based on a heterogeneous sample of 534 participants recruited using Amzon.com's Mechanical Turk suggest that helping employees mitigates negative experiences, like role conflict [39].

Results of several studies show that among the other job stressors, heavy workload is always negatively associated with job satisfaction [40]. In a study by Fila and colleagues [41] on a sample of employees of a public sector human services organization that provides services to protect children from neglect and other form of abuse, the authors find that overall job satisfaction is negatively related to role overload. In another research on social workers in non-profit organizations, organizational factors such as workload and working conditions appear to be negatively related with job satisfaction [42]. Among the job demands—and job stressors—workload represents a construct defined as 'a consumption of energy in terms of time and psychological resources [...]. An increase in such demands translates into additional resources being required or consumed'. [43: 66]. Indeed, since personal resources are limited, this situation leaves fewer resources available to individuals therefore impacting negatively on their role performance and reducing the energy available to engage in work's activities and other-than-work domains. Considering this reasoning, we decided to use workload as a job demand that predicts a reduction in job satisfaction in this study.

Hence, we posit:

- HP1. Workload is negatively related to job satisfaction.

In the last decades, significant changes have occurred in the field that consider the coexistence of work and family. The trend of women entering the labor market, the growing number of dual-career couples and the presence of many non-traditional family structures are weakening the traditional role patterns among the family members, and consequently between work and family life [44]. As a result, employees are continuously trying to balance their work request and their familial responsibilities, a topic that continue to stimulate the interest of many researchers and practitioners of different disciplines [45]. Also "Family-Friendly Policies"—sometimes driven by family-friendly laws [46] or promoted by government's efforts [47]—are becoming increasingly popular among organizations that are more interested in attracting and retaining old and new talents. The central theme of this stream of research on maintaining equilibrium between work and family life is the concept of work-family balance, also known in its negative side as work-family conflict. According to work-family border theory, people daily cross the border between the two domains: the world of work and that of family [48]. This theory represents an attempt to explain the complex interaction systems and give a framework to attain balance.

Explaining the meaning of work-family balance, Greenhaus et al. [49] refer to the one adopted by Marks and MacDermid [50]. It considers the importance of 'equally positive commitments to different life roles' (512). In other words, the authors suggest that employees should hold a balanced orientation to multiple roles. Indeed, Marks and MacDermid [50: 421] define role balance as 'the tendency to become fully engaged in the performance of every role in one's total role system, to approach every typical role and role partner with an attitude of attentiveness and care'. Other scholars define work-family balance as a "positive role balance" in which equal involvement and attention is devoted to each role (see, for example: [48, 51]).

The same studies also refer to the outcome of this balance that is satisfaction [48, 51]. Quite a number of researches have documented the relationship between work-family balance and job satisfaction [52, 53]. At the same time, a perceived lack of work-family balance, and its corresponding reduction in job satisfaction, are further assumed to produce negative job behaviors, such as: absenteeism and turnover.

Indeed, Greenhaus et al. [49] argue that a 'positive balance implies an equally high level of satisfaction with work and family roles, and negative balance suggests an equally low level of satisfaction with each role' [49: 513].

Therefore, we posit:

- HP2. Work-life balance is positively related to job satisfaction.

2.2   ICT Usage and Job Satisfaction: Drawbacks and Advantages

Following the prior considerations, our aim is now to investigate the interactive role that ICT usage can play in the relationships that job satisfaction has with workload and work-life balance, and to look for any evidence to strengthen or reduce the intensity of these linkages.

The current debate on human resource management is concerned with the impact of new technologies on work. Among the main contributions in this domain, contrasting evidence emerges about the effect of new technologies on individual wellbeing, job satisfaction and job involvement. Some studies demonstrate that a greater usage of ICTs, of the internet in particular, is associated with a decline in social involvement, with an increase in depression and loneliness among individuals [54] and a weakening of civic engagement and social participation [55]. Other authors, in contrast, highlight the positive impact of the introduction of new technologies on the increase of individuals' overall job satisfaction. In particular, it has been shown that the implementation of ICT usage favors a growth in the rate of communication among employees and the development of bottom-up flows of communication. It also stimulates participation in problem-solving and decision-making, reduces status differences and thus promotes equality [12, 56]. Therefore, since prior studies have shown the positive effect of ICT usage may have on job productivity and job satisfaction, we believe that it may rather weaken the negative relationship between workload and job satisfaction. Hence, the impact of workload on job satisfaction may be less negative if ICT is used.

Indeed, previous evidence proves that a solution to reduce the possible negative impact of workload on individuals' attitudes at work and on their productivity could be a greater use of ICT. This has been demonstrated in detail for specific profession, such as teaching, in which workload is considered a recurrent concern. In the study by Selwood and Pilkington [57], the greater practice of ICT facilities helps to reduce workload impact and to increase productivity. Thus, we suggest that:

- HP3. ICT usage moderates the negative relationship between workload and job satisfaction so that the higher the ICT usage the lower the negative relationship and vice versa.

It is generally recognized that ICT usage produces its effects on organizational structure, patterns of employment and employees' work-life balance [58]. Indeed, ICT usage may increase the complexity of claims on one's time [59, 60], but it is also widely believed to facilitate the juggling of responsibilities—as it increases the efficiency with which activities are executed—and reduce the spatiotemporal fixity of activities which lies at the heart of many work-life balance issues [61].

In the work-family literature, role theory represents a useful framework to understand how individuals try to balance multiple roles. According to this theory, the time and energy individuals have, are constant. Therefore, an increase in roles (i.e. a situation of multiple roles) results in a potential increase in role conflict.

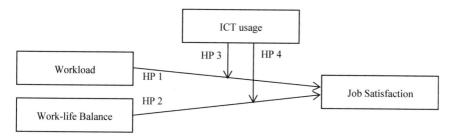

Fig. 1 The research model

This, in turn, increases the likelihood of negative effects [62, 63]. This literature does not share a unique position about the role of ICTs usage in defining strategies to favour equilibrium between life and work, with a positive situation on both sides [64]. Indeed, although current evidence suggests that while ICT usage can improve work flexibility and work-life balance, technology can also facilitate the spillover of work to the family domain and increase work-family conflict [65].

Constant ICT connectivity to the workplace can prevent employees from mentally detaching from work [66], which increases by consequence fatigue and negative mood [67]. However, there is evidence that, employees who use ICT at home for work purposes tend to balance work and life roles better, developing flexitime and, having the perception of a good control over both dimensions.

Consequently, we propose that:

- HP4. ICT moderates the relationship between work-life balance and job satisfaction so that the higher the ICT usage the higher the relationship and vice versa.

In Fig. 1, a brief path diagram representing the relationships among the factors present in our analysis is shown. The hypotheses are depicted in the figure by the causal arrows, meaning that we hypothesize that workload affects job satisfaction in a negative and significant manner (HP1) and that an increase—or decrease—in ICT usage by employees might mitigate—or worsen—that relationship (HP3); further we posit that work life balance has a positive and significant effect on job satisfaction (HP 2) and increase—or a decrease—in ICT usage by employees might further boost—or weaken—that relationship (HP4).

3 Analysis and Results

Our research project has been developed using a secondary source, which allows a large observation of the phenomenon in which we are interested. In the following paragraphs, we first introduce the methodological approach and we then describe the results obtained in order to verify the previously introduced hypothesis.

3.1 Method

Data were taken from the fifth EWCS that covered the 2010, which is the last data available. Only people who declared their employment status were included in the analysis since our focus is on the relationship with job satisfaction. Final sample results composted by 33,265 individuals, belonging to the EU 27: Belgium, Bulgaria, Czech Republic, Denmark, Germany, Estonia, Greece, Spain, France, Ireland, Italy, Cyprus, Latvia, Lithuania, Luxemburg, Hungary, Malta, Netherlands, Austria, Poland, Portugal, Romania, Slovenia, Slovakia, Finland, Sweden and the United Kingdom. Women comprise 50.3% of the sample. The average age of the population is 42.18 years.

Dependent Variable

The dependent variable considered here is *job satisfaction*. It is measured with a one-item question taken from the EWCS questionnaire: "On the whole, are you very satisfied, satisfied, not very satisfied or not at all satisfied with working conditions in your main paid job?". The range of response was based on a four-point scale ranging from 1 = 'Not at all satisfied' to 4 = 'Very satisfied'.

Independent Variables

Work life balance is measured with a one-item question taken from the questionnaire: "In general, do your working hours fit in with your family or social commitments outside work very well, well, not very well or not at all well?". The range of response was based on a four-point scale ranging from 1 = 'Very well' to 4 = 'Not at all well'.

Workload is measured with two available questions in the dataset. These are: "Does your job involve... working at very high speed?" and "Does your job involve ... working to tight deadlines?". The range of responses was based on a seven-point scale ranging from 1 = 'All of the time' to 7 = 'Never'. Alpha was computed as 0.776.

ICT usage is measured with two questions available in the questionnaire. The two questions used are: "Does your main paid job involve ... working with computers: PCs, network, mainframe?" and "Does your main paid job involve ... using internet/email for professional purposes?". The responses could range on a seven-point scale ranging from 1 = 'All of the time' to 7 = 'Never'. Alpha was computed as 0.913.

For the purpose of this analysis, data were reversed so that a higher score in response was the maximum and the lower score the minimum.

Control variables

In the study, we use some variables as control variables. In detail, these are: *age*, *gender* (1 = male; 2 = female), *years in the organization*, managerial position (1 = manager; 0 = non manager) and *education level* (ranging from 1 = no formal education to 7 = tertiary education, advanced level).

3.2 Results

The Statistical Package for the Social Sciences (SPSS Version 20) was used to analyse the data. Table 1 shows the mean, the standard deviation and the values of Alpha Cronbach when needed. It also shows the correlation between the relevant variables included in the analysis.

The findings demonstrate that job satisfaction is positively and significantly related to work-life balance ($r = 0.337$; $p < 0.01$) and ICT ($r = 0.089$; $p < 0.01$). Also, the results show that workload is negatively related to job satisfaction ($r = -0.168$; $p < 0.01$).

To demonstrate the presented hypothesis, a regression analysis was computed considering job satisfaction as the dependent variable. Also, to measure the moderation effect, all the main independent variables were mean-centered [68].

In the first step of the analysis only the control variables were included in the model, thus explaining only 2% of the variance ($R^2adj = 0.021$). In the second step the independent variables and the moderator were included with the increase in the overall variance explained ($R^2adj = 0.153$). In Table 2 only the results of the third step have been displayed. It highlights the positive relation of job satisfaction to both work-life balance ($\beta = 0.30$; $p < 0.001$) and ICT ($\beta = 0.11$; $p < 0.001$) and

Table 1 Mean, standard deviation and correlation among variables

	N	Mean	S.D.	1	2	3	4
1. Job Satisfaction	34,804	2.9896	0.71667				
2. Work-life balance	34,976	3.0728	0.76761	0.337**			
3. Workload	35,043	3.5909	1.85725	-0.168**	-0.168**	(0.776)	
4. ICT	35,064	3.1941	2.29314	0.171**	0.098**	0,054**	(0.913)

Note SD Standard deviation; Alpha Cronbach in blankets; Sig. **$p < 0.01$

Table 2 Regression analysis

	Model 1	Model 2
Gender	-0.016**	-0.016**
Age	-0.002	-0.003
Years in the organization	-0.001	0.000
Managerial position	0.062***	0.062***
Education	0.040***	0.040***
Workload	-0.130***	-0.129***
Work-life balance	0.300***	0.301***
ICT	0.119***	0.117***
Interaction term ICT*WLB	-0.020***	
Interaction term ICT*workload		0.015**
R^2adj	0.155	0.154

Note Sig. ***<0.001; **<0.01; *<0.05

Fig. 2 Graphical representation of the moderating role of ICT in the relationship between workload and job satisfaction

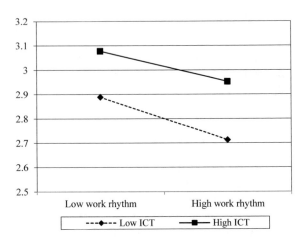

the negative link to workload ($\beta = -0.13; p < 0.001$). Thus, both hypotheses 1 and 2 are supported.

Furthermore, the moderation effect is analyzed. It demonstrates that the higher the use of ICT among workers, the stronger the relation between workload and job satisfaction. This supports hypothesis 3, which suggests that the use of ICT may reduce the negative relationship between work-load, which arises from high working rhythms, and employees' satisfaction with their work. Figure 2 shows this relationship.

On the other hand, hypothesis 4—which predicts that the higher the use of ICT among workers the stronger is the positive relation between work-life balance and job satisfaction—is not supported. In contrast, the results show that the higher the use of ICT the weaker the relationship between work-life balance and job satisfaction. So, the relationship becomes negative, as shown in Fig. 3.

4   Conclusions, Limitations and Further Research

The paper aims to investigate the role of ICT in influencing the relationship between job-related variables and individuals' job satisfaction. More specifically, we have considered two of the most important job characteristics that are proved to be related to ICT use and practice. These are: workload and work-life balance. Indeed, we believe that there is value in continuing to study the effect of ICT's use produces on employees' attitudes at work and the interaction it may encourage, in view of the increasing relevance of technologies on the labour side and on private life.

The evidence shown in our study offers some important acquisitions. First, as stated in the previous two hypotheses, while workload has a negative role in predicting job satisfaction, work-life balance, in contrast, has a positive effect. In other words, perceived workloads are an important part of the job satisfaction. They also

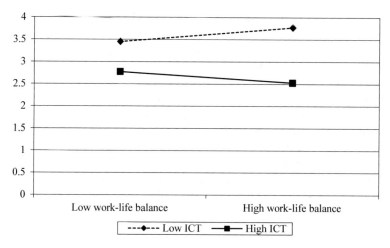

Fig. 3 Graphical representation of the moderating role of ICT in the relationship between work-life balance and job satisfaction

offer a good balance between the two fields. This result confirms what current literature on employees' attitudes at work shows (see for example: [43: 535]) and suggests that enterprises should be careful in managing these aspects by taking into consideration workers' anticipations.

Furthermore, our analysis demonstrates that ICT usage has a beneficial effect on employees' job satisfaction when the workload is considered as a job characteristic. Indeed, despite the number of contributions that suggest a positive correlation between workload and ICT, so that as soon as ICT is introduced in the work place the perceived workload may increase, the positive impact of ICT on job satisfaction seems to prevail. This means that the introduction of ICT in work practices reduces the strength of the negative correlation between workload and job satisfaction, confirming the importance of technology usage nowadays. On the other hand, regarding our last hypothesis—according to which the widespread use of ICT may strengthen the positive relationship between work-life balance and job satisfaction-we find that the introduction of ICT rather weakens the linkage so that it becomes negative. More specifically, when ICT is highly adopted, the increase in work-life balance, that is, the balance in the boundary between work and family roles, reduces job satisfaction and vice versa. This result is consistent with that specific stream of current literature that is beginning to deepen the investigation on work-family conflict and balance for different kinds of professions and among different individuals (see for example: [49, 65]), considering in this perspective different attitudes and preference toward job's characteristics. For example, studies highlight the fact that some employees—differently from others—might be more or less attracted by working extra hours [69]. Indications on this attitude may be interesting for enterprises wishing to develop personalized human resources policies, able to favourite best conditions for workers.

This study is not without limitations. The major limit is the fact that it has been developed using a secondary data source. This means that the studied population and collected measures may be not exactly what researchers might have chosen to gather. Also, the variance explained by the variables included in the model is small (15%). Further, the inclusion of relevant control variables—such as industry and country of the respondents—as well as other statistical analysis (e.g. SEM) should increase the explanatory power of the model and make the empirical analysis more significant. However, through this dataset, it has been possible to get evidence in an ample population of employees, of an interesting and intriguing phenomenon that is synthetized by the question 'what happens when ICT enters heavily in working conditions and which implications it shows?'. Of course, in the light of unexpected results that arose about work-life balance, further and in-depth investigation is expected.

References

1. Guest, D.E.: Human resource management and performance: still searching for some answers. Hum. Resour. Manage. J. **21**(1), 3–13 (2011)
2. Lee, C.S., Watson-Manheim, M.B., Chudoba, K.M.: Investigating the relationship between perceived risks in communication and ICT-enabled communicative behaviors. Inf. Manag. **51** (6), 688–699 (2014)
3. Davis, K., Nestrom, J.W.: Human Behaviour at Work. Organizational Behavior. Mc Graw Hill, New York (1985)
4. Vroom, V.H.: Work and Motivation. Wiley, New York (1964)
5. Armstrong, M.: A handbook of Human Resource Management Practice. Kogan Page Publishing, London (2006)
6. Dawal, S.Z., Taha, Z., Ismail, Z.: Effect of job organization on job satisfaction among shop floor employees in Automative Industries in Malaysia. Int. J. Ind. Ergon. **39**(1), 1–6 (2009)
7. Purani, K., Sahadev, S.: The moderating role of industrial experience in the job satisfaction, intention to leave relationship: an empirical study among salesmen in India. J. Bus. Ind. Mark. **23**(7), 475–485 (2008)
8. Cohen, A., Golan, R.: Predicting absenteeism and turnover intentions by past absenteeism and work attitudes: An empirical examination of female employees in long term nursing care facilities. Career Dev. Int. **12**(5), 416–432 (2007)
9. Zablah, A.R., Carlson, B.D., Donavan, D.T., Maxham III, J.G., Brown, T.J.: A cross-lagged test of the association between customer satisfaction and employee job satisfaction in a relational context. J. Appl. Psychol. **101**(5), 743–755 (2016)
10. McGuigan, C.J., McGuigan, K., Mallett, J.: Re-examining the job satisfaction–job performance link: a study among Irish retail employees. Ir. J. Psychol. **36**(1–4), 12–22 (2015)
11. Judge, T.A., Thoresen, C.J., Bono, J.E., Patton, G.K.: The job satisfaction–job performance relationship: a qualitative and quantitative review. Pshycol. Bull. **127**(3), 376–407 (2001)
12. Kiesler, S., Siegel, J., McGuire, T.W.: Social psychological aspects of computer-mediated communication. Am. Psychol. **39**(10), 1123–1134 (1984)
13. Bissola, R., Imperatori, B.: Generation Y at work: the role of e-HRM in building positive work attitudes. In: Strohmeier, S., Diederichsen, A. (eds.) Evidence-Based e-HRM? On the way to rigorous and relevant research, Proceedings of the Third European Academic Workshop on electronic Human Resource Management, Bamberg, Germany, May 20–21, 1–22 (2010)

14. Chesley, N.: Information and communication technology use, work intensification and employee strain and distress. Work Employ. Soc. **28**(4), 580–610 (2004)
15. Fuglseth, A.M., Sørebø, Ø.: The effects of technostress within the context of employee use of ICT. Comput. Hum. Behav. **40**, 161–170 (2014)
16. Barber, L.K., Santuzzi, A.M.: Please respond ASAP: workplace telepressure and employee recovery. J. Occup. Health Psychol. **20**(2), 172–195 (2015)
17. Kushlev, K., Dunn, E.W.: Checking email less frequently reduces stress. Comput. Hum. Behav. **43**, 220–228 (2015)
18. Hackman, J.R., Oldham, G.R.: Motivation through the design of work: test of a theory. Organ. Behav. Hum. Perform. **16**, 250–279 (1976)
19. Schaufeli, W.B., Bakker, A.B.: Job demands, job resources, and their relationship with burnout and engagement: a multi-sample study. J. Organ. Behav. **25**(3), 293–315 (2004)
20. Schaufeli, W.B., Bakker, A.B., Van Rhenen, W.: How changes in job demands and resources predict burnout, work engagement, and sickness absenteeism. J. Organ. Behav. **30**(7), 893–891 (2009)
21. Brunetto, Y., Teo, S.T.T., Shacklock, K., Farr-Wharton, R.: Emotional intelligence, job satisfaction, well-being and engagement: explaining organizational commitment and turnover intentions in policing. Hum. Resour. Manag. J. **22**(4), 428–441 (2012)
22. Brunetto, Y., Rodwell, J., Shacklock, K., Farr-Wharton, R., Demir, D.: The impact of individual and organizational resources on nurse outcomes and intent to quit. J. Adv. Nurs. **72**(12), 3093–3103 (2016)
23. Alegre, I., Mas-Machuca, M., Berbegal-Mirabent, J.: Antecedents of employee job satisfaction: do they matter? J. Bus. Res. **69**(4), 1390–1395 (2016)
24. Demerouti, E., Bakker, A.B., Nachreiner, F., Schaufeli, W.B.: The job demands-resources model of burnout». J. Appl. Psychol. **86**(3), 499–512 (2001)
25. Saari, L.M., Judge, T.A.: Employee attitudes and job satisfaction. Hum. Resour. Manag. **43**(4), 395–407 (2004)
26. Hobfoll, S.E.: Conservation of resources: a new attempt at conceptualizing stress. Am. Psychol. **44**(3), 513–524 (1989)
27. Bakker, A.B., Demerouti, E., De Boer, E., Schaufeli, W.B.: Job demands and job resources as predictors of absence duration and frequency. J. Vocat. Behav. **62**(2), 341–356 (2003)
28. De Jonge, J., Schaufeli, W.B.: Job characteristics and employee well-being: a test of Warr's vitamin model in health care workers using structural equation modelling. J. Organ. Behav. 387–407 (1998)
29. Leiter, M.P.: The impact of family resources, control coping, and skill utilization on the development of burnout: a longitudinal study. Hum. Relat. **43**(11), 1067–1083 (1990)
30. Lee, R.T., Ashforth, B.E.: A meta-analytic examination of the correlates of the three dimensions of job burnout. J. Appl. Psychol. **81**(2), 123–133 (1996)
31. Peeters, M.C., Montgomery, A.J., Bakker, A.B., Schaufeli, W.B.: Balancing work and home: how job and home demands are related to burnout. Int. J. Stress Manag. **12**(1), 43–61 (2005)
32. Firth, L., Mellor, D.J., Moore, K.A., Loquet, C.: How can managers reduce employee intention to quit? J. Manag. Psychol. **19**(2), 170–187 (2004)
33. Tadić, M., Bakker, A.B., Oerlemans, W.G.: Challenge versus hindrance job demands and well-being: a diary study on the moderating role of job resources. J. Occup. Organ. Psychol. **88**(4), 702–725 (2015)
34. Bakker, A.B., Hakanen, J.J., Demerouti, E., Xanthopoulou, D.: Job resources boost work engagement, particularly when job demands are high. J. Educ. Psychol. **99**(2), 274–284 (2007)
35. Crawford, E.R., Lepine, J.A., Rich, B.L.: Linking job demands and resources to employee engagement and burnout: a theoretical extension and meta-analytic test. J. Appl. Psychol. **95**(5), 834–848 (2010)
36. Podsakoff, N.P., LePine, J.A., LePine, M.A: Differential challenge stressorhindrance stressor relationships with job attitudes, turnover intentions, turnover and withdrawal behavior: a meta-analysis. J. Appl. Psychol. **92**(2), 438–454 (2007)

37. Eatough, E.M., Chang, C.H., Miloslavic, S.A., Johnson, R.E.: Relationships of role stressors with organizational citizenship behavior: a meta-analysis. J. Appl. Psychol. **96**(3), 619–632 (2011)
38. Trivellas, P., Reklitis, P., Platis, C.: The effect of job related stress on employees' satisfaction: A survey in health care. Proc. –Soc. Behav. Sci. **73**, 718–726 (2013)
39. Ritter, K.J., Matthews, R.A., Ford, M.T., Henderson, A.A.: Understanding role stressors and job satisfaction over time using adaptation theory. J. Appl. Psychol. **101**(12), 1655–1670 (2016)
40. Cole, D., Panchanadeswaran, S., Daining, C.: Predictors of job satisfaction of licensed social workers: perceived efficacy as a mediator of the relationship between workload and job satisfaction. J. Soc. Serv. Res. **31**(1), 1–12 (2004)
41. Fila, M.J., Paik, L.S., Griffeth, R.W., Allen, D.: Disaggregating job satisfaction: effects of perceived demands, control, and support. J. Bus. Psychol. **29**(4), 639–649 (2014)
42. Vinokur-Kaplan, J.X.: Job satisfaction among social workers in public and voluntary child welfare agencies. Child Welf. J. Policy Pract. Program **155**, 81–91 (1991)
43. Goh, Z., Ilies, R., Wilson, K.S.: Supportive supervisors improve employees' daily lives: The role supervisors play in the impact of daily workload on life satisfaction via work–family conflict. J. Vocat. Behav. **89**, 65–73 (2015)
44. Somech, A., Drach-Zahavy, A.: Strategies for coping with work-family conflict: the distinctive relationships of gender role ideology. J. Occup. Health Psychol. **12**(1), 1–19 (2007)
45. Amstad, F.T., Meier, L.L., Fasel, U., Elfering, A., Semmer, N.K.: A meta-analysis of work–family conflict and various outcomes with a special emphasis on cross-domain versus matching-domain relations. J. Occup. Health Psychol. **16**(2), 151–169 (2011)
46. De la Rica, S., Gorion, L.: The impact of family-friendly policies in Spain and their use throughout the business cycle. IZA J. Eur. Labor Stud. **5**(1), 1–26 (2016)
47. Chou, K.L., Cheung, K.C.K.: Family-friendly policies in the workplace and their effect on work–life conflicts in Hong Kong. Int. J. Hum. Resour. Manag. **24**(20), 3872–3885 (2013)
48. Clark, S.C.: Work/family border theory: a new theory of work/family balance. Hum. Relat. **53** (6), 747–770 (2000)
49. Greenhaus, J.H., Collins, K.M., Shaw, J.D.: The relation between work–family balance and quality of life. J. Vocat. Behav. **63**(3), 510–531 (2003)
50. Mark, S.R., MacDermid, S.M.: Multiple roles and the self: a theory of role balance. J. Marriage Family **58**, 417–432 (1996)
51. Kirchmeyer, C.: Work-life initiatives: greed or benevolence regarding workers' time? Trends Organ. Behav. **7**, 79–94 (2000)
52. Ezra, M., Deckman, M.: Balancing work and family responsibilities: flextime and child care in the federal government. Public Adm. Rev. **56**(2), 174–179 (1996)
53. Saltzstein, A.L., Ting, Y., Saltzstein, G.H.: Work-family balance and job satisfaction: the impact of family-friendly policies on attitudes of federal government employees. Public Adm. Rev. **61**(4), 452–467 (2001)
54. Kraut, R., Patterson, M., Lundmark, V., Kiesler, S., Mukophadhyay, T., Scherlis, W.: Internet paradox: a social technology that reduces social involvement and psychological well-being? Am. Psychol. **53**(9), 1017–1031 (1998)
55. Putnam, R.D.: Bowling alone. America's declining social capital. J. Democracy, **6**(1), 65–78 (1995)
56. Moonal, A., Masrom, M.: ICT development and its impact on e-business and HRM strategies of the organizations of Pakistan. J. Adv. Manage. Sci. **3**(4), 344–349 (2015)
57. Selwood, I., Pilington, R.: Teacher workload: using ICT to release time to teach. Educ. Rev. **57**(2), 163–174 (2005)
58. Oso, O.O., Ifijehi, G.: ICT use, cognitive style and job motivation as determinants of workers' creativity in newspaper industries. Int. Multilingual J. Contemp. Res. **2**(1), 93–0.114 (2014)
59. Jarvis, H., Pratt, A.C.: Bringing it all back home: the extensification and "overflowing" of work. The case of San Francisco's new media household. Geoform **37**(3), 331–339 (2006)

60. Schwanen, T., Kwan, M.P.: The internet, mobile phone and space-time constraints. Geoforum **39**(3), 1362–1377 (2008)
61. Kwan, M.P.: Gender, the home-work link and space-time patterns of non-employment activities. Econ. Geogr. **75**(4), 370–394 (1999)
62. Frone, M.R., Russell, M., Barnes, G.M.: Work–family conflict, gender, and health-related outcomes: a study of employed parents in two community samples. J. Occup. Health Psychol. **1**(1), 57–69 (1996)
63. Frone, M.R., Russell, M., Cooper, M.L.: Antecedents and outcomes of work-family conflict: testing a model of the work-family interface. J. Appl. Psychol. **77**(1), 65–78 (1992)
64. Hubers, C., Schwanen, T., Dijst, M.: Coordinating everyday life in the Netherland: a hostistic quantitative approach to the analysis of ICT-related and other work-life balance strategies. Geogr. Ann. Series B Hum. Geogr. **93**(1), 57–80 (2011)
65. Day, A., Paquet, S., Scott, N., Hambley, L.: Perceived information and communication technology (ICT) demands on employee outcomes: the moderating effect of organizational ICT support. J. Occup. Health Psychol. **17**(4), 473–491 (2012)
66. Park, Y., Fritz, C., Jex, S.M.: Relationships between work-home segmentation and psychological detachment from work: the role of communication technology use at home. J. Occup. Health Psychol. **16**(4), 457–467 (2011)
67. Sonnentag, S., Bayer, U.V.: Switching off mentally: predictors and consequences of psychological detachment from work during off-job time. J. Occup. Health Psychol. **10**(4), 393–414 (2005)
68. Aiken, L.S., West, S.G., Reno, R.R.: Multiple Regression: Testing and Interpreting Interactions. Sage Publications, Newbury Park, CA (1991)
69. Van Hulst, M., Geurts, S.: Associations between overtime and psychological health in high and low reward jobs. Work Stress **15**(3), 227–240 (2001)

Artificial Intelligence a Disruptive Innovation in Higher Education Accreditation Programs: Expert Systems and AACSB

Charbel Chedrawi and Pierrette Howayeck

Abstract The world is currently enduring the fourth industrial revolution causing disruption on various economic and societal pillars. For Burrus (Brand Q Mag 27, [7]), such change is coming too fast and organizations that will leverage Artificial intelligence (AI) will profit the most. One of the sectors that will get disrupted by the introduction of AI will be higher education. From this point this conceptual paper propose a model for the implementation of AI through expert systems (ES) within the AACSB accreditation programs. ES are knowledge-based computer program that achieves human expertise in a limited domain (Res J Recent Sci 3 (1):116–121, [14]). We tried to answer two main questions, whether AI can be implemented through ES and how such systems can reshape the AACSB accreditation process. We concluded that in fact ES will reshape such process while ensuring more reliable and efficient results and reducing time, cost and errors.

Keywords Artificial intelligence · AACSB · Knowledge based system · Expert systems · Disruptive innovation

1 Introduction

The age of automation, machine learning and Artificial Intelligence (AI) is upon us [1]. AI is the future, it is the disrupter of the current status quo in which we are living. According to [2], AI investment is growing fast (with a compound annual growth rate of almost 40% from 2013 to 2016), dominated by tech giants (Google and Baidu) whose are estimated to spend $20 billion to $30 billion on AI in 2016, 90% of which are spent on R&D and deployment. The largest investment ever made by Google in the European Union is the acquisition in 2014 of DeepMind

C. Chedrawi (✉) · P. Howayeck
Faculty of Business and Management, Saint Joseph University, Beirut, Lebanon
e-mail: charbel.chedrawi@usj.edu.lb

P. Howayeck
e-mail: pierrette.howayeck@usj.edu.lb

© Springer Nature Switzerland AG 2019
Y. Baghdadi and A. Harfouche (eds.), *ICT for a Better Life and a Better World*,
Lecture Notes in Information Systems and Organisation 30,
https://doi.org/10.1007/978-3-030-10737-6_8

technologies, a London-based AI startup specialized in machine learning and advanced algorithms, with $400 million [3]. Furthermore, [4] estimated that by 2025 automating knowledge work with AI will generate more than $5.2 trillion.

For [1] AI is "a general term that currently refers to a cluster of technologies and approaches to computing focused on the ability of computers to make flexible rational decisions in response to often unpredictable environmental conditions" (p. 37). Moreover, optimists have termed the current era as the 'fourth industrial revolution' [5] and the 'second machine age' [6]. In fact, this fourth industrial revolution is profoundly affecting all elements of contemporary societies and economies.

This AI is a typical example of hard trend or a future certainty [7] which society and organizations should embrace trying to legitimize its disruption to a certain limit. In fact, the issue of disruption is a central element that pertains to the potential of AI. In fact, AI has thoroughly disrupted many kind of services by completely shattering their status quo [7]. Deloitte [8] described disruptive innovation as the process by which a new product or service becomes popular and thus gains such momentum that it threatens established competitors. In the same pace AI is gaining ground on all over the sectors.

Within this context, the use of AI in organizations has grown tremendously [9]; unlike the previous revolutions, where the structure and organization of universities were relatively unaffected, the combinations of technologies in AI is likely to shake them to their core [10]. It's becoming impossible to ignore its future role in higher education [3].

Comparatively, during the last decade, higher education accreditation programs (especially AACSB) gained a solid ground in universities in general and in business schools in particular towards achieving legitimacy: "the generalized perception that the actions of an entity are appropriate within some socially constructed system of norms, values, beliefs and definitions [11] (p. 574)". Chedrawi and Howayeck [12] described the AACSB accreditation in business schools as an isomorphic innovation phenomenon visioning to secure competitive advantage and legitimacy. However, institutions have to prepare effectively for future challenges in order to buttress and maintain their existing legitimacy [11]; AI is one of these challenges in higher education in general and business schools more precisely.

In this context, and in order to optimize the accreditation program implementation, we suggest the integration of artificial intelligence throughout accreditation process and more precisely the AACSB accreditation process by using the Expert System (ES). ES are "systems which are capable of offering solutions to specific problems in a given domain or which are able to give advice, both in a way and at a level comparable to that of experts in the field" [13] (p. 1). For [14], ES, one of the three branches of AI (with robots and natural language processing), are a knowledge-based systems (KBS) or computer programs that achieves human expertise in a certain domain; they answer to inferential questions on specific issues.

With the aforementioned purpose in mind, our article addresses the following questions: Can AI be implemented in higher education accreditation programs? How can ES be implemented and reshape the AACSB accreditation process?

The remainder of this conceptual paper is organized as follows: AI as a disruptive innovation, an overview in this section will be made on the concept of innovation and disruptive innovation in order to match the characteristic of the latter with the nature of AI. The second section will discuss accreditation as a general concept with a focus on business schools and AACSB. In the last section a conceptual model will be created suggesting the implementation of AI through knowledge based system and specifically ES in the AACSB accreditation process in order to optimize results, to reduce cost and to ensure more reliable and efficient results.

2   Literature Review

2.1   AI as a Disruptive Innovation in Higher Education

Technology is the root cause behind disruptions, it is about the futuristic waves from virtual reality, to robotics, to the Internet of Things (IoT) and finally to AI [15]. Such cause shall disrupt existing business models by creating new competitors, reordering supply chains and lowering prices. PwC [16] described AI effect as a titanic shift and an ongoing disruption similar to the effect of the personal computer introduction in the 1980s; it will lay the foundations for an immense acceleration in innovation, creating a significant boost for the global economy. For [17], digital technologies disrupt established ways of creating value within and across markets.

Within this context, [18] termed AI as a technology with permanent potential, while [16] described the evolution of AI as active intelligence or the ability to act in real time with little or no human intervention. At its core, AI is about simulating intelligent behavior in machines of all kinds.

Whatever the precise growth trajectory, it's clear that AI is gaining ground rapidly. It has increased the ability of organizations to analyze data to support decisions [19]; as it continues to evolve, the benefits for businesses will be transformational. Given the power and scalability of AI solutions, tasks that used to take humans weeks or months to complete will be actionable in minutes or seconds.

The concept of disruptive innovation goes back to the seminal work by Abernathy and Clark [20]; afterwards, it was developed and elaborated by Christensen [21]. The existing literature on innovation suggests that innovation lies on a spectrum with disruptive innovations on one side and sustaining innovations on the other [22]. In fact, [23] defines disruptive innovation as "a successfully exploited radical new product, process, or concept that significantly transforms the demand and needs of an existing market or industry, disrupts its former key players and creates whole new business practices or markets with significant societal impact" (p. 227).

Though quality education will always require active engagement by human teachers, AI promises to enhance education at all levels [24]. In fact, the fourth industrial revolution, powered by AI, will transform the workplace from tasks based characteristics to the human centered characteristics. This will necessarily require much more interdisciplinary teaching, research and innovation [25]. Furthermore, the future of higher education is intrinsically linked with developments on new technologies and computing capacities of the new intelligent machines. In this field, advances in AI open to new possibilities and challenges for teaching and learning in higher education, with the potential to fundamentally change their governance and their internal architecture; it shall impact the profound nature of services within higher education [3]. For instance, Natural Language Processing, machine learning, and crowdsourcing have boosted online learning and enabled teachers in higher education to multiply the size of their classrooms while interactive machine tutors are being matched to students for teaching science, math, language, and other disciplines [24].

With this regard, [26] proposed some major challenges that AI in education should work to address, including: (1) virtual mentors for every learner (omnipresent support that integrates user modeling, social simulation and knowledge representation); (2) addressing 21st century skills (assist learners with self-direction, self-assessment, teamwork and more); (3) analysis of interaction data (bring together the vast amounts of data about individual learning, social contexts, learning contexts and personal interests); (4) provide opportunities for global classrooms (interconnectedness and accessibility of classrooms worldwide); and (5) lifelong and lifewide technologies (taking learning outside of the classroom into the learner's life).

However, AI implementation in higher education accreditation programs was not mentioned, knowing that such programs (AACSB or other) form the driver behind attracting more students and creating legitimacy for higher education institutions [12]; and that's the gap we are trying to fill.

2.2   Accreditation and AACSB

Accreditation is one approach to evaluate quality in higher education; it became relevant as international demands for quality, productivity, affordability and access in higher education increase. The aftereffect of this process is typically the granting of a status, of acknowledgment and a license to operate while insuring legitimacy [27]. At an overall level, the higher education framework needs to embrace an accreditation framework so as to give an arrangement of measures to evaluate the quality of degree programs [28].

According to [29], the main objectives of accreditation system is to ensure a high end quality of education, to improve the quality of research, to attract better students and academics, to facilitate academic exchange and high-level cooperation, to help the comparability of diplomas and titles, to improve creativity and innovation and to meet the requirements of job market. The benefits of accreditation include opportunities for institutional self-evaluations, feedback from peers, government recognition and continuous institutional renewal.

In their quest for quality, business schools are pioneers, and have been leaders in the field of ranking and accreditation for quite some time now [30]. With this regards, different international bodies have in recent years been successful in promoting accreditation as a means of gaining status and providing high quality of the international schools and programs. Among these bodies figures the AACSB International, a US-based non-profit organization formed in 1916 for the purposes of improving collegiate education for business [31]; it is the largest with the longest history in accrediting business schools; it addresses three key areas: (1) strategic management; (2) business school participants and (3) assurance of learning, keeping in mind the main goal of enhancing the quality of management education [32]. In fact, accreditation organizations (AACSB, AMBA, EFMD …) have established themselves as independent voluntary quality assurance bodies, where joining (freely) and achieving accreditation, enables Higher Education Institution (HEI) to signal their quality to the market [31].

The main stages of AACSB accreditation process according to [31] are shown in Fig. 1.

As shown in Fig. 1, an institution must be a member of AACSB International in order to apply for accreditation. Then, in the step of pre-accreditation, the HEI should submit an Eligibility Application to Pre-Accreditation Committee (PAC). The latter review the application, assign a mentor to work with the applicant (mentor visits) and forward recommendation on eligibility criteria and scope of review to the Accreditation Coordinating Committee (ACC) for concurrence. In this

Fig. 1 The AACSB accreditation process [31]

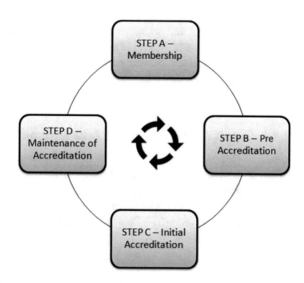

phase, the HEI and mentor work together to address PAC issues and design an Accreditation Plan (within the HEI's Strategic Plan) and submit it to PAC for review; then PAC forwards Accreditation Plan to Initial Accreditation Committee (IAC) along with its recommendations.

In the third step, the IAC reviews the Accreditation Plan before implementation. In this long phase (up to 3 years), the HEI should submit an annual reports to IAC for review and approval; the mentor submits his annual recommendation. Once approved, the HEI applies for Initial Accreditation (submits application to AACSB); here, the IAC appoints a team Chair to work with the HEI on preparing a Self-Evaluation Report (SER) and refine Strategic Plan, and select the peer review team (PRT) who review the SER and the annual reports. Them the PRT visits the HEI and submits report to IAC with its recommendations. The latter forwards the recommendations to accredit to AACSB Board for ratification. When Board concurs, member is accredited and joins the AACSB Accreditation Council. Accreditation is valid for six years, with a maintenance visit in year five.

In the last step (maintenance of Accreditation), HEI should annually refine its strategic plan and should participate in AACSB accreditation data collection while submitting maintenance review application (after the third year) and maintenance report, policies and executive summary (in the 5th year)... then MAC forwards recommendation to extend accreditation to AACSB Board for ratification; board ratifies or remands to MAC. When Board concurs, accreditation is extended for six more years, with the next maintenance visit in year five [31].

Finally, for [31], business schools are seeking accreditation in order to achieve legitimacy benefits rather than performance benefits. It is also caused by the bandwagon effect, whereby organizations adopt an innovation, not because of their individual assessments of the innovation's efficiency, but because of the social and economic pressures caused by the number of organizations that have already adopted this innovation [33]. In fact, accreditation in business schools is a "temporary isomorphic legitimacy tool" [12] where the notion of legitimacy refers broadly to the legal and social acceptability of an institution in society [11]. With this regards, [34] asserts that it is necessary to explore some of the issues regarding accreditation processes currently in place in order to provide some guidance to those involved in higher education.

2.3 Expert Systems: An AI Tool Disrupting Accreditation

Artificial knowledge is created through a recursive and reflexive process that extracts, organizes and aggregates tacit and explicit knowledge in order to articulate and amplify those [17]. During the past decade the interest in the results of AI research has been growing to an increasing extent. In particular, the area of KBS, one of the first areas of AI to be commercially fruitful, has received a lot of attention.

According to [13], KBS indicate "information systems in which some symbolic representation of human knowledge is applied, usually in a way resembling human reasoning" (p. 1). For [35], KBS is a computer based system capable of understanding the information under process and can take decision based upon; it uses and generates knowledge from data and information. In fact, with advanced computing facilities, all sectors are becoming knowledge oriented relying on different experts' decision-making ability; KBS can save money by leveraging expert, allowing users to function at higher level while promoting consistency.

KBS are more useful in many situations than the traditional computer based information systems. Some major situations include [35]:

- When expert is not available.
- When expertise is to be stored for future use or when expertise is to be cloned or multiplied.
- When intelligent assistance and/or training are required for the decision making for problem solving.
- When more than one experts' knowledge have to be grouped at one platform.

According to the classification by Tuthhill and Levy [36], there are five main types of KBS [35]: (i) Expert Systems, (ii) Hypertext Manipulation Systems, (iii) Case Based Systems, (iv) Database in conjunction with an Intelligent User Interface and (v) Intelligent Tutoring Systems. Of these KBS, ES have been the most successful. ES are defined as systems which are capable of offering solutions to specific problems in a given domain or which are able to give advice, both in a way and at a level comparable to that of experts in the field [13]. For [14], ES are computer applications that simulate manner of thinking of an expert in a particular domain; they are programs that could infer about a particular problem like human beings; they use special rational paradigms similar to tools, methods and patterns defined and used by humans for solving problems.

For [37, 38], the characteristic of ES are high performance, understandable, reliable and highly responsive; they are capable of advising, demonstrating, deriving a solution, diagnosing, interpreting input, predicting results and justifying the conclusion.

Expert system = knowledge + inference

Consequently, an ES typically comprises the following two essential components [13]:

- A knowledge base capturing the domain-specific knowledge, and
- An inference engine consisting of algorithms for manipulating the knowledge represented in the knowledge base.

Although, ES and KBS are synonym in the AI lexicon, ES are the main branch of AI due to capability of solving and inferring problems. Most AI achievements are related to decision making and solving problem as the major subjects of the ES [14].

Building ES for specific application domains has even become a separate subject known as knowledge engineering [14]. In this context, we are proposing to apply an ES to the AACSB accreditation processes in the next section.

3   Introducing the ES in the AACSB Accreditation Process

ES, one of the prominent research domain of AI has been used to carry out more efficiently the accreditation process. The block diagram of the proposed ES [29] is shown in Fig. 2.

As shown in Fig. 2, the role of expert person required by the accreditation process is reduced and replaced by the ES; the knowledge base is where the data is located. Furthermore, the use of efficient procedures and rules by the Interface Engine is essential in deducting a correct, flawless solution. Finally the user interface provides interaction between user of the ES and the ES itself [29].

We propose to apply [29] block diagram model on the various stages of AACSB accreditation process proposed by Hodge [31] as shown in Fig. 3.

Figure 3 shows the four consecutive stages of the AACSB accreditation process, which converge in its core to the normal steps of any accreditation process, are depicted. Applying the ES to these stages shall optimize and refine the quality of the AACSB accreditation by reducing time and errors. In fact, we shall define three ES (ES1, ES2 and ES3) within the various stages:

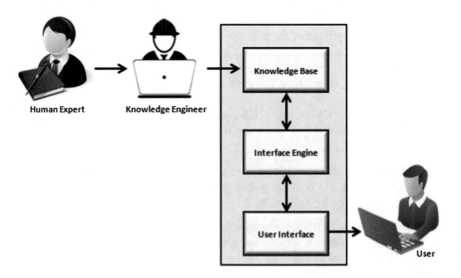

Fig. 2   The block diagram of the proposed ES [29]

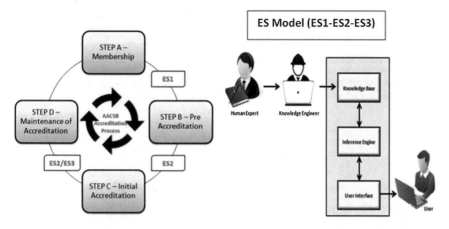

Fig. 3 The block diagram of the proposed ES applied to the AACSB accreditation process

- In ES1 the end user will be the Pre Accreditation Committee or PAC at the AACSB level;
- In ES2 the end user will the HEI (business school) seeking accreditation;
- In ES3 the end user will be the Maintenance of Accreditation Committee or MAC also at the AACSB level.

On a technical level the inference engine strategy will differ between the three ES:

- ES1 will use the "Backward chaining strategy" that permits to answer the following question "why this happened" or more precisely in our case "why this university is not eligible?";
- In ES2 the inference engine strategy would be "Forward chaining" that answer the following question "what can happen next" providing recommendations for the HEI (business school) to fill in the gaps (deviation from the standards) in order to achieve the accreditation;
- As for the ES3, the inference engine strategy should be the "Backward chaining", giving an answer on the deviating points that could put the university' accreditation in question.

Table 1 represents the main modification proposed by the ES when applied to the first stage of the AACSB accreditation process, while Tables 2 and 3 shown represents those applied to the second and the third stage of the AACSB accreditation process respectively. As for Table 4, it denotes the main proposed ES modifications when applied to the fourth stage of the AACSB accreditation process.

Table 1 The main ES modification related to the first stage of AACSB accreditation process

AACSB accreditation process	ES modification
STEP A—membership	ES1
The HEI (business school) must be a member of AACSB International in order to apply for accreditation	The membership information should be integrated in the knowledge base of the ES1 because it forms a trigger to determine whether or not a university is eligible for AACSB accreditation

Table 2 The main ES modification related to the second stage of AACSB accreditation process

AACSB accreditation process	ES modification
STEP B—Pre-accreditation	ES1
• Submit Eligibility Application to Pre Accreditation Committee (PAC) • PAC reviews application for accreditation standards issues • PAC assigns a mentor to work with the applicant; mentor visits • PAC forwards recommendation on eligibility criteria and scope of review to Accreditation Coordinating Committee (ACC) for concurrence • Applicant and mentor work together to address PAC issues and design an Accreditation Plan within the applicant's Strategic Plan—applicant submits Accreditation Plan to PAC • PAC reviews Accreditation Plan • PAC forwards Accreditation Plan to Initial Accreditation Committee (IAC) along with PAC recommendations	On this level the role of the Pre-Accreditation Committee (PAC) will be reduced with ES1. In fact, PAC's role will be limited to determining and updating the criterias and standards of eligibility, in other word no more direct involvement of the PAC in the decision of eligibility of every business school. Their role is taking care of by the human expert and the knowledge engineer. However, AACSB should get all the needed, accurate data for the knowledge base The Inference engine of ES1 will work with a backward chaining strategy that will give its result to the end user, the PAC The PAC who reports the ES recommendation on eligibility to Accreditation Coordinating Committee (ACC), give notice also to the HEI (business school) who will apply these recommendations and provide new insights to be integrated in the knowledge base. When the eligibility is attained the Applicant design a strategic plan and submit it to the Initial Accreditation Committee (IAC)

4 Conclusion

In this conceptual paper, we tried to answer two main questions stipulating that: yes AI can be implemented in higher education accreditation programs through Expert systems and yes ES can be implemented and they shall reshape the AACSB accreditation process by optimizing results, refining quality, reducing time, cost and errors.

Table 3 The main ES modification related to the third stage of AACSB accreditation process

AACSB accreditation process	ES modification
STEP C—initial accreditation	ES2
• IAC reviews the Accreditation Plan • Accreditation Plan is implemented • Applicant submits Annual Reports to IAC for review; mentor submits annual recommendation (AP implementation may take up to 3 years) • IAC reviews materials and recommendation to continue with AP implementation or apply for Initial Accreditation • At this time two years remain in the Pre-Accreditation process and the IAC appoints a team Chair • Applicant works with Chair to prepare a Self-Evaluation Report (SER) and refine Strategic Plan • Applicant, Chair and IAC select the peer review team (PRT). PRT and IAC review the SER and annual reports • PRT, with IAC concurrence, submits previsit letter to applicant at least 45 days prior to visit • Visit occurs. PRT submits report to IAC and applicant with its recommendations • IAC reviews team report and recommendation and concurs or remands to the PRT • IAC forwards recommendation to accredit to AACSB Board for ratification • Board ratifies or remands to IAC—when Board concurs, member is accredited and joins the AACSB Accreditation Council. Accreditation is valid for six years, with a maintenance visit in year five	At the AACSB level: ES2 will eliminate the role of many actors on this level. The human expert and the knowledge engineer role will be the Initial accreditation Committee The inference engine will work with a forward chaining strategy to help the business school identify the gaps and optimize the application of all the AACSB standards. It is a continuum process until the university successfully achieves all the standards and gets its accreditation At the HEI (Business school) level: ES2 can help providing the annual report, the SER and the refinement of the strategic plan. No PRT visit is necessary, reports is automatically submitted through ES2 Time could be reduced enormously

We have studied AI as a disruptive innovation in HEI in general and in accreditation processes in particular. In fact ES will reshape such processes as presented in the proposed conceptual model that allowed the implementation of AI through KBS and specifically expert systems in the AACSB accreditation process ensuring more reliable and efficient results.

The main advantages and disadvantages of the proposed model are represented in Table 5.

Finally, the ultimate objective of accreditation is the granting of a quality status, of acknowledgment in order to insure legitimacy. However, with the introduction of expert systems in its process the legitimacy question can be raised again opening doors for more study on the matter.

Table 4 The main ES modification related to the fourth stage of AACSB accreditation process

AACSB accreditation process	ES modification
STEP D—maintenance of accreditation	ES2 and ES3
• Refine Strategic Plan annually • Participate in AACSB accreditation data collection annually **Year three (from last visit):** • Accredited member submits maintenance review application and cover letter, including list of degree programs, exclusion requests, comparison groups, and catalogs • MAC forwards copy of materials with recommendations to ACC to review eligibility issues and scope of review **Within two years of scheduled maintenance review:** • Accredited member and MAC choose peer review visit team (PRT) • Set visit date • 60 days prior to visit, accredited member provides PRT with 5th Year Maintenance Report, policies and executive summary • Accredited member and PRT confer to determine what additional information and/or clarification is needed prior to the visit • PRT visits - submits report to MAC and accredited member with its recommendations • Accredited member submits a response to the PRT report (optional) • MAC reviews team report and recommendation and concurs or remands to the PRT • MAC forwards recommendation to extend accreditation to AACSB Board for ratification • Board ratifies or remands to MAC – When Board concurs, accreditation is extended for six more years, with the next maintenance visit in year five	The ES3 will ensure a continuous test maintaining the quality of AACSB accreditation and its reputation Knowledge base will be provided by data through ES2 (at the HEI level) that will gather information from the HEI Maintenance Review application shall be submitted automatically by ES2 (at the HEI level) as well. It will be integrated in the knowledge base at the AACSB level Continuous follow up and transparency is guaranteed No visits are necessary: cost shall be reduced The end user will be the MAC that will review the results and give a feedback automatically to the HEI (Business School) Time frame will no longer be useful

5   Future Works

Future works will consist of two phases the first will be practical through collecting all the standards and rules that a human expert of any of the 3 ES will impose on the knowledge engineer and the second phase will consist on developing from the latter standards the right algorithms for these expert systems to function correctly. After these two phases a ground study will be conducted to test the results of such integration at the AACSB level or at any business school.

Table 5 Main advantages and disadvantage of ES implementation in the AACSB accreditation process

Advantages	Disadvantages
Efficient and prompt results to the end user	High development cost
Equal treatment for all HEI (Business Schools) seeking this accreditation	Resistance to change
More objectivity of the results → the mentors subjectivity and all the committees will be avoided	Need of highly skilled knowledge engineer
Better analysis of all the parameters and their complexity	Need of accurate data from the HEI (business schools) to implement on the knowledge base
Reduced cost of expert employee and mentors visits and fees and the follow up cost	
Enhance the reputation of the AACSB on the level of transparency and credibility	

References

1. Tredinnik, L.: Artificial intelligence and professional roles. Bus. Inf. Rev. **34**(1), 37–41 (2017)
2. McKinsey Global Institute: Artificial Intelligence The Next Digital Frontier. McKinsey&Company, New York (2017)
3. Popenici, S., Kerr, S.: Exploring the impact of artificial intelligence on teaching and learning in higher education. Res. Pract. Technol. Enhanced Learn. **12**, 22 (2017)
4. Manyika, J., Chui, M., Bughin, J., Dobbs, R., Bisson, P., Marrs, A.: Disruptive Technologies: Advances That Will Transform Life, Business, and the Global Economy. McKinsey Global Institute, New York (2013)
5. Schwab, K.: The fourth industrial revolution what it means and how to respond. foreign affairs (2015)
6. Brynjolfsson, E., McAfee, A.: The Second Machine Age: Work, Progress, and Prosperity in a Time of Brilliant Technologies. W. W. Norton & Company, New York (2014)
7. Burrus, D.: Disruption imminent: artificial intelligence. Brand Q. Mag. **27** (2017)
8. Deloitte: Digital Disruptions, Threats and Opportunities for Retail Financial Services (2016)
9. Harfouche, A., Skandrani, S., Quinio, B., Marciniak, R.,: Toward a recursive theory of artificial knowledge creation in organizations. In: Twenty-Sixth European Conference on Information Systems (ECIS2018), Portsmouth, UK (2018) (In press)
10. Dodgson, M., Gann, D.: Artificial intelligence will transform universities. Here's how Universities have sown the seeds of their own disruption. World Economic Forum (2017)
11. Suchman, M.C.: Managing legitimacy: strategic and institutional approaches. Acad. Manag. Rev. **20**, 571–610 (1995)
12. Chedrawi, C., Howayeck (el), P.: Accreditation in higher education between Innovation and isomorphism: the case of a Lebanese Business school. Gestion 2000 "L'innovation en gestion" (unpublished) (2017)
13. Lucas, P., Van der Gaag, L.: Principles of Expert Systems. Addison-Wesley Longman Publishing Co., Inc., Boston, MA, USA (2014)
14. Mahmoodi, R., Nejad, S., Ershadi, M.: Expert systems and artificial intelligence capabilities empower strategic decisions: a case study. Res. J. Recent Sci. **3**(1), 116–121 (2014)

15. Ernest & Young: The upside of disruption megatrends shaping 2016 and beyond (2016)
16. PwC: Leveraging the upcoming disruptions from AI and IoT how artificial intelligence will enable the full promise of the internet-of-things (2017)
17. Riemer, K., Gal, U., Hamann, J., Gilchriest, B., Teixeira, M.: Digital Disruptive Intermediaries: Finding New Digital Opportunities by Disrupting Existing Business Models. Australian Digital Transformation Lab (2015)
18. Anthes, G.: Artificial intelligence poised to ride a new wave. Commun. ACM **60**(7), 2017 (2017)
19. Harfouche, A., Quinio, B., Skandrani, S., Marciniak, R.,: A framework for artificial knowledge creation in organizations. In: Thirty eighth International Conference on Information Systems, Seoul (2017)
20. Abernathy, W., Clark, K.B.: Innovation: mapping the winds of creative destruction. Res. Policy **14**, 3–22 (1985)
21. Christensen, C.M.: The innovators dilemma: when new technologies cause great firms to fail. Harvard Business School Press, Boston, Massachusetts (1997)
22. Cowden, B., Alhorr, H.: Disruptive innovation in multinational enterprises. Multinational Bus. Rev. **21**(4), 358–371 (2013)
23. Assink, M.: Inhibitors of disruptive innovation capability: a conceptual model. Eur. J. Innov. Manag. **9**(2), 215–233 (2006)
24. Stone, P., Brooks, R., Brynjolfsson, E., Calo, R., Etzioni, O., Hager, G., Hirschberg, J., Kalyanakrishnan, S., Kamar, E., Kraus, S., Leyton-Brown, K., Parkes, D., Press, W., Saxenian, A., Shah, J., Tambe, M., Teller, A.: Artificial intelligence and life in 2030. One hundred year study on artificial intelligence: Report of the 2015–2016 Study Panel, Stanford University, Stanford, CA (2016)
25. Xing, B., Marwala, T.: Implications of the fourth industrial age for higher education. The Thinker: For the Thought Leader vol. 73, pp. 10–15. www.thethinker.co.za (2017)
26. Woolf, B.P, Lane, H.C., Chaudhri, V., Kolodner, J.: AI Grand Challenges for Education. AI Magazine (2013)
27. Vlăsceanu, L., Grünberg, L., Pârlea, D.: Quality assurance and accreditation: a glossary of basic terms and definitions. Unesco-Cepes, Bucharest (2004)
28. Caporali, E., Manfrida, G., Bartoli, G., Valdiserri, J.: Environmental issue through the international accreditation of engineering education. In: 2015 International Conference on Interactive Collaborative Learning (ICL), pp. 1036–1043 (2015)
29. Tastimur, C., Karakose, M., Akin, E.: Improvement of relative accreditation methods based on data mining and artificial intelligence for higher education. In: 15th International Conference on Information Technology Based Higher Education and Training (ITHET) (2016)
30. Noorda, S.: Future business schools. J. Manag. Dev. **30**(5), 519–525 (2011)
31. Hodge T.: Accreditation of business schools. An explanatory case study of their motivation. Thesis. http://ir.canterbury.ac.nz/bitstream/10092/3755/1/Thesis_fulltext.pdf (2010)
32. Trapnell J.: AACSB International accreditation: the value proposition and a look to the future. J. Manag. Dev. **26**(1), 67–72 (2007)
33. Abrahamson, E., Rosenkopf, L.: Institutional and competitive bandwagons: using mathematical modeling as a tool to explore innovation diffusion. Acad. Manag. Rev. **18**(3), 487–517 (1993)
34. Alteste, J.: Accreditation matters achieving academic recognition and renewal. ASHE-ERIC Higher Education Report, vol. 30, No. 4 (2004)
35. Sajja, P., Akerkar, R.: Knowledge-based systems for development. In Sajja, P.S., Akerkar, R. (eds.) Advanced Knowledge Based Systems: Model, Applications & Research, vol. 1, pp. 1–11 ((2010)

36. Tuthhill, S., Levy, S.: Knowledge-Based Systems: A Managers Perspective. TAB Professional & Reference Books (1991)
37. Hernández, T.H., Bermeo, N.V., Monroy, B.: An expert system to detect risk levels in small and medium enterprises (SMEs). In: Fourteenth Mexican International Conference on Artificial Intelligence (MICAI), pp. 215–219 (2015)
38. Agarwal, M., Goel, S.: Expert system and it's requirement engineering process. Recent Adv. Innov. Eng. 1–4 (2014)

Interactive Scheduling Decision Support System a Case Study for Fertilizer Production on Supply Chain

Ahlam Azzamouri, Imane Essaadi, Selwa Elfirdoussi and Vincent Giard

Abstract This paper presents the architecture of an interactive scheduling decision support system (ISDSS) allowing users to find the optimal solution for fertilizer production on parallel heterogeneous processors. The proposed approach takes into account different production process constraints such as launch time, delivery date, preventive maintenance and the impact of scheduling on supply chain management. The ISDSS implemented is run by a relational database used to customize the structural data and the problem parameters. A user interface is available for ISDSS users to define the scheduling problem and design the solution based on tables and graphs for detecting possible issues. The ISDSS architecture was implemented on java using independent modules.

Keywords Interactive Scheduling Decision Support System (ISDSS) · Scheduling · Production plant · Modular architecture

A. Azzamouri · I. Essaadi · S. Elfirdoussi (✉) · V. Giard
EMINES, University Mohammed VI Polytechnic, 43140 Ben Guerir, Morocco
e-mail: Selwa.Elfirdoussi@emines.um6p.ma

A. Azzamouri
e-mail: Ahlam.Azzamouri@emines.um6p.ma

I. Essaadi
e-mail: Imane.Essaadi@emines.um6p.ma

V. Giard
e-mail: Vincent.Giard@emines.um6p.ma

V. Giard
Paris-Dauphine, PSL Research University, 75016 Paris, France

A. Azzamouri · I. Essaadi
Paris Ouest Nanterre University, 92001 Nanterre Cedex, France

© Springer Nature Switzerland AG 2019
Y. Baghdadi and A. Harfouche (eds.), *ICT for a Better Life and a Better World*,
Lecture Notes in Information Systems and Organisation 30,
https://doi.org/10.1007/978-3-030-10737-6_9

131

1   Introduction

After a brief presentation of the decisional problem (Sect. 1.1) we present (Sect. 1.2) a functional view of the Interactive Decision Support System (ISDSS) we have designed. In Sect. 2, we examine the technical bases of the ISDSS used to schedule fertilizer orders, before illustrating ISDSS implementation and use in Sect. 3 and concluding in Sect. 4.

1.1   Analysis of the Decisional Problem

After clarifying the characteristics of this specific scheduling problem, one will briefly review two possible models, one of which has been implemented in the DSS.

Characteristics of the Scheduling Problem in a Fertilizer Production Plant

OCP SA (http://www.ocpgroup.ma/fr) accounts for one third of world phosphate exports across product segments. The Jorf fertilizer production plant, located near the sea at the end of the Northern axis of OCP's supply chain (SC), is the Moroccan group's largest plant. It produces some twenty three fertilizer references at 7 parallel lines (3 "107" identical lines and 4 "07" identical lines); 8 out of 33 references may only be produced at a single type of line, which yields 58 routings. Fertilizer demand is seasonal and produced to order, with shipping performed by boat at the harbor located near the fertilizer plant.

Each order is characterized by a fertilizer reference to be manufactured, a tonnage and a time window during which production must be completed. The schedule must factor in production stoppage required by preventive maintenance operations, and such stoppage has no impact on ongoing production time. Order fulfillment time varies from line to line, in particular due to their different technical features and due to production rate modulation options. The schedule must also factor in substantial cleaning operation time between two batches of production of different quality on the same line. Such line preparation lead time depends on the line itself and on the previously produced reference. Such a complexity is not considered in the scheduling literature [1, 2]. Besides, the issue dealt with is always local and ignores the consequences of the proposed schedule both downstream and upstream in the SC. However, in our context, this solution has immediate consequences that may make it unfeasible due to pump priming issues (upstream) or finished product inventory saturation (downstream).

Fertilizer manufacturing requires, among other inputs, sulfuric acid and phosphoric acid, the latter using sulfuric acid as a component. The Jorf site SC comprises production units for both acids. Moreover, the phosphoric acid that it produces is also exported and shipped and both acids may be used by the Joint Ventures (JV) also operating at Jorf. An analysis of the fertilizer BOM's reveals a strong dispersion on the consumption rate for these inputs. This means that the adopted scheduling has a strong impact on consumption rate for these acids and that the schedule is only workable if it does not deplete inventory for these raw materials.

The manufactured fertilizers are carried by conveyer belts out of the six storage areas. The storage areas are dedicated to the fertilizer references belonging to a particular family. Area capacity varies depending on the number of stored references, as any mixing of fertilizers is highly hazardous. The allocation of such areas to product families' changes over time and several areas may be dedicated to a single family. The chosen schedule determines fertilizer inventory buildup and will not be workable if inventory buildup is not matched by storage capacity.

Production stoppage risk due to pump priming issues (upstream) and/or saturated storage (downstream) serves to place the scheduling problem in the wider framework of SC management for the relevant fertilizer plant. We have built two MILP models [1, 2], using the Algebraic Modeling Languages (AML) of Xpress-IVE, that takes simultaneously into account all the characteristics of the local scheduling problem described above. Moreover, one of them considers temporal constraints on input supplies and on output storage to prevent priming and saturation issues. Unfortunately, the model only works with small instances due to the size of the generated problem. The second model is simpler though it solves a very complex local problem but it can be used for reasonably large instances. To guarantee the feasibility of the solution, an optimization module based on this model is embedded in a Decision Support System (DSS) to help managers define a feasible optimal problem.

In an integrated SC, this approach is the best one as it is inefficient to monitor an integrated SC locally when ignoring the upstream and downstream consequences of local decisions. What is more, this approach promotes solutions of constraint negotiation between inter-dependent SC entities, which could work as a substitute for global optimization, as this is impossible to achieve.

1.2   ISDSS Functional Architecture

The bases for DSS were laid by Gorry and Scott Morton as early as 1971 [3] and transformed into a structured approach by Keen and Scott Morton in 1978 [4]. IS/IT development, of course, immensely increased the potential of DSS [5–7] without altering its rationale. Basically DSSs comprise: (i) an interface to formally express a complex issue that is partially structured to define a structured problem; (ii) one or multiple modules to solve the structured problem, usually based on optimization or simulation models [8]; (iii) an interface capable of exploring all the consequences of a solution obtained and of either adjusting it marginally or of validating it; (iv) if none of these solutions is acceptable, the DSS is then used to define a new structured problem using the feedback from prior formulations that failed to deliver a satisfactory solution.

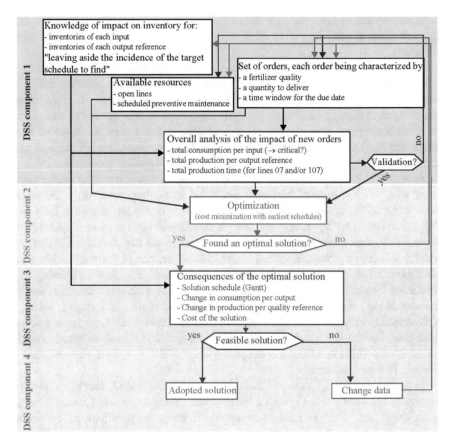

Fig. 1 ISDSS functional components

We have designed an ISDSS that applies this functional breakdown. Starting from a partially structured problem, it allows the definition of a structured problem to be optimized after an initial feasibility check. This structured problem is an instance of a generic MIP problem that uses the AML of Xpress-IVE. The scope of the problem is local as it lifts input availability and output storage capacity constraints. Optimization yields a solution whose results are used by the third functional component that takes into account the lifted constraints. If the solution found, which can be marginally changed, is not feasible, one returns to the structured problem formulation stage. The flowchart below follows the original pattern of the DSS designers, with its four components, as shown in Fig. 1.

2 Technical Bases of ISDSS

We begin with a literature review (Sect. 2.1), as this bring out the originality of our ISDSS. We then go on to explain the architecture we implemented (Sect. 2.2).

2.1 Literature Review

The following analysis reviews a number of papers published in scientific newspaper or proceedings focusing on Decision Support Systems for production scheduling.

An optimization-based Decision Support System (OBDSS) generator, designed by [9] automatically generates a database, a solver and an interface (GUI) using PowerBuilder. They applied the OBDSS generated in the production plant. The approach, called GESCOPP, uses SML technology to represent the optimization model and generate the database.

Olteanu (2011) addresses in [10] production plant in the biofuel industry. His system optimizes the main activities of the biofuel value chain and supports the decision-making process at management level. It reduces total production cost to the lowest possible level under current technological and market constraints. The shortcoming of the bioPur.OLT.SYS proposed is that is doesn't optimize the production plant process based on the processors and machine constraints.

A simulation-based DSS (GeSIM) is proposed [11] for customer-driven manufacturing. The approach aims to integrate data, generate the simulation model, and display the results and supports interactive changes. The tool requires user interaction for the information to be correctly defined, and the problem correctly expressed before input into the GeSIM. It is therefore too complex for untrained users and too time-consuming.

In [12], Krishnaiyer and Chen propose a Web-based Visual DSS to schedule the process of letter delivery to customers. The approach takes process production planning into account. The information from different systems is collected and analyzed to yield the optimal solution and ensure a high level of customer service quality. The strength of this project is its reliance on advanced technology such as web-based applications to model a number of services but the scheduling process is inefficient.

The power industry is a highly complex and critical field, where financial risk is high. Production Scheduling is an important area of research in this sector. The power generation department of the National Institute of Technology proposes [13] a DSS for operation scheduling and optimization of Sewa Hydro Electric Plan (SHEP). The system was implemented to assist SHEP to make decisions for the optimal use of available water resources at State level combined with the minimization of environmental impact.

IBM research authors describe in [14] a DSS for paper production scheduling (A-Team) which was deployed in IBM environment. A-Team is made up of three types of agents which work asynchronously: constructors, improvers, and destroyers. The 'Constructors' agent only deals with problem definition and creates new solutions. The 'Improvers' agent attempts to improve upon the current set of solutions by modifying or combining existing solutions. The 'Destroyers' agent attempts to limit the number of solutions and focus the efforts of 'Improvers' by eliminating poor solutions. Freed et al. [15] present a scheduling decision- support system implemented on VBA called the Dispatcher.

Galasso et al. [16] suggest a model of the decision-making parameters involved in the production management process. Their DSS framework aims to schedule the supply chain based on flexible demand. These authors deal in [17] with the design of a DSS that integrates machine scheduling with inventory management for a multi-product manufacturing industry. Other algorithms are proposed [18] to determine a model for production scheduling based on constraint parameters. The paper [19] describes an intelligent DSS for real-time control of a flexible manufacturing system.

Based on the above literature review, we have defined four analytical dimensions for the DSS to be designed, all of which may not all be used in a DSS: (a) application type implemented to run the DSS (desktop application vs web-based); (b) problem solving; (c) interface used to define the problem or design the solution; (d) DSS proposing generic system.

(a) Some authors experiment their DSS using such desktop applications as Excel or Microsoft Access (MA) [11, 13, 15, 16, 18, 19]. Although Excel may be used to manage very simple data base, as it is limited to just 2 dimensions and doesn't support the relational concept. Similarly, MA is limited to the Windows platform and doesn't provide high scalability and security. In the same analytical dimension, other solutions consist in web-based approaches integrating data from different systems [12, 17].

(b) Each DSS requires problem-solving capacities. The proposed optimization processes are based on different local approaches (simulation [11, 15, 19], optimization [13], heuristics [20]) or general software (ERP) and their APS (Advanced Planning System, [12]). Some of those DSSs are implemented through such programming languages as VB (Visual Basic), VBA (Visual Basic for Application), Visual C++. Although VBA or VB are user-friendly languages, they are Windows-compatible only and exclude an object-oriented approach.

(c) Few DSSs propose interfaces able to transform a semi-structured problem into a structured one. Downstream, the results processing interface is generally quite basic. The DSSs proposed in [9, 11–13, 15, 17, 19] use Web-based technology, Visual Basic or Visual C++ or DSS generator.

(d) Finally, some papers describe approaches using generic system aiming to take the three first dimensions (a, b, c) into account [9, 14] using technology such as IBM or DSS generators. Nowadays IBM products deliver multiple benefits especially in dealing with big data and computing capacity. Nevertheless, the most IBM packages will only work in IBM environments and deployment is very expensive. Turning to the DSS generator, this is a general approach based on structural data medialization and its implementation using a tagging system such as XML (eXtensible Markup Language). In itself, the general nature of such generators is restrictive because, for each request, one needs to formalize the new data and make fresh definitions of the constraints according to the working environment. From the technical point of view, these technologies are very costly and time-consuming to deploy.

2.2 ISDSS Technical Architecture

The structured problem of our ISDSS optimization modules is modeled using an AML (Algebraic Modeling Language), which allows dissociating the formulation of a generic problem from a data set, thereby enabling the instantiation of a specific problem. The cardinalities of the set of parameters and variables are totally cus-tomizable. To preserve this thorough customization capacity, it makes sense to use a relational database for the ISDSS, as this is also characterized by no-predefined cardinalities of the entities and associations and guarantees the integrity of the data in the database under a set of given rules. These characteristics lend the ISDSS an ability to adjust immediately to any changes in the number of parallel processors, inputs, outputs, routings, bills of materials (BOM) and costs. They also enable definition of a scheduling problem for any number of orders. The general archi-tecture of the ISDSS is presented on Fig. 2.

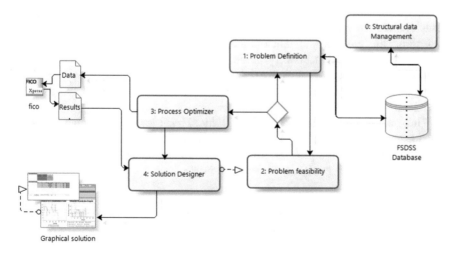

Fig. 2 ISDSS architecture

Data Management Module

This module is used to define the structural characteristics of the scheduling problem: production lines, references of fertilizers that these lines can produce, inputs (acids …) used in producing these fertilizers, fertilizer BOM for a given line (the chemical performance of these lines may vary), launching time of a reference on a line succeeding another fertilizer reference. This data is relatively stable and only evolves in the event of cancellation, transformation or addition of fertilizer lines and/or references.

The interfaces used (e.g., Figs. 4 and 5) ensure the integrity of this structural information, in the conventional sense of being retained in the relational database but also while integrating physical constraints. For example, in BOM definition, the sum of the inputs needed to produce a tone of fertilizer in a given line (and hence with a certain technology) must be equal to that of its outputs (tone of fertilizer, slag and gaseous emissions).

Problem Definition Module

The definition of a scheduling problem requires the structural data referred to above and supplements them with the following relative data:

- Available production resources: open lines, running mode (production flow), planned maintenance program, orders in production;
- The orders to be fulfilled: an order is characterized by a quantity of fertilizer to be produced, this production having to be completed in a time window, and a coefficient allowing to set its scheduling at the earliest or at the latest opportunity when a slack exists;
- The projected change in stocks of inputs and fertilizers, excluding the impact of the scheduling to be defined; this information is necessary to ensure feasibility of the optimal solution found.

Problem Feasibility Module

This module allows the user to test the possibility of finding a solution, to avoid launching the optimization unnecessarily. The test, described by the algorithm described below, leads to three possible diagnostics: a solution exists, a solution seems possible and no solution exists. In the first two cases, the optimization process must be launched. In the last one, we must return to the structured problem definition.

This module checks the problem feasibility at local level (i.e. without checking the upstream and downstream impacts of the solution)—see algorithm 1—and avoids trying to solve a problem for which no solution exists.

```
Algorithm 1: Problem Feasibility
Begin
```

```
1. Count the period concerning production and verify that
this number is smaller than the production time required for
each order. If not go to 6.
```

2. Place each order using a backward scheduling with the latest due dates and including the preventive maintenance allowance. If possible go to 4, if not go to 3.
3. Place each order using a forward scheduling with the earliest due dates and including the preventive maintenance allowance. If possible go to 4, if not go to 5.
4. End: the problem is feasible.
5. End: the problem posed seems feasible.
6. End: the problem is not feasible.

End.

If the problem is feasible, a file containing all problem parameters is generated. Its structure is defined by the generic optimization model integrated into the ISDSS. The combination of this generic model and this dataset generates an instance of the fertilizer scheduling problem.

Process Optimizer Module

A generic problem [1, 2] based on the AML of FICO Xpress [20] is activated by a dataset including all the information defining the specific problem to generate a specific problem to be solved. The file of the proposed solution is then available for the solution analysis module. This model, created with the Fico Xpress-IVE modeller [20], imports the dataset created by the previous module. The optimization results are then exported to a file that is used by the next module.

Interactive Solution Analysis

The solution contains a proposed schedule for each production line and for each order, using tables and colored Gantt diagrams. The Gantt take into account the preventive maintenance allowance and initial occupation of lines. After this, different graphs are proposed to illustrate the progress of each fertilizer produced and the input consumptions implied by the schedule. This result presentation is in the form of a user-friendly graphical interface for efficient use. It helps users make informed decisions or reformulate the problem according to the supply chain manager's need. This flexibility is one of the DSS's crucial benefits.

The optimal solution being that of a local problem that relaxes the constraints of availability of the acids consumed and the storage capacity of the fertilizers produced. The analysis of the stock levels makes it possible to check immediately whether the proposed solution is feasible. If this is not the case, a first possibility is offered to the user who can point to the task corresponding to the programming of a command to move it, while respecting the constraints of non-overlap of the productions and those of the windows of the production end dates for all the orders programmed on the line. The solution thus obtained remains optimal (the same production costs) and only uses the possible slacks of the obtained solution which yields the earliest possible schedules of orders (driven by the parameterization of the objective function). Of course, scheduling changes are immediately reflected in the of acid consumption and fertilizer production graphs.

If this approach does not yield a feasible optimal solution, we have to return to the definition of the structured problem to be solved; for this, several non-exclusive tracks are available. The first is a change in the coefficients applied to orders to push their scheduling at the earliest or at the latest available opportunity. The second is to change problem parameters of the: splitting orders into two to allow parallel production, changing the date interval of end of production for the orders or the maintenance programs or increasing the number of production lines (if possible).

3   ISDSS: Implementation and Experiment

In this section, we address the technologies implemented in our ISDSS (Sect. 3.1) and we illustrate the use of ISDSS using a case study (Sect. 3.2).

3.1   ISDSS Implementation

Obviously, the success of any information system depends on the technologies deployed and on the integrity of the data managed by the database. Our work differs from that of the papers discussed in Sect. 2.1. Indeed, we propose a framework relative to an ISDSS using generic and portable implementation combined with data management which ensures integrity and uses an object-oriented concept enabling proper flexibility of the cardinalities. All the ISDSS modules are grouped into a package that can run separately or following the ISDSS workflow.

For the deployment environment, the ISDSS is implemented on java which is easy to learn, object-oriented, robust, safe and platform-independent. The ISDSS API implements different libraries, such as mosel.jar to interact with external tools or jfreechart.jar to use graphical presentation. It can be integrated into any type of system and supports all database server providers. We have chosen MySQL for our prototype based on our conceptual database presented on Fig. 3.

ISDSS has a Graphical User Interface (GUI) that allows the users to manipulate the structural data easily, define the problem, test its feasibility, solve it and analyze the solution proposed. It also provides different menus to manage all ISDSS objects. A key feature of the ISDSS framework is data management. In fact, all the information used in the ISDSS have specific properties that we have modeled as objects defined by different attributes and methods. The ISDSS API is defined using different packages.

Each of them includes the classes relative to the ISDSS module. Most of the classes extend the "Jframe" and propose a list of drow-up menus to ensure data integrity. The most important class is "Problem Definition" which delivers a sequence of interfaces that display the components for this module, each interface interacting with the database to generate the parameters required by the optimizer

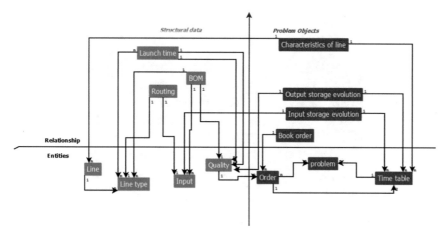

Fig. 3 ISDSS conceptual database

module. Subsequently, the ISDSS interacts with Xpress using generated files containing the previous parameters (data and result), these steps are transparent for the user.

The most interesting feature of our framework is that the structural data is modeled to support industrial standards.

3.2 ISDSS: Experiment

A study of different datasets was used to evaluate our proposed approach and architecture. In this section, we present a scenario using the ISDSS to define a fertilizer scheduling problem, the feasibility algorithm and the solution is then generated.

The case study presented in this section concerns fertilizer production at OCP. The initial setup of ISDSS consists in integration of the structural data related to our customer including the lines, the fertilizer, the inputs, BOM (Fig. 4) and launch time required between qualities (Fig. 5).

The problem discussed in this model was defined to find the optimal scheduling solution for an order book. The order book concerned contains twenty orders for different customers (Fig. 6) with production in progress on four operational lines and over a 360-h production horizon. Each order concerns a fertilizer and a customer, specifying the constraints such as the earliest and the latest delivery dates, the weighting directing the orders launches at their earliest or at their latest possibilities given by their time windows. The module also takes into account the order being produced at each production line.

Once this has been done, the user can generate the problem depending on the available resources (Fig. 7). Each problem is identified by a unique number and

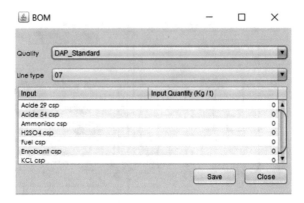

Fig. 4 Fertilizer composition interface

	DAP_Standard	DAP_EURO	DAP_Std_Noir	DAP_Chambal	MAP_Std_Normal_11_52	MAP_T
DAP_Standard	0	8	8	8	8	
DAP_EURO	8	0	8	8	8	
DAP_Std_Noir	8	8	0	8	8	
DAP_Chambal	8	8	8	0	8	
MAP_Std_Normal_11_52	8	8	8	8	0	
MAP_TAP_11_52	8	8	8	8	8	
MAP_Clair_11_54	8	8	8	8	8	
ASP	8	8	8	8	8	
TSP	8	8	8	8	8	
NPS_12_48_5S	8	8	8	8	8	
NPS_12_46_7S_1Z	8	8	8	8	8	
NPK_15_15_15	8	8	8	8	8	
NPK_12_24_12	8	8	8	8	8	
NPK_14_18_18_6S_1B	8	8	8	8	8	
NPK_14_23_14_5S_1B	8	8	8	8	8	
NPK_10_20_10	8	8	8	8	8	
NPK_10_18_24_7S	8	8	8	8	8	
NPS_12_46_7S	8	8	8	8	8	
NPK_10_20_10_Zn_Br	8	8	8	8	8	
MAP_Clair_11_52	8	8	8	8	8	

Please enter the launch cost for the fertilizer concerned (in column) and the previous fertilizer (rows)

Fig. 5 Launch time interface

assigned to an author and can be assigned to one or more workshops. The production time is an important constraint and it depends on delivery time for each
order. In the same user form, the author can also change the line characteristics
(Fig. 7), their speed (Fig. 7), specify their preventive maintenance schedules
(Fig. 8) and include the storage information for the input or output.

Fig. 6 Order book management interface

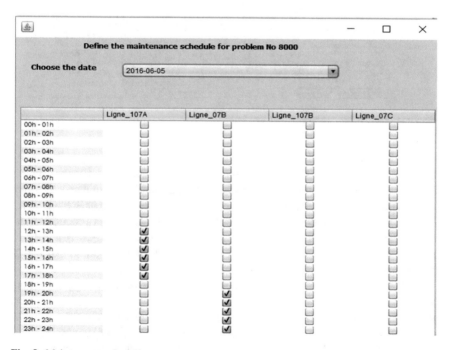

Fig. 7 Problem definition interface

Fig. 8 Maintenance scheduling

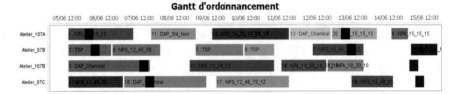

Fig. 9 Gantt diagram proposing the scheduling production

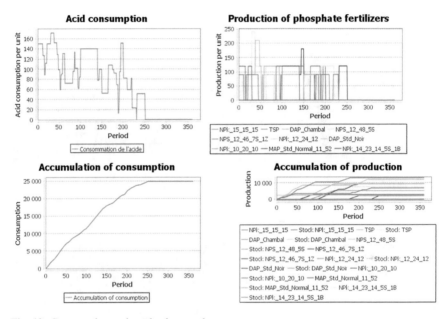

Fig. 10 Consumption and production graphs

Once the problem is defined, ISDSS supports the feasibility study before going ahead with optimization. Figure 9 presents the optimal solution in a Gantt form; this Gantt can be zoomed to view solution for each order number, with a specific color for each product quality. The maintenance program schedules appear in black in the Gantt. The solution on display also contains the graph of fertilizer production and sulfuric acid 29 consumption, both per period and aggregated (Fig. 10). All this information can be printed or exported to Excel to perform any additional operations as required or to share with different workshop managers.

In addition to the optimizer process and to improve the decision support system, ISDSS enables interactive change of the proposed solution using the Gantt diagram. Indeed, the user can drag and drop the different tasks on the date axis or the line axis according the production constraints and proposed planning coherence such as order overlap. Those changes are automatically integrated into the consumption and production graphs for real-time display of the impact of the changes.

4 Conclusions and Future Work

Our ISDSS is currently being tested to confirm its relevance for real-life environments. It can be used not only for scheduling purposes over a two to three-week horizon, but also over a longer horizon to test the impact of commercial scenarios with coupling of due dates and prices. This involves starting with formulations using weak constraints that are gradually tightened. The use of the ISDSS approach to improve the overall consistency of the decisions taken locally by different supply chain entities is clearly necessary, especially as it also supports intelligent negotiation of constraints at the interface of these entities.

The characteristics of our ISDSS architecture make it fit for use in other industrial environments confronted with scheduling problems involving parallel heterogeneous processors, taking into account time intervals for the definition of control, preventive maintenance and launch timing depending on the sequence of references produced and on the processor used.

The implementation and test of IDSS are in progress. It can be used within the horizon of a very few weeks (at the operational level) or more (at the tactical level, in the framework of spot market negotiations). Later, we aim to insert it in a system of constraints negotiations between fertilizer plant and the upstream units (acid plants) and downstream units (storage, conveyors, boat loading) in the phosphoric supply chain.

References

1. Giard, V., Ahlam, E., Essadi, I., Fénies, P., Fontane, F.: A DSS approach for heterogeneous parallel machines scheduling with due windows, processor-&-sequence-dependent setup and proximate supply chain constraints. Cahier de recherche 375, Paris Dauphine (2015)
2. Giard, V., Azzamouri, A., Essadi, I.: A DSS approach for heterogeneous parallel machines scheduling with due windows, processor-&-sequence-dependent setup and availability constraints. In: Information system Logistics and Supply Chain, Bordeaux, pp. 1–8 (2016)
3. Gorry, G., Morton, M.: A framework for management information systems. Sloan Manag. Rev. 30(3), 49–61 (1989)
4. Keen, P., Scott Morton, M.: Decision Support Systems: An Organizational Perspective. Addison-Wesley Publishing, Reading (1978)
5. Shim, J., Warkentin, M., Courtney, J., Power, D., Sharda, R., Carlsson, C.: Past, present, and future of decision support technology. Decis. Support Syst. 33, 111–126 (2002)
6. Eom, S., Kim, E.: A survey of decision support system applications. J. Oper. Res. Soc. 57 (11), 1264–1278 (2006)
7. Bhargava, H.K., Power, D.J., Sun, D.: Progress in web-based decision support technologies. Decis. Support Syst. 43(3), 1083–1095 (2007)
8. Power, D.J., Sharda, R.: Model-driven decision support systems: concepts and research directions. Decis. Support Syst. 43(3), 1044–1061 (2007)
9. Maturana, S., Ferrer, J., Barañao, F.: Design and implementation of an optimization-based decision support system generator. Eur. J. Oper. Res. 145(1), 170–183 (2004)
10. Olteanu, A.: A Decision Support System (DSS) for project management in the biodiesel industry. Informatică Economică 15(4), 189–202 (2011)

11. Heilala, J., Montonen, J., Järvinen, P., Kivikunnas, S., Maantila, M., Sillanpää, J., & Jokinen, T.: Developing simulation-based decision support systems for customer-driven manufacturing operation planning. In: Winter Simulation Conference (WSC), Baltimore, pp. 3363–3375 (2010)
12. Krishnaiyer, K., Chen, F.: Web-based Visual Decision Support System (WVDSS) for letter shop. Robotics and Computer-Integrated Manufacturing (2015)
13. Sharma, R., Chand, N., Sharma, V., Yadav, D.: Decision support system for operation, scheduling and optimization of hydro power plant in Jammu and Kashmir region. Renew. Sustain. Energy Rev. **43**, 1099–1113 (2015)
14. Keskinocak, P., Wu, F., Goodwin, R., Murthy, S., Akkiraju, R., Kumaran, S., Derebail, A.: Scheduling solutions for the paper industry. Oper. Res. **50**(2), 249–259 (2002)
15. Freed, T., Doerr, K., Chang, T.: In-house development of scheduling decision support systems: case study for scheduling semiconductor device test operations. Int. J. Prod. Res. **45** (21), 5075–5093 (2007)
16. Galasso, F., Mercé, C., Grabot, B.: Decision support framework for supply chain planning with flexible demand. Int. J. Prod. Res. **47**(2), 455–478 (2009)
17. Krishna, L., Janardhan, G., Rao, C.: Web integrated decision support system for machine scheduling and inventory management. IUP J. Oper. Manag. **8**(1), 35 (2009)
18. Tang, L., Liu, G.: A mathematical programming model and solution for scheduling production orders in Shanghai Baoshan iron and steel complex. Eur. J. Oper. Res. **182**(3), 1453–1468 (2007)
19. Shirazi, B., Mahdavi, I., Solimanpur, M.: Intelligent decision support system for the adaptive control of a flexible manufacturing system with machine and tool flexibility. Int. J. Prod. Res. **50**(12), 3288–3314 (2012)
20. FICO: Robust Optimization With Xpress. In: Fico. Accessed 22 June 2015 Available at: https://community.fico.com/docs/DOC-1818

Part II
Innovation for e-Government

The E-Banking and the Adoption of Innovations from the Perspective of the Transactions Cost Theory: Case of the Largest Commercial Banks in Lebanon

Charbel Chedrawi, Bissane Harb and Mariam Saleh

Abstract Based on the transactions cost theory, this article aims to explore the adoption and the integration of innovations and e-banking by the largest commercial banks in Lebanon. Referring to Rogers' models (Diffusion of innovations. The Free Press, A Division of Macmillan Publishing Co., Inc., New York, 1983 [16]; Diffusion of innovations. New York Free Press, 1995 [17]), we studied the effects of this adoption on transactions costs and we presented the key role played by information and communications technology (ICT) in organizations, especially at the cost level. Using a qualitative approach, our study reveals the complexity of this concept, particularly regarding the integration strategies of the latest technological innovations within the banking sector, which appear to be essential for the development and the continuity of the sector at the national and regional levels

Keywords Adoption of innovations · E-banking · Transactions cost theory · Banking sector in Lebanon

1 Introduction

In order to be effective and to survive, organizations should innovate [1]. One of the most significant developments in the banking industry during the recent years has been the development of new distribution channels made possible by technological innovation. Electronic banking (e-banking) services have been rapidly established

C. Chedrawi (✉) · B. Harb · M. Saleh
Faculty of Business and Management, Saint Joseph University, Beirut, Lebanon
e-mail: charbel.chedrawi@usj.edu.lb

B. Harb
e-mail: bissane_harb@hotmail.com

M. Saleh
e-mail: mariam_saleh@hotmail.com

© Springer Nature Switzerland AG 2019
Y. Baghdadi and A. Harfouche (eds.), *ICT for a Better Life and a Better World*,
Lecture Notes in Information Systems and Organisation 30,
https://doi.org/10.1007/978-3-030-10737-6_10

by the leading international banking institutions both as stand-alone operations and as an integral part of an established banking service [2, 3].

The introduction of e-banking has changed and redefined both the banks' way of working and the basic principles of their business [4]. Internet banking has received universal approval as a new distribution channel for banking services. Given the conditions of increased global competition, ever-changing market situations and customers' constant demand for quality services [5], technology is seen today as a determining factor for success and competitiveness of organizations [6].

The integration of technological innovations and virtual contact in the banking sector has been fostered by the rapid spread of the Internet and through innovations in the field of information and communication technologies (ICT) which come in several forms such as ATM, phone banking and e-banking [7, 8]. The use of the Internet in service industries reduces the cost of customer interaction and information asymmetry between the buyer and the seller. Thus, the internet radically reduces infrastructure and transaction costs in banking operations; According to the Bank for International Settlements, the average cost of a branch transaction is estimated to be approximately $1.07 compared to $0.01 for the same transaction processed over the Internet.

Furthermore, there is constant pressure to reduce cost in order to maintain a minimum level of profitability, especially in the banking sector. According to [9], time, which is a limited resource, means money and each company must find ways to efficiently utilize its employees working time in order to maximize the productivity and profits of the company. But time is also valuable to the individual (the client) on a personal level and using it effectively means gains in "is quality of life".

In this context, the Lebanese banking sector, which represents an important pillar of the economy, is in the process of technological development [3, 7]. Moreover, this sector has maintained its growth despite the instability and inefficiency of the political and economic situations of the region. Thus, it seems interesting to examine how the Lebanese banks react to these technological developments and to question the motivations that drive them to embark on this path. This research aims to examine the different transaction costs related to the process of integrating technological innovations by Lebanese commercial banks.

Choosing the banking sector as a framework of our field study is valid. It is concurrently related to a personal and theoretical interest. Indeed, it is a framework that one of the three authors knows well, for having worked in for several years. This choice is also explained by the fact that this sector is heavily involved in the dynamics of implementing technological innovations.

Then, the choice of proceeding with a case study is linked to our wish to create a detailed research of our object, revealing all the complexity of the different studied concepts. The use of semi-structured interviews conducted with CEOs, managers and employees allowed us to integrate the views of various players operating within the largest banks in the sector in Lebanon and to situate them in a more general context of the implementation of these innovations.

Hence, as a first phase, we will review the literature related to the concepts pertaining to our research; we will perceive the e-banking theme by exposing its various definitions, then we will discuss the concept of innovation and its adoption and we will conclude the theoretical part with input from the transaction cost theory. In a second phase, we will present the empirical study carried out among directors, managers and employees working in five of the largest Lebanese banks. Finally, we will reveal the main contributions of this article by gathering the elements that are prone to answer our research questions.

2 Technological Innovation, E-Banking and Transactions Cost Theory

2.1 The Technological Innovation and Its Adoption

The concept of innovation has given rise to an abundant literature. The different definitions of innovation revolve around the novelty of ideas, projects, services and products resulting from pioneering knowledge in a given social environment [10]. According to [11], innovation is a multi-step process by which organizations transform ideas into new/improved products, services, or processes in order to face their competitors and differentiate themselves from them on the market.

Shumpeter [12], who was at the origin of the founding theory of innovation, defines innovation as a dynamic process of creative destruction in which new technologies replace the old ones and induce changes in economic structures. According to [13, 14], innovation is an idea, practice or object that is perceived as new by an individual or another unit of adoption; it is the creation or adoption of new ideas [1]. O'Sullivan and Dooley [15] define innovation as "he process of making changes to something established by the introduction of something new" Hence, innovation plays an ongoing role in all aspects of the organizational experience.

However, the adoption of innovation is the decision to use innovation on an ongoing basis. The theoretical model of Rogers [16, 17] on the process of adoption of innovation has been widely used in the field of adoption of technologies and the dissemination of various innovations. According to [14], a person or an organization (a) adopts an innovation by making the decision to acquiring it, (b) implements the innovation by putting it into practice and testing it, and (c) institutionalizes an innovation by fully supporting and integrating it into the usual typical practice. In general, innovations that are perceived by receivers as accessible, compatible, and having relatively higher advantages will be adopted faster than other innovations [16].

Several scholars have attempted to explain the phenomenon of the adoption of information technologies. According to Davis' [18] Technology Acceptance Model (TAM), the behavior of the individual depends directly on the intention to perform this behavior. The intention is a function of the attitude of the individual towards the system that is determined by two types of beliefs: perceived usefulness and perceived ease of use. Another model developed by [19] discusses the role of expected performance, expected effort, social influence and facilitating conditions in the adoption of information technology.

The Rogers' [17] model assumes that some factors such as the perception of innovation's attributes, the type of decisions, the communication channels, the social systems and the agents of change affect the speed of adoption of an innovation by the population. According to [17] the attributes of innovation refer to the individual perceptions of the relative advantage of innovation such as the perception of the benefits of adoption, compatibility, low complexity, testing possibility and the strong influence of innovation. These elements are positively associated with the adoption of innovation.

ICT has become the major enabler of efficient exchange and retrieval of information in organizations. They are a powerful tool to support the economic system managing information especially in the transaction cost approach [20, 21]. Such studies argue that ICT supports the economic system, providing a more efficient information flow that facilitates the interaction among economic agents under complex and uncertain circumstances, and reducing transaction costs.

2.2   E-Banking

The banking sector has often been exposed to technological innovations as a result of improvements achieved in ICT. Indeed, e-banking represents the latest initiative in the range of innovative banking services, such as telebanking, ATM and electronic cards [22]. This innovation is considered as an efficient distribution channel for traditional banking products and is booming all over the world.

The terms e-Banking, online banking or internet banking refer to the use of the Internet to remote banking services, such as transferring funds or creating and closing deposit accounts. For the online banking services to exist, there are two major requirements that have to be met, the first being the access to these services, which means the infrastructure, hardware and applications that banks have to create, maintain and make available to companies and individuals. The second one is centered on the security issue and the trust that users can confer to this channel as well as the performance of the system [9, 23].

Many researchers have attempted to give a definition to e-banking; [24] defines it as "global, cheap, multimedia distribution/delivery channel". According to [8], e-banking is a term that encompasses the process by which a consumer can electronically manage his or her banking transactions without having to visit a physical branch. It is a bank offering various services to customers through a simple electronic contact. It enables users to access banking services without the intervention of a third party. Thulani and Chitura [25] define e-banking as a self-service that enables bank customers to access their accounts, get the latest information on bank products and services, and to conduct all financial transactions anytime from anywhere through the use of a bank's website. Thanks to this service, the client can access his accounts every day and track their positions, transfer funds between accounts, receive and pay bills online, and directly download statements and reports [26].

In addition, e-banking enables customers to manage their financial operations in a more flexible way, on a 24/7 basis, instead of getting restricted by the timings of the physical branch. It is thus a self-service that eliminates time and space constraints in the performance of banking operations and ensures comfort and availability for customers [27, 28].

In general, e-banking covers a wide range of banking transactions that the customer can perform electronically without the obligation to visit a branch.

Several advantages related to the use of e-banking compared to the traditional banking system are recorded. According to [29], e-banking services and technologies offer the banking sector several opportunities to meet the needs of existing customers and attract new potential clients; as a matter of fact, banks and their customers (individuals or companies) benefit from the use of alternative channels and electronic banking services.

According to [30], internet banking services decrease operational costs and amplify customers' satisfaction and retention in the retail banking sector in Turkey. Simpson [31] suggests that e-banking is largely driven by the factors of minimizing the operating costs and maximizing operating profit.

For clients, e-banking means that time and space are no longer important, as they can access banking services day and night from anywhere where internet access is available. Given the congestion of large cities and traffic problems, e-banking could be an important way to save time simply by avoiding going to the bank and doing business from the personal computer [29].

For the bank, the online channel means fewer employees dealing with customers and fewer operating transactions. This leads to cost reductions, and to the increase in the number of employees concentrating more on advanced services with higher added value. Another benefit for banks is the savings in office supplies [23].

2.3 The Transactions Cost Theory (TCT)

According to [32], a transaction cost is a cost incurred in making an economic transaction carried out in a market. He has focused on transaction costs mainly to show that recourse to the market is not free. For [33, 34], agents have bounded rationality and adopt opportunistic behaviors; they have limited cognitive abilities and cannot contemplate all possible events and fully calculate the consequences of their decisions. In addition, they are opportunistic and seek to advance their own interests to the detriment of the others' interests.

Williamson [33–35] describes the characteristics of a transaction in terms of asset specificity, frequency, and uncertainty. Asset specificity is a "specialized investment that cannot be redeployed to alternative uses or by alternative users without a loss in productive value" [34]. The frequency of the transactions reduces transaction costs due to the ability to re-deploy knowledge and capitalize on standardized processes and contracts [36]. As for uncertainty, we distinguish between internal uncertainty and external uncertainty [37]. The first covers the complexity and tacit nature of the tasks performed internally by the firm or by two different firms during a technological transfer transaction. The second is external uncertainty, which includes technological uncertainty, legal regulatory and fiscal uncertainty, and competitive uncertainty.

There is an extensive literature defining transaction costs [32, 35, 38–41]. Back to this vast literature for e-banking application. Ciborra [42] was the first author to propose the TCT as an approach to explain the design of computer based information systems. He contends that in depicting the transactional dimension of economic exchanges, TCT discusses varying organizational forms as alternative responses that are enacted to overcome problems in the efficient allocation of economic resources. As a result, ICT is proposed as a solution that can reduce transaction costs.

Ciborra [21] states that the key feature of technological innovations and ICTs, is the possibility of reducing the transactions costs. The introduction of these technologies will reduce the costs of exchange and increase the gains for both parties, if the consumed resources are less than the incurred transaction costs. He suggests that the impact of ICT on transaction costs should be appraised not only in quantitative terms but also by taking into account qualitative changes that can be induced by ICT when it fosters a shift in the paradigm of the organization that hosts it.

Malone et al. [20] argue that ICT lowers transaction costs; these are the costs of executing the transaction and may include commission costs, the costs of physically negotiating the terms of an exchange, the costs of formally drawing up contracts, etc. as well as the costs of executing the operation.

According to [43], the reduction of transaction costs and the efficiency factor are probably the most important advantages of e-business. Internet-based transaction systems cost less in the long run because they reduce the need for a large organizational system (a study conducted by Booz Allen & Hamilton Consulting Company for a banking system revealed that a transaction costing 13 Cents on the Internet shall cost $1.08 if processed in a branch).

For [44], the internet is an ideal way of delivering banking products and services in terms of cost savings. These cost savings come about through the combined effects of reduction (a payment operation will cost the bank up to 11 times more in a branch than on the internet) and better utilization of the workforce, equipment, more economical usage of space, and operational savings. The internet reduces physical and bureaucratic resistance by drastically reducing the importance of location and the number of procedural steps requiring the direct intervention of the bank operators. Costs related to task execution time and paper flow are reduced.

Finally, for e-banking, transaction costs are incurred as a result of time and labor related expenditures associated with the activities and costs of the resources used to create, develop, implement and maintain this type of transaction throughout of the operating cycle of its services. Indeed, the utilization of the internet in banking operations considerably reduces infrastructure and transaction costs; the average cost of a transaction at the branch level is estimated to be approximately $1.07 compared to $0.01 for the same transaction processed via the Internet [45].

3 Research Methodology

In order to dynamically analyze the e-banking and the adoption of innovations from a perspective of transaction costs in the banking sector in Lebanon, we will use an exploratory approach. Our methodology is based on the collection and analysis of qualitative data. These data were collected through centered semi-structured interviews with five General Managers (GM1, GM2, GM3, GM4, GM5), five directors of IT departments or persons in charge of e-banking (D1, D2, D3, D4, D5) and 10 employees (two employees per bank E11, E12, E21, E22, E31, E32, E41, E42, E51, E52) operating in five of the largest banks in Lebanon. Our sample represents almost 50% of the Lebanese banking sector in terms of deposits, profitability and size. Centered semi-structured interviews may enable us to collect data that is adapted to the case studies [46]. To data collected by interviews, we will add secondary data from several sources (written, reported, verbal). This approach will bring us closer to the process of adopting e-banking as a technological innovation and its effects on transaction costs in the sector.

3.1 The Context of the Study: Adoption of E-Banking in Lebanon

About a decade ago, commercial banks in Lebanon started to take interest on integrating electronic channels of distribution and communication into their work. Azzam [47] realized that the Internet has significantly transformed the banking servicing process and all marketing strategies opening up new opportunities for banking institutions. According to him, distribution channels (ATMs, bank accounts websites, smartphones) are developed to become real smart computer media that interact with customers and facilitate all types of banking transactions.

3.2 The Context of the Study: The Sample

As shown in Table 1, the choice of our sample of five among the largest banks operating in Lebanon, strongly reflects the general state of the banking sector. Indeed, the selected banks are successively the first, second, third, eighth and tenth banks among the 69 financial institutions that operate in the Lebanese banking sector.

The total assets of banks exceeded $227 billion in December 2015 (assets of banks represent more than 400% of Lebanon' GDP), which is a very large figure that affects the Lebanese economy. The selected sample represents approximately 48% of the total assets of the banks in Lebanon, 50% of total deposits and 44% of total equity.

Table 1 Key figures on the sample of selected banks compared to the total banking sector in Lebanon (2015)

	Audi	Blom	Byblos	BLF	BBAC	Total sample	Total banking sector	% sample/ banking sector
Rank in terms of deposits	1	2	3	8	10			
Deposits in billion $	35.6	25.1	16.6	9.8	5.3	**92.4**	186.4	49.6
Assets in billion $	42.3	29.1	19.9	11.6	6	**108.9**	227.8	47.8
Equity in billion $	3.3	2.7	1.7	1.1	0.48	**9.3**	21	44.3

Our sample is composed of Bank Audi, BLOM Bank, Byblos Bank, Banque Libano-Française and Bank of Beirut and the Arab Countries:

- **Bank Audi**; Bank Audi ranks first in Lebanon and it is one of the first banks to introduce e-banking. It has one of the largest branch networks in Lebanon, with 83 branches in Lebanon. It is making tremendous efforts to achieve a model progress in integrating technological innovations into the Lebanese market. It has developed a customer centric model supported by innovative distribution channels and cutting-edge technologies. The strengths of Bank Audi are materialized by its electronic platform which offers internal and external transfer options. This is combined with the creation of an electronic branch (NOVO) open 24/7, the creation of Interactive Teller Machines (ITM), and the extension of its ATM network across the country. Bank Audi's customers are currently served by an omnichannel network comprising 400 "self-service advanced machines", digital channels (Internet and mobile) and more than 180 branches. In 2015, for the first time, online transactions exceeded those made through the counter.
- **Banque du Liban et d'Outre Mer (BLOM)**; It is the second bank in Lebanon and the first bank to launch online transactions in 1998. Currently, BLOM devotes a huge budget to launching new online services. In this bank, a "home strategy" is adopted; the new innovative products are designed and launched by the IT team belonging to the Bank. Thus, the costs are lower but the "time to market" to launch new digital channels is longer. BLOM is the only bank in Lebanon that offers its customers the possibility to transfer cash via its ATMs without the receiver needing a bank card.
- **Byblos Bank**; It is the third bank in Lebanon, it has an extensive network of 80 branches distributed homogeneously throughout Lebanon. Byblos Bank offers its customers an array of innovative products and a full range of online banking services. The range includes innovative and secure tools such as the Mobile

Banking application, Smart ATMs, the Internet Banking platform, as well as e-branches. Innovation in e-banking is reflected in products suitable for each type of customer, for example "sra3App" which is an application dedicated to car dealers and "kramApp" an application dedicated to Bank Byblos cardholders.

- **Banque Libano-Français (BLF)**; It is the eighth bank in Lebanon and one of the fastest growing ones. It enjoys wide geographical expansion and good technical advancement at the operational level. The BLF tends to develop its online banking services in order to line up with large banks. The marketing managers are interested in the contribution of e-banking and are trying to take great advantage of it in order to commercialize the products and services offered by the bank (broadcasting advertisements on the bank" website via a mobile screen). The main digital services are the consultation of balances and account movements, transfers via internet and foreign exchange transactions for small amounts.

- **Bank of Beirut and the Arab Countries (BBAC)**; it is ranked as the tenth bank in Lebanon. However, the development of online banking services falls as a response to competition. BBAC is following a cautious expansion strategy that focuses on establishing its presence in selected markets with sustainable growth potential.

4 Analysis and Discussion of Results

In order to deeply understand the current stakes of the use of electronic distribution channels by the banking sector in Lebanon and to better define this phenomenon which is currently witnessing a rapid expansion, we studied the factors that affect the adoption of e-banking and the challenges related to the integration of ICT by the Lebanese banking sector in a perspective of transaction costs.

The results of our exploratory study conducted with five of the largest commercial banks in Lebanon enabled us to bring forward the influence of the adoption of technological innovations on the banking sector in general and on the transaction costs in this sector. The results provide a significant insight on this subject.

The first noted conclusion is that the degree of innovation varies among Lebanese banks. Indeed, the size of the bank influences the degree of innovation, according to the results obtained by [7, 48]. "The largest Lebanese banks were the first to integrate e-banking, and made remarkable progress in this field, while in other banks the electronic banking services remains limited" (DG1, D3, D4, D5, D6).

In fact, the development of e-banking generates significant investment costs to renew and develop the used technologies, and large banks are better positioned to bear these costs and to expand their productive capacity. "The large Lebanese banks are the best equipped with human and financial resources to ensure a better experience to the public" (DG4, DG5, D4, D5). "Banks that are leaders in terms of assets or profits are also leaders in terms of technological innovations" (DG2, D2, D3, D4).

"We have devoted a large budget for the on-going development of digital banking services and the adoption of the most advanced models; this budget corresponds to that allocated for all the other activities of the bank" (DG1, DG2, D1). "Large banks are more capable to attract highly skilled human resources" (D3, D4, D5, DG5).

According to [8], several factors, such as bank size, technical infrastructure, the degree of international experience of the decision-makers and their control over innovation, the presence of competent technical staff and the risk associated with the adoption of e-banking, have favored the integration of technological innovations within the Lebanese banking sector. "Our bank was the first in the Middle East to launch Novo, it is a technology based on video banking. We are still working to be leaders in e-banking. For example, we recently adopted the omnichannel which is a synergy between digital and physical points of sale" (DG1). "Our success in e-banking depends on the efforts of our IT team. The small banks buy the new digital products while in our bank, our team designs and launches them. It enables us to regularly make the necessary changes to adapt them to market needs" DG1, DG2).

Regarding **the adoption of e-banking by the largest banks in Lebanon**, the results of the interviews confirm that the main factors affecting this adoption are:

- **The existence of technological opportunities (the internet) and the perception of their advantages**; "the technological evolution is very fast all over the world, the largest company that rents cars is virtual and does not own cars. The banking sector could not remain as it is, it is essential to adapt to the evolutions in customer behavior and to meet these new challenges" DG1).

"The Lebanese consumer is more and more aware of the importance of technology in his daily life, the rate of use of the internet is constantly increasing, so as a banking sector we should always follow the evolution of our clients' needs and habits" DG2, DG3, D1). "It is a service that represents an added value for us, we cannot do without" (DG1, DG2, D2).

"No product is as attractive as automated banking services, especially for young customers, innovation is now synonym of digital for the banking sector" (D1, D2, D3, E11). "We are aware that e-banking improves the image of our bank, and the use of digital services by our customers gives them a sense of modernity" (DG1, DG2).

- **The improvement of services and productivity**; [3] emphasized that the major impact of new technologies on the distribution function is customer satisfaction by fostering the speed and reliability of the services. As for productivity, from now on it would be doubled. "Currently, the integration of alternative distribution channels has become a priority for us. We can no longer ignore the fact that virtual contact is a key aspect of the banking industry beside physical contact" DG2). "It is not the products that are the vectors of innovation but their distribution channels" (DG3, D3, D4, D5).

Toufaily et al. [8] found that the adoption of e-banking contributes to improving the quality of offered services, reducing processing costs per customer and promotion costs, and strengthening the relationship with the customers. "The adoption of online banking services will greatly help us alleviate the increased pressure in our many branches, particularly for simple banking services (DG1, DG2, DG3, D1, D2, D3, E11, E21, E22). In big branches, people wait too long to carry out regular and simple banking transactions that do not require physical contact with the bank" (E11, E12, E31, E32). As pointed out by [49], financial innovation and technological progress have improved productivity and social welfare at the banks. "The new technologies of information and communication allow an improvement of the relationship with the customers" (DG1, D2). Therefore, by shifting from face-to-face financial services to self-service technology, banks also try to meet their customers' needs and expectations and improve their relationships with them [50].

- **Competitive pressure**; non-banking financial institutions put pressure on the Lebanese banks by increasing their banking activities using developed computer systems. "We have begun to adopt electronic distribution channels to compete with these new comers to the market and to meet customer expectations" (DG3, D4, D5). "Our customers, distributed all over the world are now demanding fast and easy services compatible with their lifestyle and their regular moves" (DG1, D1, DG2). In his model, [48] found that elements related to the organization' environment such as competitiveness and market size influence the adoption.

Hilal [3] found that the first strategic objective that drives Lebanese banks to integrate new technologies is to develop their sphere of action and surpass their competitors. "The increasing internationalization of the banking market and the strong competition from the "Clicks and Mortar"[1] and the "Pure Players" prompt us to diversify our distribution channels and to use technological innovation as a strategy of differentiation" (D1, D2, DG1).

This competitive pressure gives a neo-institutional dimension to the adoption of e-banking in the Lebanese banking sector and recalls the work of DiMaggio and Powell [51] in a coercive isomorphism: "small and medium-sized banks are obliged to adopt alternative distribution channels to deal with their competitors who have largely embarked on this path" and mimetic one: "some banks adopt new electronic distribution channels because their competitors have done so" (DG3, DG4, D4, E21, E32) [24]. "All the banking institutions in the market currently provide automated delivery of banking products and services. So we should do the same, otherwise we will be excluded from the market" DG4, D4, E41, DG5, D5, E51).

---

[1]Banks that combine physical channels and online services across Web.

Thus, in order to remain competitive, commercial banks integrate the elements of cutting-edge technology by imitating their competitors. The adoption of innovation can therefore be the direct result of a management choice or may be imposed by external conditions [1].

- **Reduction of transactions' cost**; [20, 21, 23, 29, 30, 31, 44, 43] and many other authors confirm the role of cost reduction as a decisive factor in the adoption of e-banking. This role is confirmed by our research field. "The introduction of these technologies will reduce the bank' costs," says the majority of interviewees.

This reminds us of the "transaction cost innovation theory" developed by [52]. It states that the key determinant of financial innovation is cost reduction. The adoption of technologies such as mobile banking or e-banking favors the reduction of transaction costs by allowing external (off-site) access to company databases and to other relevant sources and thus increases the banks' profitability [6].

In order to face the resistance to change both internally and externally, banks are multiplying advertisements and messages addressed to their customers through all available media and are involving employees in the implementation of e-banking strategies. They are trying to build trust by investing in continuous education programs in order to reduce uncertainties and fears about these new changes: "we need to reduce uncertainties regarding customers' computer literacy" (DG2); In fact, computer or digital literacy and e-information literacy (ease/difficulty in searching and locating the right information on the web) are considered by [53] as obstacles that can increase the e-service divide. "In order to create an environment that is favorable to the electronic banking exchanges, we should mobilize our clients' attention and make them more aware of the importance of these changes" (DG2, DG3, D1, D2). "We are also facing resistance from some employees, especially those who have been working for years in a certain way and want to continue working as they are used to" (D3, D4, DG5). "But all these charges are minimal compared to the reduced costs and saved time".

On another hand, the ongoing development of the current infrastructure and technological systems weigh heavier on the budgets. In fact, the technological aspect is of particular importance in the process of implementing electronic distribution channels. The strategic projects involve the need of replacement of basic banking services and other services such as Customer relationship management (CRM), the banking platform, the new automated business process and the management system. "The slight modifications of a large system such as ours involve multiple and expensive changes" (DG2, D1, D2, D3). "Our computer system has been in existence for 20 years, its upgrade would be very expensive; moreover, replacing it without affecting the continuity of banking operations is a great challenge for us" (DG3, D3, D4, D41, E42, DG5). "Dealing with suppliers is a major challenge for us. Their only aim is to earn money and they impose many charges on us. We should then know how to order and negotiate well" D1, D3, D4, D5).

According to [54], e-banking contributes to reducing the cost of designing and distributing financial services and significantly reduces infrastructure and transaction costs. "Without having to move, customers can use the bank" website to download, via any Internet access point, the applications that are required for their banking transactions" (E11, E21, E22, E31, D4). "E-banking saves bank employees a lot of time and enables them to concentrate more on higher value-added services" (D1, D2, E12, E32).

Finally, the use of these services does not require high costs. E-banking has already been developed, in most countries, by banks, because they have found that it grants them great advantages. For this reason, users, individuals and companies or even government agencies are all encouraged by the use of this type of service at lower costs.

To conclude, problems at the legal level were raised; indeed, the majority of interviewees stated that the current legislative framework is ambiguous and uncertain. "It should be developed in accordance with the perpetual changes in the field of information and communication technologies" (D1, D2, D3, D4, D5). "The major judicial issue is that the electronic signature is not yet legal in Lebanon" (DG1, DG2). "Lebanese laws do not authorize the electronic signature" (D3, D4, DG3, DG4). "In order to circumvent this legal obstacle by inserting a clause about electronic signature recognition in every contract signed by clients" (DG1, DG2, DG3, DG4). According to [55], the government should increase the opportunities for e-banking development by shaping regulations so as to enable the experimentation and integration of new e-services.

5 General Conclusion

ICT invaded the daily life of companies all over the world making surprising progress. Commercial banks have embarked on a more and more innovative technological process to meet current and future market demands. The banking sector in Lebanon, which plays a major role in the national economy, is currently in the process of technological development, and the largest Lebanese banks are more and more developing strategies for integrating the latest technological innovations [3, 7].

In this framework, we examined the main factors affecting the adoption of information and communication technologies by the largest commercial banks operating in Lebanon.

While in the past, branches were the exclusive distribution channel for commercial banks, most of them are now embarking on the creation of virtual distribution channels. The development of online banking services meets several requirements, such as the fierce competition between Lebanese commercial banks, the perception of the advantages of these services and the willingness of bank managers to reduce their transaction costs through the use of information and communication technologies.

The qualitative study enabled us to verify the relevance of certain factors and variables taken from the literature on the adoption of information technologies and previous researches in the Lebanese context.

Our research presents a methodological limit that does not allow the generalization of the findings throughout the sector or countries with similar contexts. In fact, the findings presented in this research depend on the Lebanese context. Although our sample is representative, the generalization of the findings depends on further researches, either in the same Lebanese context or in similar contexts in other countries.

6   Future Works

Future work will consist on going through more banks in the Lebanese banking sector in order to identify the relevance of many elements revisited in the literature review so we can cover the whole Lebanese sector; similar studies can be conducted in the MENA region or in similar in developing countries in order to compare and generalize results.

References

1. Damanpour, F., Shneider, M.: Phases of the adoption of innovation in organizations: effects of environment, organization and top managers. Br. J. Manag. **17**, 215–236 (2006)
2. Hughes, T.: Marketing challenges in E-banking: standalone or integrated? J. Mark. Manag. **19**, 1067–1085 (2003)
3. Hilal, M.: Technological transition of banks for development: new information and communication technology and its impact on the banking sector in Lebanon. Int. J. Econ. Finan. **7**(5) (2015)
4. Berz, K., Chin, V., Maguire A.: Come Out a Winner in Retail Banking. The Boston Consulting Group BCG. (2009)
5. Tushman, M., O'Reilly, C.: Winning through innovation: a practical guide to leading organizational change and renewal. Harvard University Press, Boston (2002)
6. Kombe, S.K., Wafula, M.K.: Effects of internet banking on the financial performance of commercial banks in Kenya. Int. J. Sci. Res. Publ. **5**(5) (2015)
7. Sankari, A., Gazzawi, K., El Nemar, S., Arnaout, B.: Factors affecting the adoption of internet banking in Lebanon. J. Impact Factor **6**(3), 75–86 (2015)
8. Toufaily, E., Daghfous, N., Toffoli, R.: The adoption of e-banking by Lebanese banks: success and critical factors. Int. J. E-Serv. Mobile Appl. (2009)
9. Patriche, D., Bajenaru, A.: The take-up importance of ICT enabled services in crisis time, an evaluation of e-banking, internet conferencing and e-public services. Bull. Transylvania Univ. Braşov **3**(52), Ser V: Econ Sci (2010)
10. Harrison, T., Waite, K.: Consumer expectations of online information provides by Bank websites. J. Finan. Serv. Mark. **6**(4), 309–322 (2002)
11. Baregheh, A., Kombe, S.K., Wafula, M.K.: Effects of internet banking on the financial performance of commercial banks in Kenya. Int. J. Sci. Res. Publ. **5**(5) (2015)

12. Shumpeter, J.A.: Théorie de l'évolution économique: recherche sur le profit, le crédit, l'intérêt et le cycle de la conjoncture. Dalloz, Paris (1935)
13. Rogers, E.: Diffusion of Innovations. The Free Press. A Division of Macmillan Publishing Co. Inc., New York (1971)
14. Rogers, E.M.: Diffusion of Preventive Innovations. Addictive Behaviors (2002)
15. O'Sullivan, D., Dooley, L.: Applying Innovation. Sage Publications Inc., Thousand Oaks (2009)
16. Rogers, E.M.: Diffusion of Innovations. The Free Press. A Division of Macmillan Publishing Co. Inc., New York (1983)
17. Rogers, E.M.: Diffusion of Innovations. New York Free Press (1995)
18. Davis, D.: Perceived usefulness, perceived ease of use, and user acceptance of information technology. MIS Q. 13, 319–336 (1989)
19. Venk, A., Rowley, J., Sambrook, S.: Toward a multidisciplinary definition of innovation. Manag. Decis. 47(8), 1323–1339 (2009)
20. Malone, T.W., Yates, J., Benjamin, R.I.: Electronic markets and electronic hierarchies: effects of information technology on market structure and corporate strategies. Commun. ACM 30, 484–497 (1987)
21. Ciborra, C.U.: Teams Markets and Systems. Cambridge University Press, Cambridge (1993)
22. Rahmath, S., Hema, D.: Internet banking adoption in an emerging economy: Indian consumer's perspective. Int. Arab J. e-Technol. 2(1) (2011)
23. Lee, M.C.: Factors influencing the adoption of internet banking: an integration of TAM and TPB with perceived risk and perceived benefit. Electron. Commer. Res. Appl. 8(3), 130–141 (2008). https://doi.org/10.1016/j.elerap.2008.11.006
24. Stamoulis, D.S.: How bank fit in an internet commerce business activities model? J. Int. Banking (1999)
25. Thulani, D., Chitura, T.: Adoption and use of internet banking in Zimbabwe: an exploratory study. J. Internet Bank. Commer. 14(1) (2009)
26. Lioyd, G.G.: Internet banking adoption by Chinese American: an empirical study on banks customers from Chinese and American, pp. 79–102, 134–155 (2007)
27. Hu, Y., Liao, P.: Finding critical criteria of evaluating electronic service quality of internet banking using fuzzy multiple-criteria decision making. Appl. Soft Comput. 11, 3764–3770 (2011)
28. Aderonke, A.: An empirical investigation of the level of users' acceptance of e-banking in Nigeria. J. Internet Bank. 15(1), 102–145 (2010)
29. Angelakopoulos, G., Mihiotis, A.: E-banking: challenges and opportunities in the Greek banking sector. Electron. Commer. Res. 11(3), 297–319 (2011)
30. Onay, C., Ozsoz, E., Helvacioğlu, A.: The impact of internet-banking on bank profitability: the case of Turkey. Oxford Business & Economics Conference Program. ISBN: 978-0-9742114-7-3 (2008)
31. Simpson, J.: The impact of the internet in banking: observations and evidence from developed and emerging markets. Telematics Inform. 19, 315–330 (2002)
32. Coase, R.H.: The nature of the firm. Economica New Ser. 4(16), 386–405 (1937)
33. Williamson, O.: The economics of organization: the transaction cost approach. Am. J. Sociol. 87(3), 548–577 (1981)
34. Williamson, O.: The Mechanisms of Governance. Oxford University Press, New York (1996)
35. Williamson, O.: Transaction cost economics: how it works; where it is going. Economist 146 (April), 23–58 (1998)
36. Rorstad, P.K., Vatn, A., Kvakkestad, V.: Why do transaction costs of agricultural policies vary? Agric. Econ. 36, 1–11 (2007)
37. Ghertman, M.: Oliver Williamson et la théorie des coûts de transaction. Rev. Fr. de Gestion Issue 142, 43–63 (2003)
38. Coase, R.H.: The problem of social cost. J. Law Econ. 3, 1–44 (1960)
39. Dahlman, C.J.: The problem of externality. J. Law Econ. 22, 141–162 (1979)

40. Stiglitz, J., Arnott, R.: The Welfare Economics of Moral Hazard. Working Papers 635, Queen' University, Department of Economics (1986)
41. North, D.: A transaction cost theory of politics. J. Theor. Polit. **2**, 355–367 (1990)
42. Ciborra, C.U.: Markets, bureaucracies and groups in the information society. Inf. Policy **1**, 145–160 (1981)
43. Damanpour, F., Damanpour, J.: E-business e-commerce evolution: perspective and strategy. Manag. Finan. **27**(7), 16–33 (2001)
44. Jayawardhena, C., Foley, P.: Changes in the banking sector—the case of Internet banking in the UK. Internet Res. **10**(1), 19–31 (2000)
45. Hawkins, J., Dubravko, M.: The banking industry in the emerging market economies: competition, consolidation and systemic stability, an overview. BIS Papers No. 4, pp. 1–44 (2001)
46. Romelar, P.: L'entretien de recherche. Management des ressources humaines (Chap. 4), de boeck ed (2005)
47. Azzam, E.: l'impact des nouvelles technologies de l 'information et de la communication sur le marketing bancaire. Proche Orient Magazine, Faculty of Business and Management, Saint-Joseph University (2010)
48. Grover, V.: An empirically derived model for the adoption of customer- based interorganizational systems. Decis. Sci. **24**(3), 603–640 (1993)
49. Frame, S.W., White, L.: Technological Change, Financial Innovation, and Diffusion in Banking. The Oxford Handbook of Banking (Chap. 19), Oxford University Press (2009)
50. Wessels, L., Drennan, J.: An investigation of consumer acceptance of e-banking. Int. J. Bank Mark. **28**(7), 547–568 (2010)
51. Dimaggio, Paul J., Powell, Walter W.: The iron cage revisited: institutional isomorphism and collective rationality in organizational fields. Am. Sociol. Rev. **48**, 147–160 (1983)
52. Niehans, J.: Financial innovation multinational banking, and monetary policy. J. Bank. Finan., 537–551 (1983)
53. Harfouche, A.: The same wine but in new bottles. Public E-Services divide and low citizens' satisfaction: an example from Lebanon. Int. J. Electron. Gov. Res. **6**(3), 73–105 (2010)
54. Deyoung, R., Lang, W.W., Nolle, D.E.: How the internet affects output and performance at community banks. J. Bank. Finan. (2006)
55. Pickens, M., Porteous, D., Rotman, S.: Scenarios for Branchless Banking in 2020. Focus note 57, CGAP, Washington, DC (2009)

Economic Effect by Open Data in Local Government of Japan

Tetsuo Noda, Akio Yoshida and Masami Honda

Abstract Public data collected or possessed by administrative agencies and subsequently released as Open Data is expected to bring about positive economic effects. We aim to establish a point of view and methods for the estimation of the economic effect through the utilization of Open Data. For this purpose we conducted a questionnaire survey on local governments in Japan. The result of the survey shows that Open Data in local governments in Japan is still in earlier stage and it should be difficult to produce the economic effect within the area of them. But, it also shows the possibility of estimating the economic effect by the utilization of Open Data quantitatively.

Keywords Open Data · Open innovation · Economic effect · Local government · Japan

1 Introduction

Public data collected or possessed by administrative agencies and subsequently released as Open Data is expected to bring about positive economic effects. There are some investigative researches of this economic area as referred to in what follows. However, each research method to date has largely depended on the first

T. Noda (✉)
Faculty of Law and Literature, Shimane University,
Nishikawatsu-cho 1060, Matsue, Japan
e-mail: nodat@soc.shimane-u.ac.jp

A. Yoshida
School of Social Science 1, Centre for Media Studies,
Jawaharlal Nehru University, JNU, New Delhi 110067, India
e-mail: akio.yoshida@gmail.com

M. Honda
Center for the Promotion of Project Research, Shimane University,
Nishikawatsu-cho 1060, Matsue, Japan
e-mail: ask@honda-masami.jp

© Springer Nature Switzerland AG 2019
Y. Baghdadi and A. Harfouche (eds.), *ICT for a Better Life and a Better World*,
Lecture Notes in Information Systems and Organisation 30,
https://doi.org/10.1007/978-3-030-10737-6_11

this area's research of ACIL Tasman's research and their conclusions are not reviewed from the perspective of directly gathering data of Open Data. We aim to establish a point of view and methods for the estimation of the economic effect through the utilization of Open Data to estimate the positive economic effects provided by the utilization of Open Data quantitatively.

We assume economic effect through the utilization of Open Data by accumulating measurable economic effects of industry sectors that using open data from its corresponding public sectors, and we also assume that most of industry sectors are using or are ready to use Open Data not only from national government but also local governments. Measuring economic gains of big businesses using Open Data are, of course, important for estimating economic effect of GDP. As well, it must also be important to accumulate economic effects of local industries and local governments in this areas. For this purpose we first conducted WEB questionnaire survey targeting on local governments of Japan which have already implemented Open Data.

In this paper, we estimate the economic effects by the utilization of Open Data in Public Sector, targeting on local governments of Japan by questionnaire survey. Though the range of this research in this area is limited, it shows the degree of the utilization and the economic effect of Open Data in local governments of Japan, and it also shows possibility of estimating the economic effect by the utilization of Open Data quantitatively, as a whole.

2   Estimation of Economic Effect by Questionnaire Survey

2.1   Previous Studies of the Estimation and Their Issues

ACIL Tasman [1, 2] have kicked off the research of this area. These investigations are not intended to estimate economic effect of Open Data directly but to explore how modern spatial information technologies have impacted economic activities. It should be noted that the researches adopted the Computable General Equilibrium Model to estimate the total economic ripple effect. This model analyses modifications of relationships among industrial sectors caused by the direct economic effect. The research also adopts the method of estimating passive damages from proprietary data associated with modern spatial information technologies. If we read this data and this approach as true then the economic effect of open data in modern spatial information technologies should be construed as 0.045–0.09% of GDP with respect to its total economic ripple effect and passive cost.

Vickery [3] explores the economic effect of Open Data via PSI (Public Sector Information) within EU 27 countries. This study significantly depends on estimated figures extrapolated from the prior ACIL Tasman's investigations. Because of this Vickery's estimation is not analyzed from gathered data of Open Data. Instead, it estimates economic effects by applying estimated parameters derived from Tasman's into the GDP data from the EU 27 then averaging the total.

By the same token, in Japan, the Jitsuzumi et al. [4] estimates the economic effect of Open Data in Japan using Tasman's parameters as the basis for its considerations. Its conclusions are that the direct economic effect of PSI data are equal to 16–31.4 billion Euro (0.51–0.99% of GDP) annually in Japan with an additional economic effect when PSI data is opened equivalent 1.2–2.3 billion Euro annually. This means that the additional economic effect of Open Data is 0.04–0.07% of GDP and in-line with the Tasman research's conclusions.

2.2 Methods for the Estimation of the Economic Effect

Aiming to establish a point of view and methods for the estimation of the economic effect through the use of Open Data in Japan, Noda [5] and Noda et al. [6] carried out a study of the relevant prior research and establish whether that expectation holds true and how to best estimate the positive economic effect provided by the utilization of open data. It defines Open Data based on Open License,[1] and it also defines as the data opened from public data sources owned by national and local governments. It can then be assumed that such public data is utilized in corresponding industry sectors and subsequently accumulates measurable economic effects there and in adjacent sectors, resulting in an economic ripple effect and passive damages. Then economic effects should be measured and accumulated in two each sector, Public sectors (national and local governments) and Business Industries, as bellow.

- To estimate economic effects quantitatively sources of (a) *public data*, (b) *the rate of opened data*, (c) *and the cost to open data* are needed. For public sector organizations opening data is likely to be an initial cost-center with the expectation of positive economic effects such as improved public services or market creation to offset such costs in the mid-to-long term.
- For business industries the presumed impact is cost reduction considered in the following manner: (d) *cost reduction by using open data*, (e) *economic losses by data not opened*, (f) *and the economic effect of using other means of obtaining data in such a situation*. These are direct economic effects that can be potentially leveraged by businesses to improve their competitiveness to obtain (g) *market expansion*, (h) *the creation of new business markets or* (i) *changes in industrial structures*. These processes are visualized in Fig. 1.

---

[1]Open License is explained in detail in the FAQ prepared by Creative Commons of Guide to Open Data Licensing. http://opendefinition.org/guide/data/#fn:4.

Public Sectors   Business Industries

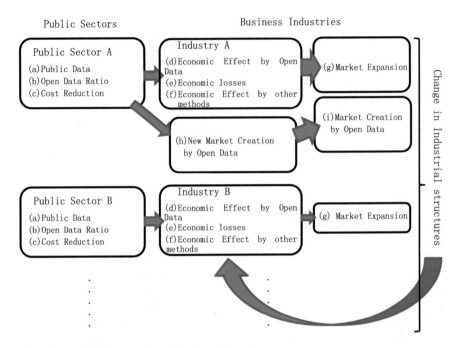

Fig. 1 Economic effects by the utilization of Open Data

2.3 Investigation Object of the Estimation and Questionnaire Survey

Subsequently, on the basis of previous studies' results, a questionnaire survey for local governments of Japan was conducted [7]. A comparison of previous studies and this study are shown in Table 1. The feature of this survey are that it aims to

Table 1 A comparison of the major previous studies and this study

	ACIL Tasman [1, 2]	Vickery [3]	Jitsuzumi et al. [4]	This Study (2016)
Area	Australia and New Zealand	EU	Japan	Japan
Investigation object	Use operators	Use operators	Use operators	Data provider
Data provider	All	Public agencies	Public agencies	Local governments
Kind of data	Spatial information	All	All	All
Method	Interview	Applying parameters from Tasman's	Applying parameters from Tasman's	Questionnaire (WEB)

Table 2 Open Data rate of public sectors in Japan

	All	Prefecture	City	Major city	Administrative district
All	1963	47	1721	20	175
Request for survey	**182**	23	115	18	26
Rate of LG with OD (%)	9.3	48.9	6.7	90.0	14.9
Number of respondents	104	14	75	10	5
Rate of recovery (%)	57.1	60.9	65.2	55.6	19.2

estimate the economic effect in line with the current situation in Japan, that the investigate object is the local government which is a provider of data, and that the estimation process of the economic effects become clear by using a uniform question of WEB questionnaire.

The purpose of this study in the project is to obtain the knowledge that will contribute to estimate the economic effects of Open Data in Public Sector, targeting on local governments of Japan. For this purpose WEB questionnaire were requested to local governments of Japan which have already implemented Open Data. Using the SPIRAL of Piped Bits Co., Ltd. WEB site for answer were constructed and e-mails of the request for answer were delivered. The main questions in this survey were, percentages and progress degrees of Open Data, the cost at the time of implementation of Open Data, the reduction cost of the past business. Period was up to February 22 from February 9, 2016. The subjects were to Open Data municipality list of Fukuno [8] at the time of survey, **182** local governments of Japan (Table 2). Recovery rate is at 57.1%, up to 63.5% excluding the administrative districts of major cities.

3   Results of Questionnaire Survey

3.1   The Rate of Open Data and Format Type

First, we asked the rate of Open Data in each sector: Spatial Information, Agroforestry, Commerce and Industry, Medical and Welfare, Education Tourism, and Others, of local governments (Fig. 2). In some advanced local governments answered so high rates of Open Data that average rates are pushed up. Therefore median rates are shown in following figures, too. Many local governments just started Open Data. Median represents the reality better. Median rate of Spatial Information sector and Others which include population data are 5.0%, and those of other sectors are at most 1.0%.

Then, we also asked the rate of the format type of Open Date set at five steps: (1) not any format in open licenses, (2) including textual information, for example PDF, Word or structured Excel format, (3) independent from particular applications, for example CSV or TXT, (4) all data elements can be linked in URI like

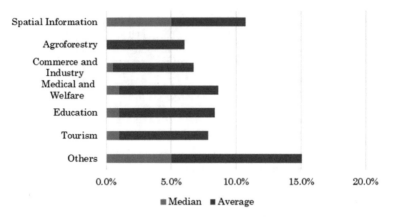

Fig. 2 The rate of Open Data in each sector of local governments

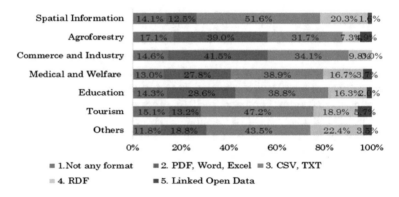

Fig. 3 The rate of format steps of Open Data in each sector of local governments

RDF, (5) Linked Open Data: including linked information of data of related other Web sites (Fig. 3). The rates of the format independent from particular applications are almost half in most sectors, and the rates of the machine readable format aiming secondary usage consciously, which are RDF and Linked Open Data, are almost 20% in certain sectors.

3.2 Expenditure and Work Cost for Open Data

We asked many questions sequentially about a certain data set which is advanced the best of all Open Data sets in each local government. Regarding the direct expenditure for Open Data, most of local governments spend no cost directly, as shown in Table 3.

Table 3 Expenditure for Open Data

	Answers
<1 million dollar	13
<5 million dollar	3
No expenditure	80

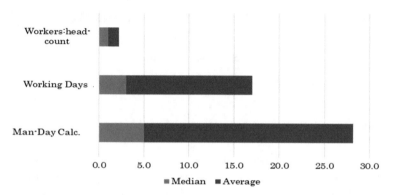

Fig. 4 Work cost for Open Data: men and days

Aside from above, their municipal employee are engaged in some operations of Open Data in working hours. We asked working men and days for operations of Open Data within local governments' office.

Figure 4 shows 1 or 2 workers are engaged in operations of Open Data, and they work only three days in most of local governments. Totally, about 5 worker days is needed for operations of Open Data as it now.

3.3 Work Saving by Open Data

At the same time, we asked how many workers and how many hours in a month were needed for the operations which are streamlined by Open Data within local governments' office.

Though each operation's hours is so little, totally at least one hour a month, about 12 h a year, has been saved by Open Data, as shown in Fig. 5. If they work 8 h per day, 12 h mean 1.5 day's work.

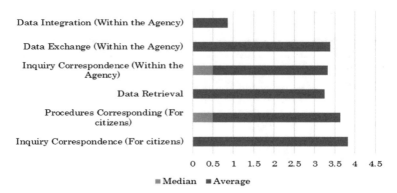

Fig. 5 Work saving by Open Data: men and days

4 Conclusion

First, in Japan, the rate of local governments that release their public data as Open Data, based on open license, is less than 10% in the whole. In these governments, the rate of Open Data in each sector: Spatial Information, Agroforestry, Commerce and Industry, Medical and Welfare, Education Tourism, and Others, is also very low (Average rate: less than 10%, Median rate: at most 5%).

And the degree of the format type of Open Data is still low, because the rate of the format independent from particular applications and the rate of the machine readable format aiming secondary usage consciously are both low. Moreover, considering the difference between Average rate and Median rate in each sector is large as a whole, some particular local governments proceed but almost other governments are still behind schedule overall.

Next, at the present stage, though most of local governments spend no cost directly, they spend work cost of municipal employee engaged in some operations of Open Data, which is about 5 worker days a year. Compared with this, the work cost saved by Open Data, which is about 1.5 day a year, is measurable quantitatively. Work cost in operating Open Data can be offset in 3–4 years. These results are only about a certain data set which is advanced the best of all Open Data sets in each local government. Therefore, total amount of costs in Open Data will be larger numbers. We cannot underestimate the scale of Open Data in local governments' offices.

These research results show that Open Data in local governments in Japan is still in earlier stage and it should be difficult to produce economic effects within the area of them: Public Sectors, the left side of Fig. 1. But, these results also show the possibility of the estimation of economic effects by the utilization of Open Data quantitatively. Then we must continue questionnaire survey targeting on business industry sectors which use Open Data from corresponding local governments' sectors and estimate economic effects by the utilization of Open Data quantitatively, the right side of Fig. 1.

References

1. ACIL Tasman.: The value of spatial information: the impact of modern spatial information technologies on the Australian economy. In: The CRC for Spatial Information and ANZLIC, Australia, the Spatial Information Council http://www.crcsi.com.au/assets/Resources/7d60411d-0ab9-45be-8d48-ef8dab5abd4a.pdf (2008). Accessed 2016-11-10
2. ACIL Tasman.: Spatial information in the New Zealand economy: 'realizing productivity gains, a report prepared for land information New Zealand'. In: Department of Conservation; Ministry of Economic Development http://www.crcsi.com.au/Documents/spatial-information-in-the-new-zealand-economy-200.aspx (2009). Accessed 2016-11-10
3. Vickery, G.: Review of Recent Studies on PSI Re-Use and Related Market Developments http://ec.europa.eu/newsroom/dae/document.cfm?doc_id=1093 (2011). Accessed 2016-11-10
4. Jitsuzumi, T., Hatta, M., Noda, T., Watanabe, T.: Innovation Nippon Study Group Report Economic Effect Estimation of Open Data http://innovation-nippon.jp/reports/2013Study Report_OpenData.pdf (2013). Accessed 2016-11-10
5. Noda, T.: A consideration about the method of economic effect estimation by using open data. Shimane Univ. Fac. Law Lett. Bull. J. Econ. **41**, 33–52 (2015)
6. Noda, T., Honda, M., Yoshida, A., Coughlan, S.: A Review of estimation method of economic effects created by using open data. In: Proceedings of the 12th International Symposium on Open Collaboration (OpenSym 2016), ACM, 2016
7. Yoshida, A., Noda, T., Honda M.: A research of economic effects created by using open data in local governments. In: Proceedings of the Conference on Society of Socio-Informatics 2016 (2016)
8. Fukuno, T.: Japan of open data city map http://fukuno.jig.jp/2013/opendatamap (2013). Accessed 2016-11-10
9. Honda, M., Noda, T., Yoshida, A.: Positioning of the precedent local government in the influence of open data promotion. In: Information Processing Society of Japan 137th Information System and Social Environment Research Workshop (2016)
10. McKinsey Global Institute.: Open Data: Unlocking Innovation and Performance with Liquid Information http://www.mckinsey.com/insights/business_technology/open_data_unlocking_innovation_and_performance_with_liquid_information (2013). Accessed 2016-11-10
11. MEPSIR: Measuring European Public Sector Information Resources.: Final Report of Study on Exploitation of Public Sector Information—Benchmarking of EU Framework Conditions http://www.ec.europe.eu/information_society/newsroom/cf//document.cfm?doc_id=1198 (2006). Accessed 2016-11-10
12. Omidyar Network.: Open for Business: How Open Data Can Help Achieve the G20 Growth Target http://www.omidyar.com/sites/default/files/file_archive/insights/ON%20Report_061114_FNL.pdf (2014). Accessed 2016-11-10
13. Open Knowledge Foundation: Open Knowledge Foundation. 2013. Open Data Census 2013 by Open Knowledge Foundation http://blog.okfn.org/2013/02/20/open-data-census-tracking-the-state-of-open-data-around-the-world/ (2013). Accessed 2016-11-10

Innovation, New Public Management and Digital Era Government, Towards a Better Public Sector Performance Through ICT: The Case of the Lebanese Ministry of Environment

Nada Mallah Boustani and Charbel Chedrawi

Abstract The public sector, especially in developing countries, is encountering several problems in general and is crippled by the lack of government intervention; hence a grown awareness about the role of the public sector in gaining capacity to innovate, as innovation is a dynamic and iterative process, which includes the implementation of new ideas or approaches. In view of the challenging context, this paper assesses the needs in terms of research namely in the field of innovation in the public sector in Lebanon, especially in the Ministry of Environment; it examines the existing literature and theory regarding innovation while focusing on the new public management, the new era government, ICT and innovation theories. Using a qualitative approach, this paper reveals the actions currently undertaken by the Lebanese Government to innovate in public services using ICT which can set the scene for a better public sector performance.

Keywords Innovation theory · New public management · Digital Era Governance · ICT · Public sector · Ministry of environment

1 Introduction

Communities are faced with a daunting number of problems for which traditional government action is failing [1]. Consequently, public sector organizations are operating in an increasingly changing environment, which is leading off to a growing understanding of the need for the public sector to innovate.

Scholars often cite the need for innovation as a major reason for the emergence of the network type of governance [2, 3].

N. M. Boustani · C. Chedrawi (✉)
Faculty of Business and Management, Saint Joseph University, Beirut, Lebanon
e-mail: charbel.chedrawi@usj.edu.lb

N. M. Boustani
e-mail: Nada.mallahboustany@usj.edu.lb

© Springer Nature Switzerland AG 2019
Y. Baghdadi and A. Harfouche (eds.), *ICT for a Better Life and a Better World*,
Lecture Notes in Information Systems and Organisation 30,
https://doi.org/10.1007/978-3-030-10737-6_12

To succeed in innovation, one should complete a three-stage process: idea generation, acceptance, and implementation [4]. As noted by [5], "innovation requires more than the creative capacities to invent new ideas; it requires managerial skills and talents to transform new ideas into practice."

Hood [6, 7] identified that New Public Management (NPM) is the sole reference for public reform. It is "the theory of the most recent paradigm change in how the public sector is to be governed" [8]. NPM has been guiding the public sector reform for over 25 years [9] through introducing a results-oriented culture that emphasizes on outcomes rather than on inputs or processes and performance management based on targets, monitoring and incentives and decentralized decision.

NPM favored the managerial emphasis on organizational arrangements and strong corporate leadership against technological changes [10]. However, NPM always prioritized managerial elements and assigned little intellectual significance to digital developments. The Digital-Era Governance (DEG) model represents a shift of ideas that entails the emergence of a single competing approach gathering momentum over time, and generating 'swarms of ideas' and supporting implementations [10].

According to [11], digital technologies have spread rapidly in much of the world and has boosted growth, expanded opportunities, and improved service delivery. In fact, in 2014, all 193 United Nations (UN) member states had national websites: 101 enabled citizens to create personal online accounts, 73 to file income taxes, and 60 to register a business. For the most common core government administrative systems, 190 member states had automated financial management and 148 had some type of digital identification.

In this context and in line with the international donors' focus on the Lebanese Ministry of Environment—designing, financing and implementing innovative projects covering the technical and management pillars—we have decided to choose the Ministry as our qualitative experimental object. The technical innovative projects are related to uplifting environmental policies, regulations and technical capacity development of the Ministry's staff. Nevertheless, the Ministry's management innovative projects related to ICT/NPM and DEG are focused on improving the Ministry's management system through administrative workflow automation, and ICT equipment upgrade.

This article reports on an exploratory case study in which we observed the ICT-innovation relationship with NPM in the public sector. The central purpose of this study is to address the following questions: are the Ministry of Environment's senior executives aware of the need to innovate the public sector? What is the relationship between ICT innovation and NPM/DEG in the Lebanese public sector?

In part one, we discuss the conceptual framework; in part two we dig into the conceptual framework while focusing on the innovation theory and NPM/DEG. In parts three and four, we discuss the methodology and the context of the study. Finally, in parts five and six, we bring forward our survey findings and recommendations.

2 Conceptual Framework

The concept of innovation has generated a vast amount of research. The discussion below is based on two key aspects of the study:

(1) The study's focus is related to the public sector's innovation using ICT and;
(2) This paper is intended to focus on innovation for a better public service through the exploitation of NPM and DEG potential in Lebanon.

This study, based on the input of several authors, defines innovation as: the generation, acceptance and implementation of a new idea or approach among social actors that challenge the prevailing wisdom as it advances the public good and creates public value [4, 5, 12].

In order to capture the essence of this definition, one must recognize the dual nature of this concept; innovation is both a process and an outcome.

2.1 Innovation Theory

The usage of the term innovation has grown exponentially over the past few years. You can see it in politics, institutions, and international organizations and so on. Despite its growing popularity, innovation management is still an immature "science". There is no dominant theory and little agreement among managers and academics alike regarding what affects a company's ability to innovate.

Schumpeter [13] argued that economic change revolves around innovation, entrepreneurial activities, and market power. He sought to prove that innovation-originated market power can provide better results compared with the invisible hand and price competition. He argues that technological innovation often creates temporary monopolies, allowing abnormal profits that would soon be competed away by rivals and imitators. These temporary monopolies were necessary to provide the incentive for firms to develop new products and processes.

The increasingly complicated modern economies created the need for more economic interaction. Today's knowledge-based economies are dependent on a dynamic technological progress. Innovation no longer depends on a one-man show but involves many actors.

Among the most influential innovation management theories, the ones that provide a comparative analysis where the insights gained from one theory can be used to fill the gaps of another. There are many authors in the field of innovation [14–16] and different concepts of innovation (incremental, modular, architectural, radical, product, process, market, disruptive, organizational, complementary, etc).

Henderson and Clark [14] provide an excellent starting point for classifying and categorizing innovations. They drew on earlier work to provide a fourfold typology. Two of the categories, radical and incremental innovation have substantial literatures of their own whereas the modular and architectural innovations have been overviewed by them:

- Incremental innovation is covered by the work of [16, 17] to name a few. It introduces quality improvements in core components. The word renovation would more precisely describe this type of innovation.
- Radical innovation on the other hand overlaps with other aspects of innovation such as technological discontinuities and crops up in sources as diverse as [13]. It introduces a new meaning, potentially a paradigm shift.
- Architectural innovation is an innovation typology that is based on an innovation's impact on core design components and/or inter-relationships. It changes the nature of interactions between core components, while reinforcing the core design concepts.
- Modular innovation may result in the complete redesign of core components, while keeping unchanged the linkages between components.

When it comes to the product, process and service categorization of innovation, one finds that product innovation is comparatively well served, while service and process innovations have attracted much less attention. The main reason being that product innovation falls within the remit of histories of invention while service and process innovations do not. Product innovation rather focuses on the evolution of technology and the links between different innovations.

Service innovation is much more poorly served, largely because technology is often less in evidence and because there is no tangible object. As for process innovation, it is the hardest to research and the most widespread though it is difficult to acquire detailed data about it.

It is worth noting that it is crucial for innovation to be properly diffused. Rogers [18] argues that diffusion is the process by which an innovation is communicated over time among the participants in a social system. Rogers [18] proposes that adopters of any innovation or new idea can be filed under innovators (2.5%), early adopters (13.5%), early majority (34%), late majority (34%) and laggards (16%), based on the mathematically based Bell curve.

2.2 New Public Management

The NPM model was heralded as a managerial alternative to the traditional model of public administration [19]. Hood [6, 7] identified that NPM is the sole reference to public reform. It is "the theory of the most recent paradigm change in how the public sector is to be governed" [8].

According to [9], NPM has been guiding public sector reform for over two decades. Its position on the design of effective management control rests on three key ideas:

- Performance improvement requires a result-oriented culture that emphasizes outcome rather than input or process;

- Public sector organizations need to introduce performance management based on targets, monitoring and incentives; and
- Public sector organizations should decentralize decision rights and reduce their reliance on rules and procedures.

According to [19], the United Kingdom (UK) played a crucial role in the development of the NPM paradigm. The UK was at a certain point considered to be the birthplace of this new concept especially that "the seminal paper which coined the term NPM was the product of the UK experience [6]—though the work in the United States (US) by [3, 19] was also important".

NPM contributed to putting in place several new concepts that characterize public administration from performance management to competition and to offering quality choices to citizens.

These new concepts aimed at mixing accountability and efficiency in public administration. Politt and Dan [20] consider that implementing NPM would finally result in a public administration that is "cheaper, more efficient, and more responsive to its 'customers'". Within the same line of thinking, [21] stated that the main goals of the NPM reforms are mainly "to improve the effectiveness and efficiency of the public sector, enhance the responsiveness of public agencies to their clients and customers, reduce public expenditure and improve managerial accountability".

In addition, NPM prescribes cultural changes aimed at making the government apparatus more user-friendly and market-oriented [22, 23].

Most NPM reform efforts have had similar goals [21]. The means used to achieve these goals were a series of reforms connected to structural devolution— strong vertical and horizontal specialization of administrative systems, competitive tendering, customer choice, and so on.

It is essential to note that NPM does not describe what goes on in the public sector reform. It nevertheless recommends a new approach, if government wishes to increase efficiency in service delivery [8].

According to [8], NPM changes the coordination mechanism in public resource allocation from authority or command to contracting or exchange. NPM is the theory that makes contracting the medium of communication in the public sector; it puts in place a contracting state, where personnel and other resources are to be managed by means of a series of contracts. The NPM reforms have focused on the methods of organizing, governing, controlling and reporting activities rather than on the products and production process of the public sector. It is actually a rather loose concept encompassing several different administrative doctrines, inspired, in turn, by a combination of newer institutional economic theory and management theory [24].

2.3 Digital Era Governance

NPM marginalized technological changes in favor of a managerial emphasis on organizational arrangements and strong corporate leadership [10]. NPM stressed on a trinity of macro-themes—disaggregation (chunking-up government hierarchies into smaller organizations); competition (especially with private-sector contractors but also in internal quasi-markets within government); and incentivization (built on pecuniary motivations instead of professionalism). From 1980 to around 2005, the NPM wave was moving strongly forward across many countries (with distinct emphases in different countries). However, NPM always prioritized managerial elements and assigned little intellectual significance to digital developments.

The DEG model represent a shift of ideas entailing the emergence of a single competing approach gathering momentum over time, and generating 'swarms of ideas' and implementations that support it [10]. Albeit mainly concerned with the potential of transformative change through technology [25], suggest that the emerging period of DEG is characterized by three related features: "reintegration," "needs-based holistic structures," and "digitalization" of administrative processes. The latter is said to provide a transformation toward a new era of interaction between government and its subjects.

In current times, the advanced use of the Internet, e-mail and the Web and the generalization of IT systems is shifting from the simple state of merely affecting back-office processes to conditioning in important ways the whole terms of relations between government agencies and the civil society. Internet growth has had especially important implications in the political and administrative changes occurring in areas far beyond leading-edge advanced industrial countries [26]. With the shaping of the DEG, many changes occur owing to IT and information-handling, they have spread much more widely and are gaining additional dimensions simultaneously compared with previous IT influences.

Digital-era changes have already triggered numerous significant shifts: a largescale switchover to e-mail in internal and external communications; the rising salience of Websites and intranets in organizational information networks [2, 26]; the development of electronic services for different client groups; the growth of electronic procurement systems; a fundamental transition from paper-based to electronic record-keeping; and so on.

Margetts and Dunleavy [10] stated that the DEG model stressed on the importance of digital change, but not in any determinant way, rather assigning equal importance to two other components—organizational reintegration within governments (which fosters disintermediation) and needs-based holism (re-unifying government services around client groups, instead of 'business processes').

The DEG intellectual and innovation momentum is building, its coherence and acceptance as a quasi-paradigm is expanding, and its growth is continuing under potentially adverse austerity conditions [10].

According to [25] the transition to DEG is characterized as involving three themes: Reintegration (putting corporate hierarchies back together); Needs-based holism (agile governance, and efforts to simplify, re-engineer, transform and change agency/client relationships); and Digitization (electronic channels as genuinely transformative). Their thesis is that DEG represents a potential paradigmatic shift away from and a replacement for, NPM [25].

3 Methodology

This research paper is based on a qualitative methodology with an exploratory approach [27]. We adopted the interpretive method, more particularly the case study of [28] that allows us to consider a phenomenon in its natural setting.

According to [29], in a case study, the researcher explores in-depth a program, event, activity, process, or individuals. This method allows us to understand the overall context of innovation and ICT in the NPM DEG approach in the public sector. This method is most often used by researchers seeking to better understand the social and cultural context.

Data were collected by means of centered semi-structured interviews (between September and November 2016). These data were supplemented by means of secondary data. Centered semi-structured interviews are a reliable data collection method that can bring us closer to the understanding of NPM and DEG in public administration [30].

In this study, we interviewed five executive officers acting as agents for change at the Lebanese Ministry of Environment (MoE):

- M1. Team Leader of an EU Financed Project of Support to Reforms & Environmental Governance at the MoE;
- M2. Head of Environmental Guidance Service (Guidance, Awareness, Media, Private Sector);
- M3. Acting Head of Planning and Programming Service (Policies, Strategies, Statistics, MIS/IT);
- M4. Head of Registrar Service (Finance, HR, Archive, Legal, Procurement);
- M5. Key Expert Quality Management of the Support to Reforms & Environmental Governance Project for MoE.

The above officials stated clearly that they play a leading role in implementing innovation and ICT at the Ministry. Their names have been coded using (M1, ..., M5) for the sake of anonymity.

Moreover, and in addition to the data collected by interviews, secondary data from different sources (written, oral, reports, etc.) has been included, treated and analyzed. Data consolidation was carried out using the NVivo software.

4 The Context of the Study

In the previous sections, the concept of innovation has been developed in addition to a deep analysis of the theories related to the public sector innovation through ICT, NPM and DEG tools.

The Lebanese MoE has been chosen to be the experimental object of this paper whereby the researcher, through a designed interview guide, tried to test a hypothesis that assesses the awareness of the Ministry's senior executives of the public sector's innovation tools and the need for Government institutions to innovate.

4.1 MoE Current Situation

A number of laws, decrees and ministerial decisions govern environmental management in Lebanon. Chief among them are the laws and decrees establishing the Ministry of Environment. Law No 216/1993 was first amended by Law No 667/1997 that reviewed the Ministry's mandate and suggested the establishment of the National Environmental Council. These laws were fully revised through the Environmental Protection Law (444/2002) that sets (i) a code for the protection of the Environment that represents a legal framework and (ii) principles based on the concept that the right to a healthy environment is a basic human right, and that the protection of the environment is a public interest issue. The mandate and organization of the Ministry was subsequently revised again by laws No 690/2005 and 2275/2009 that suggested new central and regional set up and mandates. At the same time, Lebanon has made significant advances on the road to full compliance with binding international legislation related to the environment.

In September 2011, the MoE presented a 3-pillar work plan for the years 2011–2013 under the following slogan "The Political Environment at the Service of the Environmental Policy". According to the plan, the favorable political environment is synonymous of a "Strong, transparent, fair, multi-partner and educating Ministry of Environment" (pillar #1). The environmental policy is viewed from two angles: strictness in conserving the natural wealth of Lebanon (pillar #2) and management of environmental risks through prevention and remediation (pillar #3).

In spite of these efforts, and significant advances on both the institutional and legal frameworks, considerable legal, institutional, technical and financial challenges remain present, especially with regards the legislation in terms of reorganization, decentralization, departmental function and services as well as staffing, information technology upgrades and monitoring tools to reach and serve the citizen in a very efficient and effective manner.

Fig. 1 MoE organizational chart

4.2 The Ministry of Environment Summary Structure

Figure 1 shows a summary of the Ministry of Environment organizational structure. Currently, the Lebanese Ministry of Environment is implementing innovative projects covering the technical and management pillars. It is worth noting that some of our interviewed candidates are experts and specialists committed to manage a European Union (EU) financed project for the MoE.

Some of the major objectives of this EU project were related to innovation through NPM and DEG. The program is dedicated to improving the Ministry's management system through automating the administrative workflow, archive and transactions in addition to the upgrade of the related ICT equipment. The technical innovative project's pillar is focused on uplifting the environmental policies, regulations and technical capacity of the Ministry's staff.

4.3 Public Sector Innovation Through ICT to DEG

Two important outcomes or expectations should raise awareness regarding the ultimate rationale for public sector innovation:

First, innovation within the public sector should represent a new idea or approach, which challenges the prevailing wisdom [31].

Second, innovation, within the public sector, should accomplish two goals:

- uphold public good and;
- create public value.

Innovation, within the public sector, is just too expensive and time-consuming "to be defined as mere novelty" [31]. The creation of public value must be based on sound evidence that an innovation is likely to work. The potential costs of a failed innovation in the public sector are likely to be far greater than in the private sector. In the public sector, when an innovation fails a segment of the public is likely to suffer as a result.

As stated previously, innovation represents the successful completion of a three-stage process: idea generation, acceptance, and implementation [4]. When examined more closely, the processual nature of innovation provides a framework for enhancing our understanding of how "innovations emerge, develop, grow, or terminate over time" [5].

5   Results and Findings

The results obtained were stunning, yet diversified. Clearly for Lebanon, the strategic intent for innovation is non-existent at the governmental level and the knowledge of ICT, NPM and DEG tools has been found variant among MoE executives ranging between weak and strong. In absence of a top governmental embrace for innovation and a basic knowledge of the implementation tools' process and service innovation at the governmental sector, change and reform have become very difficult to achieve.

Most of the surveyed candidates, regardless of their ICT, NPM and DEG proficiency, claimed that change for innovation in the public sector is an extremely difficult exercise for the following reasons:

- Institutional governmental laws and regulations, if not updated, obstruct change and innovation in the public sector (M1, M3, M5).
- Lack of financial resources forbid proper investment of public institutions in ICT, NPM and DEG innovative tools (M2, M3, M4).
- Most of the Lebanese institutional reforms and changes rely on international donors funded projects and programs like the World Bank, UNPD and the European Union (M1, M2, M3, M4 M5).
- Current public servants require intensive training on updated public management principles, cutting edge ICT, NPM and DEG tools (M1, M4).

As a result, our findings could be analyzed using the summarized cross-examining shown in Table 1, to better understand the positions of our interviewed candidates and try to wrap up and appraise their opinions on the different innovation's subject elements, tools and implicating factors.

In the absence of a strategic will to innovate at the public level, it becomes hard to fight for change or implement innovation through the institutional structural pyramid—top-down approach—(M1, M2, M4). However, with the proper ICT/ DEG tools and resources, the Ministry of Environment could be partially reformed using a special unit that can handle the automated transactions and affairs, thus securing a quality tracking system, electronic data warehousing, a cutting edge decision support system, all leading to a drastic improvement in service management (M1, M2, M3).

Table 1 Interviews findings summary

	Innovation in the public sector	ICT/DPM & DEG tools
M1	Innovation is a necessity to improve the Lebanese public sector	ICT/DPM & DEG tools would be the main tools in helping upgrade and change the management system at the public sector
M2, M3, M4	Innovation is considered very important, but expectation are low as a result of the many cumbersome governmental obstacles	The ICT/DPM & DEG tools are obviously considered pre-requisites for change; however considering the lack of resources, the nonexistent will or ability to change, it is believed to be impossible to modernize using those tools
M5	Innovation of the public sector should be based on an urgent/emergency strategy for uplifting Lebanon's public institutional system and management	No Public sector innovation is possible without the ICT/DEG & DEG tools. Therefore, financial and non financial resources should be acquired and used in designing and implementing a comprehensive strategy focused on changing and innovating the public sector using the cutting edge and modern tools of management and ICT for public institutions

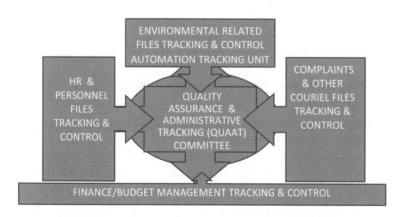

Fig. 2 Proposed model and role of the innovative unit within the MOE

The elaboration of the new model as shown in Fig. 2, is the result of the interviewees' responses and suggested measures. Therefore, the recommended innovative unit for the Ministry shall be defined and structured to serve the purpose of quality control and transactions tracking of the Ministry's automated administrative, legal, financial and non-financial processes throughout the use of ICT/NPM tools while at the same time avoiding serious human, structural and legal resistance (M1, M2, M3, M4, M5).

The major functional mandate of this unit, and through the use of ICT/DEG tools, is to manage, control and track the MoE related files and operations in the areas of: environment, legal, financial, HR, citizens' complaints, licenses etc....

Its main functional duties shall be to:

a. Capture, treat, process and track the Ministry's written (incoming/outgoing) communications, complaints and EIA files using a compliant Documentations Tracking &Archiving Software (M1, M2, M5).
b. Log and register updated Ministry's personnel information and their related administrative transactions on (HR) software of Council of Civil Service or any other solution if found suitable (M1, M2, M3).
c. Log, register and track all transactions related to budget management laying from commitment requests to disbursement authorization using the designated and available budget financial management software (M1, M4).

The pros and cons of this MoE innovative Automated Tracking Unit are (M1, M2, M3, M4, M5) as follows:

a. It cannot eliminate and bypass the functions of any Service at the Ministry of Environment.
b. It will not be a committee for advisory services, nor will it have any authority to approve or reject transactions. It will control and track the workflow and processes and define their functions.
c. In the future, with time and due to the availability of the stored data and quality information generated and monitored, the Unit would have the ability to influence and quicken decision making and related actions with its decision support system.
d. This Unit shall be automated to serve as an innovation structure within MoE and encourage the integration of its ICT/DEG tools in the whole organization.

Innovation requires the design, development, and institutionalization of several processes that help facilitate the completion of the innovation process (M1, M3); as such, it is expected that the above-mentioned Unit and the use of ICT/DEG tools shall laterally improve the Ministry operational lines in different areas such as:

• Innovated and automated archive management tracking system (M1, M5);
• Innovated and automated document management tracking system (M1, M2);
• Innovated and automated environmental and legal transaction management tracking system (M1, M3);
• Innovated and automated budget management and personnel management tracking system (M1, M4).

6   Conclusion, Recommendation and Limitation

Where investments to automate government service delivery have advanced, improvements in regulations, interdepartmental cooperation, and streamlining become more important; automation provides an opportunity for simplifying steps, increasing the impact as well as the transparency; the greater use of the internet develops digital engagement with the country's citizens [11].

To conclude, the findings of this paper state that the ICT/DEG administrative capacity of the MoE should be strengthened and reformed to serve the citizen in a more professional manner. Because throughout this interview, it has also been mapped and found that most of the citizens' complaints at the Ministry were treated in a chaotic and un-organized manner.

Therefore, the Ministry's innovation using the ICT/DEG tools is mandatory at both the central and regional levels and aim for more improvement of management systems, innovative processes, electronic availability of information, and service of excellence for citizens.

In line with the identification of a crucial need and requirement for innovation at the Lebanese MoE, and in agreement with the above, the proposed system using ICT/NPM and DEG tools could and would provide a set of automated and re-engineered procedures that will streamline operational and control processes in many tasks that will all help reach-out to the Lebanese citizens and provide them with quality, efficient and effective services. However, these citizens/users need to have access, the needed skills and the willingness to use the ICT [32].

Our research presents a methodological limitation regarding the generalization of the results. Indeed, considering the limited validity of qualitative methods, the generalization of the results was never our primary objective [27]. We are aware that the results of this research depend strongly on the context of the MoE. Further research is needed at the MoE or any other public entity in order to fully use the NPM and DEG potential in Lebanon or similar countries.

7   Future Work

Future works will consist on assessing the literature review factors and variables in other ministries, which will allow us to generalize in the first place the current findings and in the second place make a solid assessment of the NPM and DEG usefulness and potential in Lebanese public sector.

References

1. Golden, O.: Innovation in public sector human service programs: the implications of innovation by groping along. J. Policy Anal. Manag. 219–248 (1990)
2. Goldsmith, S., Eggers, W.: Governing By Network: The New Shape of the Public Sector. The Brookings Institution, Washington, D.C. (2004)
3. Osborne, S.P., Brown, K.: Managing Change and Innovation in Public Service Organizations. Routledge, New York (2005)
4. Shepard, H.A.: Innovation-resisting and innovation-producing organizations. J. Bus. 470–477 (1967)
5. Van De Ven, A., Angle, H.: An introduction to the Minnesota innovation research program. In: Research on the Management of Innovation: The Minnesota Studies, pp. 3–31. Oxford University Press, New York (2000)
6. Hood, C.C.: A public management for all seasons? Public Adm., pp. 3–19 (1991)
7. Hood, C.C.: The new public management. In the 1980s: variations on a theme. Acc. Organ. Soc. 20(2/3), 93–109 (1995)
8. Lane, J.-E.: New Public Management: An Introduction. Routledge, London (2000)
9. Verbeeten, F.H.M, Speklé, Rf.: Management control, results-oriented culture and public sector performance: empirical evidence on new public management. Organ. Stud. 36(7), 953–978 (2015)
10. Margetts, H., Dunleavy, P.: The second wave of digital-era governance: a quasi-paradigm for government. Philos. Trans. R. Soc. A 371: 20120382 (2013). Http://Dx.Doi.Org/10.1098/Rsta.2012.0382
11. World Bank.: World Development Report 2016: Digital Dividends. Washington, Dc: World Bank. https://doi.org/10.1596/978-1-4648-0671-1. License: Creative Commons Attribution Cc By 3.0 Igo (2016)
12. Hannah, S.B.: The correlates of innovation: lessons from best practice. Public Prod. Manag. Rev. 216–228 (1995)
13. Schumpeter, J.A.: The Theory of Economic Development, Tenth Printing 2004, Transaction Publishers, New Brunswick, New Jersey Karol Śledzik Schumpeter's View on Innovation and Entrepreneurship (1912)
14. Henderson, R.M., Clark, K.B.: Architectural innovation: the reconfiguration of existing product technologies and the failure of established firms. Adm. Sci. Q. 35, 9–30 (1990)
15. Abernathy, W.J., Utterback, J.M.: Patterns of innovation in technology. Technol. Rev. (1978)
16. Tushman, M.L. Anderson, P.: Technological discontinuities and organizational environments. Adm. Sci. Q. 31, 439–465 (1986)
17. Ettlie, J.E., Bridges, W.P., O'keefe, R.D.: Organizational strategy and structural differences for radical Vs. Incremental innovation. Manage. Sci., 682–695 (1984)
18. Rogers, E.M.: Diffusion of Innovations, 5th edn. Free Press, New York (1984)
19. Harfouche A., Robbin, A.: E-Government implementation in developing countries. In: Mola, L., Pennarola, F., Za, S. (eds.) From Information to Smart Society: Environment, Politics and Economics. Springer's Lecture Notes in Information Systems and Organisation Series, vol. 5, pp. 315–327 (2015)
20. Politt, C., Dan, S.: The Impacts of the New Public Management in Europe: A Meta-Analysis. Cocops Work Package 1—Deliverable (2011)
21. Wright, J.: Reshaping the state: the implications for public administration. West Eur. Polit. 17(3), 102–137 (1991)
22. Christensen, T., Lægreid, P.: The whole-of-government approach to public sector reform. Public Adm. Rev. 67 (2007)
23. Christensen, T., Laegreid, P.: Transcending New Public Management: The Transformation Of Public Sector Reforms. Ashgate Publishing, Aldershot (2007)

24. Boston, J.: Origins and destinations: New Zealand's model of public management and the international transfer of ideas. In: Weller, P., Davis, G. (eds.) New Ideas, Better Government. Allen & Unwin, St. Leonards, Nsw (1996)
25. Dunleavy, P., Margetts, H., Bastow, S., Tinkler, J.: New public management is dead-long live digital-era governance. J. Public Adm. Res. Theor. **16**, 467–494 (2005)
26. Franda, M.: Launching Into Cyberspace: Internet Development And Politics In Five World Regions, 295 pp. Lynne Rienner, Boulder (2002)
27. Eisenhardt, K.M.: Building theories from case study research. Acad. Manag. Rev. **14**(4), 532–550 (1989)
28. Walsham, G.: Interpretive case studies in is research: nature and method. Eur. J. Inf. Syst. **4**(2), 74–81 (1995)
29. Creswell, J.: Research Design: Qualitative, Quantitative, and Mixed Methods Approaches. Sage (2003)
30. Romelaer, P., L'entretien De Recherche, Dans Roussel, P., Wacheux, F. (eds.): Management Des Ressources Humaines: Méthodes De Recherche En Sciences Humaines Et Sociales, De Boeck, pp. 101–137 (2005)
31. Light, P.C.: Sustaining Innovation. Jossey-Bass, San Francisco (1998)
32. Harfouche, A.: The same wine but in new bottles. Public E-services divide and low citizens' satisfaction: An example from Lebanon. Int. J. Electron. Gov. Res. **6**(3), 73–105 (2010)
33. Mclaughlin, K., Osborne, S., Ferlie, E.: The New Public Management: Current Trends and Future Prospects. Routledge, London (2002)
34. West, D.: Global E government 2002, Providence. Center For Public Policy, Brown University, Ri (2002)

Choosing Valuation Models in the UAE

Khaled Aljifri and Hafiz Imtiaz Ahmad

Abstract This study aims to empirically examine the valuation models used by UAE investment analysts. A questionnaire and interviews were used to answer its research questions. Thirty-five investment analysts, in cooperation with the CFA Society Emirates, participated in the questionnaire. The sample covered most of the analysts who have professional qualifications such as CFA and CAIA (coupled with an academic degree such as the MBA) and have an average of more than eight years of experience in the relevant sectors. Descriptive and comparative analysis was employed in this study. The results reveal that discounted cash flow and P/E ratios are the most preferred valuation methods used by these analysts. For the accounting variables used in this study, the analysts perceived free cash flow and operating cash flow to be the most important variables. The results also show that the analysts perceive the solvency ratios (i.e., gearing ratio and interest cover) and liquidity ratio to be the most important ratios. The study concludes that the analysts in the UAE use both sophisticated valuation models and unsophisticated valuations models, with a preference for cash flow models.

Keywords Financial analysts · Valuation models · Cash flow models · UAE

1 Introduction

A large body of literature has focused on different issues related to company valuation models. The focus has mainly been on evaluating the efficacy of different valuation models (e.g., [1, 2]). The literature has provided mixed results which conclude that financial analysts have used valuation techniques that depend on

K. Aljifri
United Arab Emirates University, Al Ain, UAE
e-mail: k.aljifri@uaeu.ac.ae

H. I. Ahmad (✉)
New York Institute of Technology, Abu Dhabi, UAE
e-mail: hahmad02@nyit.edu

© Springer Nature Switzerland AG 2019
Y. Baghdadi and A. Harfouche (eds.), *ICT for a Better Life and a Better World*,
Lecture Notes in Information Systems and Organisation 30,
https://doi.org/10.1007/978-3-030-10737-6_13

accrual based valuation models and cash based valuation models. Some studies have documented that the Discounted Cash Flow model (DCF) is the most popular in practice, followed by Residual Income Valuation (RIV) [1, 3–6, 24]. This popularity results from their relevance and efficacy as two valuation models which produce almost the same results [5, 7–9]. Other studies, however, have suggested that analysts and fund managers use unsophisticated valuation models such as the Price/Earnings ratio (PE) and Dividend Yield (DY) in preference to more sophisticated models (e.g., DCF and residual income models). Another line of research has found a relationship between the level of disclosure in financial reports and accuracy of the analysts' forecasts (e.g., [2]). However, the level of effect of the financial disclosure on valuation methods is not obvious [10]. Preiato et al. [11] have suggested that other factors such as "measures of firm performance and current market conditions" can have more effect on the accuracy of the analysts' forecasts. In this regard, Chan and Hameed [12] considered macroeconomic factors in developing countries to be more important than firm-specific information when the valuation is related to stocks. However, analysts in emerging countries may face challenges in predicting the state of the economy and macroeconomic variables [13].

In this paper, we document the various valuation models used by UAE investment analysts. The list of valuation models used in this study is determined on the basis of the study of [6]. The survey employed in this paper was structured on the basis of certain previous studies [14–18]. This study includes both sophisticated and unsophisticated valuation models in its list.

The study replicates, with modifications, the study [6], to which it provides additional insights. The research methods of this study focus on surveys (by semi-structured questionnaire and interview). To generate a broader understanding of financial statement analysis than that given only by valuation models, the questionnaire includes a section related to accounting ratios [19]. Foster [20] stated that investment analysts depend heavily on accounting ratios in their valuations. The current study, unlike all previous ones, provides the results from an emerging economy in the Middle East which has been ranked as one of the most developed in the world and is in top three most attractive countries for infrastructure investment. Omran [21] studied the equity valuation in the context of the UAE, focusing on the determinants of three valuation multiples (i.e., price earnings; price book value; the price sales). However, to the best of the authors' knowledge, no study in this region has addressed analysts' choices of valuation models. The major findings of this study are remarkably consistent with those of [6], considering that the current study did not examine the equity research reports of the sample, because it was difficult to collect them and also because the sample of this study contained more buy-side analysts; this is one of the limitations of this study. This study contributes to the literature as follows: (1) it provides evidence of the valuation models used by analysts in an emerging economy (that of the UAE, which has become one of the most attractive countries for investment in the world). The study suggests that the analysts in the UAE prefer to use sophisticated valuation models, their first choice being DCF; (2) it provides evidence of the accounting variables and accounting ratios used by the UAE's analysts. The results provide evidence that these analysts prefer variables related to cash flows and ratios related to solvency.

The study addresses the following four questions:

(1) What are the valuation models that analysts in the UAE select?
(2) What accounting variables do these analysts employ?
(3) What types of financial ratio do these analysts use?
(4) Why do they use these models?

The study of this particular developing country presents an interesting case study for understanding its analysts' choice of valuation models. Although this study has specific relevance to the UAE business environment, it is believed that many other developing countries, especially those countries in the Middle East that face similar problems and needs, could benefit from the findings below.

The remainder of the paper is structured as follows. Section 2 provides a literature review followed by a description of the research methodology in Sect. 3. Section 4 reports and discusses the results. Section 5 presents a summary and conclusions.

2 Literature Review

Comparing various valuation models used by analysts and investors has been a focus of attention for academics and researchers. From the financial theory perspective, the DCF model is used as a base model for equity valuation. The model can be used either in the form of dividend discount model or free cash flow model. Researchers have compared residual income-based valuation models to DCF models [1, 3, 4]. They conclude that the accruals based residual income valuation model provides better valuations than do DCF models. The residual income valuation model has also been studied as a tool for company valuation in other studies such as [22, 23]. Lundholm and O'Keefe [24] comment that cash flow and residual income valuation models should produce the same valuation since the models are theoretically equivalent. Penman [9] argues that such empirical comparison is an important test for the relevance of accrual accounting for equity valuation even if predicted assumption inconsistencies can explain valuation differences.

The theoretical work of [25–28] underlie the usefulness of P/E, price-to-book value, and PE/Growth ratios as valuation tools. However, due to the development of closer links between financial statement analysis and equity valuation [7, 8, 29], analysts have had recourse to alternative and more sophisticated valuation models. Recently, Imam et al. [6] observed that analysts perceive the DCF to have become significantly more important than other previous studies suggested. These authors also observe, however, that contextual factors, notably the analysts' need for their research to be credible to buy-side clients, cause the subjective unsophisticated valuation to be used instead.

Analysts' preferences among valuation models are well covered in the academic research. According to [5, 17], who suggested industry related factors behind this preference, it is also possible that analysts covering similar industries use different models [8, 30, 31]. Now, some academics and analysts agree that valuation models have to be consistent with the purpose and perspective of the analysts' valuation [32, 33].

In their recent study, Trejo Pech et al. [34] examined the relationship between financial ratios and leading stock returns. They found that these are related and that financial ratios can predict 1-year stock returns. According to these authors, profitability and leverage are the most popular ratio; in addition, free cash flow yield and dividend yield ratios are important to analysts in Mexico. Wang and Lee [35] used the categories of financial ratios (leverage, solvency, turnover, and profitability) to get an estimate of a firm within the shipping industry. Katchova and Enlow [36] used the Du Pont ratios to compare the return on equity component of agribusiness firms and found that asset turnover was the most predictive ratio, leading to better financial performance. From a practical standpoint, financial ratios have been used to predict aspects of business such as bankruptcy, credit ratings, risk, future cash flow, etc. [37, 38]. Chen and Shimerda [39] used principal component analysis of 34 financial ratios that were useful in predicting bankruptcy. Since financial ratios help to predict the future rates of returns [40, 41], the statistical relationship between financial ratios and stock returns has become a popular area of research.

Researchers have also surveyed security analysts about their opinion of the usefulness of financial ratios. Matsumoto et al. [42] carried out such a survey on security analysts and reported that the most important ratios were growth in earnings per share and sales growth, followed by valuation ratios (price to earnings and market to book), profitability ratios and leverage ratios. Inventory turnover, receivables turnover, cash flow and dividend ratios were moderately important, with capital turnover and cash position ratio least important. Gibson [43] conducted a survey among CFA charter-holders and found that analysts assigned the highest significance rating to profitability ratios, then the price to earnings ratio, debt ratio, and liquidity ratio; the rest are less important.

We find only one study discussing the equity valuation in the context of the UAE, that of [21], who tested the determinants of three valuation multiples for 46 UAE companies listed in local share directories. The three valuation multiples are price sales (PS), price book value (PBV) and price earnings (PE). He used a regression analysis of panel data for the years 1996–2001 and found that PS, PBV, and PE are significantly linked to the net profit margin, return on equity, and the payout ratio.

The above literature indicates that understanding analysts' choices of valuation methods in a country such as the UAE is crucial for practitioners and academics. As mentioned in the introduction, this study will complement the previous studies by examining the most popular valuation models in a country that has a rapid economic development and is considered one of the world's major business centers.

3   Research Methodology

This section reports the empirical methods used to examine the research questions of this study, describes the questionnaire design, presents a detailed description of the sample, and discusses the sample selection. Analysts in the UAE were asked to complete a questionnaire which was electronically and randomly distributed to them with the help of the CFA Society Emirates. A total of 35 analysts of different nationalities, including the following: Emirati, Egyptian, Moroccan, Lebanese, Libyan, American, British, French, Indian, Pakistani. Of the total, eight (23%) were sell-side analysts, and 27 (77%) were buy-side analysts. Twenty-three percent of the analysts had less than five years of work experience, 34% had 5–10 years of work experience, and the remainder (43%) had more than ten years of work experience; the average was more than eight years. The sample covered most of the analysts who have professional qualifications such as CFA and CAIA (coupled with an academic degree such as the MBA). Table 1 summarizes details of the sample who completed the questionnaire and reveals that 86% of the analysts came from the Financial Sector followed by the Real Estate sector (8%), the Media sector (1%), and other sectors (1%). Table 2, with descriptions of the sample used in the semi-structured interviews and shows that most of the analysts (97%) were buy-side and 3% were sell-side analysts.

Table 1 Descriptions of the sample used in the questionnaire

Participants	Sectors				Total participants in the questionnaire
	Financial	Real estate	Media	Others	
Buy-side analysts	23 (85%)	3 (11%)	1 (4%)	–	27 (77%)
Sell-side analysts	7 (87.5%)	–	–	1 (12.5%)	8 (23%)
Total	30 (86%)	3 (8%)	1 (3%)	1 (3%)	35 (100%)

Table 2 Descriptions of the sample used in the interviews

Participants	Sectors				Total participants in the interviews
	Financial	Real estate	Media	Others	
Buy-side analysts	13 (93%)	–	–	–	13 (93%)
Sell-side analysts	1 (7%)	–	–	–	1 (7%)
Total	14 (100%)	–	–	–	14 (100%)

The questionnaire in the present study fell into three sections: demographic questions; questions on valuation models, accounting variables, and accounting ratios, with answers in the form of a 5-point Likert scale; and an open question, asking for comments to determine and assess the valuation models used by analysts in the UAE. In addition, semi-structured interviews were employed to get more insight into the participants' answers and improve the level of consistency and reliability in the results [44]. Fourteen semi-structured interviews were conducted with the analysts.

4 Results

4.1 What Are the Valuation Models Choices that Analysts in the UAE Select?

This section employs descriptive and comparative statistical analysis to examine the research questions of this study. Table 3 highlights the responses of the analysts using the 5-point Likert Scale (ranging from 1 = Not Important to 5 = Extremely Important). The table shows that the respondents agreed that DCF is the most important valuation model, followed by the P/E ratio, and EV/EBITDA. The table adds that the mean of DCF is 4.03 with standard deviation of 1.52. The mean of the P/E ratio is 3.51 with a standard deviation of 1.36 while the EV/EBITDA has the same mean with a standard deviation of 1.7. The table reveals that the respondents agreed that EV/book value (mean = 2.17 and standard deviation = 1.38), price to

Table 3 The valuation models used by the analysts

	N	Minimum	Maximum	Mean	Std. deviation
Discounted CF	35	.00	5.00	4.03	1.52
Price earnings ratio	35	.00	5.00	3.51	1.36
Enterprise value/EBITDA	35	.00	5.00	3.51	1.72
Price to book value	35	.00	5.00	3.34	1.41
Dividend discount model	35	.00	5.00	3.20	1.39
CF return on investment	35	.00	5.00	3.06	1.39
Price to cash flow	35	.00	5.00	2.86	1.42
PE to growth	35	.00	5.00	2.51	1.38
Economic value added	35	.00	5.00	2.51	1.22
Enterprise value/sales	35	.00	5.00	2.43	1.40
Price to sales	35	.00	5.00	2.34	1.49
Enterprise value to book value	35	.00	5.00	2.17	1.38
Others	35	.00	1.00	.11	.32

A Mann-Whitney test was used to compare the results of the buy-side analysts and sell-side analysts; the test shows no significant differences between these two types of analyst

Table 4 Accounting variables used by the analysts

	N	Minimum	Maximum	Mean	Std. deviation
Free cash flow	35	.00	5.00	4.31	1.39
Operating cash flow	35	.00	5.00	3.91	1.44
Operating earnings	35	.00	5.00	3.63	1.37
Net income	35	.00	5.00	3.46	1.27
Revenues	35	.00	5.00	3.43	1.24
Book value of equity	35	.00	5.00	3.06	1.47
Others	35	.00	1.00	.03	.17

A Mann-Whitney test was used to compare the results of the buy-side analysts and sell-side analysts; the test shows no significant differences between the two types of analyst

sales (mean = 2.34 and standard deviation = 1.49) and EV/sales (mean = 2.43 and standard deviation = 1.40) are the least important valuation models. These results are consistent with the study of Imam et al. [6], which found that UK financial analysts consider DCF the most important valuation model; however, they still consider the importance of earnings based models. Yet Ionascu and Ionascu [13] found that the Romanian analysts prefer to use earning-based models (e.g., P/E and EV/EBITDA) because these models are not complicated but easy to use. Lundholm and O'Keefe [24] argued that both cash flow and residual income valuation models have the same practical implementation and should produce the same valuation. A number of studies that compare residual income-based valuation models with DCF models documented that accrual based residual income valuation models perform better than DCF models [1, 3, 4]. The results of this study indicate that the UAE market depends on both cash-based models and earnings based models; in other words, the market uses both sophisticated models (e.g., DCF) and unsophisticated models (e.g., P/E). The table reveals that only six valuation models were rated above "Moderately Important" (scale "3") while seven valuation models including "Others" were rated below "Moderately Important". The six models include three sophisticated models (i.e., DCF, DDM, and CFRI), and another three which are unsophisticated (i.e., P/E, EV/EBITDA, and P/CF). The seven models excluding "Others" that were rated "Slightly Important" (scale "2") only include one sophisticated model (EVA) while the other five models are unsophisticated ones. The results suggest that the UAE market seems to have a balance between sophisticated and unsophisticated valuation models and uses both cash flow and accrual based models with the preference going to cash flow models. This is also supported by the results presented in Table 4.

4.2 What Accounting Variables Do These Analysts Employ?

Table 4 presents the ranking of the analysts regarding the importance of accounting variables. The table shows that analysts perceive free cash flow (4.31), operating cash flow (3.91), and operating earnings (3.63) to be the most important variables to consider in their valuation. It also shows that book value of equity (3.06), revenues (3.43), and net income (3.46) are the least important variables. This indicates that analysts in the UAE give more priority to cash-based valuation models than accrual-based valuation models. Another insight from this result is that the financial system in the UAE provides a wide range of information from which analysts can select more complicated valuation models.

4.3 What Types of Financial Ratio Do They Use?

Financial ratios were selected for this research study according to those of [16]. These financial ratios present additional evidence on the valuation models presented in Tables 3 and 4, which report analysts' questionnaire responses concerning the importance in valuation of a range of financial ratios. Table 5 shows that gearing (3.68), interest coverage (3.60), and liquidity (3.57) are the most important ratios that analysts in the UAE consider in valuation. Nonetheless, the ratios of credit turnover (2.57), dividend cover (2.65) and depreciation (2.66) are found to be the least important for these analysts to consider in valuation. These results are consistent with the study of [34], who found that leverage and liquidity ratios are two of the most popular ratios employed by research analysts in Mexico. They also found that the analysts in Mexico perceive profitability ratios to be among the most important ratios; this is not completely consistent with the results presented in Table 3, which show that the profitability ratio is not ranked in the top four ratios.

Table 5 Financial ratios used by the analysts

	N	Minimum	Maximum	Mean	Std. deviation
Gearing	35	.00	5.00	3.69	1.37
Interest cover	35	.00	5.00	3.60	1.31
Liquidity	35	.00	5.00	3.57	1.39
Return on capital employed	35	.00	5.00	3.51	1.40
Asset turnover	35	.00	5.00	3.20	1.32
Trading margins	35	.00	5.00	3.14	1.54
Stock turnover	35	.00	5.00	2.86	1.37
Debt turnover	35	.00	5.00	2.74	1.29
Capital expenditure to depreciation ratio	35	.00	5.00	2.66	1.33
Dividend cover	35	.00	5.00	2.66	1.30
Credit turnover	35	.00	5.00	2.57	1.36
Others	35	.00	1.00	.06	.23

A Mann-Whitney test was used to compare the results of the buy-side analysts and sell-side analysts; the test shows no significant differences between the two types of analyst

Another study by Gibson [43] also found, through a survey among CFA charter-holders, that profitability ratios are among the most effective ratios. The findings of this study are also not consistent with the results of [36]: that asset turnover was the most effective ratio. However, Table 3 makes it clear that this ratio was not as highly ranked as the other financial ratios.

The analysts in the UAE ranked the gearing, interest coverage, and liquidity ratios highly because of their important role in the UAE business environment. The banking sector is the cornerstone in developing an advanced financial system and securing the country's sustainable growth. The banking sector in the UAE is strong and has shown itself well prepared to face all "economic headwinds" (Augustine, 2016). The gearing ratio and coverage ratio are the main ratios in measuring company solvency, which has a direct effect on liquidity. This argument is supported by the following quotations extracted from the responses in the semi-structured interviews:

> I mean sustainability and growth in the margins are important with regard to debt and all. I think the interest coverage ratio is one of the important factors which show whether the company has enough cash to interest coverage. The days payable and receivable are also important from the perspective of how often a company rotates the cash flow.
>
> (Financial Analysts)

> It is important to assess the ability of the company to pay back its loan and debts. So it is important to look at the capital structure of the company and check whether it is sustainable or not. In this context, Debt/Equity and Debt/EBITA ratios are also important.
>
> (Financial Analysts)

> Gearing is as important as trading margins. More debt will impact on the discount rates of the business and adds risk.
>
> (Financial Analysts)

The analysts ranked the dividend cover ratio and the capital expenditure to depreciation ratio as the least important ratios for the purpose of business valuation. A reasonable justification for these results is provided in the following excerpts:

> I normally never look at the dividend coverage ratio. Coverage ratios are important where there is a mandatory payment required. A dividend is not mandatory and you really have no need to look at the coverage ratio but interest is mandatory … a company has to make the payments otherwise it will default. In this region, investors look at it this way: 'I give you money, and you give me something every year, whether it is in the form of a dividend or interest – they don't care which'.
>
> (Financial Analysts)

> Capital Expenditures to Depreciation ratio basically defines what your investment cycle is. It tells you about your assets (short or long term). It is an important ratio if you are looking in terms of DCF analysis. For short-term investors or those who are using the P/E & P/B ratio, this is not important. It is an important ratio for a long-term growth oriented stock and if it is a capital intensive business.
>
> (Financial Analysts)

4.4 Why Do They Use These Models?

The findings of this study provide evidence that the analysts in the UAE make the cash flow models their first choice. Therefore, the interviewees were asked why the analysts prefer this type of valuation model. They pointed out the importance of the cash basis over the accrual basis, reasoning that the latter is vulnerable to subjectivity and earnings management. The analysts reveal that the free cash flow is the most relevant variable and they depend on it when they make their valuation. Three excerpts from the analysts' answers are given below:

> In investment, everything is cash. I put myself in the investor's shoes and then only I feel the pain of losing money. Cash is king here, and we have to keep an eye on cash. Accounting base provisions may give some credit to the business, but that is not real credit. And, even in valuation, we look at the cash. If you look at any private equity firm, they consider the cash on cash yield, how much we are paying and how much we are getting. The concept of cash is applied to developed and emerging markets alike.
>
> (Financial Analysts)

> Cash flow based estimates give a better picture of a company, so cash flow and cash flow yields are better indicators than accrual-based estimates because of earning management, receivable, working capital requirements, etc. So cash flow would not be distorted by these things.
>
> (Financial Analysts)

> When we value a company using the DCF model, we use FCF instead of net profit which is very prone to accounting treatment (IFRS & US GAAP). FCF is more relevant as any business is worth only the money it is bringing in.
>
> (Financial Analysts)

According to the results of this study, the analysts in the UAE ranked DCF and P/E ratios as the most popular valuation models, which indicates they used both cash and accrual models. The analysts justified the importance of the P/E ratio and the following may be quoted from their interview answers:

> P/B – I specifically use it more for the banking industry. In general, it is an important matrix for the banking industry because it gives a slightly better picture. Even in the banking sector, only the model will tell you how much provision is required, how much they can grow the loan book. So, multiples come at the second level.
>
> (Financial Analysts)

> In the stock market, P/E ratio matters. Perhaps P/E ratio is the standardized benchmark for analyzing a company.
>
> (Financial Analysts)

> The transactions we have done, till today, are only listed companies, and we focus on the P/E ratio. So we look at what the global peers are and what their variables for valuation are. As per my experience, DDM & CF models are prone to manipulation because of management sales projections for three and four years which might happen or might not happen. Every management wants to give a better picture of the future, and we don't know what will be because of macroeconomic parameters.
>
> (Financial Analysts)

The study provides evidence in the questionnaire (see Tables 3 and 4) and the semi-structured interviews that the analysts in the UAE depend mainly on sophisticated models (cash flow models). The analysts reiterated that cash is king, and it is not prone to judgment and earnings manipulation. The study also discovered that the analysts also rely on unsophisticated models (accrual-based models) which were highly ranked.

5 Conclusion

Prior studies have provided mixed results on the most popular and dominant valuation models used in practice. Some show that unsophisticated valuations models (e.g., P/E) dominate sophisticated models (e.g., DCF), while other studies show the opposite. This study examines the valuation models preferred by the analysts in the UAE, using the survey research method of questionnaires and interviews. The survey covers the Financial, Real Estate, Media sectors, and others. It suggests that the analysts use both sophisticated valuation models and unsophisticated valuations models with a preference for cash flow models. The study finds that the analysts prefer DCF and ranked free cash flow as the most important accounting variable. In addition, it reveals that the analysts ranked P/E highly as their second choice. These results are expected for a good equity valuation model that strikes a balance between using cash flow based models and accrual-based models. Furthermore, DCF depends on earnings, which enhance forecasts of future free cash flows. The analysts gave as the main reason for their preference for cash flow models to accrual-based models, that subjectivity and earnings management could easily affect accrual-based models, unlike cash flow models. The findings also reveal that the analysts consider the solvency accounting ratios to be the most important accounting ratios. This is not a surprising result since DCF is adequate to credit risk analysis.

A limitation of this study is that it did not include the content analysis of the equity research reports because of the difficulty of collecting these and because of more participation from buy-side analysts in our survey and interview. Another limitation is that the sample concentrates on a few industries, most of them in the financial sector. The study also did not include enough sell-side analysts, especially in the semi-structured interviews.

Further research should include, in addition to the survey, the content analysis of equity research reports. In other words, it should include questionnaires, interviews, and content analysis. This study could be extended by increasing the sample size, considering all the GCC countries and including more analysts from other sectors. Another avenue for future research would be to examine by means of other research methods and other factors that determine analysts' valuation models.

References

1. Francis, J., Olsson, P., Oswald, D.: Comparing the accuracy and explainability of dividend, free cash flow, and abnormal earnings equity value estimates. J. Acc. Res. **38**(1), 45–70 (2000)
2. Peek, E.: The influence of accounting changes on financial analysts' forecast accuracy and forecasting superiority: evidence from the Netherlands. Eur. Acc. Rev. **14**(2), 261–295 (2005)
3. Penman, S.H., Sougiannis, T.: A comparison of dividend, cash flow, and earnings approach to equity valuation. Contemp. Acc. Res. **15**(3), 343–383 (1998)
4. Courteau, L., Kao, J., Richardson, G.: Equity valuation employing the ideal versus ad hoc terminal value expressions. Contemp. Acc. Res. **18**, 625–661 (2001)
5. Demirakos, E.G., Strong, N., Walker, M.: What valuation models do analysts use? Acc. Horiz. **18**, 221–240 (2004)
6. Imam, S., Braker, R., Clubb, C.: The use of valuation models by UK investment analysts. Eur. Acc. Rev. **17**(3), 503–535 (2008)
7. Copeland, T., Koller, T., Murrin, J.: Valuation: measuring and managing the value of companies. Wiley, London (2000)
8. Palepu, K., Healy, P., Bernard, V.: Business Analysis and Valuation using Financial Statements. South-Western College Publishing, Cincinnati (2004)
9. Penman, S.H.: On comparing cash flow and accrual models for use in equity valuation. Contemp. Acc. Res. **18**(4), 681–692 (2001)
10. Hope, O.K.: Disclosure practices, enforcement of accounting standards and analysts' forecast accuracy: an international study. J. Acc. Res. **41**(2), 235–272 (2002)
11. Preiato, J.P., Brown, P.R., Tarca, A.: Mandatory Adoption of IFRS and Analysts' Forecasts: How Much Does Enforcement Matter? Available at: http://ssrn.com/abstract=1499625 or http://dx.doi.org/10.2139/ssrn.1499625 (2012)
12. Chan, K., Hameed, A.: Stock price synchronicity and analyst coverage in emerging markets. J. Financ. Econ. **80**, 115–147 (2006)
13. Ionascu, M., Ionascu, I.: The use of accounting information by financial analysts in emergent markets: the case of Romania. Acc. Manag. Inf. Syst. **11**(2), 174–186 (2012)
14. Arnold, J.A., Moizer, P.: A survey of the methods used by UK investment analysts to appraise investments in ordinary shares. Acc. Bus. Res. **14**, 195–207 (1984)
15. Pike, R., Meerjanssen, J., Chadwick, L.: The appraisal of ordinary shares by investment analysts in the United Kingdom and Germany. Acc. Bus. Res. **23**, 489–499 (1993)
16. Barker, R.G.: The role of dividends in valuation models used by analysts and fund managers. Eur. Acc. Rev. **8**(2), 195–218 (1999)
17. Barker, R.G.: Survey and market-based evidence of industry-dependence in analysts' preferences between the dividend yield and price-earnings ratio valuation models. J. Bus. Finan. Acc. **26**(3–4), 393–418 (1999)
18. Block, S.B.: A study of financial analysts: practice and theory. Finan. Anal. J., 86–95 (1999)
19. Breton, G., Taffler, R.J.: Creative accounting and investment analyst response. Acc. Bus. Res. **25**(Spring), 81–92 (1995)
20. Foster, G.: Financial Statements Analysis, 2nd edn. Prentice-Hall International, Englewood Cliffs, NJ (1986)
21. Omran, M.F.: Equity valuation using multiples in the emerging market of the United Arab Emirates. Rev. Middle East Econ. Finan. **1**(3), 267–283 (2003)
22. Frankel, R., Lee, C.M.C.: Accounting valuation, market expectations, and cross-sectional stock returns. J. Acc. Econ. **25**(3), 283–319 (1998)
23. Biddle, G.C., Bowen, R.M., Wallace, J.S.: Does EVA beat earnings? Evidence on associations with stock returns and firm values. J. Acc. Econ. **24**(3), 301–336 (1997)
24. Lundholm, R.J., O'Keefe, T.: Reconciling value estimates from the discounted cash flow model and the residual income model. Contemp. Acc. Res. **18**(2), 311–335 (2001)

25. Miller, M.H., Modigliani, F.: Dividend policy, growth, and the valuation of shares. J. Bus. **34** (4), 411–433 (1961)
26. Ohlson, J.A.: Earnings, book values and dividends in security valuation. Contemp. Acc. Res. **11**, 661–687 (1995)
27. Penman, S.H.: A synthesis of equity valuation techniques and the terminal value calculation for the dividend discount model. Rev. Acc. Stud. **2**(4), 303–323 (1997)
28. Ohlson, J.A., Juettner-Nauroth, B.: Expected EPS and EPS growth as determinants of value. Rev. Acc. Stud. **10**(2/3), 349–365 (2005)
29. Penman, S.H.: Financial Statement Analysis and Security Valuation. McGraw-Hill, New York (2007)
30. Liu, J., Nissim, D., Thomas, J.: Equity valuation using multiples. J. Acc. Res. **40**(1), 135–172 (2002)
31. Lee, C.M.C.: Choosing the Right Valuation Approach. Working Paper Presented at the AIMR Conference, Amsterdam, the Netherlands (2003)
32. Stowe, J.D., Robinson, T.R., Pinto, J.E., McLeavey, D.W.: Analysis of Equity Investments: Valuation. Association for Investment Management & Research, Charlottesville (2002)
33. Cowen, A., Groysberg, B., Healy, P.A.: Which types of analyst firms are more optimistic? J. Acc. Econ. **41**, 119–146 (2005)
34. Trejo Pech, C.O., Noguera, M., White, S.: Financial ratios used by equity analysts in Mexico and Stock returns. Contaduría y Administración **60**(3), 578–592 (2015)
35. Wang, Y., Lee, H.: Evaluating financial performance of Taiwan container shipping companies by strength and weakness indices. Int. J. Comput. Math. **87**(1), 38–52 (2010)
36. Katchova, A., Enlow, S.: Financial performance of publicly-traded agribusinesses. Agric. Finan. Rev. **73**(1), 58–73 (2013)
37. Beaver, W.: Financial ratios as predictors of failure. J. Acc. Res., Supplement to Volume **4** (Empirical research in accounting: selected studies), 71–111 (1966)
38. Call, A.: Analysts' Cash Flow Forecasts and the Predictive Ability and Pricing of Operating Cash Flows. Available at SSRN: http://ssrn.com/abstract=1362177 or http://dx.doi.org/10.2139/ssrn.1362177 (2008)
39. Chen, K., Shimerda, T.: An empirical analysis of useful financial ratios. Finan. Manag., Spring, 51–60 (1981)
40. Barnes, P.: The analysis and use of financial ratios: a review article. J. Bus. Finan. Acc. **14**(4), 449–461 (1987)
41. Delen, D., Kuzey, C., Uyar, A.: Measuring firm performance using financial ratios: a decision tree approach. Expert Syst. Appl. **40**(10), 3970–3983 (2013)
42. Matsumoto, K., Shivaswamy, M., Hoban, J.: Security analysts' views of the financial ratios of manufactures and retailers. Finan. Pract. Educ. (Fall/Winter), 44–55 (1995)
43. Gibson, C.: How chartered financial analysts view financial ratios. Finan. Anal. J. **43**(3), 74–76 (1987)
44. Harris, L.R., Brown, G.T.L.: Mixing interview and questionnaire methods: practical problems in aligning data. Pract. Assess. Res. Eval. **15**(1), 1–19 (2010)

Empowering Farmers in India Through E-Government Services

J. Nair and B. N. Balaji Singh

Abstract Government organizations are stepping up to the challenge of facilitating e-Government services, with consumers as partners. E-Government allows customer co-creation where a citizen with Self-Service Technologies (SSTs) as tools, steps into the service-delivery process. The goal of such e-Government Services results in a self-service economy. The Government of India (GoI), as part of its government-to-citizen (G2C) e-business model, has rolled out multiple electronic web services (e-services) through the Digital India program. However the question arises: Has the Government met its objectives in providing efficient e-Government services through SSTs? A case-study methodology is adopted in this research to analyze consumer considerations through a process workflow model in an e-Government program initiated for farmers through an Agricultural Extension Centre. The study is conducted in Karnataka, a Southern State in India. The study proposes an enhanced ICT-based process workflow model at RSK (Raitha Samparka Kendras).

Keywords E-Government services · Information dissemination · Self-service economy · Self-service technologies

1 Introduction

e-Governance is the process of delivering services of a government to its citizens through a digital medium. The resulting outcome of such an initiative is to bring-in effective governance and enhanced transparency for the benefit of its citizens [1]. According to UNESCO *"e-Governance involves new styles of leadership, new ways of debating, and deciding policy and investment, new ways of accessing education,*

J. Nair (✉) · B. N. Balaji Singh
Faculty of Management Studies, PES University, Bangalore, India
e-mail: jessynair@pes.edu

B. N. Balaji Singh
e-mail: bbalaji@tatatrusts.org

© Springer Nature Switzerland AG 2019
Y. Baghdadi and A. Harfouche (eds.), *ICT for a Better Life and a Better World*,
Lecture Notes in Information Systems and Organisation 30,
https://doi.org/10.1007/978-3-030-10737-6_14

205

new ways of listening to citizens and new ways of organizing and delivering information and services. e-Governance is generally considered as a wider concept than e-Government since it can bring about a change in the way citizens relate to governments and to each other. e-Governance can bring-forth new concepts of citizenship, both in terms of citizen needs and responsibilities. Its objective is to engage, enable and empower the citizen". In recent times, e-Government has become a key medium to inform, interact and transact policies and programs of a government to its citizens. e-Government services refer to the delivery of national or local government information and services via the internet or other digital means to its citizens [2]. The United Nations defines e-Government as "utilizing the Internet, and the world-wide-web for delivering government information and services to citizens." The e-Government services offered are based on fulfilling functions such as disseminating information, interaction with intermediaries, conducting transactions for services and the overarching goal of bringing transformation in the services offered to citizens. Delivering digital services to stakeholders is the current Prime Minister of India's dream. The Government of India's (GoI) flagship program, Digital India, aims to develop an ecosystem of technology, skill, and accessibility of services of governments through digital media. The objective of this national program is to enable citizens in supporting government operations, engage citizens and provide government services [2]. Technically known as e-Government, it is the interaction of a government agency with its citizen stakeholders by means of Information and Communication Technologies (ICT) to provide one-stop, online access to information and services to citizens through information and transactional services [2, 3].

The Central Government launched the National e-Governance Plan (NeGP) in the year 2006 through thirty-one citizen-centric projects implemented through various State Governments. However, the outcomes of these projects have had minimal impact. To improve the effectiveness and efficiency of the program, [3] it was suggested e-Governance should transition from static websites that provide only information, to ones providing interactive transactions [4]. It is agreed that a seamless provision of services could be achieved by integration of services from all the agencies of the government, which will result in a transition of e-Government services. Hence e-Government becomes an effective tool in implementing e-Governance. Through the Digital India program, the vision of the Government is to transform the nation by offering e-Government services from a citizen-centric perspective by digitally empowering the nation, creating customer co-creation by diminishing the digital divide and transforming the nation into a knowledgeable economy.

Facilitating the service delivery with Self-Service Technologies (SSTs) will further empower the end user, that is the farmer [5]. Study on extension activities for farmers suggests that governments and citizens need to play an interactive role in the transformation process. The proposed outcome of the Digital India program known as *e-Kranti* (meaning revolution in Hindi), or electronic delivery of services, is to develop digital infrastructure, offer services and governance, and empower citizens [6]. This research article focuses on *e-Kranti* services for farmers where real-time price information, online ordering of inputs, and online cash, loan, relief payment with mobile-banking, are the key objectives to be fulfilled by the Government nationwide by 2019. The Central Government programs are implemented through the 29 States and seven Union Territories and the state government. The State of Karnataka has been one of the key front-runners in implementing digital services to its stakeholders [7] and is a nodal agency that facilitates the e-Governance programs of the Central Government [8]. Some of the e-Services offered by the Government of Karnataka are interaction centers for farmers, distribution of ration, transfer of government primary school teachers, cooking gas subsidies, digitization of land records, et al. The primary objective of this research is to analyze the workflow model at the Raita Samparka Kendra (RSK), translated from local language to mean farmers interaction center, based on the premise of e-Government services maturity model. The Gartner model suggests four functions of e-Government services as; information through web presence, interaction, transaction and transformation [9].

The research article is organized as follows. Section two of the article sets the theoretical foundation and reviews literature related to e-Government services and the significance of digitization of services. In section three, the research method adopted is detailed and the current workflow at RSK is analyzed. In section four, we discuss the issues and challenges faced by farmers at RSK and the current workflow at RSK is illustrated in a model. The fifth section discusses the challenges of implementing SST in service co-creation and based on this an enhanced workflow process model is proposed. Finally, the implications, research limitations and directions for future research are stated.

2 E-Government: A Paradigm Shift Towards Governance to Stakeholders

Reaching out to stakeholders through governance by means of an e-Government medium is a paradigm shift allowing governments of emerging nations to empower citizens with service delivery through an electronic medium. Gupta [10] list transparency, increasing performance efficiency, raising service 0performance and eliminating bottlenecks and highlight the significance of skilled human resource to manage technological infrastructure. The scope of implementing electronic medium infrastructure includes the provision of information, interaction, transaction and transformation. Heeks and Bailur [11] points to the growing satisfaction of internet usage among people and calls for research in identifying satisfaction of citizens towards e-Government services. Electronic media will enable the government to decentralize its operations, achieve efficiency and flexibility, while citizens could become part of the service-delivery process known as co-creation and complete the service delivery. Gartner's e-Government model to analyze how governments are using SST to create value to its stakeholders, forms the foundation for this research article [12].

2.1 Service Delivery Through Co-creation

Emerging countries like India, China, and Brazil, which are also growing economies, are implementing ICTs to bring about the inclusion of stakeholders in the
service delivery process to leverage economic and social outcomes [13]. Social and
economic outcomes of e-Government services lead to empowered citizens
accessing information using Self-Service Technologies (SST) and completing the
service delivery process. For citizens *"they feel they are getting a service rather
than a favor* [14, pp. 4]." The authors highlight the pressure such a system could
build upon the public officials, who had earlier controlled the information, whereas
in the present service delivery model officials have greater accountability to the
services offered.

This new paradigm shift of service delivery model using SSTs will enable
farmers to be more active stakeholders rather than being passive. "Co-creation
relates to the value received by the customer through usage, consumption or
experience [15, pp. 23]." Meuter et al. [16] states that co-creation process in the
G2C model of service leads to a connected government. In this research article the
authors explore the challenges faced by farmers who use the services of Interaction
Centers and through a case study, the authors propose a workflow model of service
delivery so that service value can be effectively improved by the government
agency.

2.2 Empowering Stakeholders by Digitizing Information Dissemination

The Digital India campaign by the Government of India aims at delivering
e-Government services digitally. The campaign rests on nine pillars signifying the
provision of dissemination of government-related services to all stakeholders viz.,
the citizens of the country. In this respect, the Central Government collaborates with
State governments to initiate, implement and dissipate the programs seamlessly
using internet technology as a medium. As a pioneer in implementing
e-Government services for its stakeholders, the State Government of Karnataka has
been successful in its many initiatives. One of the key stakeholders in the Indian
context is farmers in the agricultural sector. Over 58% of the rural households in
India depend on agriculture as their principal means of livelihood. With the intent of
modernizing agriculture and bringing about socio-economic changes among the
farming community, an earnest effort has been initiated by the Government in
offering farmers those services to enhance their livelihood and information, interaction and transaction of the services through Centres known as *Raitha Samparka
Kendras (RSK)*.

Raitha Samparka Kendra in the local Kannada language means, "Farmer's
Interaction Center". Construction of such Centers is a program of the Department of

Agriculture, Government of Karnataka. These Centers are to serve as an Information Centre for farmers on crops, irrigation, cultivation practices, technologies, and markets. In this context, RSKs are one of the channels to provide farmers updated technical resources on crop-production knowhow, market information, seed and soil testing on-site and arranging interface with experts in implementing technologies [17].

The process and extent of providing specific services to farmers is streamlined and ought to be delivered through computer systems at RSKs. Electronic channels or e-channels as a medium for information dissemination in the present technological era are a strategic tool in customer relationship management for private organizations. The Government has modelled RSK based on *e-choupal*, a successful e-business model created by a private company called ITC, one of India's largest consumer product and agribusiness companies.

An e-choupal is an Internet-kiosk, village-gathering place and e-commerce hub all rolled into one unit. In fact, the word *choupal* means "village gathering place" in Hindi. The e-choupals are run by an operator who is himself a farmer recruited by ITC to be the interface between the computer terminal and the farmers [18]. The choupals are a blend of click and mortar capabilities and village internet kiosks managed by farmers. They enable the agricultural community to access information readily in their local language about weather and market prices, disseminate knowledge on scientific farm practices, facilitate the sale of farm inputs and purchase farm produce from the farmers' doorsteps. Real-time information and customized knowledge provided by an 'e-Choupal' enhance the ability of farmers to take decisions and align their farm output with market demand and secure quality and productivity. However, when government organizations adopt a similar strategy to connect to its customer-citizens the intent of government is to empower citizen stakeholders known from here on in the case study as citizen-customers of their rights and benefits. Therefore the objective of this case study is to propose a process flow model to analyze farmer's considerations in their decision-making, so as to leverage ICT to disseminate information to farmers while utilizing e-Government services.

3 Research Method

This research article adopts an exploratory method and the objective is to analyze the current process workflow model at RSK and identify how the e-Government services could be enhanced further through SSTs. Miah [19] classifies such a type of research as a positivist deductive approach since research questions are defined clearly before the data collection. The research questions were converted to qualitative interview design. A general interview guide approach is applied since questions can be structured and the respondents are observed and interviewed in their natural setting. The informal environment allows the researcher to ask follow-up or probing questions based on the responses to pre-designed questions [20].

3.1 Current Workflow at RSK: Opportunities for Improvement

Hopes and travails of farmers as stakeholders are analyzed through farmers who visited the RSK. Ravikumar and Subramanya are two young farmers of Nimbaekayipura village, in Bidarahalli Hobli of Bengaluru, in a Southern State of India. They travel roughly about five to seven miles once in a month to the RSK Centre to collect subsidies offered by the State Government. Since they belonged to a lower income class group, they were aware that they could avail of a subsidized rate of 0.23 USD for one quintal (100 kg) of Ragi grain, a cereal used in the staple food of the local population. Unfortunately, they ended up paying approximately one USD per half a quintal bag for 5 bags, effectively paying 2 USD for a quintal, instead of only 0.23 USD. Both the young farmers had come on a motorbike and when the Centre in-charge requested them to come back another time to avail the subsidy, both were unwilling to avail it due to the extra cost involved through another visit.

Similarly, Krishnappa, an elderly farmer from Kannamangala travels about four miles to reach the Bidarahalli RSK Centre. He has availed a lot of subsidies from the RSK such as subsidized seeds, fertilizers, manure and advice on technology implementation such as rainwater harvesting. Yet his constant grievance is about the number of documents required to be produced to the authorities each time a subsidy is to be availed from the RSK. These are stories of two farmers, while at the Centre, throughout the day, many of them come to avail such facilities or for consultations. Though they are satisfied with the Services and subsidies provided, the dissatisfaction arises from cumbersome processes at the RSK to avail the benefits at the Centre. An identical story unwinds at the Kengeri Hobli covering a similar number of villages in Bangalore South.

3.2 Farmers as Stakeholders and Citizen-Customer

Championing the cause of farmers is a core agenda of governments across the world. With very well-structured plans, policies and ICT infrastructure, the program initiatives of the Central and State Governments of India are yet to reach the masses of farmers. In earlier times an Assistant Agriculture Officer (AAO), usually a non-graduate appointed by the Agricultural Department, would play the role of an information disseminator and advisor to the farmers on the schemes laid by the Government. This also meant the AAO had to pay routine visits to the fields of farmers despite any requirements from their side and disseminate information on behalf of the Government. In the present context, the Government has set up farmer extension centers called RSK. Each RSK is meant to cover a cluster of few villages together called *hobli* ranging from twenty to less than fifty in number, and headed by a graduate in agriculture studies, with a designation of Agriculture Officer (AO), Assistant Agriculture Officer (AAO) or an Agriculture Assistant (AA).

The technical staff is of help to address the technical problems in agriculture production, while the para-technical staff plays an important role in assisting and implementing the works of the RSKs, besides providing technical information on limited subjects. Furthermore, as agricultural lands are being converted to commercial or industrial estates, RSK Centers at these *hoblis* are being shut down and some villages whose agricultural lands are not commercialized clustered under these *hoblis* are transferred to nearby RSK increasing the responsibilities of the technical staff at RSK.

The primary purpose of this Centre is that of a distribution and advisory role (Fig. 1). Hence, farmers visit the Centre to seek information, advice, transact loans, and avail farming-related subsidies. The RSK Centers have attached godowns to disperse agricultural tools and implements, seeds and fertilizers. Consequently, the objective of establishment of an RSK is to provide services to the farmers. During a day-long visit to an RSK, it was observed that though the personnel at the RSK had a busy day with visits from farmers for various services, both stakeholders were affected. For the RSK staff, the sheer number of visits by farmers throughout the day implied a delay in completion of their routine office work. For the farmers who have to travel a long distance to avail services or to find that the documents they have brought to avail loans or subsidies are incomplete, and products such as seeds, fertilizers, and pesticides are unavailable, leads toward an incomplete service. Is there a way to communicate and update on matters significant to the stakeholders so

Fig. 1 RSK and current information dissemination mechanism

that the service encounter for both are beneficial? Could there be a shift in service delivery pattern from traditional methods to electronic self-service delivery? The answer to this challenge is to leverage upon newer digital technologies to avail the services efficiently. In such a context, the provider's personnel may not necessarily have to complete the service. However, the service delivery function would be placed on the farmer-customer to transact the service. Technologies, where the customer intervenes to complete the transaction with the organization, are referred to as SST.

4 Analysis of Process Work Flow Model

4.1 Workflow Approach to Understand Issues and Challenges of an Indian Farmer at RSK

Primary research is adopted in this case study since the key objective is to observe issues and challenges of an Indian farmer at RSK Centers and propose incremental changes that can be implemented in the e-Government service by the providers to the farmers. As part of the case study, a visit to two Centers is carried out and an observation method of research is adopted. The researchers spent an entire day at the Centre observing the functioning of the Centre and stakeholders of the RSK. This enabled in developing the workflow model of the RSK.

Workflow modeling is the process of simplifying reality, based on facts gathered during observations. Though this representation can never be perfect, it could be enhanced by ethnographic research methods [21]. Hence an observation study adds value since the researcher shadows-in the characters of the study. A typical ethnographic research employs three kinds of data collection: through interviews, by observation, and from documents. This, in turn, produces three kinds of data: quotations, descriptions, and excerpts of the document resulting in one product- a narrative description. This narrative description, obtained during the case study, is used to create the proposed workflow model. Figure 2 illustrates the workflow model of the functioning of an RSK in present times. The case study uses this workflow model as a pointer to analyse the present methods of information-dissemination in RSKs in Karnataka.

4.2 Workflow Model Enhancement: Leveraging Self-Service Technology

The introduction of SST for delivery of a service places additional responsibilities on the customer to transact the service. In the context of expected service from government organizations, farmer's expectations in the adoption of SST may be

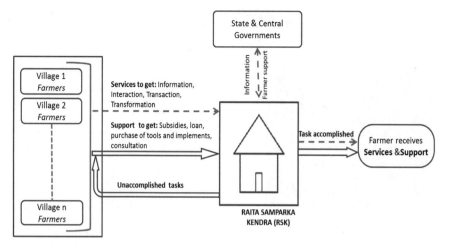

Fig. 2 Present workflow at RSK

leveraged. Implementation of SST from the Government as a provider of the service has been initiated by the Department of Agriculture by way of transaction websites known as K-Kisan, Krishibhagya and RTI (Right to Information) for information dissemination. Ravikumar and Subramanya the two young farmers, and Krishnappa the elderly farmer are aware of these SST. The AO at Bidarahalli and Kengeri RSK have lately initiated to communicate updates from the service provider to the farmers.

They have formed farmer groups on social media such as WhatsApp to communicate to the farmers (Fig. 3). Although changes in service delivery are supposedly made to benefit the customer, they often require increased work or involvement on the part of the customer. While the younger generation of farmers like Ravikumar and Subramanya visiting the RSK are ready to use social media and had broadband Internet connection on their mobile phones, they suggested that the Department of Agriculture could develop applications (apps) for easier information dissemination. They added that elder farmers still preferred traditional communication tools. This was affirmed by the elderly farmer Krishnappa and others who visited the RSK at both locations. A middle path to accommodating and educating the aging and young generation, the usefulness of adoption of SST by the government agency as a service provider, can be a solution to successful diffusion of Digital India Program. The Information Technology & Innovation Foundation (ITIF) report of 2010 estimates that if the self-service technology were more widely deployed, the U.S. economy would be approximately $130 billion larger annually, the equivalent of an additional $1100 in annual income for every household. This can be a story for India too since the vision of Digital India programme rests on providing digital infrastructure as a utility to every citizen, enabling governance and services on demand and fulfilling digital empowerment of citizens.

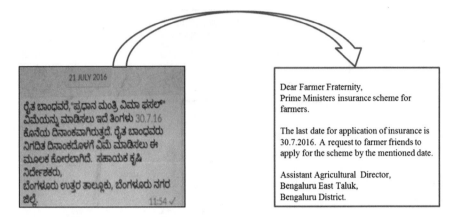

Fig. 3 Dissemination of information through social media in regional language initiated in 2016. Adjacent block illustrates the English translation of the message about an insurance scheme announced for farmers by the Central Government through social media on a mobile

5   Discussion

5.1   Issues and Challenges of Implementing SST

The AOs day at RSK begins in the morning. On most of the five working days in a week, farmers like Ravikumar, Subramanya and Krishnappa await procurement of supplies, sanctioning of loans, advice on crops or request AO to visit their fields to train the farmers on soil, use of seeds, fertilizers, technology or implementation of farming systems like rain water harvesting. The elderly farmer Krishnappa is visiting RSK to apply for a loan to procure farming equipments. All these activities are handled by three members at the Centre who have additional responsibilities of sending written communication as reports every week to help farmers develop documents for loans. However, though a computer system has been sent to the Centre, the system is yet to be installed. Manual data and records of farmers are maintained, including providing bills and receipts for the purchase of items from RSK. On any given day, the AO is the only point of contact at the Service Centre. If the AO is away on a field visit to a farmers land or away on routine meetings held at the Agricultural Office, a farmer who visits RSK is helpless, and avails a minimal or no service at all from the Centre. Hence, issues faced by the provider of the service include a lack of infrastructure, loss of time and money due to travel and waiting time. Overall, it is a lost opportunity caused due to incomplete work in their fields on a particular day.

Self-service is the process by which consumers engage in all or a portion of the provision of a service or product. ICT has created an opportunity to leverage technology for large gains in efficiency and convenience in the following ways. First, customer's readiness to play a specific service role becomes a challenge while implementing SST. According to [22] technology, readiness is a generalized individual difference concept that balances contributors (optimism and innova-tiveness) and inhibitors (discomfort and insecurity). Second, considering that SST is an innovation that needs to reach out to 0.25 million villages in India through IT infrastructure such as broadband and universal phone connectivity, this plan is infallible since government preparedness is well laid out. Yet factors such as ease of use, usefulness, need for interaction and risk of using SST may be antecedent to developing the farmers attitude or intention towards adoption of innovations such as SST. Third, SST being an innovation in Indian context specifically among farmers as customers, specificity of type of SST as a communication channel is essential. Finally, demographic profile of farmers accounts for adoption or rejection of SST.

5.2 A Proposed Workflow Model Incorporating SST

The way forward would be to incorporate internet kiosks at the panchayat (village) level, offer service delivery and reduce farmer visits to RSKs for essential services (Fig. 4). Integrating mass media and interpersonal media communication tools will facilitate gaps in the generation of farmers availing the services. Though mass media channels play a more effective role in creating awareness for SSTs as an innovation, young farmers like Ravikumar and Subramanya, savvy with technol-ogy, may adapt to such changes sooner. However, Krishnappa of the older gen-eration would require interpersonal communication channel tools such as newsletters, pamphlets, internet kiosks, audio and video programs, as they are more effective in forming and changing attitudes toward a new idea, and thus help in

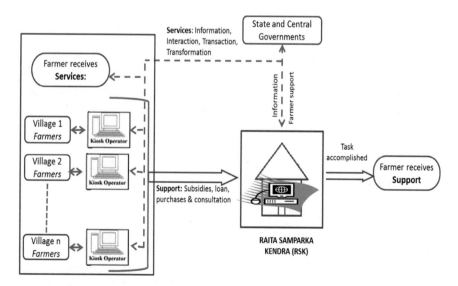

Fig. 4 Proposed workflow with SSTs

influencing the decision to adopt or reject a new idea. An AAO at the RSK can devote sufficient time in training farmers to use SST such as internet kiosks, websites and mobile apps through peers who serve as role models and whose innovation behavior tends to be imitated by other farmers in the system. Overall, SST will empower farmers and AAO at RSK in substantially lessening rework and helps to work efficiently in utilizing the resources the Government provides in enabling the success of the e-Government services. This method is increasingly seen as an answer to a plethora of problems that the governments or public agencies, in general, face in serving their constituencies effectively.

Notably, among 64 countries, the State Government of Karnataka's e-Governance MobileOne Application (App) won the gold award instituted for the first time at the World Government Summit held at Dubai in February 2016 [23]. The MoblieOne app brings together 4000 services, including government and private services, and is integrated under one platform. The plan is to upscale it to a national level since it can be accessed through mobile apps, web portals, Short Message Service (SMS) and Internet Voice Response Service (IVRS). The one-point platform is being used for utility payment, booking railway tickets, recharging prepaid mobile phone connections, etc. The Government plans to extend the service to the farmers too. The case develops a futuristic process flow model to empower citizen-farmers who can adapt to change through ICT.

Hopefully, the proposed new sustainable process flow model illustrated in Fig. 4 will see increased service and a quicker response time in service delivery, leading to increased transparency in the e-Government program to farmers. Perhaps as pointed out by [24], the application of the proposed workflow by the Government will contribute to the practical application of the research. While the concept of SST was explained to understand their awareness, Ravikumar, Subramanya and other young farmers at the RSK were enthusiastic and familiar with SSTs and keen in using SSTs. As [25] stated, though customers may take time to adopt SSTs leading to slower customer engagement in the service encounter, identifying their preferences will be the key for increasing the efficiency of e-Government-delivered services. Readiness in customer engagement necessitates an equal commitment and institutionalization of programmes and policies of the Government from public managers and leaders representing the Government, which leads to reduction in corruption and higher transparency in e-Government services [26].

6   Conclusion

Digital media is an enabler of customer outreach for organizations, and digital technology-based service encounter is in recent times becoming the standard process of service delivery. Technology integration in all spheres of service delivery may be a reality for future transactions for which end-user adoption and satisfaction is essential. E-services of the Government are available to consumers as published information for transactions and interaction, and have undergone pervasive changes over the course of the last decade. The Digital India campaign championed by the current Honorable Prime Minister of India offers scope for large-scale digitization and adoption of Information and Communication Technologies (ICT). This campaign has enabled government outreach to a larger mass of the population and has shown itself to be a very successful initiative at the Central and State levels. The farmer's role as a customer and being part of co-creation of e-Government services using SSTs such as web portals, social media, such as being part of the social media group and at farmer's interaction Centre, is studied in this research. This research article may be among a few qualitative type of research that has analyzed e-Government services disseminated through a process workflow model and hence contributes to the information systems research.

Administration of the e-Government service delivery to the farmers takes place through interaction centers known as RSK where farmers who belong to a Hobli (a group of villages) level utilize the Centre for service transactions and delivery. One of the goals of these centers is to empower the farmer to use ICTs to make vital decisions and furthermore, act as a key source of information dissemination through ICTs to the farmers on various aspects of agriculture. The motivation behind the case study is to assess the effectiveness of information dissemination by utilizing ICT specifically SSTs. The case discusses the issues and challenges faced by farmers while using the SSTs and identifying a workflow for successful adoption of e-Government services through the state's e-governance program. Government stakeholders may use this workflow model as a guideline to allow for enhanced dissemination of information to farmers. One of the goals of these centers is to empower the farmer to use ICTs to make vital decisions and furthermore act as a key source for information dissemination through ICTs to the farmers on various aspects of agriculture.

The study concludes that diffusion of ICT through SST and the prevalent service delivery can be through one-stop service delivery centers for farmers. A visit to an RSK could be for getting highly essential services and SSTs are to be used at village *panchayats* to empower farmers with information dissemination and transactions of e-Government services. This is done by customizing the SST by localizing the content delivery of services which adds value to the e-Government services. This will allow both information-oriented and user-oriented theoretical approach to service delivery being adopted in the interest of a user's perspective [27]. In this regard, the State of Karnataka, by providing e-Government services through one-stop Service centers and a mobile application called MobileOne, has achieved the information orientation. The MobileOne application accommodates self-service to most government services like payment of tax, bills, helps in uploading services of the Government that are not found efficient, access land records, etc. Emerging economies implementing and leveraging SSTs in e-Government services are known as self-service economies since SSTs increase efficiency and lower costs for the government while engaging its citizens who are customers in the transaction process [28]. Agriculture being a key driver in Indian economy [29] points to the significance of ICT enabled services as an emerging extension method of customer engagement and information dissemination.

6.1 Limitations and Scope of Research

The research method being exploratory is limited to analyzing the process workflow at two RSKs or farmers interaction centers while more than seven hundred such RSKs exist in the State alone. Future studies can overcome this limitation by adopting a survey technique at RSKs in the State. Government stakeholders can implement the proposed enhanced process workflow model to offer more efficient e-Government services to the farmers and simultaneously enrich the role of RSK of Centre Heads as experts rather than having a transaction-based role. Hence the proposed model through this research fulfills another function of e-Government service delivery called as transformation. This answers the "so what" of the research since farmers become empowered by stepping into the self-service delivery process through co-creation.

References

1. Aundhe, M.D., Narasimhan, R.: Case Studies on e-Governance in India, Nemmadi—Challenges in IT Adoption & Execution. A Project for Digital Services at Village Level (2013)
2. Basu, S.: E-government and developing countries: an overview. Int. Rev. Law. Comput. Technol. 18(1), 109–132 (2004)
3. Baum, C., Di Maio, A.: Gartner's Four Phases of e-Government Model. Gartner Group (2000)
4. Carter, L.: e-Government diffusion: a comparison of adoption constructs. Transforming Gov. People Process Policy 2(3), 147–161 (2008)
5. Castro, D., Atkinson, R. Ezell, S.: Embracing the self-service economy. The Information Technology & Innovation Foundation (2010)
6. http://www.cmai.asia/digitalindia/pdf/Digital-India-DeITY-Details.pdf. Accessed 27 Jan 2017
7. Cecchini, S., Scott, C.: Can information and communications technology applications contribute to poverty reduction? Lessons from rural India. Inf. Technol. Dev. 10(2), 73–84 (2003)
8. Curran, J.M., Meuter, M.L.: Self-service technology adoption: comparing three technologies. J. Serv. Mark. 19(2), 103–113 (2005)
9. Devasena, C.L., Balraj, P.L.: E-Governance in Southern States of India—Towards Whole-of-Government (WoG). Int. J. Emerg. Trends Technol. Comput. Sci. 3(2), 255–262 (2014)
10. Gupta, S.K.: e-Governance leaders as change agents. http://nceg.gov.in/sites/nceg.gov.in/files/Background%20Book.pdf (2013). Accessed 29 Jan 2017
11. Heeks, R., Bailur, S.: Analyzing e-government research: perspectives, philosophies, theories, methods, and practice. Gov. Inf. Q. 24(2), 243–265 (2007)
12. Hilton, T., Hughes, T.: Co-production and co-creation using self service technology: the application of service-dominant logic. In: Otago Forum, Vol. 2 (2008)
13. Kumar, R., Best, M.L.: Impact and sustainability of e-government services in developing countries: lessons learned from Tamil Nadu, India. Inf. Soc. 22(1), 1–12 (2006)
14. Maio, A.D.: Gartner Open Government Maturity Model. Gartner Report (2010)
15. Malhotra, S., Jordan, D., Shortliffe, E., Patel, V.L.: Workflow modeling in critical care: piecing together your own puzzle. J. Biomed. Inf. 40(2), 81–92 (2007)
16. Meuter, M.L., Bitner, M.J., Ostrom, A.L., Brown, S.W.: Choosing among alternative service delivery modes: an investigation of customer trial of self-service technologies. J. Mark. 69(2), 61–83 (2005)

17. http://raitamitra.kar.nic.in/ENG/index.asp. Accessed 27 Jan 2017
18. http://www.cio.com.au/article/176852/fields_online_dreams/. Accessed 27 Jan 2017
19. Miah, S.J.: The role of end user in e-government application development: a conceptual model in the agricultural context. J. Organ. End User Comput. (JOEUC) 24(3), 69–85 (2012)
20. Ndou, V.: e-Government for developing countries: opportunities and challenges. Electron. J. Inf. Syst. Developing Countries 18(1), 1–24 (2004)
21. Nkohkwo, Q.N.A., Islam, M.S.: Challenges to the successful implementation of e-government initiatives in Sub-Saharan Africa: a literature review. Public Adm. Rev. 65 (1), 64–75 (2013)
22. Palvia, S.C.J., Sharma, S.S.: e-Government and e-governance: definitions/domain framework and status around the world. In: International Conference on E-governance, pp. 1–12 (2007)
23. http://economictimes.indiatimes.com/tech/internet/karnataka-mobile-one-m-governance-model-wins-gold-atworld-government-summit-in-uae/articleshow/50940654.cms. Accessed 27 Jan 2017
24. Raghuprasad, K.P., Akarsha, B.M., Raghavendra, K.: Raitha samparka kendras and their role in agro-information delivery. Karnataka J. Agric. Sci. 25(1), 82–85 (2012)
25. Rowley, J.: Using case studies in research. Manag. Res. News 25(1), 16–27 (2002)
26. Subbiah, A., Ibrahim, O.: e-Government towards service co-creation of value. Afr. J. Bus. Manage. 5(22), 9401–9411 (2011)
27. Tat-Kei Ho, A.: Reinventing local governments and the e-government initiative. Public Adm. Rev. 62(4), 434–444 (2002)
28. Turner, III, D.W.: Qualitative interview design: a practical guide for novice investigators. Qual. Rep. 15(3), 754–760. Retrieved from http://nsuworks.nova.edu/tqr/vol15/iss3/19 (2010)
29. http://www.digitalindia.gov.in/. Accessed 27 Jan 2017

E-Society Realities in Sub-Saharan Africa: The Case of Cote d'Ivoire

Z. R. Ahouman and Z. Rongting

Abstract Over the past ten years, sub-Saharan Africa has undergone cultural transformations resulting from the development of ICTs at the political, economic and societal levels. The e-Society, beyond the organizational perspectives or the form that can be attributed to it, uses ICT and particularly the Internet. Through this study, we have looked at the formation of the e-Society in sub-Saharan Africa by querying some scientific publications or other qualitative data to see, as most of the illiterate and poor citizens are concentrated in this area. The study revealed two modes under which the e-Society operates, namely: a Government-Type Organization (e-Government, e-Commerce, e-Education, e-Health, e-Agriculture) and Private-Type Organization (private communities or platforms, working groups and exchanges Academics, social networks). Exploring the e-Society realities will surely rethink the way in which these societies are organized in terms of the evolution of digital technology.

Keywords ICT · Internet · e-Society realities · Sub-Saharan Africa · Cote d'Ivoire

Z. R. Ahouman (✉)
Department of Science, Technology Policy and Communication, School of Public Affairs, University of Science and Technology of China, No. 96 Jinzhai Road, Hefei 230026, Anhui, People's Republic of China
e-mail: ahouman.jason@gmail.com; ahouman7@mail.ustc.edu.cn

Z. Rongting
Department of Science, Technology Policy and Communication, School of Humanities and Social Science, New Media Institute, University of Science and Technology of China, No. 96 Jinzhai Road, Hefei 230026, Anhui, People's Republic of China
e-mail: rongting@ustc.edu.cn

© Springer Nature Switzerland AG 2019
Y. Baghdadi and A. Harfouche (eds.), *ICT for a Better Life and a Better World*,
Lecture Notes in Information Systems and Organisation 30,
https://doi.org/10.1007/978-3-030-10737-6_15

1 Introduction

The World Summit on the Information Society was held in Geneva in 2003 and Africa has been involved in this conference [1, 2]. The aim of this global initiative was to create favorable conditions for the use of ICTs by all in the different sectors of activity and in the daily life of the populations in order to harness from the information and communication technologies revolution [3]. After about 10 years, Jim Yong Kim, President of the World Bank Group, observes that nearly 6 billion people do not have a broadband Internet connection and therefore cannot fully participate in the digital economy, another 4 billion people are deprived of the Internet [4]. Access to the Internet is therefore an imperative for many populations of this world. Indeed, the Internet has become one of the most important primary needs to fully live the notion of e-society, factor of *"ICT for a better life and a better world"*. Innovative ICT companies have already realized this dream thanks to the concepts of "Smart City" [5, 6] and social innovation [7], whereas our policy-makers or leaders still reflect on how to develop a "digital economy" that focuses on regulations and laws [8–10]. These authors by their commitments made translated and showed the notable advances of ICTs and digital technologies and their positive impacts on our lives and in society.

During these ten years we have witnessed a flourishing literature on the "digital divide" [11–14]. But this has not changed because the latest report on human development in the world points to the limitations of transformation and considers that "the access to the digital revolution is heterogeneous when we compare regions, gender, Age groups and living environments (urban/rural)" [15]. This has been reiterated by the latest World Bank report [4]. In spite of this daily reality, the countries of the North and those of the South have remained in perpetual change, although we can say that globalization is irreversible [16].

However, can the rate of human and technological pauperization suffered by African countries enable a true e-society or even a digital economy? The aim of this work is to take a look at the use of ICTs and the construction of the e-Society in sub-Saharan Africa, and then the way in which the e-Society manifests itself. This will allow us to see the products or services that bear witness to the e-Society. Finally, we will address the specific case of Cote d'Ivoire.

2 Theoretical Framework and Methodology

Qualitative research is generally based on an exploratory model of language that considers the most relevant data collected (e.g. interviews, documents, designs …). On the theoretical level, a sociological and communicational approach like that of Habermas [17] who also served authors such as Calhoun [18], Bailo [19] was used in this study. This approach claims the benefits and human well-being of the individual within the Community in the contemporary debate that is taking place on the Internet. This underlines the evolutionary, historical and social character already proposed by many authors. Communication within a society and in particular in our world has long aroused the researcher's interest's vis-a-vis the phenomena of constructions and organizational transformations.

Thus, every researcher is always confronted with social, economic, political and cultural important tasks.

Jürgen Habermas, in the book "Technology and Science as Ideology" [20], reflects on the role of technology and science in the society. He analyzes to understand the changes in the institutional framework of traditional societies when they are transformed into modern societies under the growing influence of science and technology. Habermas, Calhoun and Francesco questioned the transformation of modern society under the influence of techno-science and even ICT. These structural transformations of society could be applied in the same way to the context of e-Society with the Theory of the Diffusion of Innovations. According to Rogers, "innovation is an idea or object perceived as new that brings benefits, compatibility with values, so complex which has the ability to be assess, and which becomes easy and visible". This adoption follows five phases: knowledge (exploration), persuasion (involvement), decision (commitment), implementation (use) and confirmation (adoption or rejection) [21]. So, the use and adoption of digital devices here has favored the growth of ICTs and, above all, has redesigned the shape of the e-Society in sub-Saharan African countries.

For this purpose, the Figs. of the International Telecommunication Union (ITU) ICT development index show that some countries in sub-Saharan Africa have made good progress in adopting and using ICT. For example, a high mobile penetration rate was recorded this year by International Telecommunication Union (ITU) report 2016 in countries such as Burundi, Côte d'Ivoire, Ethiopia, Gambia, Ghana, Guinea, South Africa and Tanzania. The study also shows that Cote d'Ivoire occupies 10th place in the African regional ranking and 132nd in the world ranking with an average of 2.86%. World population has reached more than 7 billion people, and only 3 billion have access to the Internet, a penetration rate of 40%. Africa has a total of 281 million Internet users with an average rate of 23.4%. In Côte d'Ivoire, the percentage of household's access to Internet has increased from 12% in 2014 to 17% in 2015 and Internet users have also increased from 15 to 21% [22]. Despite the fact that 60% of the world's population does not have access to the Internet, the e-Society appears to be an essential part, an indisputable reality in our society. This is why we would therefore like to make the following hypothesis: the e-Society is not real in Sub-Saharan Africa because of its lag in ICT.

E-Society is an Anglo-Saxon term that translates as "electronic society" [23]. The e-Society therefore refers to Digital Society in French. According to these authors (Magoulas, Lepouras, & Vassilakis), *"E-Society is a broad term used to describe a research area covering aspects of digital technologies for large user communities"* [23]. In other words, it is a generic term that is used in the field of digital technologies, which brings together large user communities that interact with each other. The e-Society is consecutive to the impact of digital technologies, especially Internet on society. And ICTs are both the tools and the vector that allow these connections, exchanges and cooperation between peoples, Communities, States, Administrations and Institutions that constitute this new form of society. Example have been given by Alfred Rovai in the context of educational apprenticeship with the definition of classroom community [24] and also UK e-Society which revealed 23 associations in its geographical classification [25].

This paper is based on a qualitative method and focuses on five key areas of the e-Society as a corpus basis through which this reality is possible (e-Government, e-Commerce, e-Education, e-Health, e-Agriculture), although e-Society is also the interaction of the Communities via platforms and social networks as well [26–28]. The study's space takes into account Sub-Saharan African countries and Cote d'Ivoire as a case study. Several scientific literatures revealed cases of e-Society practices in both particular and various forms.

On the other hand, some scholarly work and disciplines on the subject have been of great use to understand the realities surrounding the construction of the e-Society via ICT. Finally, empirical data based on secondary sources were used, with relevant review of literature from publications, reports, journals and scientific articles.

3 Result

3.1 Presentation of Sub-Saharan Africa

Today, Sub-Saharan Africa presents a new face through the development of many ICT projects. It is a set of 48 countries including islands. For political or geopolitical issues, it is often divided into four sub-regions and sometimes affected by political and military crises. So, this region of the world tirelessly tries to find its way to development. According to the African Development Bank Group, in 2006 all the 53 African countries had only 35 research and development centers, compared to 861 in North America, 655 in Asia and 1576 in Europe [29]. Those [Africans] who want unicity and see Africa take off for development consider this continent as a single heritage. Therefore, the birth of the African Union as hope. ICTs are today essential keys of transformation of humanity and the life of human being. To this end, developed countries have a long period enjoyed ICTs fruits as a development enabler because of their skills of technological capital. Sub-Saharan Africa has only its devoted young people who started following these advanced countries through the e-Society by the development of start-up as shown in Fig. 1, thanks to the support of private companies and international institutions [see 30: 99].

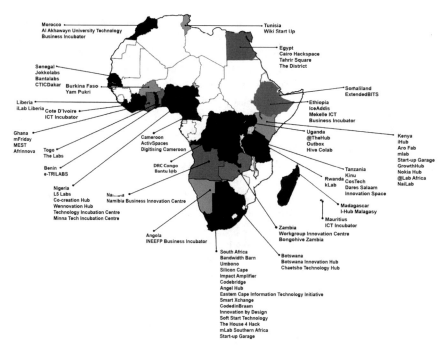

Fig. 1 Mapping of start-up incubators in 23 sub-Saharan African countries (*Source* Agence Française de Développement, Agence Universitaire de la Francophonie, UNESCO and Orange [30: 99]

3.2 Genesis of an E-Society in Sub-Saharan Africa

The scientific and technological development initiatives were at the heart of African political reforms just after independence in 1964 for Africa industrialization [31]. Indeed, Africa has missed the train of the Industrial Revolution since it was long struck by the slave trade and colonization. In the absence of real human and technological capital to achieve industrialization, and take advantage of the Technology Revolution, Africa opted for "the strategy of industrialization by substitution of imports" [32]. It should be noted that it was in the late 1970s and 1980s that the world embraced this Technological Revolution with Internet popularization. According to Internet Society, *"In October 1972, Kahn organized a large, very successful demonstration of the ARPANET at the International Computer Communication Conference (ICCC). This was the first public demonstration of this new network technology to the public. It was also in 1972 that the initial "hot" application, electronic mail, was introduced"* [33].

In Sub-Saharan Africa, the Digital Revolution tone has been launched by President Houphouët Boigny. Houphouët argued that after having missed the industrial revolution, Africa should not once more miss the computer revolution

[34, 35]. Therefore, from 1987 to 1992, 600 African experts were commissioned to work on the African Satellite Project (RASCOM) in order to address ICT and interconnection concerns in Africa [36]. Unfortunately, it was in 1996 that Africa Information Society Initiative (AISI) initiated a policy and strategy to encourage all African countries to develop and implement policies and strategies about ICT usage, including national and regional plans to promote the genuine adoption of ICT in all sectors of society [37]. A few years later, Presidents Abdoulaye Wade, Thabo Mbeki, Abdelaziz Bouteflika and Olusegun Obasanjo launched the NEPAD (New Partnership for Africa's Development) project to unite the energies of the African community to that end. Thus, the e-Africa commission was created in the context of the New Partnership for Africa's Development (NEPAD). In an e-Society spirit, this Commission, African governments, business and civil society have worked in collaboration with other organizations such as COMESA, SADEC and ECA on many projects [38].

E-Society uses various ICT media to facilitate communication between communities in the society. As Dzidonu said, ICTs include a variety of technologies, therefore we must not limit e-Society exclusively to the use of the Internet [39, 40]. In many African countries, under the umbrella of the African Union, the Pan-African e-Network in collaboration with several States and International Non-Governmental Organizations, e-Health projects have been financed, developed and realized between western doctors and their colleagues from Africa [41]. During the implementation of the projects, the actors and institutions involved have interacted by remote consultations, diagnosis patients far from them. They have also recovered and store important data and files, transmitted or shared data or experiences through ICT. Figure 2 shows that all Sub-Saharan Africa countries have benefited from these projects. These e-health projects have completely been carried out remotely with various technologies such as the Internet, mobile phones, open source software, etc.

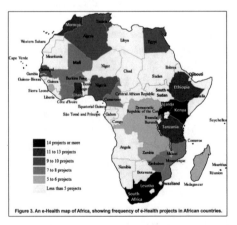

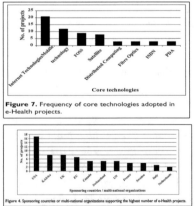

Fig. 2 e-Health projects carried out in sub-Saharan African countries, ICTs used and donor countries (*Source* Jahangirian and Taylor [41: 211–212] (Adapted by the author)

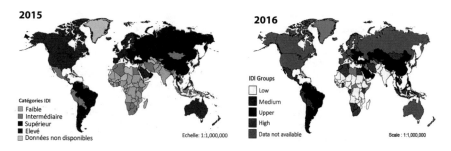

Fig. 3 ICT development index level of Sub-Saharan African countries in the world (IDI 2015 & 2016) (*Source* ITU 2015: 15, [22: 35]

In addition, the "New Public Management" imposed itself on Sub-Saharan Africa in response to public mismanagement, corruption, overcrowding staffing levels and misappropriation of public funds in public management under the auspices of Democracy-Good Governance, donors and international institutions [42]. In many Sub-Saharan African countries, the Intranet and multimedia projects have allowed to facilitate the information flow between the state, the different agents and the interconnected administrations. It can be noted that the use of ICT by the various actors into a kind of e-Society dimension has made possible to circumscribe the evil of these administrations. The emergence or the birth of National Information and Communication Infrastructure (NICI) plans, the adoption of e-Government initiatives and their generics (e-Administration, e-Services, e-Health ...) have been made in this same spirit. Despite all these efforts, Africa remains the least connected continent in the world and the most laggard in terms of ICT development. Without the use of statistics or numbers, the ITU Report 2015 and 2016 shows high evidence of ICT Development Index. On the IDI global map, as shown in Fig. 3 there is only one Sub-Saharan African country (Gabon) which would have made progress in 2016, compared to more than half of Asia countries [43].

3.3 The E-Society Realities or Manifestations

Over the past 15 years, we are witnessing a new form of relationship and socialization in Sub-Saharan Africa as a result of the use of New Technologies Information and Communication (ICT), in particular the Internet and the mobile phones. Indeed, the e-Government initiatives adoption or development by the states has shaped a major and beneficial paradigm shift to the public sector with the transformation of economies, work habits and life especially relations between governments, citizens and society as a whole. In addition, the social networks have come to boost these relations. UNESCO argued that these changes are under way thanks to the upheavals brought by the third industrial revolution—that of new technologies [44]. E-Society come in two forms in sub-Saharan Africa, namely: a Governmental-Type Organization (e-Government,

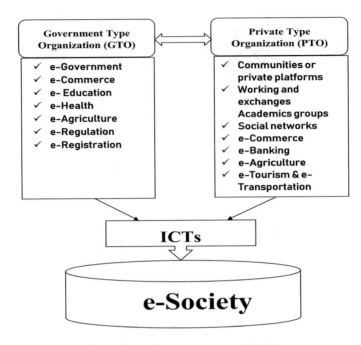

e-Society Conceptual framework and Model

Fig. 4 e-Society operational framework in Sub-Saharan Africa (*Source* Author)

e-Commerce, e- Education, e-Health, e-Agriculture), and a Private-Type Organization (Communities or private platforms, working and exchanges Academics groups, Social networks, e-Commerce/ e-Banking, e-Agriculture). Figure 4 allowed us to assess the e-Society operational implementation framework in Sub-Saharan African countries.

At the Governmental Type Organization Level
Several states of Sub-Saharan Africa have adopted e-Government and attend the UN e-Government world rankings (see UN e-Gov Survey from 2002 to 2016). Indeed, e-Government is addressed to both members of government (G2G), state administrations (G2E), companies (G2B) and citizens (G2C). E-Participation is the result of the e-information, e-consultation, and e-decision-making factors within e-Government [45, 46]. This social and technology interaction between the Government and the citizens is undoubtedly one of the greatest e-Society evidence. Many Government members and parliamentarians, including authorities around the world fully live e-Society realities on secure platforms such as Intranets, e-Parliaments and e-Councils (e.g. National or Regional Advisory Councils). Ochieng 'Ogodo [47] emphasizes that authorities and Scientific's in African countries are collaborating and interacting well on forum groups. In developed countries where democracy is advanced, after their workplace, parliamentarians frequently interact and exchange with their citizens also [48]. Inter-Parliamentary

Union note that e-Society manifests more between young parliamentarians with their elders, including between genders [49]. The use of the various ICTs (Internet, mobile phones, tablets...) between the governors and the governed offers new modalities or possibilities for co-production of knowledge, information and collective memories beyond the political dimension. This is the context surrounding Alain LOUKOU proposal for stakeholder's engagement on the appropriation and the use of ICTs as tools for innovation, efficiency and value creation for local development in Africa [50]. The Co-production works (Public-private partnership), a source of innovation and development, has made possible to carry out community projects in the e-Government field for example in Ghana (Ghana Community Network), Tanzania (TAKNET), and Kenya (Corruption Reporting and Kenya Open Data Initiative) [51].

In addition, the e-Society appears under a socio-communicational dimension and also both build on a market value, because the use of ICT by all stakeholders lead to effective and makes more efficient; But above all it contributes to the economy and social development through the e-Commerce component.

In Sub-Saharan Africa, several national single windows (one-stop shop) have been opened by governments to facilitate the task of users and enterprises to access to government services [52–54]. Henceforth, as a replacement for the face-to-face traditional windows, businesses and citizens alike can use ICTs to pay taxes, make customs clearance registrations for imports and exports of goods and vehicles, Companies can also to obtain the various documents. This process foster proper managerial and guarantee more transparency and efficiency. Conversely, government agencies collect taxes and all necessary information in the shortest possible delay. This also enables port and airport communities to interact with each other. In this regard, Schuppen [51] mentioned that: *"With the introduction of a new IT system—the GCNet—all customs affairs which are necessary for the import and export of good scan, to a very large extent, be performed electronically. The GCNet was first used in October 2002 at Kotoka international airport and was later also implemented in Ghana's sports"*. The convergence efforts in term of exchanges between regional and sub-regional organizations by using ICT as a channel or bridge to speak with one voice during policy decisions are gestures indicates the e-Society. To this end, Sub-Saharan Africa integration involves several negotiations, exchanges of information and documentation provided by regular ICTs (mails, fax, telephone, etc.), including participation to some Global Forums or the summits of exchanges and discussions in the context of negotiations North-South Partnership Agreements and the WTO discussions. ICTs provide an opportunity for trade specialists to exchange views, but also some members of regional organizations take advantage of the opportunity to express their viewpoints related on international trade issues, and exchanges [55, 56].

The e-Society remains visible through the interaction between trainers and learners, but also between trainers and experts of international organizations and institutions during the learning process and capacity building of actors in the education system. Sub-Saharan Africa, conscious of its backwardness in several areas, is constantly building collaborations with many international and regional partners to bring innovation to its universities and improve its education system. On that point, Ng'ethe [57] argued that many national and international partners have emphasized the importance of ICTs to engaging correspondence education, facilitate online enrolment, and improve the quality of courses through on-line access to teaching materials. This collaboration and innovation cannot be done without the transformations made by ICT (e.g. computers, mobile phones, online games, consulting works …) in the area of education. Thanks to ICT, the education system has initiated e-Society in education through the terms "e-Education or e-learning". E-Learning is the delivery, learning, training, electronical education using media such as computer, mobile phone, CD-ROM, DVD and especially Internet [58]. Today, this phenomenon has entered into the educational mores in sub-Saharan Africa. Academics and organizations have published some case studies, have also revealed implementation and challenges related to e-Education or e-learning in some Sub-Saharan African countries. These studies show examples of relevant electronic content and how ICTs have contributed to distance-learning among groups of disadvantaged people through the Association for the Development of Education in Africa [59–61].

In Medicine and generally in the field of health, African governments are called upon to appropriate ICTs and especially mobile phone penetration to consolidate the e-Society. To achieve this, several solutions are available to decision-makers, practitioners, citizen and stakeholders to train and especially developed the techniques. Alan RYAN et al. [62] have studied and tested e-Learning cases in the medical field in Sub-Saharan Africa. According to the Government of Canada, E-health is defined as the use of information and communication technologies to support, educate, inform and connect health care professionals and the people they serve [63]. In reality, Sub-Saharan Africa does not take much advantage of this opportunity offered by the e-Society. The Happy and great beneficiaries are for the time being the healthcare professionals since they can inform themselves online, get self-educate and to exchange easily between them.

Nevertheless, encouraging e-Health results have been reported in some Sub-Saharan African countries regarding the m-Health with the public-private partnership such as Be Healthy Be Mobile and Alcatel, Senegal health ministry with Orange Company etc. But above all, the result of this collaboration reveals that 363 m-health projects were identified in June 2013 [64]. The healthcare professionals participate fully experience to the e-Society through capacity-building initiated between health institutions and laboratories with the assistance of international organizations, inter-regional and national collaborations [65, 66]. This also happened between universities and academics or researchers. From doctor to doctor, the results of a patient can be transmitted in various ways by using ICT. As well, the exchange or delivery of information in the medical field to prevent a number of risks among populations living in remote areas has been made possible through emergency SMS messages and information of public utility provided through the media. With the evolution of the e-Society, some section of the population benefit from e-health diagnosis, distance prescriptions medicines or online medical counselling. This interaction between practitioners and users, the administrative management of the hospital or patients, the hospital technical records, but also actions between hospitals, doctors or specialists via TICs are results need mainly be attributed to the e-Society. E-health is faster thanks to the interaction and co-operation of healthcare providers through e-Care, e-Learning, e-Administration and e-Surveillance. When we talk about poverty and hunger in the world, all eyes are therefore turned on sub-Saharan Africa. According to Hugon [67], it is the meeting place for various evils such as the political distortions, unfavourable prices, rural emigration, low public investment, marketing and supply difficulties, inadequate or obsolete technology, climatic factors (e.g. drought), ecological (desertification), social (land or lineage structures) or political (e.g. war and insecurity). The World Bank emphasised that 89 per cent of the rural population of the predominantly agricultural countries are located in sub-Saharan Africa [68]. These are often obstacles linked to the transformation of the agricultural landscape of this zone.

Today, governments and actors in agricultural sectors are experimenting with e-Agriculture in Sub-Saharan Africa [69, 70]. ICTs are used for the exchange of information and mutual collaboration between farmers, states, and intermediaries. On the one hand, information relating to the development of the national agricultural sector, climatic and meteorological conditions and the costs of imports and exports on domestic or international markets. On the other hand, information on stocks, supply, inputs and different modes of coordination between all actors in order to provide the market. Unfortunately, we observe that a lot of people in these areas are illiterate. So they cannot afford a computer and an internet connection. Thus, the mobile phone comes as a palliative to fill this deficit. Therefore, the e-Society takes its full form over here between the state, intermediaries, some leaders of agricultural cooperatives and the farmers. Across Sub-Saharan Africa, Kenya seems to be enjoying the transformations of ICTs in the agricultural sector regarding to the e-Agriculture and m-Farmers organization in the country [71].

Some countries have followed the same bold initiatives by developing projects such as Esoko in Ghana, DrumNet in Kenya, LiberFor in Liberia, NamLITS in Namibia [72].

At the Private Type Organization Level

In sub-Saharan Africa, ICTs continue to bring various mutations and interactions between private companies and communities, as access to the Internet is possible through cybercafés, mobile phones or at home via a computer. Indeed, the various social strata or socio-professional categories, by the advent of social networks have managed to consolidate the e-Society. According to some researchers, like Mbarika et al. [73], and Mbarika et al. [74], Sub-Saharan Africa has shifted from a technological desert to an emerging growth for the future thanks to ICTs.

We consider this e-Society as a Private Organization in the sense that it involving private companies' work that often bring their clients together on a same platform in order to listen to their needs, to advertise, Loyalty or gathering Internet users via communities ... (e.g. mobile phone companies, banks, tourism agencies ...). Apart from companies, there are some communities, academic groups and individuals who use personal websites, mobile applications such as WeChat, WhatsApp, Imo … or have opened a space on social networks like Facebook, LinkedIn, Mxit in South Africa … to communicate and interact with many friends.

It should be noted that private companies have been the backbone of ICTs adoption in sub-Saharan Africa. For example, banks have initially interacted with their customers via landlines or fax, electronic bank cards (ATM), e-mails, recordings and downloads form of documents on Internet, telephone calls, sms (short message service) And e-Payments or m-Payments. Gérard Tchouassi points out that mobile phones used for banking services (e-banking) are likely to increase the bank account penetration rate in sub-Saharan Africa [75]. Some telephone companies such as Orange, MTN, Vodafone, Safaricom and others have brought their customers to exchange on discussion platforms housed on their own sites. They also do not hesitate to communicate by being followed on social networks. The customers interact through call centers or by mobile phones as well. Over the past decade, e-banking and e-commerce have become the dominant fields of activity, bringing all companies closer to people. Several scholars in sub-Saharan African countries, through their studies, have observed the progress made in the process of deployment and adoption of services. Some mentioned the security problems, scepticism among many clients, before showing the benefits expected by each individual or stakeholder. Moreover, the main problem remains the infrastructures that is inaccessible to rural inhabitants, the high cost of the Internet and low data rates [76–78].

In addition, Fig. 5 shows the ingenuity of some individuals has enabled them to use networks such as Facebook to bring people together in small communities to exchange or promote their ideals, but also to make marketing around their different products or business. Some have embarked on cyber-activism to interact with all Internet users at national, interregional and international levels to denounce certain facts or to engage in social debates and to discuss topics of current interest.

Others operational entities, namely companies and recruitment agencies also benefit from LinkedIn to hunt talent or build their image and reputation as shown in Fig. 6.

We observed that many noble associations (labour movement), political associations, and religious associations exist especially on Facebook, since they don't have their own website. Several socio-professional categories or communities, and even some citizens exchange with their Diasporas on topical subjects or local development. These groups interact with each other to share information and common interests. These groups interact with each other to share information, and to discuss common interests.

However, it was also observed that some academic communities [79–81], professionals from the same Corporation such as mFamers in Malawi, Kenya and other countries; as well as civil society associations operate on their own websites. They have the opportunity to share their research, publications and some

Fig. 5 Melding of 2 groups or private communities via a social network participating in the e-Society (*Source* Facebook 2016, adapted by the author)

information concerning their meetings. This overcoming or reduces the barriers, costs and distance that separate them from their members [82, 83]. In Sub-Saharan Africa, We identified several examples or groups: The members of the Institute of Political and Strategic Studies (IEPS); The African Center for Trade, Integration and Development (Enda Cacid), the Platform of Civil Society Organizations in West Africa on the Cotonou Agreement (POSCAO), the Common Market of East and Southern Africa (COMESA) etc. The advent of this e-Society is one of the concerns of communities or groups of booksellers, and universities. Oyinloye [84] argued that it strongly supports and participates in the Information and Knowledge Society insofar as ICT facilitates and transforms learning habits and the dissemination of knowledge. Finally, to understand the ideology of this e-Society, Jeremy RIFKIN [85] reports that there is no adversary in a network, it is like a big family [86].

Fig. 6 Melding of 4 pages, including a web surfer activist and her friends, a private company and two pages suggesting private groups or communities with various themes or interests (*Source* LinkedIn 2016, adapted by the author)

3.4 e-Society in Côte d'Ivoire [Ivory Coast]

E-Society was observed in Ivory Coast in 1993 with the "RIOnet" network [87] before Internet adoption became one of the main drivers in 1996 [88]. The liberalization of telecommunications in 1995 has facilitated the rapid advancement of ICT and has led to transformations that have gradually changed the way of collaborating and interacting between successive governments, enterprises and populations. In fact, the e-Society has been promoted in Ivory Coast by the website Abidjan.net set up by two Ivorian's, called Jil N'Dia and Daniel Ahouassa. According to the report of Panos Institute West Africa and the United Nations on e-governance and citizen participation in West Africa, "*in 1998, the founders of Weblogy launched the website* www.Abidjan.net *to enable the Ivoirian diaspora community to access information on what was happening in Cote d'Ivoire. This site was launched towards the end of 1999, the time of the country's first ever coup. This portal is now the most visited portal in Cote d'Ivoire, with a minimum of*

300,000 visits per day" [89: 47]. As regards the political authorities, the African Information Society Initiative (AISA) has invited all the African countries to develop plans to enhance their national information and communication infrastructure (NISI Plan) in order to adopt the ICTs in 1996 to move toward Electronic Government. This initiative aimed to use the ICT channel to promote economic and social development [90]. Moreover, in 2001, Ivory Coast was unexpectedly ranked for the first time in the Globe, e-Government Survey as one of the countries that adopted e-Government [91]. The following year, the United Nation survey entitled "Benchmarking E-government: A Global Perspective" proved that Cote d'Ivoire was not only ahead of some great country like China but also surpassed some e-government leaders in Sub-Saharan Africa, such as Mauritius, Cape Verde and Ghana [92]. The e-Society was initiated by the Government on the basis of States interaction tools, populations and enterprises: the invention of a multimedia information system used by the government and at the same time managed by the CICG [36], a Call Center, the customs' one-stop shop under DG Gnamien Konan in order to facilitate ICT procedures for enterprises and citizens [93, 94]. The project to use electronic methods to vote [95, 96], passports and driving licenses will henceforth be secured by ICT [97, 98]. As for e-education in Cote d'Ivoire, Bogui Jean-Jacques and Mian Bi assert that ICT has long been used to train and develop teachers' capacities in Ivory Coast [99, 100]. These actors of education have always armed themselves with courage to integrate the e-Society. Despite their numerous battles to become educators through researches, learning as trainers and also learning online via Internet, it was in 2005 that the Felix University and the University of Cocody have received a high speed internet room from the Agence Universitaire de La Francophonie and Ivory Coast Telecom [99]. The inability to access or broadcast on the internet remains the real problem that thwarts enjoying e-society.

Many have denounced that a lot of citizens in Ivory Coast are unable to access Internet because of high costs, the obsolete equipment and infrastructures, the digital divide, illiteracy or the lack of competence [101–103]. However, it is observed that Ivory Coast has a very young population. According to World Factbook, the structure of the Ivorian population is as follows: "0–14 years 37.94%; 15–24 years 20.95%; 25–54 years 33.53%; 55–64 years 4.25%; 65 years and over 3.34%" [104]. There are nearly over twenty-three (23) million inhabitants in Ivory Coast [105]. There is the phenomenon of "Digital natives and Generation Z" [106] and "La Google Generation" [107] that ought not to be omitted and that is becoming popular around the world. In Ivory Coast and particularly in Sub-Saharan Africa, this has contributed significantly to the adoption of smart mobile phones. In Ivory Coast, the Internet's penetration rate has been increasing in recent years. For example, by 5.3% in 2010 [108], this rate increased to 23.08% [109] and then to 31.65% in 2015 [110]. Failing to obtain a computer for some researches, learning or information, brought about the palliative measure to fill the vacuum. To solve the lack of a functional university it has adapted their needs especially in the e-Education or e-Learning fields. Many populations, including teachers and students started using cybercafés' and mobile phones [111–114]. This problem encouraged Hocine Khelfaoui's assertion that, *"Despite its relative financial ease, Ivory Coast remains one of the countries where ICTs are underdeveloped in universities and research centers. The research sector has been relegated to second place, being surpassed only by administration. Computers in number and power are more available in administrations than in research laboratories"* [115].

E-Health and e-Agriculture have appeared in the last five years. These "Revolutions" were observed in Ivory Coast from 2005 to 2009 [116]. Provided that administration is a continuity, the State has just started these projects after the crisis [117]. Moreover, the e-Society seems to be consolidated as a result of the partnership between the public and the private sector. The e-Commerce, e-Banking, e-Money and m-Money components were introduced in 2008 and continue to provoke a frenzy among populations at the moment, which can be described as springtime for Private partnership companies [118]. People with mobile internet access in cybercafés and in offices are constantly interacting with social networks to connect online or to discover more about themselves. Commendation to the Facebook social network, abidjan.net and LinkedIn, Ivorian's, the diaspora and the whole world interact.

Moreover, by virtue of the economic spin-offs or the contribution of ICTs to the economic growth of countries, the Ivorian government has become aware of the UN's 2003 criticisms [119] to reflect on the situation of ICT in Ivory Coast as well as to initiate the first ICT development programs to elaborate its e-Government strategy [120]. Additionally, in October 2009, Prime Minister Soro Kigbafori Guillaume signed the Order No. 18/PM/CAB/of 13 Oct. 2009 to provide Ivory Coast with a legal, institutional framework and normative for the e-Government initiative to enable the very important national actors to fully participate in the success of the e-Government project, launched since 2000 [121]. In 2011, the second part was initiated by the new government [122]. Cote d'Ivoire continues to improve its ICT environment with the implementation of a flagship project called "e-Gouv", centering around two (2) major axes, particularly; e-Administration and e-Service and seven categories, which include: e-Health, e-Education, e-Agriculture, e-Justice, e-Diplomacy and e-Land as well as an Intranet service for the needs of government institutions [122].

4 Discussion

Over the last ten years, sub-Saharan Africa has undergone cultural transformations resulting from the development of ICTs in political, economic and societal terms. The e-Society, in its organizational form uses ICT and the Internet to make communities of the planet interact. The e-Society was designed in two forms of organization: a Government-Type Organization (e-Government, e-Commerce, e-Education, e-Health, e-Communities) as well as a Private-Type Organization (working groups and academic exchanges, social networks). The term "Governmental Organization" refers to the notion of the Public Sector plus (+) organizations or institutions affiliated with the governments of State (UN, UNESCO, IMF, World Bank, UNCEA, AU, NEPAD, AISI ...) with Governments face-to-face, especially online through ICT.

Secondly, the Private Organizations associates the Private Sector (Companies) with individual initiatives or those of civil societies and Non-Governmental Organizations that are organized throughout the countries. The e-Society seems to be the result of what is observed in the theory of motivation and needs called the "Pyramid of Maslow's needs". Indeed, the theory of motivation and needs expresses various needs [123]. Within the framework of the e-Society, two needs seem to motivate the construction of this society, namely: the physiological needs, that affect the well-being of the body such as, hunger, the thirst for the Internet at the level of populations as well as the needs of belonging, which arouse one's will to leave a family, a group, a tribe or community whose knowledge is vital. Contemporary societies are abundant in knowledge. ICT and the Internet appear to be the essence for food, society and communities to flourish. As an alternative solution for sub-Saharan Africa, the rulers would prefer to advance from e-Government to m-Government due to the fact that most successful projects with populations have been implemented with mobile phones [124–126]. The e-Society proves to be a "demand" insofar, as it lies between the two poles of desire and need among all actors or stakeholders. ICTs arouse and sustain this demand as technological innovations in society increase. Criticisms and failures in relation to the implementation of e-Government in poor and developing countries [127] should enable the rulers to strengthen the participatory and inclusive framework of citizens and populations by opting for the e-Society. In other words, one must re consider how to organize and use ICTs in societies so that every citizen can participate in the life of the virtual community. In the perspective of paradigm shift and innovation, let's move on to a form of socialization, a facilitation of life because technologies allow mankind to go beyond its limits with the e-Society. Sub-Saharan Africa can achieve the digital economy very quickly, appreciating China's method by reducing the cost of the Internet, forging human and technological capital, but above all, by encouraging mass adoption of ICTs by the populations.

In Sub-Saharan Africa, the adoption of ICTs and the consolidation of the e-Society is facilitating digital inclusion for the profit of populations. It improves the flow of information, money, goods and services. The real impact of ICTs on the behavior of this society is shown by a new structure and form of work management, relationships and all socio-economic activities. Tasks are automated with certain software's or software packages, faster and easier access to information and sharing, flexibility in tasks, reduced time, distance and cost/Activities. Improved quality, performance and intensified competitivity between companies and institutions are observed within society. Innovation and the creativity produce constant changes and shifts. In sub-Saharan Africa, this can be seen with the boom in technology centers across the continent (e.g. AfriLabs, The Innovation Hub in South Africa, Botswana Innovation Hub, BongoHive in Zambia, I-Hub in Kenya, EtriLabs in Benin, ILab in Liberia, IceAddis in Ethiopia, Kinu in Tanzania, ActivSpaces in Cameroon, CcHUb in Nigeria, JoziHub in Johannesburg) [129] and above all the positive impact of ICT on the women's lives which unfortunately are still considered as Excluded. These women are now able to communicate through the various ICTs with their family members and those who use them; they find refugees or freedoms, express themselves, learn, develop contacts and for some of them, do business [130]. Unfortunately, all these opportunities offered by ICT have often been reduced to electronic governance. It is rather the expression of democratic stakes with citizen participation in public debate through the use of ICT in the electoral processes that fuel the debates [36, 131]. As for the degree of ICT contribution to competitiveness and innovation, Ushahidi created in Kenya in 2008. MTN, Orange and Vodafone have developed mobile money services that help people to bank, Jumia is emerging as the leader in e-commerce on the continent, bringing together the beginners and their customers, the positive reaction indicates that 195 million people use Internet [132]. Moreover, it is clear that in some countries of Sub-Saharan Africa, the digital not only brought opportunities. The delinquent acts of young people in society have been reproduced in the e-Society and worse we are witnessing threats against the weakest [133–135].

5 Conclusion

The objective of this paper was to show the structure and realities of the e-Society in Sub-Saharan Africa followed by the specific case of Ivory Coast. Firstly, the observation is that Sub-Saharan Africa is undergoing an organizational transformation with the adoption of digital technology. The majority of governments have committed themselves to ICT projects and in particular e-Government development. There are very few successful Government-Type Organization projects, fundamentally because the real needs of the populations have not been taken into account. The local actors highlighted by the scientific literature have been the poor qualities of infrastructures, the high cost of computers and the Internet, illiteracy, a digital divide that persists at a rate of 60% globally and 74% in sub-Saharan Africa Saharan Africa. There is a sense that there is a lack of political will to free up Internet governance in the world. Secondly, Sub-Saharan Africa has become dependent on ICTs and particularly the Internet, as all the countries of the world because it has adopted e-Society. This society facilitates and simplifies life. This has been possible due to globalization, the liberalization of telecommunications and the adoption of ICTs by the government, businesses, and citizens. ICTs have made it possible for humanity to be at the center of the problems of development, industrial, technological and digital changes in our countries. Communication, health, education and training, trade, access to services, to name but a few, are now being realized in the construction of the e-Society. Moreover, what is alarming is the fate of many illiterate and poor people who are concentrated in the sub-Saharan Africa area. Conversely, the e-Society, through this study, has shown two forms in its organizational perspectives, namely: a Government-Type Organization (e-Government, e-Commerce, e-Education, e-Health, e-Agriculture) which hardly dominates the field as well as a

Private-Type Organization (Communities or private platforms, working groups and academic exchanges, social networks, e-Banking ...) which is expanding.

It is generally the work of private companies and communities that aspire knowledge. It would, therefore, be wise for African governments to encourage the e-Society because it is the basis for bringing people together. It also removes the barriers that complicate life and procedures, subsequently shortening time and distance as well as solving many problems in the city. Finally, significant ongoing engagement of decision-makers in all sub-Saharan African countries is required for a real development of conditions for the motivation of citizens and all stakeholders. This serves to simplify and reduce the cost of the Internet and computer hardware which these people need, to change their lives. For future works, we plan to investigate e-Society and the digital economy in Sub-Saharan Africa in order to ascertain that e-Society investment has been done, but also to know that these investments have left a legacy of economic and social benefits. As well, we will also shortly be looking at another questionable issue in this respect to demonstrate how smart cities come as a product of e-Society in various developed countries. This information will be used to capture the attention of decision-makers and investors in sub-Saharan African countries likely to boost the digital transformation.

References

1. Samassekou, A.: Avant-Propos le Sommet Mondial sur la Société de l'Information: Préparation, Enjeux et Résultats de la Première Phase. Revue québécoise de droit international **18**, 13 (2005)
2. Isabelle, C.: La Société numérique en question(s) pp. 11–12. Sciences Humaines Éditions, Auxerre, France (2011)
3. UN and UIT.: Sommet Mondial sur la Société de l'Information. Rapport final de la troisième réunion (suite) du Comité de préparation. Genève, 10–14 novembre, 5-6 et 9 décembre 2003. (2004), http://www.itu.int/dms_pub/itu-s/md/03/wsispc3/doc/S03-WSISPC3-DOC-0015!!PDF-F.pdf
4. Banque Mondiale.: Rapport sur le Développement dans le monde 2016: Les dividendes du numérique (Abrégé), (2016), https://doi.org/10.1596/978-1-4648-0671-1. http://documents.worldbank.org/curated/en/527621468195004729/pdf/102724-WDR-WDR2016Overview-FRENCH-WebResBox-394840B-OUO-9.pdf
5. Komninos, N.: Intelligent Cities and Globalization of Innovation Networks. Routledge, Abingdon on Thames (2008)
6. Li, Y., Lin, Y., Geertman, S.: The development of smart cities in China. CUPUM (Comput. Urban Plan. Urban Manag.), 1–20 (2015). http://web.mit.edu/cron/project/CUPUM2015/proceedings/Content/pss/291_li_h.pdf
7. Osburg, T., Schmidpeter, R.: Social Innovation Solution for Sustainable Future. Springer, Berlin (2013)
8. Colin, N., et al.: Économie numérique. Notes du conseil d'analyse économique **26**(7), 1–12 (2015)
9. Bomsel, O.: Gratuit! Du déploiement de l'économie numérique. Folio Actuel, Editions Gallimard (2007)
10. Bonjawo, J.: Révolution numérique dans les pays en développement: l'exemple africain. Dunod, Paris (2011)

11. Conte, B.: La fracture numérique en Afrique. Univeristé Montesquieu, Bordeaux (2001). http://ged.u-bordeaux4.fr/ceddt65.pdf
12. Fuchs, C., Horak, E.: Africa and the digital divide. Telematics Inf. **25**(2), 99–116 (2008). https://doi.org/10.1016/j.tele.2006.06.004, http://fuchs.uti.at/wp-content/uploads/divide.pdf
13. Kiyindou, A.: La place des savoirs africains sur Internet ou penser «la fracture numérique» par le contenu. Réduire les fractures numériques nord-Sud, quels enjeux **5**, 1–63 (2004)
14. Guichard, É.: Le mythe de la fracture numérique. Regards croisés sur l'internet, 69–100 (2011)
15. UNDP.: Rapport sur le développement humain 2015: Le travail au service du développement humain. UNDP, New York (2016)
16. Staff, I.M.F.: Globalization: Threat or Opportunity? Issues Brief (2000). http://www.imf.org/external/np/exr/ib/2000/041200to.htm
17. Habermas, J.: The Structural Transformation of the Public Sphere: An Inquiry into a Category of Bourgeois Society. MIT press (1991)
18. Calhoun, C.J. (eds.): Habermas and the Public Sphere. MIT Press (1992)
19. Bailo, F.: Mapping online political talks through network analysis: a case study of the website of Italy's Five Star Movement. Policy Stud. **36**(6), 550–572 (2015)
20. Habermas, J.: La technique et la science comme "idéologie". Gallimard, Paris (1973)
21. Rogers, E.M.: Diffusion of Innovations, 4th edn. The Free Press, New York (1995)
22. ITU: Measuring the Information Society Report. Geneva (2016), https://www.itu.int/en/ITU-D/Statistics/Documents/publications/misr2016/MISR2016-w4.pdf
23. Magoulas, G.D., Lepouras, G., Vassilakis, C.: Virtual reality in the e-society. Virtual Reality **11**(2), 71–73 (2007)
24. Rovai, A.: Building sense of community at a distance. Int. Rev. Res. Open Distance Learn. **3** (1), 4 (2002). http://doi.org/10.19173/IRRODL.V3I1.79
25. Longley, P.A., Webber, R., Li, C.: The UK geography of the e-society: a national classification. Environ. Plann. A **40**(2), 362–382 (2008)
26. El-Diraby, T.E., Wang, B.: E-Society portal: integrating urban highway construction projects into the knowledge city. J. Constr. Eng. Manag. **131**(11), 1196–1211 (2005)
27. Giuffre, K.: Communities and Networks: Using Social Network Analysis to Rethink Urban and Community Studies. Wiley, New York (2013)
28. Lee Shun, Y.: E-Society. (Bachelor of Computer Science). University Malaysia Pahang (2012). http://umpir.ump.edu.my/5097/1/CD6543.pdf
29. African Development Bank Group.: Strategy for higher education, science and technology. In: Indicative OSHD. 2 Pipeline of Projects 2008–2010 (2008). http://www.afdb.org/filead min/uploads/afdb/Documents/Policy-Documents/10000019-EN-STRATEGY-FOR-HIGHER-EDUCATION-SCIENCE-AND-TECHNOLOGY.PDF
30. Agence Française de Développement, Agence universitaire de la Francophonie, UNESCO & Orange: Le numérique au service de l'éducation en Afrique. In Savoir commun no. 17, p. 99 (2015). http://www.afd.fr/webdav/shared/PUBLICATIONS/THEMATIQUES/savoirscomm uns/17-Savoirs-communs-VF.pdf
31. Kodjo, E.: L'Afrique face aux défis de la science et de la technique. In: John, L (ed.) Francophonie scientifique: le tournant, pp. 45–54. AUPELF-UREF, Paris (1989). http://www.bibliotheque.auf.org/doc_num.php?explnum_id=472
32. Maxime, B.S.: «La Problématique de l'Industrialisation de l 'Afrique, la nécessité d'une reformulation», 11ème Assemblée générale du codesria Maputo (MOZAMBIQUE) du 6 au 10 Décembre 2005. p. 1 (2005). https://codesria.org/IMG/pdf/bikoue.pdf
33. Leiner, B.M., et al.: A brief history of the internet. ACM SIGCOMM Comput. Commun. Rev. **39**(5), 22–31 (2009). http://doi.org/10.1145/1629607.1629613
34. Ifinedo, P.: Measuring Africa's e-readiness in the global networked economy: a nine-country data analysis. Int. J. Educ. Dev. Using Inf. Commun. Technol. (IJEDICT), **1**(I), 53–71 (2005)

35. Gichoya, D.M.: Government Informatics: Toward the Successful Implementation of ICT Projects in Kenya. Doctoral Dissertation, Loughborough University, p. 67 (2007)
36. Mbengue, M.: Enjeux et pratiques de la gouvernance électronique en Afrique de l'Ouest/The Issues and Practices of e-governance in West Africa. International Federation of Library Associations and Institutions. Dakar: IFLA, pp. 1–12 (2009). http://www.ifla.org/files/assets/ faife/publications/misc/issues-and-practices-of-e-governance-in-west-africa-fr.pdf
37. ECA.: The African Information Society Initiative (AISI): A decade's perspective. Economic Commission for Africa, Addis Ababa, Ethiopia (2008). https://www.uneca.org/sites/default/ files/PublicationFiles/aisiplus10.pdf
38. Bogui, M.J.J.: Intégration et usages des Technologies de l'information et de la communi- cation (TIC) dans l'éducation en Afrique: Situation de l'enseignement supérieur en Côte d'Ivoire (2003–2005). Doctoral dissertation, Université Michel de Montaigne-Bordeaux III (2007)
39. Dzidonu, C.: An analysis of the role of ICTs to achieving the MDGs. The Division for Public Administration and Development Management of the United Nations Department of Economic and Social Affairs (UNDESA), pp. 15–18 (2010). http://unpan1.un.org/intradoc/ groups/public/documents/UN-DPADM/UNPAN039075.pdf
40. Kayisire, D., Wei, J.: ICT adoption and usage in Africa: towards an efficiency assessment. Inf. Technol. Dev. 22(4), 630–653 (2016)
41. Jahangirian, M., Taylor, S.J.: Profiling e-health projects in Africa: trends and funding patterns. Inf. Dev. 31(3), 199–218 (2015)
42. Keyter, C.: New Solutions, Enduring Challenges—The Case for Public Sector Reform in Sub-Saharan Africa Re-examined, 3–11 (2007). http://unpan1.un.org/intradoc/groups/ public/documents/AAPAM/UNPAN029854.pdf
43. Union Internationale des Télécommunications (UIT).: Rapport Mesurer la société de l'information 2015: résumé analytique. Genève, Suisse, p. 35 (2015). https://www.itu.int/en/ ITU-D/Statistics/Documents/publications/misr2015/MISR2015-ES-F.pdf
44. UNESCO, Rapport Mondial: Vers les sociétés du savoir, Paris, Editions UNESCO, p. 5 (2005)
45. United Nations.: E-Government Survey 2014: e-Government for the Future We Want. United Nations: New York. pp. 67–72 (2014). https://publicadministration.un.org/egovkb/ Portals/egovkb/Documents/un/2014-Survey/E-Gov_Complete_Survey-2014.pdf
46. Peña-López, I., et al.: UN e-Government Survey 2016. E-Government in Support of Sustainable Development (2016)
47. SciDev.Net, http://www.scidev.net/afrique-sub-saharienne/communication/actualites/lance ment-d-un-forum-scientifique-parlementaire-panafricain.html
48. Union Interparlementaire.: Rapport mondial 2016 sur l'e-Parlement. Genève, Suisse (2016). http://www.ipu.org/pdf/publications/eparl16-fr.pdf
49. Inter-Parliamentary Union.: Youth participation in national parliaments 2016. 15, 12–15 (2016). http://doi.org/10.1332/policypress/9781447300182.001.0001
50. Loukou, A.F.: Les TIC au service du développement en Afrique. Simple slogan, illusion ou réalité?. tic&société 5(2–3) (2012)
51. Schuppan, T.: E-Government in developing countries: experiences from sub-Saharan Africa. Gov. Inf. Q. 26(1), 118–127 (2009). https://doi.org/10.1016/j.giq.2008.01.006
52. African Alliance for Electronic Commerce (AACE), http://swguide.org/guichet_unique/ AACE_guide_pratique_Guichets_Uniques_2013.pdf
53. United, N.: La pratique du commerce électronique 2013-CEDEAO. Genève, Suisse (2013)
54. UNECA.: Guichet unique: un outil pour la facilitation des échanges, pp. 40–44 (2008). http://www1.uneca.org/Portals/atpc/CrossArticle/1/Events_Documents/WorkshopMarch09/ GuichetUnique.pdf
55. ICTSD et Enda Caid: La facilitation des échanges: une priorité pour le continent? Passerelle 17(6) (2016). http://www.ictsd.org/sites/default/files/passerelles_aout_2016.pdf
56. OMC: Rapport annual 2011 de l'OMC. Genève, Suisse, pp. 120–132 (2011). https://www. wto.org/french/res_f/booksp_f/anrep_f/anrep11_f.pdf

57. Ng'ethe, N.: Amélioration en matière d'innovations dans l'enseignement supérieur: Les innovations dans les Universités en Afrique. Conférence Régionale de Formation, *Accra*, 23–25 Septembre (2003)
58. Stockley, D.: E-learning definition and explanation (E learning, Online training, Online learning) 15, 2010 (2003), http://www.derekstockley.com.au/elearning-definition.html
59. Association for the Development of Education in Africa (ADEA).: The integration of ICT into education and training systems in Africa: the cases of Argentina, Burkina Faso, Cote d'Ivoire, Paraguay, Senegal, Tunisia, Uruguay (2014)
60. Betchoo, N.K.: Sub-Saharan Africa's Perspective of distance learning. Int. Lett. Soc. Humanistic Sci. **48**, 185–191 (2015)
61. Janssens-bevernage, A., Stern, R.: Facilitated e-learning in Sub-Saharan Africa, 5–8 (2006). http://www.reading.ac.uk/ssc/resources/Docs/Facilitated%20e-learning%20in%20sub-Saharan%20Africa.pdf
62. Ryan, A., et al.: Developing e-Learning in palliative care education in Sub-Saharan Africa: ideas and examples for the selection of appropriate media and technology. Palliative care report, 1–55 (2012). https://doi.org/10.1314/rg.22.2.36302.05449
63. Government of Canada.: eHeath. https://www.canada.ca/en/health-canada/services/first-nations-inuit-health/health-care-services/ehealth.html
64. Leem (Les entreprises du médicament).: La sante mobile pourrait sauver un million de vie en Afrique Sub-saharienne d'ici 2017. Rencontre LEEM/OIF/Delegations Francophones 2015. http://www.leem.org/sante-mobile-pourrait-sauver-un-million-de-vies-en-afrique-subsaharienne-d-ici-2017
65. OMS.: Cybersanté: outils et services proposes. Rapport du Secrétariat, no.EB117/15, pp. 1–6 (2005). http://apps.who.int/iris/bitstream/10665/21629/1/B117_15-fr.pdf
66. OMS.: Cybersanté et noms de domaine Internet pour la santé. Rapport du Secrétariat, no. A66/26 du 14 Mai 2013, pp. 1–4 (2013). http://apps.who.int/gb/ebwha/pdf_files/WHA66/A66_26-fr.pdf
67. Hugon, P.: L'agriculture en Afrique sub-saharienne: enjeux et perspectives. Oléagineux, Corps Gras Lipides **6**(9), 409–415 (2002). DOI:htt://dx.doi.org./https://doi.org/10.1051/ocl. 2002.0409, http://www.ocl-journal.org/articles/ocl/pdf/2002/06/ocl200296p409.pdf
68. Mondiale, B.: L'Agriculture au service du développement (Rapport sur le développement dans le monde 2008). Banque Mondiale, Washington (2007)
69. Namisiko, P., Aballo, M.: Current status of e-agriculture and global trends: a survey conducted in TransNzoia County, Kenya. Int J Sci Res **2**, 2319–7064 (2013)
70. World Bank and African Development Bank.: The Transformational Use of Information and Communication Technologies in Africa. Washington, DC, USA, pp. 44–46 (2013). https://www.afdb.org/fileadmin/uploads/afdb/Documents/Publications/The_Transformational_Use_of_Information_and_Communication_Technologies_in_Africa.pdf
71. Baumüller, H.: Agricultural Innovation and Service Delivery through Mobile Phones. Analyses in Kenya. Doctoral Dissertation, Center for Development Research-The Faculty of Agriculture, University of Bonn, pp. 59–100 (2015). http://hss.ulb.uni-bonn.de/2015/4046/4046.pdf
72. Yonazi, E. et al.: The transformational use of information and communication technologies in Africa (2012). https://openknowledge.worldbank.org/bitstream/handle/10986/26791/NonAsciiFileName0.pdf?sequence=1&isAllowed=y
73. Mbarika, V.W., et al.: Community-Based Information Technology Access: The Case of Cybercafe Diffusion in Sub-Saharan Africa (2006). https://repository.upenn.edu/cgi/viewcontent.cgi?referer=https://scholar.google.com/&httpsredir=1&article=1014&context=ictafrica
74. Mbarika, V., Jensen, M., Meso, P.: Cyberspace across sub-Saharan Africa. Commun. ACM **45**(12), 17–21 (2002)
75. Tchouassi, G.: Can mobile phones really work to extend banking services to the unbanked? Empirical lessons from selected Sub-Saharan Africa Countries. Int. J. Developing Soc. **1**(2), 70–81 (2012)

76. Agwu, M.E., Carter, A.L.: Mobile phone banking in Nigeria: benefits, problems and prospects. Int. J. Bus. Commer. **3**(6), 50–70 (2014)
77. Akuffo-Twum, E.: The Effect of Internet Banking on the Ghanaian Banking Industry-a Case of Cal Bank, Unibank and Prudential Bank. Doctoral dissertation, Institute of Distance learning, Kwame Nkrumah University of Science and Technology (2011)
78. Fekadu, G.W.: Electronic Banking in Ethiopia: Practices, Opportunities and Challenges (2009). https://doi.org/10.2139/ssrn.1492006
79. Desbordes, F., et al.: Sociétés africaines de l'information, Vol. 2: Recherches et actions en Afrique de l'Ouest francophone (2012). http://www.diplomatie.gouv.fr/fr/IMG/pdf/SAI_cle89a963-1.pdf
80. Toure, K.: Formality and Flexibility in Planning for Research: Case of the International Development Research Centre (IDRC) (2010)
81. Palmer, N.: Using ICT to enable agricultural innovation systems for smallholders ICT innovations. E-Agriculture, 1–11(2012)
82. Meijer, S.S., et al.: The role of knowledge, attitudes and perceptions in the uptake of agricultural and agroforestry innovations among smallholder farmers in sub-Saharan Africa. Int. J. Agric. Sustain. **13**(1), 40–54 (2015)
83. Donner, J.: The use of mobile phones by microentrepreneurs in Kigali, Rwanda: changes to social and business networks. Inf. Technol. Int. Dev. **3**(2), 3–19 (2006)
84. Doss, C.R.: Designing agricultural technology for African women farmers: lessons from 25 years of experience. World Dev. **29**(12), 2075–2092 (2001)
85. Oyinloye, A.M.: Electronic networking of libraries and the development of an information society in Africa. Inf. Dev. **15**(4), 217–222 (1999). https://doi.org/10.1177/026666 6994239985
86. Rifkin, J.: L'ère de l'accès – La révolution de la nouvelle économie, La Dé- couverte, Paris, p. 22 (2000)
87. Péjout, Nicolas: "Les nouvelles techno-logies de l'information et de la communication en Afrique du Sud: Les mots de la fracture ou la rhétorique du numérique." Les fractures numériques nord/sud en question Netsuds no. 1, 7–25 (2003). http://www.africanti.sciencespobordeaux.fr/resultats/colloque2003/Communications/PEJOUT5.pdf
88. Renaud, P.: Historique de l'internet du Nord au Sud. Enjeux des technologies de la communication en Afrique: du téléphone à internet, CHENEAU-LOQUAY, Annie (dir.). Paris, l'Harmattan (2000)
89. ATCI.: Historique Abonnes—Internet, p. 30 (2014). http://www.artci.ci/index.php/Internet/historique-abonnes-internet.html
90. Panos Institute West Africa (PIWA) and the United Nations Development Programme (UNDP).: E-governance and Citizen Participation in West Africa: Challenges and Opportunities. Dakar, Senegal and New York: PIWA and UNDP, p. 47 (2011). http://unpan1.un.org/intradoc/groups/public/documents/UN-DPADM/UNPAN045433.pdf
91. Hafkin, N.: E-government in Africa: an overview of progress made and challenges ahead. In Prepared for the UNDESA/UNPAN workshop on electronic/mobile government in Africa: Building Capacity in Knowledge Management through Partnership. United Nations Economic Commission for Africa, 17–19 Feb 2009. http://unpan1.un.org/intradoc/groups/un/documents/un/unpan034002.pdf
92. World Markets Research Centre and Brown University, USA.: Global e-Government Survey. Rhode Island Providence, p. 11 (2001). http://unpan1.un.org/intradoc/groups/public/documents/caricad/unpan008523.pdf
93. United Nations-DPEPA: Benchmarking E-government.: A Global Perspective ... Assessing the Progress of the UN Member States, pp. 30–33 (2002). https://publicadministration.un.org/egovkb/Portals/egovkb/Documents/un/English.pdf
94. Duhamel, S.: Rapport au Ministre de l'Economie et des Finances - Mission de diagnostic sur le Cadre de Normes visant à sécuriser et à faciliter le commerce mondial (Programme Colombus). Direction Générale des Douanes de Côte d'Ivoire, Abidjan, pp. 7–19. (2007). http://www.douanes.ci/admin/docs/27.pdf

95. Guce.gouv.ci.: The National Single Window for Foreign Trade in Ivory Coast. (2013). https://guce.gouv.ci/ or https://guce.gouv.ci/downloads?lang=en_GB

96. Pepe, M.: «Le vote électronique: ses forces et ses faiblesses». In: Fraternité-Matin, (2005). Récupéré avec Ndiaye, M. (2006). E-Gouvernement et Démocratie en Afrique: Le Sénégal dans la Mondialisation des Pratiques. Thèse de doctorat. Université Michel de Montaigne-Bordeaux-3

97. LS/APA: Le vote en Côte d'Ivoire sera "électronique" pendant les prochaines élections (Alassane Ouattara). In Agence de Presse Africaine (2013). http://news.abidjan.net/h/458783.html

98. N'Guessan, N.: Le passeport biométrique (2008). http://www.loidici.com/piecesadm/piecesadmpasseport.php

99. Diebkile, S.: Passeport ordinaire biométrique république cote d'ivoire: document type communication. Gouv.ci - édition 2009, (2012). http://ambaci-dakar.org/fr/wp-content/uploads/2012/05/Passport_ordinaire_biometrique.pdf

100. Bogui, J.J.: Intégration et usages des Technologies de l'Information et de la Communication (TIC) dans l'Éducation en Afrique: Situation de l'enseignement supérieur en Côte d'Ivoire (2003–2005). Thèse de doctorat, Université Michel de Montaigne—Bordeaux III, France, pp. 105–106 & 164 (2007)

101. Mian, B.: Le statut des TIC en éducation: cas de la Côte d'Ivoire. ROCARE/EDUCI, Afr educ dev issues, 137–155 (2012). http://www.rocare.org/aedi4/ch6-AEDI4.pdf

102. Bogui, J.J.: Usages et appropriation des TIC par les jeunes ivoiriens: de l'espoir au désenchantement. Tic & Développement-Le Net et ses démons **4**, 1–11 (2009). http://www.tic.ird.fr/IMG/pdf/BOGU-NetEtSesDemons.pdf

103. Loukou Alain François: La diffusion de l'Internet en Côte d'Ivoire. Obstacles et implications. Netw. Commun. Stud. NETCOM, **26**(3/4), 307–328 (2012). https://doi.org/10.4000/netcom.1045

104. Yaya, O. et al.: Internet dans les métropoles africaines: le cas d'Abidjan. TIC & Développement, vol. 3 (2007). http://www.tic.ird.fr/spip5d42.html?article225

105. Central Intelligence Agency (Ed.).: The World Factbook 2014–15. Government Printing Office (2015). https://www.cia.gov/library/publications/the-world-factbook/geos/iv.html

106. RGPH: Recensement Général de la Population et de l'Habitat de la Côte d'Ivoire 2014: Rapport d'exécution et présentation des principaux résultats (2014). http://www.ins.ci/n/documents/RGPH2014_expo_dg.pdf

107. Polyconseil.: Digital natives et nouveaux usages medias: comment s'y adapter? Livre Blanc – Octobre 2012, pp. 4–8 (2012)

108. Francis, P., Dominique, P.: Comment le web change le monde: L'alchimie des multitudes. Pearson Education France (2008)

109. CCIP (Chambre de Commerce et d'Industrie de Paris).: Mission TIC en Côte d'Ivoire à l'occasion des 12ème Journées Nationales des TIC (JNTIC 2012) (2012). http://www.systematic-paris-region.org/fr/evenements/ccip-mission-de-prospection-tic-en-cote-divoire

110. ATCI: Historique Abonnes—Internet (2014). http://www.artci.ci/index.php/Internet/historique-abonnes-internet.html

111. Mian, B.: Côte d'Ivoire: le taux de pénétration de l'internet boosté par le mobile (2015). http://www.ticeduforum.ci/cote-divoire-le-taux-de-penetration-de-linternet-booste-par-le-mobile/

112. Bahi, A.: Usages d'Internet et logiques d'adaptation sociale des jeunes dans des cybercafés abidjanais. Bull. du Codesria **1**, 67–71 (2004)

113. Bahi, A.: TIC, pratiques de recherche d'information et production du savoir des enseignants-chercheurs universitaires ivoiriens. Revue africaine des médias **15**, Numéros 1&2, 125–149 (2007). http://www.codesria.org/IMG/pdf/AMR_15_1_2_2007_7_Bahi.pdf

114. Bahi, A., et Dakouri, G.: Internet et enjeux de pouvoir dans le champ universitaire ivoirien. Revue africaine des médias **16**(1), 91–107 (2008)

115. Mian, B.S.A.: L'apprentissage mobile en formation initiale des enseignants à l'ENS d'Abidjan/Mobile learning in teacher training at ENS Abidjan. Frantice. net, TICE et qualité en éducation **5**, 63–72 (2012)
116. Khelfaoui, H.: La science en Côte d'Ivoire. In: Waast, R., Gaillard, J (éds.) La Science en Afrique à l'Aube du 21e siècle. Rapport Final. IRD, Paris (2000). http://horizon. documentation.ird.fr/exl-doc/pleins_textes/divers07-09/010033547.pdf
117. Foster, V., Pushak, N.: Côte d'Ivoire's Infrastructure: A Continental Perspective. Rapport pays AICD, pp. 32–35 (Mars 2010). https://library.pppknowledgelab.org/attached_files/ translations/57/original/AICD-CDI-Rapport-Pays.pdf?1466190752
118. CICG.: Bilan 2011–2015.gouv.ci. «Plateforme Officielle pour accéder au Bilan du Gouvernement 2011–2015 (voir Dossier TIC)». Abidjan, Cote d'Ivoire (2015). http:// www.bilan2011-2015.gouv.ci/
119. Pénicaud, C.: Mobile Money in Côte d'Ivoire: A Turnaround Story, pp. 2–4 (2014). http:// www.gsma.com/mobilefordevelopment/wp-content/uploads/2014/05/MMU_Cote_dIvoire_ Turnaround_Story.pdf
120. United Nations.: UN Global E-Government Survey 2003. United Nations: New York, p. 35 (2003). https://publicadministration.un.org/egovkb/Portals/egovkb/Documents/un/2003-Survey/Complete-Survey.pdf
121. Dédé, D.: Panorama des TIC en Côte d'Ivoire. Presentation. Abidjan, Côte d'Ivoire, pp. 36–40 (2009). http://www.gouv.ci/doc/E_PRESENTATION_MINISTERE_NTIC_2.pdf
122. Cabinet du Premier Ministre: Arrêté No.18/PM/CAB/du 13 Oct.2009: portant création, attributions et fonctionnement du comité interministériel de gestion du projet de gouvernement électronique en Côte d'Ivoire (2009). http://www.egouv.ci/sites/default/ files/EGOUV_Arrete_PM_Octobre_2009.pdf
123. Koné, B.: Rôle de la gouvernance électronique dans une économie émergente: enjeux et perspectives en Côte d'Ivoire d'ici à 2020. In Les Rendez-vous du Gouvernement. Op. cit., pp. 42–44 (2014). http://www.gouv.ci/doc/PPT%20MPTIC%20%5BMode%20de% 20compatibilit%E9%5D.pdf
124. Maslow, A.H.: A theory of human motivation **13**, 370–396 (1943). http://apps. fischlerschool.nova.edu/toolbox/instructionalproducts/edd8124/articles/1943-Maslow.pdf
125. Munyoka, W., Manzira, M.F.: From E-Government to M-Government—challenges faced by Sub-Saharan Africa. In: The International Conference on Computing Technology and Information Management (ICCTIM). Society of Digital Information and Wireless Communication, pp. 86–99 (2014)
126. Jayashree, S., Marthandan, G.: Government to E-government to E-society. J. Appl. Sci. **10** (19), 2205–2210 (2010). https://doi.org/10.3923/jas.2010.2205.2210
127. Grimus, M., Ebner, M.: M-learning in Sub Saharan Africa context- what is it about. In: Proceedings of World Conference on Educational Multimedia, Hypermedia and Telecommunications 2013. AACE, Chesapeake, 2028–2033 (2013). https://www.resea rchgate.net/publication/283727687_M-Learning_in_Sub_Saharan_Africa_Context-_What_is_ it_about
128. Heeks, R.: Failure, Success and Improvisation of Information Systems Projects in Developing Countries (paper No. 11). Manchester, UK (2002). http://unpan1.un.org/ intradoc/groups/public/documents/NISPAcee/UNPAN015601.pdf
129. Ngulube, P.: The nature and accessibility of E-Government in Sub Saharan Africa. Int. Rev. Inf. Ethics **7**(9), 1–13 (2007). http://fiz1.fh-potsdam.de/volltext/ijie/08092.pdf
130. Duriez, J.: Les incubateurs se multiplient en Afrique Sub-saharienne (2015). http://www.la-croix. com/Actualite/Monde/Afrique/Les-incubateurs-se-multiplient-en-Afrique-subsaharienne-2015-11-17-1381304
131. Buskens, Ineke: et Anne Webb: Les Africaines et les TIC: enquête sur les technologies, la question de genre et autonomisation. Les Presses de l'Université Laval, Québec (2011)
132. Chikerema, A.F.: Citizen participation and local democracy in Zimbabwean Local Government System. IOSR J. Humanit. Soc. Sci. (IOSR-JHSS) **13**(2), 87–90 (2013)

133. Simon, I.: Le numérique, incubateur d'innovation en Afrique (2016). https://portail-ie.fr/
     analysis/1398/le-numerique-incubateur-dinnovations-en-afrique
134. Bogui, J.J.: La Cybercriminalité, menace pour le développement: les escroqueries internet en
     Côte d'Ivoire. Afrique contemporaine **234**(2), 155–170 (2010)
135. Gonzales, C., Dechanet, J.: L'essor du numérique en Afrique de l'Ouest: Entre opportunités
     économiques et cybermenaces. Paris, France: CEIS-Les notes σtratégiques (2015). https://
     www.securitydaysn.com/Data/kmsecuritydaysn/block/F_97c2bc46b77e0f4f18b147496d63b
     be0563cdb68d2d07.pdf
136. Ibrahim Coulibaly: La lutte contre la cybercriminalité en Côte d'Ivoire: une réalité (2014).
     http://www.village-justice.com/articles/lutte-contre-cybercriminalite-Cote,17336.html

Disclosure and Communication of the Corporate Social Responsibility (CSR) in Morocco: The Case of a Bank

Wadi Tahri and Abdelbari El Khamlichi

Abstract Companies have been concerned more and more with the way they approach social and environmental dimensions. A number of companies consider social engagement as a deliberate option based on the will to respect the society and the environment, while others believe that it is essential. Many perceptions are in competition due to the absence of the standardization of the CSR practices. Accordingly, there is a need, particularly in the case of banks, for a supplementary effort to be made in terms of disclosure and communication so as to deserve the confidence of stakeholders. This article aims at clarifying the CSR concept, its practices along with their evolution in time in the Moroccan context. Our methodology consists of a thematic analysis using Nvivo and annual reports of a Moroccan bank during the period of 2007–2015. The objective of this study is the evaluation of the bank's engagement in the sustainable development in reference to the seven principles of ISO 26000.

Keywords CSR · Bank · Information and communication · Annual reports · ISO 26000

W. Tahri (✉) · A. El Khamlichi
LERSEM, University Chouaib Doukkali, ENCG El Jadida, El Jadida, Morocco
e-mail: wadi.tahri@gmail.com

A. El Khamlichi
e-mail: abdelbari.elkhamlichi@gmail.com

W. Tahri
MRM, Montpellier, France

A. El Khamlichi
CRCGM, Clermont Ferrand, France

© Springer Nature Switzerland AG 2019
Y. Baghdadi and A. Harfouche (eds.), *ICT for a Better Life and a Better World*,
Lecture Notes in Information Systems and Organisation 30,
https://doi.org/10.1007/978-3-030-10737-6_16

1   Introduction

The Corporate Social Responsibility (CSR) has been subject to an important process of improvement since its beginning [1, 2]. Besides, the CSR's components have been investigated for years now [3]. Businesses are asked to account for their practices in the field of CSR and sustainable development. The CSR notion is usually perceived through the integration of three basic constituents (social, economic and environmental). However, a number of controversies rise about the definition and the consensus on its application across the globe. Despite the positive efforts that have been made in this respect, the CSR practices are not stabilized yet. There is still much work to be done.

What about the Moroccan experience as far as the CSR is concerned? There is much debate about the notion in this part of the world. In accordance with its international declaration of Johannesburg in 2002, the Moroccan government has adopted a strategy that incorporates the concept of sustainable development encouraging equilibrium between the environmental, economic and social dimensions. The illustration of this political shown in a number of very significant events: the implementation of the National Initiative for Human Development (INDH), the country's adhesion to the Global Compact in 2005 and 2006, along with the organization of the COP 22 (November 2016) in Marrakesh.

As such, banks have responded to this approach through the publication of a charter of responsibilities in their web sites [4, 5], so as to define their engagements, to obtain the confidence of their stakeholders, and to precise the method whereby they conceive their (economic, social, and environmental) responsibilities. Therefore, we suggest a longitudinal study of a bank to refer to the implementation of the CSR notion within the Moroccan context. Since our objective is investigating the practices and their evolutions, we are interested in the disclosure of the CSR in the annual reports. This will help make businesses' engagement in terms of social responsibility more verifiable and more credible [6].

This research consists of two parts: the first part is devoted to the theoretical study of the CSR concept and its communication. The second part is concerned with the investigation of the used research methodology and the main results of the study.

2   Theoretical Background

Definitions and theories are formulated in this part, to explain and extend existing knowledge about the CSR concept, especially in the Moroccan context.

2.1 The CSR: Definitions and General Context

There exists no consensus on any definition of the CSR as the observed practices of the notion seem very variable from one business to another and from one culture to another.

We will refer to the definition of the AFNOR which is the most commonly used. The Corporate Social Responsibility is defined according to the ISO 26000 standard as the responsibility of a business in regards to the impacts of its decisions and its activities on both society and environment through a transparent and ethical conduct that:

- Contributes to the sustainable development of the society, including health and welfare;
- Takes into consideration the expectations of the stakeholders;
- Respects laws in force and compatible with the international norms;
- Is integrated in the whole organization and application of the business's relations.

It has become vital for businesses to take the social dimension into account. A number of enterprises think that social engagement is a deliberate option based on the will to respect the society, the environment and all the stakeholders; while others believe that it is a compulsory decision in a constantly changing environment.

Due to the absence of standardization of the CSR norms, many ethical perceptions have appeared and, consequently, a number of social rating agencies have been created. Each of these agencies offers their point of view on the subject matter [7]. Therefore, supplementary efforts must be made in terms of transparency and communication [8]. There exist many referential norms and certifications, but we would basically refer to the ISO 26000 which underlines 7 rules of the CSR (Fig. 1) and helps organizations adopt the most suitable and effective practices.

It suggests, above all, the identification of its social responsibility, the communication with all its stakeholders and the extension of this responsibility to different fields of application. In fact, the fields of CSR are diverse that they can also cover education, quality of personnel, ergonomics, and environment. The tools which companies can reach are also diversified, and may take the form of ethical codes, labels, social standards, publications about the company's commitment in regards to the CSR [9].

If companies can benefit from their ethical commitment, the implementation of a CSR strategy may entail, on the other hand, additional costs. According to those who support CSR, it is rather the lack of a social commitment that leads to difficulties in the management of organizations. In fact, the recurrent crises on the international scale, whose dimensions are multiple (social, environmental, financial,

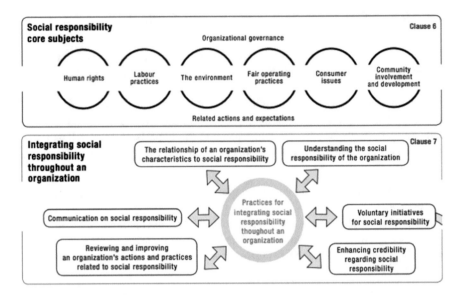

Fig. 1 Schematic overview of ISO 26000

etc.), can be seen as an illustration. The concrete benefits to be derived from a CSR policy are numerous, such as efficiency improvement, energy saving, customer satisfaction, exploration of new activities with high value added to the environment, mobilization of personnel around a unifying project, incorporation of stakeholders in a win-win approach, establishment of good relations with investors who share the same standards, etc....

However, opponents of the notion in question argue that deploying ethics in business is merely a lie or rather a dream hard to make come true. The example of "green-washing" can be stated in this respect, some companies increase their advertising spending in order to be regarded as socially responsible companies, without being accompanied by real actions in favor of the environment, employees and the society in general. This could negatively impact the financial performance of the company [10].

According to this point of view, the main mission of a company is maximizing its economic benefits, without taking social or environmental considerations into account. Furthermore, other researchers consider that the imposition of certain rules related to social responsibility can be counterproductive [11] and may create additional difficulties and constraints within these companies. Besides, the implementation of the rules of good conduct entails supplementary costs, imposed particularly by the social constraints, though these costs prove to be low [12] compared to the expected benefits.

2.2 CSR Practices in Morocco

In Morocco, a charter of social responsibility has been adopted by the General Confederation of Moroccan Companies (CGEM) since 2006. During these 10 years, the number of companies awarded the label has reached 72. In accordance with the will of labeled companies, The CGEM refers to the ISO 26000 standard specifying the guidelines of social responsibility of organizations. According to the CGEM, the attribution of the label is conditioned upon the adoption of an ethical and transparent conduct which:

- Contributes to sustainable development, including health and welfare of the society;
- Takes into account the expectations of all stakeholders;
- Respects the laws in force in consistence with the international standards of conduct;
- Is integrated throughout the organization and implemented in its relationships.

In addition to the nine pillars of the commitment being defined according to the Charter of the CGEM Label for the Social Responsibility of the Company:

1. Respecting Human Rights
2. Continuously improving employment and working conditions as well as professional relationships
3. Protecting the Environment
4. Preventing corruption
5. Respecting the rules of healthy competition
6. Strengthening the transparency of corporate governance
7. Respecting the interests of customers and consumers
8. Promoting corporate responsibility of suppliers and subcontractors
9. Developing societal commitment.

Banking is one of the most active sectors in Morocco, given the diversity of supply, banking volume, the job opportunities it generates and the role it plays in the financing of companies. It is not surprising that the Moroccan experience is exported to cover other markets, particularly in Africa. Several Moroccan banks show their social responsibility commitments through initiatives taken within the framework of the GPBM (Groupement Professionnelle des Banques du Maroc), as part of their own structures, or in response to governmental projects at the national level. To illustrate, the BMCE Bank stands out as the first Moroccan bank to undergo an evaluation of its social activities [9]. Carried out by the VIGEO (a leading international CSR assessment firm), the assessment of BMCE Bank corporate activities covered two of the six domains of the reference system used by the firm. For the third consecutive time (2012, 2013 and 2015), BMCE Bank has proved the incorporation of the following Social Responsibility Factors:

- The non-discrimination and gender equality approach, based on the professional advancement of women;
- Transparency of information to clients;
- The environmental strategy advocating a Sustainable and Responsible Finance;
- The contribution, through the BMCE Bank Foundation, to issues of general interest and, in particular, to the promotion of education in the rural world;
- The guarantee of equitable rights to shareholders enabling them to actively control of the strategic planning;
- The enhancement of skills and employability of employees through a process of dedicated training and professional mobility;
- The promotion of communication among the different social interlocutors using a method of collective interaction.

2.3   CSR Communication or Legitimation?

Among CSR companies, the communication strategy varies depending on the nature of countries, sectors, targets, the media and values of each company. According to the theory of legitimacy [13], companies are constrained to work in accordance with the expectations of the society in which they operate, seeking to make their social actions visible to stakeholders and to legitimize their positions and roles within the civil society [3, 14, 15]. In fact, according to the Stakeholder theory [16], there exists a relation between the interests of the partners of the company and their performance. The CSR commitment of companies leads them to improve their conduct towards the stakeholders in order to confirm their social approach.

In order to communicate the CSR commitment, several tools can be used (brochure, CSR reports, mass media, etc.). Several companies dedicate a part of their websites to the CSR bearing in mind the new possibilities offered by the Internet [4]. The annual report is an important medium for communicating CSR, given its periodic nature, mandatory and informative about the company's achievements during the previous year. Several researchers have linked social disclosure with social performance [17, 18, 19].

Inspired by Anglo-Saxon companies which were the first to publish annual reports alluding to social responsibility, French companies reacted following the New Economic Regulations Act in May 2001 and its decree in February 2002 [6]. Moroccan companies started considering the social responsibility aspect in their annual reports till the end of 2006. As far as banks are concerned, social responsibility is a matter of reputation risk management rather than an issue of strategic positioning [20]. It is a process of integrating CSR into banking businesses through the innovations of products and services. In addition, there is an explicit desire to introduce new rules that can deal with some banking practices.

Unlike the multitude of studies analyzing banks' sustainable development reports [15, 21], the study of the disclosure of CSR information in the Moroccan context has not been explored yet. Thus, using the Nvivo software, our article suggests a thematic analysis of BMCE Bank's annual reports (social responsibility in particular) so as to investigate the evolution of its CSR communication during the last nine years (From 2007 to 2015).

3 Methodology and Results

To conduct this research, we have opted for a qualitative methodology, with the epistemological assumption, based on a longitudinal case study in accord with Yin [22]. This choice is not yet studied according to our research in the Moroccan context and would guarantee a complementarity to the studies carried out so far. The aim of the qualitative analysis [23, 24], whether with or without using software, is to uncover the main ideas and to decipher the meaning of the text. There are two approaches to analyse a text or speech: the thematic analysis and the content analysis. We are using Nvivo 12 in our research for the thematic analysis taking in consideration this method's objectives (qualitative research/themes extraction).

On the other hand, in order to observe the difference between the theory and the practice of CSR, we have opted for a longitudinal study of a Moroccan bank to better detect this concept evolution over time since the appearance of the charter of Social Responsibility in 2006. Thus, we will deal with the case BMCE Bank from 2007 to 2015. We have decided on the BMCE bank mainly because:

- 2010: the first bank in Morocco to adhere to the Equator Principles (EPs) for the assessment of social and environmental risks in the field of project financing.
- 2011: 1st bank in Morocco, the Middle East and North Africa to obtain ISO 14001 certification for the environment.
- 2013: Awarded "Top performer CSR Morocco" by the rating agency Vigeo for its commitment to community, development and the environment.
- 2014: Awarded "Top performer CSR Morocco" also for the management and valuation of human capital.
- The bank is considering to establish diagnostics linked to OHSAS 18001 (for occupational health and safety) and ISO 50001 (for energy) references.

3.1 Treatment Process

This stage consists of presenting the data that have been collected and their processing through segmentation and de-contextualization [25].

3.1.1 Pre-analysis

This implied collecting and assembling the annual reports of the bank in question (2007–2015). We had to convert all the annual reports into a Word file and "clean" the documents (i.e., linking words, deletion of images, retyping paragraphs not converted by the software, etc.). We ultimately focused only on the part dealing with CSR (the subject matter of our research).

3.1.2 Analysis

According to Thiétart [23], the analysis consists of the deconstruction of the contents of a discourse or a text into units of analysis (words, phrases, themes …) and their integration into selected categories depending on the subject matter of the research. Coding, or lemmatization, consists of a process of deconstruction before restructuration, de-contextualization followed by re-contextualization [26]. Regardless of the used methods, the exploitation of the material stands for a process of deconstruction of a given text into units of analysis or units of meaning (words or segments) that will be the subject of a qualitative or quantitative study. The researcher is the only side to decide on the codification operations, the aim is to produce an analysis, an interpretation and not a "catalogue of ideas or quotations" [27]. The software manages the links between verbatim (Documents) and categories (Nodes) in two steps:

- First step: de-contextualization through coding themes in each Basic Document (can be annotated or linked) and/or in each node created (recipient to encode and/or link each extract). Each extract can be classified into several nodes (themes, ideas, concepts…).
- Second step: re-contextualization according to matrices and models. Proofreading of the corpus: investigating words or expressions, co-occurrences, or matrices….

Thus, we have deployed Nvivo to analyze the BMCE reports and to encode the paragraphs according to the seven key principles of social responsibility described in ISO 26000 standard.

3.2 Results

You can find below the results of the study listed in the form of tables and graphs followed by comments.

3.2.1 Evolution of the Portion of the CSR

We have reviewed all BMCE Bank annual reports and have subsequently been concerned, above all, with the CSR section. Table 1 illustrates the evolution of the integration of CSR information.

We can notice that the number of pages devoted to CSR had been increased till the year 2011 (coverage rate 5.26%) to be reduced again in 2012. The annual reports devote a full part of their communication to CSR; furthermore, the concept had been dealt with in a separate report in four languages: French, English, Arabic and Amazigh. It highlights the company's effort to be part of a global voluntarist action.

3.2.2 Evolution of CSR Over Time

What are the practices of the BMCE in this regard?

The longitudinal analysis of the most used words since 2007 (Table 2) proves that the notion of "development" is the main lever of the bank's voluntarist approach to CSR. The main focus was first upon the social phase of development and on both environmental and social sides starting from 2010. The bank has created the BMCE Bank Foundation as a means to respond to CSR related concerns (cited 101 times since 2007). However, we can observe that the economic aspect, the third principle of CSR, does not appear in the word analysis.

Second, we observe that CSR for education in the disadvantaged areas takes an important place in the report as there is a large number of education related words such as: *school*(s), *Medersat* (meaning school in Arabic). This illustrates the company's response to the poor literacy rate in the Moroccan context (the rate is close to 70% according to UNDP in its report of 2011). Similarly, the bank offers in-house training of employees favoring of human capital development. Lastly, we can deduce that the BMCE has been seeking international recognition along with new certifications and prizes since 2010.

Table 1 The study of annual reports from 2007 to 2014

Year of the report	Number of pages in report	Number of pages dedicated to CSR	From page ...to...	Value in %
2007	200	6	94 to 100	3
2008	182	6	97 to 102	3.29
2009	177	8	91 to 98	4.52
2010	200	9	126 to 134	4.5
2011	190	10	117 to 126	5.26
2012	210	10	121 to 130	4.76
2013	222	8	131 to 138	3.60
2014	224	8	131 to 138	3.57
2015	54[a]	6	46 to 51	–

[a]Abbreviated version

Table 2 Analysis of the most used words since 2007 (From Nvivo)

Results of the most used words in 2007	Results of the most used words in 2010	Results of the most used words in 2015
Bank	Development	Development
Development	Sustainable	Fondation
Fondation	Fondation	School
Réseau	Capital	Bank
Medersat	Humain	International
Actions	Environment	Sustainable
Social	Group	Medersat
School	Association	Network
Children	Bank	Employees
Training	Training	Environment
Amazigh	Philanthropy	Culture
Mobility	Festival	Engagement

3.2.3 The BMCE Bank's Definition of CSR

The BMCE definition of CSR refers to the term "sustainable development" since the term CSR almost does not appear in the reports nor in the title part. Although there exists an implementation of the principles of CSR according to international standards, practices in relation to stakeholders in this direction have not been very effective. The group's focus is mainly destined to sustainable actions, particularly education (rural areas), training of employees and patronage to strengthen the company's brand image. An enthusiasm for environmental protection actions has been noticed in the BMCE practices in recent years despite the "a priori" nature of its banking activity.

3.2.4 The BMCE Practices of CSR According to the Seven Principles of ISO 26000 Standard

To understand BMCE's CSR practices, we have analysed the annual reports according to the ISO 26000 classification, which we consider the most complete, especially since it is the reference for the CGEM in terms of Social responsibility.

Principle 1—Human rights: We have explored this principle in the annual BMCE's CSR reports since 2007. The result shows that the bank is not very involved in this principle (3% in 2015). The group advocates the integration of young people, with a supplementary effort to feminize the workforce (non-discrimination). Diversity in the recruitment of people of Sub-Saharan origin appeared in the report of 2015 (Fig. 2a). On the other hand, the BMCE group does not mention the recruitment of people with disabilities.

Référence 1 - Couverture 2,52%

Les effectifs des entreprises au Maroc sont
constitué de 25 à 40% par des femmes contre
32,7% au sein de BMCE Bank. Au niveau des postes
de management 10 à 25% sont occupés par des
femmes, contre 21,9 % pour BMCE Bank. Dans la
continuité des sa politique mixité du management,
BMCE Bank a vu son effectif se féminiser, puisque
les collaboratrices représentent aujourd'hui 34,6%
de l'effectif de 21,9% des managers

(a) Node of: "Human rights"

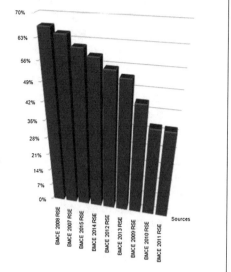

(b) Coverage of the node: "Community
involvement and development"

Référence 1 - Couverture 2,95%

Ainsi, le réseau Medersat.com compte
désormais deux écoles ayant obtenu le label
"Pavillon vert" il s'agit de l'école Laazib à
Settat, et l'école Bagdour à Tanger. Cette
prestigieuse distinction récompense les
établissements ayant adhéré aux meilleures
pratiques respectant l'environnement en
matière de jardinage éducatif, d'économie
d'eau , d'électricité, et de recyclage de
matière usées...d'autres écoles ont entamé
le processus d'adhésion au programme e Eco-
Ecoles parrainé par la Fondation Mohammed
VI pour l'environnement.

(c) Node of: "Environment"

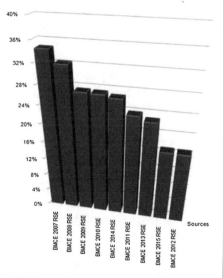

(d) Coverage of the node: "Labor practices"

Fig. 2 Some of illustrations obtained from the QSR Nvivo software

Principle 2—Community involvement and development: This principle constitutes the first practice in terms of coverage (65% in 2008) though it decreased in 2010 and 2011 (35%), before it could go up again in 2014 and 2015 (60%) (Fig. 2b). This high rate is the outcome of BMCE Bank desire to affirm its contribution to social and charitable actions at the local level.

Principle 3—Consumers issues: This notion did not appear in the report first (2007–2008) and started being included in 2011 and 2013 with a limited coverage rate of 13%. Example of Verbatim: "*In four years, BMCE Bank was invited by IFC to Cairo, Palestine, Dubai, Washington and Frankfurt to share its social and environmental risks management as a socially responsible bank engaged in Sustainable finance*".

Principle 4—Fair operating practices: The BMCE does not hesitate to set the example in this respect unlike these competitors: Implementation of best practices; An exemplary approach is highlighted by UNEP FI in 2011 and 2015 (rate: 17%).

Principle 5—The Environment: Since 2011 when it was awarded the ISO 14001 certification, the bank has steadily increased its efforts to maintain its certification over time. The bank finances renewable energy projects that have been selected among the 3 finalists of the FT Sustainable Banking Award 2010. Finally, the BMCE participates punctually in the improvement of the cleanliness and awareness on the Beaches according to the criteria of the "Blue Pavilion" label and in the rural environment for its Medresat.com network of schools having obtained the "Green Pavilion" (Fig. 2c). The disclosure of environment related information has increasingly been taking place in the bank's CSR report since its appearance in 2011.

Principle 6—Labor practices: Since 2007, all CSR annual reports on human resources aspects have been highlighted: recruitment, training, improvement of working conditions, etc. However, a decrease in the coverage rate of this principle is observed (Fig. 2d) in order to give way to other principles.

The survey shows that managers give more attention to the training of employees (weighting 34%) because of the return on investment. The BMCE Academy was created to help increase the sales of agency managers. The BMCE is also aware of the positive impact of a motivating social framework for employees. Accordingly, it provides benefits for: housing loans, holiday settlements, aid to pilgrims, reimbursement of medical expenses, etc.

Principle 7—Organizational governance: The bank often refers in its reports to the Vigeo standard, ISO 9001 for human capital, ISO 26000 for CSR and 14001 for the environment. The appearance of the word governance has increased significantly since the bank got the ISO 14001 certification (from a coverage ratio of 3% in 2010 to 15% in 2014).

Thus, the analysis of the results about the BMCE approach to communication and disclosure of information shows that there is a concrete implementation of CSR in spite of the slow evolution of the concept over time. Taking into account the nature of the recent adoption of CSR in Morocco, we have not come across any similar studies analyzing the same issue according to a longitudinal perspective to compare with our findings.

4 Conclusion

The purpose of this research was to examine the CSR concept within the Moroccan socioeconomic context. Our approach to the background of the CSR has proved the existence of different practices of the notion depending on the cultural context [28]. First, this led us to suggest a better definition of the concept through a new method of analysis of practices in a comparatively new field of study: banks [15]. Second, we tried to analyze the annual reports of a prominent Moroccan bank in the light of a longitudinal perspective (2007–2015). The analysis of the data in the reports allowed us to make the commitment of the company in terms of social responsibility more verifiable [6].

During our research, we have noticed that the Moroccan companies are making big efforts in CSR to respond to the different stakeholders. The CGEM Label for Corporate Social Responsibility (CSR) and the organization of the COP22 later are signs of acknowledgement that Moroccan companies do respect their commitment, defend and promote the universal principles of social responsibility and sustainable development. These principles represent the guidelines of ISO 26000 standard.

Thus, we verified the appropriation of the 7 principles of CSR according to this standard in the Moroccan context. We have observed that the notion of social responsibility is well established though it is still used when dealing with sustainable development and has little changed over time. Moreover, we have suggested that more importance should be given to certain principles (community and local development, relations and working conditions) rather than to others (human rights, loyalty) so as to reinforce, above all, the company's competitivity. This practice has been slowly enhanced in spite of the company's new approach to environmental activities during the recent years (search for ISO 14001 certifications, actions for the protection of the environment, etc.).

Finally, given the ever-changing context, the value creation must not be only economic and financial, but it should seek for the well-being of employees too [29]. Moroccan companies have to prove their social responsibility in the annual reports and the different media of information and communication technology [5]. In this research, we tried to contribute to the debate about CSR, specifically through the analysis of the case of a bank using a different methodology. We suggest that multi-case studies should be encouraged and that interviews be conducted to investigate other types of sectors and activities.

References

1. Igalens, J., Tahri, N.: Perception de la RSE par les salariés: construction et validation d'une échelle de mesure. Revue de gestion des ressources humaines. **83**, 3–19 (2012)
2. Moskolaï, D.D., Tsapi, V., Feudjo, J.R.: État des lieux de la Responsabilité Sociétale des Entreprises au Cameroun. Manag. Avenir **86**, 139–162 (2016)

3. Carroll, A.B.: The pyramid of corporate social responsibility: toward the moral. Management of organizational stakeholders (balancing economic, legal, and social responsibilities). Bus. Horiz. **34**(4), 39–48 (1991)
4. Coupland, C.: Corporate social responsibility as argument on the web. J. Bus. Ethics **62**, 355–366 (2005)
5. Bourdon, I., Rodhain, F., Vitari, C.: Internet et la communication RSE des entreprises du CAC40. In: 14ème conférence de l'AIM, La rochelle (2010)
6. Igalens, J.: Comment évaluer les rapports de développement durable? Revue Française de Gestion. **30**(152), 151–166 (2004)
7. Zarlowski, Ph.: Notation sociale des entreprises: Premiers pas et premier bilan. In: Mottis N. (coord.), L'art de l'innovation, pp. 199–204, Harmattan (2007)
8. De Brito, C., Desmartin, J.-P., Lucas-Leclin, V., Perrain, F.: L'investissement socialement responsable. Economica, Paris (2005)
9. Rouggani, K., Bouayad, A.N.: L'implémentation d'une démarche Responsabilité Sociale des Organisations dans le système financier: le cas de la BMCE Bank. In: Colloque international: Ethique en sciences de gestion, mythe ou réalité? Maroc (2014)
10. Walker, K., Wan, F.: The harm of symbolic actions and green-washing: corporate actions and communications on environmental performance and their financial implications. Emerald Manag. Rev. **109**(2), 227–239 (2012)
11. Donaldson, L.: Ethics problems and problems with ethics: toward a pro-management theory. J. Bus. Ethics **78**, 299–311 (2008)
12. Burlacu, R., Girerd-Potin, I., Dupré, D.: Y'a-t-il un sacrifice à être éthique? étude de performance des fonds socialement responsables américains. Banque & Marchés **69**, 20–28 (2004)
13. Suchman, M.C.: Managing legitimacy: strategic and Institutional Approaches. Acad. Manag. Rev. **20**(3), 571–610 (1995)
14. Igalens, J.: L'analyse du discours de la responsabilité sociale de l'entreprise à travers les rapports annuels de développement durable d'entreprises françaises du CAC 40. Finance Contrôle Stratégie. **10**(2), 129–155 (2007)
15. Reynaud, E., Walas, A.: Discours sur la RSE dans le processus de légitimation de la banque. Revue Française de Gestion. **41**, 187–209 (2015)
16. Freeman, R.E.: Strategic management: a stakeholder approach. Pitman, Boston (1984)
17. Abbott, W.F., Monsen, R.J.: On the measurement of corporate social responsibility: self reported disclosures as a method of measuring corporate social involvement. Acad. Manag. J. **22**, 501–515 (1979)
18. Igalens, J. et Gond, J.-P.: La mesure de la performance sociale de l'entreprise: une analyse critique et empirique des données ARESE. Revue de gestion des ressources humaines. 50, 111–130 (2003)
19. Oxibar, B., Déjean, F.: An alternative approach of corporate social disclosure analysis. In: EAA Congress (2003)
20. Gadioux, S.: Qu'est-ce qu'une banque responsable? Repères théoriques, pratiques et perspectives. Management & Avenir **38**, 33–51 (2010)
21. Pupion, P.: Développement durable-RSE: Une quête de légitimité des banques européennes. Gestion 2000. **30**(6), 39–59 (2013)
22. Yin, R.K.: Case study research, design and methods. Sage Publications, Thousand Oaks (1994)
23. Miles, M.B., Huberman, A.M.: Qualitative data analysis: an expended sourcebook. Sage publications, Thousand Oaks (1994)
24. Thiétart, R.A.: Introduction, pp. 1–10. Méthodes de recherche en management. Dunod, Paris (2007)
25. Krief, N., Zardet, V.: Analyse de données qualitatives et recherche-intervention. Recherches en Sciences de Gestion. **2**, 211–237 (2013)
26. Tesch, R.: Qualitative research: analysis types & software tools. Falmer Press, Bristol, PA (1990)

27. Auger, P.: Une méthode de recherche innovante : l'utilisation du logiciel Nvivo pour les analyses de littérature. Revue Sciences de Gestion. **57**, 113–129 (2006)
28. Maignan, I., Ralston, D.A.: Corporate social responsibility in Europe and the U.S.: insights from businesses self-representations. J. Int. Bus. Stud. **33**(3), 497–515 (2002)
29. Tahri, W., El kadiri, I.: Sensemaking et bien-être dans le contexte de changement organisationnel. Revue Question(s) de management. n°13, l'Innovation managériale en questions. Editions EMS (2016)

Does Persuasive E-commerce Website Influence Users' Acceptance and Online Buying Behaviour? The Findings of the Largest E-commerce Website in Malaysia

N. A. Abdul Hamid, C. H. Cheun, N. H. Abdullah, M. F. Ahmad and Y. Ngadiman

Abstract Previous study related to persuasive design of e-commerce websites has been shown to significantly impact online buying behavior. Nevertheless, the importance of persuasive applications has been discussed extensively in website design and e-learning application compared to e-commerce especially from Malaysia context. Thus, this paper discusses the assessment of persuasive design to one of the famous e-commerce website in Malaysia. The assessment was adapted from original Persuasive System Design (PSD) model in combination with Technology Acceptance Model for the user acceptance and website usage level. Online survey link was conveniently emailed to the selected e-commerce users. A total of 200 samples were collected and data were analysed using statistical methods. The results revealed extensive use of persuasive features; particularly features related to dialogue support, credibility support, and primary task support; thus highlighting weaknesses in the system credibility. Further the result indicated significant relationship towards user acceptance and online buying behaviour. The findings also confirmed that gender had insignificant relationship towards user acceptance and online buying behaviour. In conclusion, this study suggests possible ways for enhancing persuasive feature implementation via appropriate contextual examples and explanation.

Keywords Persuasive system design · User acceptance · Online buying behaviour · E-commerce

N. A. Abdul Hamid (✉) · C. H. Cheun · M. F. Ahmad · Y. Ngadiman
Department of Production and Operation, Faculty of Technology Management and Business, University Tun Hussein Onn, Parit Raja, Batu Pahat, Malaysia
e-mail: aziati@uthm.edu.my

N. H. Abdullah
Department of Technology Management and Business, Faculty of Technology Management and Business, University Tun Hussein Onn, Parit Raja, Batu Pahat, Malaysia

© Springer Nature Switzerland AG 2019
Y. Baghdadi and A. Harfouche (eds.), *ICT for a Better Life and a Better World*,
Lecture Notes in Information Systems and Organisation 30,
https://doi.org/10.1007/978-3-030-10737-6_17

1 Introduction

Persuasive design is define as a two way computerized software or information system that developed based on persuasive principles with the purpose of reinforcement, shape or change the user attitudes and behaviors or even both. Persuasive theory was first introduced in particular to ensure consumer retention and loyalty to a product or the online applications. From the definition above, the persuasive system was expected to increase voluntary, shaping or change of attitudes and change or shaping or the behaviors. Design principles of persuasive system (PSD) consist of four dimensions, which are primary task support, dialogue support, system credibility and social support. All those dimensions are proven to have significant impact on system persuasiveness and system qualities evaluation.

The advent of Internet technology and mobile gadgets has resulted in bilateral communication that can be conducted everywhere. This situation has indirectly encouraged persuasion communication as the network access is easier and faster. The concept of persuasion communication process includes message passing from persuaders to the recipient with the intention to influence recipient's behavior whilst leaving the power of making the decision to the recipient. All of these dimensions have shown a positive impact on system persuasiveness and evaluation system qualities.

Current trend of business trading activities in this era involves internet and online money transaction. Hence, a well-designed e-commerce system is one of the important elements for a successful business. In addition [1] claimed the significant impact of persuasive principles to attract potential consumers besides promoting new product. Online persuasion applied the same dynamic persuasive techniques as similar to those applied by face-to-face sales-persons, to enhance system credibility, facilitate the process of online buying, and motivate users to reuse the systems. By applying the principles of persuasive in designing e-commerce website, the advertisement can be appear more attractive, informative and allocated at place where easy to get clicked by potential consumers or buyers. PSD principles have been applied in previous studies, particularly in the fields of education, health, tourism and e-commerce.

In Malaysia context, e-commerce market is now at the nascent stage. According to Statista report (2017), the e-commerce market (excluding e-services) in Malaysia for 2017 is expected to reach USD894 million in revenue, while the global e-commerce industry is projected to surpass USD2.5 trillion by 2020. Local Malaysia online marketplaces such as Zalora, 11street, Lazada, Shoppee, Rakuten and others contributed more than 40% of the total 2016 revenue. To accelerate e-commerce growth, 6 thrust areas have been identified under the National e-Commerce Strategic Roadmap. These interventions were expected to double e-commerce growth and drive e-commerce GDP contribution to the nation. Therefore, realizing the mechanisms of e-commerce and the behavior of the online consumer is a priority issue for practitioners competing in the fast expanding virtual marketplace. Thus, the design of an e-commerce website is not only for fulfilling customer's needs and interest but is expected to assist customers through the steps of buying process. Herewith, e-commerce presents a perfect platform for persuasive tools such as digital catalogue which may influence user's needs, inform special sales and promotions. Designers of online shopping websites combine their knowledge of design, technology, and social science to design persuasive e-commerce websites that are ideally able to enhance consumers' satisfaction and ultimately increase retailers' revenues. Globally, online shopping has taken the retail market by storm and consumers are adopting it as it provides many advantages. On consumers' perspective, online buying provides a lower and more transparent price, allowing price comparison to be done immediately, comprehensive assortment of goods and services, and a much more convenient shopping alternative comparing to traditional shopping inconveniences of overcrowding, time wasted in long queue at cashier counter or payment, fighting for parking spaces at a busy mall. Therefore, e-commerce has taking such opportunity and had become more common in this technology era.

Accordingly, the developed e-commerce marketplaces not only need to follow persuasive system principles, but must fulfil all factors that influence consumer acceptance rates. User acceptance in this research refers to the acceptance of e-commerce, which is an activity of online purchase performed by public. The study of users' acceptance is to understand a scale of reputation reading. It is a positive reflection of online purchase behaviour. Users will rank these platforms according to their purchase experiences. Hence it is important for e-commerce businessmen to provide a suitable platform for their potential consumers. Using ZALORA.com as a case study, this paper aims at identifying the impact of persuasive principles that make an e-commerce website successful. ZALORA is one of the Asia's leading online fashion destination and it launched in early 2012. E-commerce revenue generated from cloth and accessories website reaching RM180.121 million in 2016. ZALORA websites offer consumers various payment options such as online banking, credit card, PayPal and others in order to complete the deal. These payment options are mostly online transactions which allowing instant payment to be done and the order can be released at the same date. This study can serve as a guide for e-commerce website developers to build successful e-commerce platforms or to improve on existing ones.

1.1 Issues and Challenges of E-commerce Website

There have been numerous studies conducted on the topic of e-commerce adoption, in both advanced countries and developing countries. Most scholars investigate the reaction of respective local people toward e-commerce as they could react differently due to local culture and purchase behaviour. Based from PwC Retail Survey 2016 reported that only 33% of Malaysian shopped online on monthly basis. According to [2], Malaysian consumers are less confident about online security however it is certainly gaining popularity among the younger generation. The information about the users is transferred via unsafe environment. In addition, most of the e-commerce website lacks high-end security features that provide the confidence to the user that they will be able to purchase online without any fear of the security threats. In order to increase online purchase in Malaysia and gain the customer trust, understanding persuasive principle of user acceptance and online buying behaviour should be given priority. For instance, designers of e-commerce websites can apply third party endorsement techniques to increase website credibility, such as endorsing PayPal as a secure and trusted third party payment method.

In sum, e-commerce especially for developing countries such Malaysia is considered underutilised, even though the penetration of high speed broadband application helped increase the percentage of online purchases. There are various factors associated with low adoption of users and companies to implement online business besides the factors mentioned earlier. Some of the factors mentioned by past scholars were [3, 4]; informativeness, website credibility, information comparison, payment security and privacy. These factors may influence consumers' decision in purchase activity and determining user acceptance. A study conducted by [4, 5] claimed that consumers in Malaysia are still lack of confidence and trust in utilising the Internet to purchase goods and services. For instance, recent statistics shows that approximately 30% Malay does not commit with online shopping, due to lack of trust. For this reason, designers and web practitioners should be aware of various persuasive techniques and the required persuasive characteristics.

Previous study had shown that websites with valuable information is important toward consumers while doing online purchase decision. This information may build up extra credit for the website and enhance its reputation to the public. Website also act as crucial information collecting system for SMEs, as via loyal customers' interaction with the website while shopping, for instant products' rating, leaving comments, or while purchasing an item, they will directly and indirectly leaving information regarding their favourite. However, how to use this information collected to generate good recommendation and images for customer is a crucial problem for this persuasion technology. Putting the information collected in good use may leads to a successful business, yet misleading information may divert consumers to blacklist the website from future visits. Even though persuasive principles had been applied into these e-commerce information platform, effectiveness of persuasive principles had been questioned by many, as some business still remain low in dealing. Therefore, this study focuses more on assessing the characteristics of persuasive design towards one of Malaysia's largest e-marketplace. In addition, this study attempts to fill research gaps related to the field persuasive in the context of teaching and learning.

2 Literature Review

2.1 Online Buying Behavior

Online buying behaviour refers to consumers' psychological state in terms of making decision to purchase up until the transactional stage of purchasing and logistics [6]. Online shopping behaviour also known as online buying behaviour refers to the process of purchasing products or services via the Internet in this study. Basically there are two categories on of online buyers; those who shop online in order to acquire a specific product or service (utilitarian aspect). Second category is those who sees online shopping as "enjoyment" and seeks for the potential entertainment (hedonic aspect). Many researchers have discussed the factors that influence online buying behaviour. Socio-demographic is common variables studied in online buying related researches. Behaviour towards online shopping is influenced by demographic factors, such as gender, age, educational background and income had mentioned by [5, 7]. Younger users spend more time on the Internet than older users and also younger users are more knowledgeable about the Internet commonly [8]. Therefore, younger age group will be more frequent online buyers. In additional, regarding the income perspective, consumers with higher incomes intend to shop more online compared to lower income of consumers [6]. However, there are some countries that reported the opposite findings such as studies conducted in Turkey [9].

Apart demographic characteristics, website design is one of the factor that influences online buying behaviour. The website that been designed to meet the buyer psychology does give impact on customer loyalty and positive experience [10] to maintain term relationship. In case prior online shopping experiences resulted in satisfactory outcomes and were evaluated positively, this leads consumers to continue to shop on the Internet in the future. Website design with well content such as timing, loading speed and the quality of internet line provides good accessibility and good quality of website support system. Other than that, the speed of navigation is important to success a website design [11]. Consumers are easier to access appropriate and unlimited information by having a good navigation website. Accordingly, persuasive system design has been associated with the development of e-commerce based website to enhance user acceptance and thus influence the consumer decision to purchase.

2.2 Persuasive System Design and User Acceptance

The design of e-commerce systems in particular, incorporates the art of persuasion by applying different persuasive techniques in the design to increase consumer's motivation, trust, and experience; besides changing consumer's attitude and support making decision to purchase online. In addition, persuasive principles had been applied into the design of e-commerce websites, similar to the techniques applied by face-to-face sellers. The study of users' attitudes and behaviour, related to information systems and their use, has a long history in information system research. Theory such as the Technology Acceptance Model [12] has significantly contributed in increasing the understanding of users' behaviour and willingness to accept or reject the use of such technology. User acceptance can be explained as the willingness of user to accept certain changes. It is a form of measurement to be taken in order to allow system developer to design a more suitable system for user to continue the service provided, at the same time introducing new features to their users, with the aim to improve the sales volume. In order to perform a better analyses based on reflection from user, Technology Acceptance Model (TAM) is popular model to measure user acceptance. According to the TAM, a user's perceptions about a system's usefulness and ease of use result in an intention to use (or not use) the system. Customers' motivation can be explained by three factors; *Perceived Ease of Use*, *Perceived Usefulness*, and *Attitude toward Using* the system. There are also several researchers studied TAM (e.g. [6, 13, 14]) and had refined this model into a leading model in explaining and predicting system use. Previous studies have validated the TAM and its reliable constructs of *perceived usefulness, perceived ease of use*, the *attitude toward using* the web system, and the *behavioural intention to use* the web system. These studies had have augmented the TAM with other constructs as well to better explain the relationship and significance of the TAM constructs.

On the other hand, Fogg [15, 16] has introduced persuasive theory that considers the design element of the technology such as reduction, tunnelling, tailoring, suggestion, self-monitoring, surveillance, and conditioning. Each design elements have different strategy to change attitudes or behaviours. A persuasive technology product usually is a mix of two or more tool types to achieve a desired outcome. Reduction is a form of persuading through simplifying, a guided persuasion known as tunnelling, tailoring is persuasion through customization, and suggestion provides a right timing intervening. Self-monitoring would allowing the taking of tedium out of tracking, surveillance allowing observation based persuasion and reinforcing target's behaviours is conditioning. Eventually, Harjuma et al. [17, 18] has integrates TAM model with PSD model. The selected parameters originally from TAM are, *Perceived ease of use* and *Perceived usefulness* while the other parameters were persuasive design elements; *Primary task support, Dialogue support, Perceived credibility*, and *Perceived persuasiveness* to have a more detail analyses. Indirectly, this study also examines the impact of persuasive website towards consumer acceptance and retention.

2.3 Persuasive Systems Design (PSD) and Online Buying Behavior

According to [19], persuasive design influence users' behaviour and perceptions, and various tactics may be applied by the technologies to support different outcomes and behaviour change strategies. Persuasive design has strong influence on consumers' attitude and behaviour; with persuasion seemingly key element in behaviour and attitude change [1]. Persuasive principle is used rather extensively in a multitude of domains, for instance, within the domains of ecommerce [20], education [21, 22], health [23] or motivation to buy online [10]. The computer technology had been studied in performing persuasive activity in order to influence human action and currently these principles are used to persuade people in e-commerce activity. This concept had been first proposed by Fogg [15, 24] during his doctoral study, originally term as *Captology*. Persuasive Systems Design (PSD) Model is divided into four different categories; primary task support, dialogue support, system credibility support and social support. Figure 1 shows the element consists in each dimension.

Persuasive systems design may be defined as "computerized software or information systems designed to reinforce, change or shape attitudes or behaviours or both without using coercion or deception". There are three potential successful outcomes for a persuasive system [25]: the voluntary reinforcement, change or shaping of attitudes and behaviours. A reinforcing outcome means the reinforcement of current attitudes or behaviours, making them more resistant to change. A changing outcome means changes in a person's response to an issue (e.g. to social questions). A shaping outcome means the formulation of a pattern for a situation when one does not exist beforehand. In many cases, communication that results in a shaping outcome may have a higher likelihood of success than communication that aims at a changing outcome.

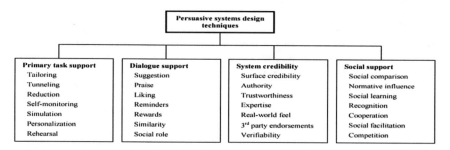

Fig. 1 Persuasive system design elements

2.3.1 Primary Task Support

According to [1], primary task support refers to the person in performing his or her primary task. The aim of primary task support is to design principles that help and support the user to perform the primary task. Persuasion techniques in the primary task support category are shown in Table 1. In previous study, primary task support increase significant affect [26] which augments the persuasiveness of the source [27]. For instance, eBay utilized self-monitoring on its page and this proven that by using persuasion technique increase the possibility to keep track with online buyers [28]. In additional, [23] had discussed about behaviour change support systems (BCSS) through a theoretical model. They constructed and tested the model perceived principles and actual behaviour of online buyers. They find out that primary task support has a positive effect on actual behaviour of online buyers. Therefore, hypothesis is formulated:

H1 Primary task support positively affects online buying behaviour.

2.3.2 Dialogue Support

Nowadays, people try to react with Information Technology (IT) application as they were interacting in social context. In dialog support, e-commerce website should be interactive and provide consumers with appropriate feedback in order to maintain them to perform the behaviour of online buying [31]. Table 2 shows the persuasion techniques in this category. The principles in this category aim to implement computer-human dialogue support in order to help the user to continue for their goal [1]. According to [1], the capability to maintain users is by providing appropriate

Table 1 Measurement items for primary task support

Variables/ Constructs	Operational definition	Authors	Selected measurement items
Primary task support	Primary task support encompasses reflecting on one's behaviour, setting personal goals, and tracking progress toward them	[23, 29, 30]	1. Information at the website is well organized and guides me in reaching my goals gradually 2. The website can support different languages such as English and Bahasa Malaysia 3. The website helps me in keeping track of my progress 4. The website provides simple and personalized content for me 5. The website provides two-dimensions pictures for the purpose of simulation 6. The e-commerce websites look similar to each other

Table 2 Measurement items for dialogue support

Variables/Constructs	Operational definition	Author	Selected measurement items
Dialogue support	Dialogue support defines the key principles in keeping the user active and motivated in using the system and, ideally, helping the users to reach their intended behaviour	[1, 23, 32]	1. The website provides virtual rewards for me 2. The website provides me reminders for reaching my personal goals 3. The website provides me with appropriate suggestion 4. The website sending messages via e-mail or short message service (SMS) for reaching individual goals 5. The website adopts some specific way include punctuation and capitalization to persuade me use system 6. The website is visually attractive for me 7. The website offers a various functions to increase interactive experience

feedback too users. Besides, in the study done by [28] mentioned that Amazon.com used persuasion technique in order to attract consumers. For instance, Amazon.com was able to give the user recommendations based on the browsing history of the products. Therefore, this proves that dialogue support significant relationship with online buying behaviour. Thus, the following hypothesis is formulated:

H2   Dialogue support positively influences online buying behaviour.

2.3.3   System Credibility

According to [23], system credibility contains both a subjective and objective component. The subjective component is based upon people's initial evaluations of the system credibility based on their first impression. System credibility also has an objective component which might be bolstered by providing endorsements from respected and renowned sources. Persuasion techniques in this category are shown in Table 3. Besides, the aim of system credibility support is to help to design a system with more credibility and also more persuasion [1]. The result of system credibility support has a significant relationship to the persuasive principle discussed in the study done by [23]. The most common persuasion techniques used by e-commerce are trustworthiness and expertise. For example, Amazon.com and Ebay use trustworthiness as a persuasion tool in order to creating a sense of truth for their users. In contrast, cheating consumers is unacceptable. When the story about

Table 3 Measurement items for system credibility

Variables/ Constructs	Operational definition	Author	Selected measurement items
System credibility	Credibility and trust are important, related constructs	[1, 22, 23]	1. The website provides fashionable content 2. The website provides regularly updated content 3. The content of the website is concise 4. The content of the Website is trustworthy 5. The website uses professional design standards that draw me into the application 6. The website provides contact information or support help desk 7. The website shows the security logo such as Web Trust 8. The content of the website able to verify by offering links to other website

tricking the consumer spreads, the company reputation will be greatly damaged, and will lost a lot of consumers [28]. Besides, expertise was also discovered in the website of Amazon.com and eBay [28]. The website was updated regularly and all the information was up to date. Hence, credibility of the websites will be increase in consumers' eyes. Consequently, the hypothesis is formulated:

H3   System credibility support positively influences online buying behaviour.

2.3.4   Social Support

Social support refers to the design of e-commerce website should incorporate a range of social influence to motivate and persuade users to purchase a solution online by offering them alternatives similar to what those 'social interaction' that are available when they shop in the physical store [31]. According to this principle, a system can be more persuasive if users can learn from other users in the system. In the case of Amazon.com, product ratings and reviews and their helpfulness are public, hence users can learn from other customers who have bought a product they are interested in [33]. According to [1], the aim is to manipulate the users by increasing the social influences of the system. Table 4 shows the persuasion techniques in this category. In previous study has discussed social support implied in e-commerce web sites such as pizza-online.fi [28]. In the study shown that social support positively affects persuasive principle towards online users. Besides, the most common persuasive principle uses by e-commerce websites is cooperation. According to [28], cooperation was utilized by providing the users a possibility to write and read reviews on the products. Consumers usually like to hear opinions

Table 4 Measurement items for social support

Variables/ Construct	Operational definition	Author	Selected measurement items
Social support	Our social relationships are increasingly maintained through technology-mediated Communications	[3, 17, 23]	1. The website motivates me by competing from my peers' actions 2. I can share and compare information posted at the website 3. I able to observe the review from other users who are using the website 4. The use of website gives me a feeling of being accepted by the community/follows the trend 5. I able to discern via the website that others are performing the behaviour along with me 6. Behavioural patterns of users are analysis with cooperation of authorities and users through the website 7. The website provides recognition or award to me

from others in order to purchase items that they prefer. If some product has received a lot of negative feedback from other consumers, normally consumers will not consider purchasing the product [28]. In previous studies had shown that social support significant effect towards behaviour of online buyers. Consequently, the hypothesis is formulated:

H4   Social support positively influences online buying behaviour.

Figure 2 showed the suggested framework for the PSD model with hypothesized relationships between constructs in this research.

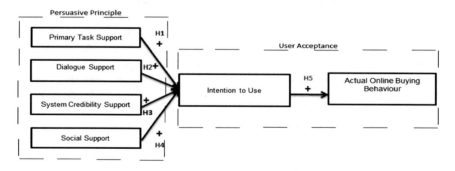

Fig. 2 Research framework and hypotheses

3 Methodology

The study was using the questionnaire on-line. The instrument used was developed based on previous studies and had been through a pilot test to ensure the validity of the questions and question the appropriateness built. The layout of questionnaire consists of five sections showed in Appendix E. Five questions about respondents profile questioned in Section A. Section B is about pattern of using Internet and online buying include six close-ended questions. Section C is regarding measurement of intention to use and Section D is about actual online buying behaviour. Lastly, Section E is regarding persuasive principle. The study employed 7 point Likert scale, ranging from "1" Strongly disagree to "7" Strongly agree. This research employed convenience sampling method due to the unavailability of the list online buyer that involved in online purchases as well as easy getting the sample who is online buyers of ZALORA. The survey was emailed individually and through their own social media ZALORA. Social media is actively involved in online purchases were distributed randomly. Based on the distribution of the survey, only 200 visitors and users ZALORA successfully complete answer. There were 20 respondents rejected due to incomplete questionnaires. The respondent responded are among active online buyers that have experienced online buying for a few years to get constructive feedback based on their experience. The collected data were then analysed using statistical methods using IBM-SPSS software. The overall reliability score for actual online buying behaviour is 0.892. Besides, the overall reliability of primary task support was 0.864 and the overall reliability of dialogue support was 0.890. For system credibility support, the overall reliability score was 0.895. Lastly, the overall reliability of social support was 0.886.

4 Results

The mean of intention to use ranged from 5.1150 (IU3: *I feel adherence with the website characteristics*) to 5.5800 (IU1: *I intend to use the website (e.g. purchasing a product or seek product information*). Besides, the standard deviation of intention to use was slightly different with the range of 0.94671 to 1.05114. Therefore, this shown that the data points were clustered closely to mean. The mean of actual online buying behaviour ranged from 5.1800 (B4: *My personal behavior is congruent with the website image*) to 5.4800 (B2: *I prefer to use the website in the future*). Standard deviation of actual online buying behaviour was ranged from 0.94980 to 1.10731 had shown that the data points were closely to mean. In additional, mean of primary task support was ranged from 5.2250 (PTS6: *The website provides two-dimensions pictures for the purpose of simulation*) to 5.5850

(PTS1: *I find the website easy to use*). Besides, standard deviation of primary task support ranged from 0.81714 to 0.95779 had shown that the data points were closely to mean.

Furthermore, mean of dialogue support ranged from 5.1050 (DS2: *The website provides virtual rewards for me*) to 5.5350 (DS5: *The website adopts some specific way include punctuation such as "!", capitalization "18% OFF" and "HAPPY BIRTHDAY" in order to persuade me use it*). Standard deviation of dialogue support ranged from 0.83419 to 1.04875 had shown that the data points were clustered closely to mean. Besides, mean of system credibility support ranged from 5.1650 (SCS1: *The content of the Website is trustworthy*) to 5.4800 (SCS3: *The website provides regularly updated content*). The standard deviation of system credibility support was slightly different with the range of 0.81381 to 1.03106. Hence, this had shown that the data points were clustered closely to mean. Lastly, mean of social support ranged from 5.1450 (SS4: *I able to discern via the website that others are performing the behaviour along with me*) to 5.3350 (SS6: *The website motivates me by competing from my peers' actions*). Standard deviation of social support ranged from 0.83732 to 0.98673 had shown that the data points were closely to mean.

Spearman's rho correlation coefficient is considered in the research as the data distributions are abnormal. Table 5 shows the results of hypothesis tests. Five of the hypotheses are accepted because the p values which was given as Sig. (2-tailed) in the tables ware less than 0.05. Furthermore, the five hypotheses also had positive relationship between the variables. The highest correlation coefficient of H_2 had shown that dialogue support is the most influence persuasive principle that affects intention to use.

Table 5 Hypotheses testing result

	Hypothesis	Sig. (2-tailed)	Correlation coefficient	Inference
H1	There is a positive relationship between primary task support and intention to use	0.000	0.602	Hypothesis accepted
H2	There is a positive relationship between dialogue support and intention to use	0.000	0.652	Hypothesis accepted
H3	There is a positive relationship between system credibility support and intention to use	0.000	0.598	Hypothesis accepted
H4	There is a positive relationship between social support and intention to use	0.000	0.607	Hypothesis accepted
H5	There is a positive relationship between intention to use and actual online buying behaviour	0.000	0.709	Hypothesis accepted

5 Discussions, Limitations, Recommendations and Conclusion

The research attempted to determine the influence of persuasive principle on determining users' acceptance and online buying behaviour. The results indicated that the hypothesis (H_1, H_2, H_3, H_4, H_5) also significant and positively. The finding concluded that persuasive principle had positive influence on users' acceptance and online buying behaviour. Besides, the most influence persuasive principle is dialogue support towards user acceptance and online buying behaviour. In the finding showed that 65% of elements in dialogue support does persuade buyer to continue by online. In additional, the demographic effects of gender and age had no significant relationship towards user acceptance and online buying behaviour. The result supported by previous study, persuasive principle can have a strong influence on consumers' attitude and behaviour. Lastly, the result also consistent with previous study persuasive principle has a significant impact on actual system usage.

Based on the research, it was clearly showed that the most influence persuasive principle is dialogue support towards user acceptance and online buying behaviour. Majority of the respondents agreed that dialogue support affected user acceptance and online buying behaviour proven by the survey in this research. For example, 85% of respondents agreed that "The website sending messages via e-mail or short message service (SMS) for reaching individual goals". Other than that, reasons like "The website provides me reminders for reaching my personal goals" and "The website provides me with appropriate suggestion" agreed by the respondents with 88.5%. There were 87.5% of respondents agreed that "The website adopts some specific way include punctuation such as "!", capitalization "18% OFF" and "HAPPY BIRTHDAY" in order to persuade me use it". Therefore, the most influence persuasive principle is concluded to be dialogue support towards online buying behaviour.

The limitation of this study is time constraint for data collection. It is very time-consuming to collect data from respondents that use the e-commerce website. Therefore, the sample size is relatively small and hence the results needed to be interpreted with caution, particularly with respect to the generalization of research findings of Malaysian consumers as a whole. The recommendation is data collection should be started earlier in order to increase the amount of time for data collection, as well as increases the number of respondents that could be taken part in the survey. Apart from that, future research might compare two or more e-commerce websites in order to enlarge cross section of online buyers and more diversified random samples to verify the findings of the current study.

Lastly, e-commerce website must adopt persuasive techniques included primary task support, dialogue support, system credibility support and social support. For instance, e-commerce designers adopts some specific way include punctuation such as "!", capitalization "18% OFF" and "HAPPY BIRTHDAY" in order to persuade users. Therefore, persuasive principle techniques that have been discussed in the research can be used in e-commerce website in order to maximize the benefits and attract more users. Lastly, e-commerce website must adopt persuasive techniques included primary task support, dialogue support, system credibility support and social support, as well as all the necessary features such as security, ease of use and truthfulness that have been discussed in the research in order to maximize the benefits and attract more users.

6 Future Work

More research is needed on this area in relation to the persuasive design across cultures, gender and technologies. Gaps among cultural boundaries are narrowing and the global population are changing in their attitudes towards accepting technologies due to the digital culture. There needs to be more research on the following if system developers and designers in general are to produce globally accepted e-commerce website as well as making a positive impact on online product sales. The PSD measurement scale used in this study can be replicated to measure the effect of PSD on mobile shopping behavior. In addition, cultural factors, loyalty, and artificial intelligence can also be integrated into a more comprehensive future study. This is because in year 2020, 85% of customer interactions will be managed without a human. Many e-commerce businesses are already using forms of AI to better understand their customers, generate new leads and provide an enhanced customer experience.

References

1. Oinas-kukkonen, H., Harjumaa, M., Oinas-kukkonen, H.: Persuasive systems design: key issues, process model, and system features. Commun. Assoc. Inf. Syst. **24**, 28 (2009)
2. Alam, S.S.: Young consumers online shopping : an empirical study. Bus. Manag. 79–98 (2008)
3. Anckar, B.: Drivers and inhibitors to e-commerce adoption: exploring the rationality of consumer behavior in the electronic marketplace. In: ECIS 2003 Proceedings. Paper 24. 24 (2003)
4. Khan, M.J., Dominic, P.D.D., Khan, A.: Opportunities and challenges for E-commerce in Malaysia: a theoretical approach. In: ICECT 2010—Proceedings of the 2010 2nd International Conference on Electronic Computer Technology. pp. 189–192 (2010)
5. Khatibi, A., Haque, A., Karim, K.: E-commerce: a study on internet shopping in Malaysia. J. Appl. Sci. **6**, 696–705 (2006)
6. Monsuwé, T.P.Y., Dellaert, B.G.C., De Ruyter, K.: What drives consumers to shop online? A literature review. Int. J. Serv. Ind. Manag. **15**, 102–121 (2004)
7. Zendehdel, M., Paim, L.H., Osman, S.B.: Students' online purchasing behavior in Malaysia: understanding online shopping attitude. Cogent Bus. Manag. **2**, 1–13 (2015)
8. San, L.Y., Omar, A., Thurasamy, R.: Online purchase: a study of generation Y in Malaysia. Int. J. Bus. Manag. **10**, 1–7 (2015)
9. Akman, I., Rehan, M.: Online purchase behaviour among professionals: a socio-demographic perspective for Turkey. Econ. Res. Istraživanja **27**, 689–699 (2014)

10. Alhammad, M.M., Gulliver, S.R.: Consideration of persuasive technology on users acceptance of e-commerce: exploring perceived persuasiveness. J. Commun. Comput. **11**, 133–142 (2014)
11. Osman, S., Yin-Fah, B.C., Hooi-Choo, B.: Undergraduates and online purchasing behavior. Asian Soc. Sci. **6**, 133–146 (2010)
12. Davis, F.D.: Perceived usefulness, perceived ease of use, and user acceptance of information technology. MIS Q. **13**, 319–339 (1989)
13. Sook Harn, T.C., Harvey Tanakinjal, G., Liason Sondoh, S., Rizal, H.: Determinants of online group buying behaviour: The moderating role of informational social influence. J. Pengur. **41**, 133–143 (2014)
14. Lim, Y.J., Osman, A., Salahuddin, S.N., Romle, A.R., Abdullah, S.: Factors influencing online shopping behavior: the mediating role of purchase intention. Procedia Econ. Financ. **35**, 401–410 (2016)
15. Fogg, B.J.: Computers as persuasive social actors. http://www.ncbi.nlm.nih.gov/pubmed/ 15275676%5Cnhttp://doi.wiley.com/10.1002/ijop.12010%5Cnhttp://linkinghub.elsevier. com/retrieve/pii/S096386871000048X%5Cnhttp://www.irrodl.org/index.php/irrodl/article/ view/1530%5Cnhttp://www.ncbi.nlm.nih.gov/pubmed/19135 (2002)
16. Fogg, B.: A behavior model for persuasive design. In: Proceedings of the 4th International Conference on Persuasive Technology—Persuas'09, p. 1 (2009)
17. Oinas-kukkonen, H.: Behavior change support systems : a research model and agenda, pp. 4–14. Springer, Berlin (2010)
18. Harjumaa, M., Oinas-kukkonen, H.: Persuasion theories and IT design. In: PERSUASIVE 2007, pp. 1–5. Springer-Verlag, Berlin Heidelberg (2015)
19. Berkovsky, S., Freyne, J., Oinas-Kukkonen, H.: Influencing individually: fusing personalization and persuasion. In: IJCAI International Joint Conference on Artificial Intelligence 2015 Jan, pp. 4153–4157 (2015)
20. Kaptein, M., De Ruyter, B., Markopoulos, P., Aarts, E.: Adaptive persuasive systems: a study of tailored persuasive text messages to reduce snacking. ACM Trans. Interact. Intell. Syst. **2**, 1–25 (2012)
21. Thomas, S.: Pervasive, persuasive eLearning: modeling the pervasive learning space. In: Third IEEE International Conference of Pervasive Computing and Communications Workshops, PerCom 2005 Work. 2005, pp. 332–336 (2005)
22. Daud, N.A., Sahari@Ashaari, N., Muda, Z.: An initial model of persuasive design in web based learning environment. Procedia Technol. **11**, 895–902 (2013)
23. Drozd, F., Lehto, T., Oinas-Kukkonen, H.: Exploring perceived persuasiveness of a behavior change support system: A structural model. Lecture Notes in Computer Science (including Subser. Lect. Notes Artif. Intell. Lect. Notes Bioinformatics), vol. 7284 LNCS, pp. 157–168 (2012)
24. Fogg, B.J., Cuellar, G., Danielson, D.: Motivating, influencing, and persuading users. Human-Computer Interact. Handb. Fundam. Evol. Technol. Emerg. Appl. 133–46 (2009)
25. Oduor, M., Oinas-kukkonen, H.: A system's self-referential persuasion: understanding the role of persuasive user Experiences in committing social web users. In: PERSUASIVE, pp. 241–252. Springer (2015)
26. Derrick, D.C., Jenkins, J.L., Jay, F., Nunamaker, J.: Design principles for special purpose, embodied, conversational intelligence with environmental sensors (SPECIES) agents. AIS Trans. Human-Computer Interact. **3**, 1–25 (2011)
27. Angst, C.M., Agarwal, R.: Adoption of electronic health records in the presence of privacy concerns: the elaboration likelihood model and individual persuasion. MIS Q. **33**, 339–370 (2009)
28. Mankila, P.: Utilization of persuasive technology in e-commerce (2012)
29. Dwivedi, Y.K., Shareef, M.A., Simintiras, A.C., Lal, B., Weerakkody, V.: A generalised adoption model for services: a cross-country comparison of mobile health (m-health). Gov. Inf. Q. **33**, 174–187 (2016)

30. Räisänen, T., Lehto, T., Oinas-Kukkonen, H.: Practical findings from applying the PSD model for evaluating software design specifications. Lectures Notes Computer Science. (including Subser. Lect. Notes Artif. Intell. Lect. Notes Bioinformatics), vol. 6137 LNCS, pp. 185–192 (2010)
31. Alhammad, M.M., Gulliver, S.R.: Persuasive technology and users acceptance of e-commerce: exploring perceived persuasiveness. J. Electron. Commer. organ. **12**, 13 (2014)
32. Kelders, S.M., Kok, R.N., Ossebaard, H.C., Van Gemert-Pijnen, J.E.W.C.: Persuasive system design does matter: a systematic review of adherence to web-based interventions. J. Med. Internet Res. **14**, 1–24 (2012)
33. Adaji, I., Vassileva, J.: Evaluating personalization and persuasion in e-commerce. In: CEUR Workshop Proceedings, vol. 1582, pp. 107–113 (2016)

Exploring Factors Affecting the Adoption of HRIS in SMEs in a Developing Country: Evidence from Cameroon

A. Noutsa Fobang, S. Fosso Wamba and J. R. Kala Kamdjoug

Abstract With the increasing effect of globalization and technology, Human Resource Information Technology plays a key role in today's modern enterprise management. However, developing countries such as Cameroon are facing challenges in its implementation. The aim of this research is to explore factors influencing the adoption of HRIS by SMEs. To understand this issue, this paper integrates the unified theory of acceptance and use of technology (UTAUT) model. Primary data have been collected through survey by administrating structured questionnaire to the employees (HR department) of a number of organizations. We found that Performance Expectancy and Internal Social Influence have a significant effect on the intention to adopt HRIS. In contrast, the specific groups—age and education—are significantly different in the relationship between Adoption Intention and Use. Of course, these findings open the door for future research issues, including explaining why SMEs organizations are sluggish to respond to HR innovation.

Keywords HRIS · Factors of adoption · UTAUT · Cameroon

1 Introduction

One of the most spectacular changes of this century is no doubt the development of Information and Communication Technologies (ICTs). Many organizations are becoming more are more dependent and use them for their daily management so as

A. Noutsa Fobang (✉) · J. R. Kala Kamdjoug
GRIAGES, Catholic University of Central Africa, P.O. BOX 11628, Yaounde, Cameroon
e-mail: aimenoutsa@gmail.com

J. R. Kala Kamdjoug
e-mail: jrkala@gmail.com

S. Fosso Wamba
Toulouse Business School, 20 Boulevard Lascrosses, 31068 Toulouse, France
e-mail: s.fosso-wamba@tbs-education.fr

© Springer Nature Switzerland AG 2019
Y. Baghdadi and A. Harfouche (eds.), *ICT for a Better Life and a Better World*,
Lecture Notes in Information Systems and Organisation 30,
https://doi.org/10.1007/978-3-030-10737-6_18

to achieve their goals and take more advantage of information technology (IT) and human resource management (HRM), the two constructs being correlated. Human resource information system (HRIS) plays an important role in the modern enterprise management [1]. More than being at the heart of HR, HRIS is increasingly occupying the "heart of the firm" because it brings together all the different actors of the social capital [2]. In the past years, researchers have attempted to give a definition of HRIS, but Tannenbaum's definition is the one that is commonly accepted in the literature review. It is composed of three main concepts, namely: HR, Information, and System. HRIS is defined as a "system used to acquire, store, manipulate, analyze, retrieve and distribute pertinent information about an organization's human resources" [3].

As a matter of fact, HRIS allows managers not only to follow up their employees' work on a regular basis, but also to offer indicative dashboards that are very necessary for a better implementation of a HR strategy aligned with the business strategy [4]. Scholars have agreed that using HRIS can provide a number of benefits, not only for the HR function, but also for line managers and the whole organization [5]. While medium and large organizations have spent a huge amount of money and reserves on implementing HR software [6], efforts and considerable resources are to be dedicated small organizations as well. Some of the disadvantages of a HRIS [4] involve data entry errors, cost factor such as costly technology to update in system, initial investment cost and training costs of users [7, 8], cost per-hire for a new employee in a specialized field, high cost and risk of implementing new software [9], malfunctions or insufficient applications to support human resources needs, staffing because of a strong demand in specialized knowledge and the finding of qualified specialist with human resources functional area knowledge, security due to unauthorized access and hacking strategic information.

Taking into consideration that Information and communication technologies (ICTs) continue to be the main drivers of the information society, Cameroon is one of the countries of the sub-Saharan regions which offers a range possibility of IT development. The World Development Report 2016: Digital Dividends, published in January 2016, revealed that the Internet penetration rate in sub-Saharan Africa is in constant growth (from 1.22% in 2006 to 10.84% in 2014). The Bretton Woods institutions believes efforts have to be done. Thus, Cameroon, due to its geography strategic position, can play a major role as a driver for the digital economy in the sub-region. According to the 2015–16 Affordability Report, released in February 2016 by the Alliance for Affordable Internet (A4AI), Cameroon is the 19th country in Africa with an Affordability Drivers Index (ADI) of 25.97%, which is certainly low but encouraging. Moreover, according to the McKinsley Global Institute (MGI), in one of its report published in August 27th, 2014, Cameroon is ranked 8th in Africa, in a ranking on the level of involvement of new technologies.

As other developing countries, Cameroon is facing many challenges in the adoption of technology (HRIS as well), specifically the involvement of end users, the management reluctance; the cost factor, the work culture, the training and learning, the lack of technological knowledge and a strong organizational internal resistance, to name but a few. Despite the importance of HRIS in any modern organizations, some authors seem to agree that HRIS adoption remains insignificant and still suffers a low level of investigation [10], particularly in developing countries [11] like Cameroon [12]. Regarding specifically the case of SMEs, IT adoption by this corporate category has been a regular topic of few studies [13]; but, in this regard, much has to be done in the context of Cameroon. This research paper aims to contribute to filling that gap in the relevant literature, by analyzing some critical factors influencing the Use of HRIS.

2 Theoretical Background

HRIS must be able to cover all the HR management processes, and the various tasks computerized so as to better respond to the needs and thereby to assist management in a better decision-making process [14]. Efficient, regular management is only ensured owing to HRIS adoption [15]. One of the usages of a well-integrated HRIS will be through simple spreadsheets and easily performed complex calculations [16]. The significance of the implementation of an IT system such as HRIS will vary from one organization to another. Therefore, HRIS helps in proper planning of HR [17], keeping records, managing talent and knowledge and enhancing decision-making [18]. Firms are facing many challenges when it comes to implementing new technologies, especially in a globally changing environment; so goes with HRIS, the adoption and use of which is possible only when the potential adopters forecast and perceive the net benefits of it, such as competitive advantage [19].

Some research works have explored factors influencing the adoption of the human resource information system (HRIS) in a growing economy, notably in sectors such as banking [20, 21] and the academic environment [22, 23]. Alam et al. [24] performed a survey to identify critical factors influencing the decision of hospitals' management in Bangladesh to adopt HRIS. They used the Human-Organization-Technology fit (HOT-fit) model and the Technology-Organization-Environment (TOE) framework. They found that IT infrastructure, top management support, IT capabilities of staff, perceived cost, and competitive pressure are the main critical factors which have a significant effect on the decision to adopt HRIS. In addition, they discovered that the technological dimension stood as the most significant dimension.

On their part, Mamum and Islam [25] revealed that management perception toward HRIS performance fully depended on the experience, gender and education of managers, but was at the same time associated with the organizational origin. Bal et al. [26] rather asserted that performance with the HRIS is influenced by system quality, information quality and perceived ease of use. The fact that HR department staff lack knowledge about HRIS [12] does not underrate the importance of this technology. Haines and Petit [27] earlier founded that the presence of a specialized HRIS unit would increase system usage.

Few researches have been carried out on the effects of usage. Ron Hanscome [28], research director of HCM technologies at Gartner Inc., said industry vendors now view the user experience as a competitive battleground. As a consequence, user experience is now used as one of those things where a major change might happen frequently. It would therefore be essential to continuously evolve and improve user experience, as it would have an effect on future implementation, because of usage experience and each software update would in turn have an incremental improvement in usability.

Among the various models and theories proposed for the adoption of ITs, the Unified Theory of Acceptance and Use of Technology (UTAUT), formulated by Venkatesh et al. [29], is a model of technology acceptance that aims to describe the intended use of an information system by users. In a consumer acceptance and use context, Venkatesk et al. [30] adapted the four constructs (i.e. Performance Expectancy, Effort Expectancy, Social Influence, and Facilitating Conditions) of UTAUT that influence behavioral intention to use a technology and/or technology use. Based on literature review, it has been confirmed that many scholars have used this model in their studies, using subset constructs, in various context. For example, Al-Khowaiter et al. [31] used the social influence construct in a context of a public administration in Saudi Arabia and found that it has both direct and indirect effect for encouraging employees to use HRIS. Moreover, Rahman et al. [21] in their

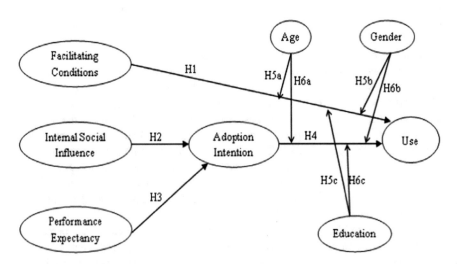

Fig. 1 Research model

study identified the four above mentioned constructs of UTAUT and proposed a simplify conceptual model without moderating effects (age, gender, experience).

Based on these prior studies, we conceptualize the research model Fig. 1. Thus, this study endeavors to test hypothesis regarding HRIS adoption and the variability of Facilitating Conditions and Adoption Intention toward HRIS's use in terms of age, gender and education.

Facilitating Conditions. Many salient factors produce a unique and direct effect on use, without the intermediation of the intention to adopt. They can be considered as a degree to which an individual believes that the perception or non-perception of subjective elements could support the use of the system [29].

H1   Facilitating Conditions have a positive influence on the Use of HRIS.

Internal Social Influence. Venkatesh et al. [29] stated that it is the degree to which an individual perceives that the people he considers important think he should use a system. And in that case, such people will encourage him.

H2   Internal social influence has a positive influence on the intention to adopt HRIS.

Performance Expectancy. It is a degree to which an individual believes that using the system will have a positive effect on its job performance, so as to attain personal gains [29]. It is an outcome expectation at the individual level, viewed as a perceived usefulness.

H3   Performance expectancy influences users' intention to adopt HRIS.

Adoption Intention. The Adoption Intention is influenced by users' attitude and perceived usefulness of the system by end users. It describes that desire to use the system. People who intend to adopt a technology are more likely to use it [29] as the Use describes the intensity of the use of HRIS in daily life.

H4   The intention to adopt HRIS has a positive influence on the Use of HRIS.

Age, Gender, and Education. The effects of Facilitating Conditions and Adoption Intention on Use will be significantly different for each specific group of moderators.

H5 (a–c)   Age, gender, and education are significantly different for the relationship between Facilitating Conditions and Use of HRIS.

H6 (a–c)   Age, gender, and education are significantly different for the relationship between Adoption Intention and Use of HRIS.

3   Methodology

Firms were not targeted neither for their industry nor their category. Perhaps the target population of respondents for this research was made up of employees working in various public and private organizations in Yaounde and Douala, two cities of Cameroon, mainly in the HR department, using the HR software to accomplish their daily tasks. The sampling frame was a list of workers at the HR department without HR Managers. Items for constructs used in the research model were developed from previous research, and then modified for use in HRIS within the Cameroonian context, in order to enhance their validity. The nature of this research work is hypothetico-deductive, and only quantitative data have been used to conduct the study. These data has been collected from primary source through conducting both online and field survey. The survey has been conducted using structured questionnaires to collect data and measure the constructs of the above proposed model, utilizing a seven-point Likert scale ranging from "(1) strongly disagree" to "(7) strongly agree". Pre-test with six former students in IS Management (Master's level) and pilot study of 20 respondents drawn from our population were carried out consecutively, and the various feedback received were used in designing and testing the efficiency of the final questionnaire.

Among the 510 questionnaires sent, 278 were returned and only 258 were usable, giving a response rate of 50.58%. Exploratory Factor Analysis has been conducted to ensure reliability and convergent validity of each item of our model. Then Structured Equation Modeling (SEM) has been performed to identify the relationship between constructs. The SmartPls 3.2.6 software developed by Ringle et al. [32] has been used to perform the analyses [33].

4   Data Analysis and Results

4.1   Demographic Information

The demographic characteristics of our respondents are shown in Table 1.

Of the 258 respondents, 138 were women (53.49%). It is a fairly average distribution. Concerning educational background, the majority of the respondents 62.79% are holders of a master's degree while 29.46% are bachelor's degree holders. It can be noted that the HR training program ends at least at the level of bachelor's degree. That is why our population is more concentrated on these two levels. The participants' average age was between 20 and 40 (80.24%), which is an eloquent proof of the HR services/departments' inclination for a relatively young staff.

Table 1 Demographic characteristics of respondents

Profile	Description	Frequency	Percentage
Gender	M	120	46.51
	F	138	53.49
Age	20–30	106	41.09
	31–40	101	39.15
	41–50	11	4.26
	51–60	40	15.50
	Over 61 years	0	0
Educational background	High school	20	7.75
	Bachelor degree	76	29.46
	Master	162	62.79
	Ph.D. and above	0	0

4.2 Demographic of Respondents

Measurement Model. To assess the measurement model, internal reliability, convergent and discriminant validity are used [34]. For each construct, we shall measure the internal reliability (*Composite Reliability-CR* and the *Cronbach's Alpha*). The acceptable value of these measures must be greater than 0.70 [34, 35]. As for the convergent validity measured by the *Average Variance Extracted (AVE)*, the preferred value is greater than 0.50 [34, 36]. *Cross loading* and correlations between constructs are also key measures for convergent validity, so as to ensure that the items being used match their correspondent constructs and that these constructs are independent. Concerning the *outer loadings*, Hair et al. [34] underlined that further analysis should be carried out for values between 0.40 and 0.70 and that items below 0.40 should be removed.

The results of the CR, Cronbach's Alpha and AVE are shown in Table 2. It shows that CR value ranges from 0.838 to 1.000 > 0.7, and that the Cronbach's Alpha of the construct ranges from 0.769 to 1.000 > 0.7, which indicates a strong internal consistency and reliability of our constructs. As for AVE, their value ranges from 0.528 to 1.000 > 0.5.

Based on these previous findings, we can conclude that the convergent validity is insured. As for the HTMT ratios of correlation between the constructs, the different corresponding values are set forth in Table 3. Such values are acceptable because they are below the threshold of 0.90 [34]. On the basis of the findings, both the reliability and validity of the constructs are guaranteed.

Structural Model. The *Bootstrapping* method allows testing the significance of the relationship between the constructs featuring in the model through the interpretation of the *t-statistics*, as well as the correlation between these constructs by looking deeply on the values of the *path coefficient*.

Table 2 Constructs reliability and validity

	Cronbach's Alpha	rho_A	Composite reliability (CR)	Average variance extracted (AVE)
Adoption intention	0.923	0.925	0.963	0.928
Facilitating conditions	0.818	0.857	0.861	0.528
Internal social influence	0.769	1.300	0.838	0.582
Performance expectancy	0.847	0.855	0.907	0.764
Use	1.000	1.000	1.000	1.000

Table 3 Heterotrait-monotrait ratio (HTMT)

	Adoption intention	Facilitating conditions	Internal social influence	Performance expectancy	Use
Adoption intention					
Facilitating conditions	0.365				
Internal social influence	0.323	0.280			
Performance expectancy	0.813	0.376	0.380		
Use	0.888	0.246	0.386	0.775	

To express some significance, the *t-statistics* must be greater than 1.96. Table 4 summarizes these values. It shows that the relationships *Adoption Intention* → *Use* ($t = 37.096$), *Internal Social Influence* → *Adoption Intention* ($t = 5.347$) and *Performance expectancy* → *Adoption Intention* ($t = 21.514$) have significant effects on the adoption of HRIS. Thus, these findings support hypotheses H2, H3 and H4. However, Table 5 highlights the values «R^2» and «R^2 adjusted» of the latent constructs «Adoption Intention» and «Use». The variable «Adoption Intention» is explained at 55% by the variables «Inernal Social Influence» and «Performance expectancy», but in turn it explains up to 72% of the variance of the variable «Use». As far as the values of R^2 are greater than 0.25, we can conclude that our model is quite good and interesting [34].

Multigroup Analysis (MGA). The multigroup analysis assesses whether predefined data groups present significant differences for the group-specific model estimations. For this purpose, we decided to use the PLS-MGA approach (Partial Least Squares Multigroup Analysis). It focuses on the bootstrapping results for each group [37]. The PLS-MGA method [38] represents an extension of Henseler's MGA [37]. This method is an important non-parametric test for the comparison of the group-specific *bootstrapping* PLS-SEM results. *p*-value smaller than 0.05 or larger than 0.95 indicates a significant difference from the probability of 0.05.

Table 4 Structural model testing hypothesis using bootstrapping

Hypothesis		Original sample (O)	Sample mean (M)	Standard deviation (STDEV)	T statistics (|O/ STDEV|)	P values
H1	Facilitating Conditions → Use	−0.015	−0.010	0.034	0.445	0.656
H2	Internal Social Influence → Adoption Intention	0.160	0.166	0.030	**5.347**	0.000
H3	Performance Expectancy → Adoption Intention	0.677	0.678	0.031	**21.514**	0.000
H4	Adoption Intention → Use	0.858	0.855	0.023	**37.096**	0.000

Table 5 R-square and R-square adjusted

Latents constructs	R^2	R^2 adjusted
Adoption intention	0.553	0.550
Use	0.727	0.725

For the sake of simplifying our study, we decided to restrict analyses to only the two groups relating to age and education profile: GROUP_AGE(20–30) versus GROUP_AGE(31–40) and GROUP_EDUC(Bachelor's degree) versus GROUP_EDUC (Maîtrise/Master). We considered the others values irrelevant.

Table 6 shows that the two groups of age are significantly different for the relationship Adoption Intention → Use (p-value = 0.000 < 0.05). The analysis of the values of each group path coefficient: GROUP_AGE (20–30) (*path coefficient* = 0.885 − R^2 = 0.910) and GROUP_AGE (31–40) (*path coefficient* = 0.451 − R^2 = 0.327) reveals that the first group is stronger than the second group, which means that respondents' age range 20–30 has a more significant effect on that relationship than the one ranging from 31 to 40 does. Apparently, the younger respondents will be more sensitive due to their age as they are likely to have a good intention to adopt new technologies.

Table 6 Multigroup analysis of the group "Age"

	Path Coefficients-diff (|GROUP_AGE (20–30) - GROUP_AGE(31–40)|)	p-Value (GROUP_AGE(20–30) vs. GROUP_AGE(31–40))
Adoption intention → Use	0.434	0.000
Facilitating Conditions → Use	0.029	0.622

Table 7 Multigroup analysis of the group "Education"

	Path coefficients-diff (GROUP_EDUC(Bachelor's degree,...)) - GROUP_EDUC (Maitrise/Master))	p-Value (GROUP_EDUC (Bachelor's degree) vs. GROUP_EDUC(Maitrise/ Master))
Adoption intention → Use	0.158	0.002
Facilitating conditions → Use	0.059	0.165

Table 8 Multigroup Analysis of the group "Gender"

	Path Coefficients-diff (GROUP_GENDER(F) - GROUP_GENDER(M))	p-Value (GROUP_GENDER(F) vs. GROUP_GENDER(M))
Adoption Intention → Use	0.033	0.318
Facilitating Conditions → Use	0.079	0.162

Table 7 shows that the two education groups are significantly different as concerning the relationship Adoption Intention → Use (p-value = 0.002 < 0.05). The values of path coefficient are fairly equal between the two groups: GROUP_EDUC (Bachelor's degree) (*path coefficient* = 0.890 − R^2 = 0.919); and GROUP_EDUC (Master) (*path coefficient* = 0.732 − R^2 = 0.0582). However, although they are not so different from each other, the analysis of the values of R^2 highlights that Bachelor's degree holders have a stronger explanation on the Use of HRIS than Master's degree holders. Given their lower level of education as compared to the other group, holders of bachelor's degree are more enthusiastic and willing to learn more in order to gain more advantage. So, they will supply more efforts.

As for Table 8, there is no significant difference between the two groups of gender as it may appear in the relationships Adoption Intention → Use (p-value = 0.318 > 0.05) and Facilitating Conditions → Use (p-value = 0.162 > 0.05). Moreover, paths coefficients' values for each gender group are fairly equal in absolute value (*path coefficient* = 0.874 for F and 0.841 for M for the relationship Adoption Intention → Use and *path coefficient* = 0.018 for F and −0.061 for M for the relationship Facilitating Conditions → Use). On the other side, for the same gender group, these values are greater for the link Adoption Intention → Use although their contributions to R^2 are fairly equal in each group.

Based on these findings, it clearly appears that the hypotheses H6a and H6c are supported.

5 Discussions

Our study contributes to IS research in general and to IT adoption in particular, especially in the Cameroonian context, where the available relevant literature is poor, like in most developing countries. Therefore, by applying the UTAUT model to investigate the various factors influencing HRIS adoption in SMEs in Cameroon, this research work certainly adds new knowledge to the existing literature. One major theoretical contribution consisted in identifying and analyzing critical factors influencing the Use of HRIS by modifying UTAUT2 [30] with the removal of the extended constructs and the application of the subsequent model at the level of consumers. This conceptual model modifies and completes the one formulated by Rahman et al. [21]. Prior research works have corroborated some results of Al-Khowaiter et al. [31], Dečman [39], Rahman et al. [21], Noutsa et al. [12] and Venkatesh et al. [29]. The findings can be summarized as follows: Social influence and performance expectancy influence the adoption of ITs (including HRIS), while the intention to adopt influences the Use. Furthermore, we demonstrated how some individual characteristics such as age and education are significantly different between the relationship Adoption Intention → Use. In-depth analyses reveal that the impact of Adoption Intention on Use is stronger for young people, but also more important for people with low educational background. Young people tend to face an accurate ability in processing new technologies, thus affecting their intention to adopt, only if they perceive its usefulness. Moreover, holders of bachelor's degree explain 91.90% of variance of the Use of HRIS. By adopting a technology, they tend to use it because it affects their learning of new technologies, while the holders of master's degree think they already have the maximum knowledge in IT adoption. As a consequence, they won't make any effort because of their complex of superiority.

Another aspect is the insignificant effect of Facilitating Conditions on Use. While the findings of the original UTAUT, in line with Kemayou et al. [13], proved the contrary—that is, Facilitating Conditions constitute a significant factor in the adoption process—our study could not ascertain such a statement. Furthermore, there is no significant difference in the relationship of the selected individual characteristics. This evidence could be explained by the fact that very few organizations have so far implemented such a technology in Cameroon and that the system was not well perceived by our interview respondents.

The SME sector in Cameroon which constitutes 95% of the economy fabric is rich and diversified, but unfortunately it is not well organized and lacks maturity in terms of IT implementation. With the recent signature of economic partnership agreements with some international counterparts, Cameroon-based organizations are expected to be more competitive. This will undoubtedly drive the domestic economy and help firms to be more proactive, efficient, and mature while providing them with innovative solutions. This external social influence will necessarily impact on the social groups inside the organization and the performance expectancy these people think they can benefit in performing their daily tasks [40].

While identifying critical factors for the adoption of HRIS in our context, the study attempts to examine the significant difference of each specific-group of the individual characteristics. Future research may focus on a number of limitations faced by this study. This includes failure to study the moderating effects of these variables and their subsequent joint effect, and to expand the scope of the study to more urban and rural areas as well as HR departments. In addition, the outcome of this study might not be the perfect reflection of the entire scenario in Cameroon as we have not covered all geographic areas of the country and could not consider the point of view of all employees. So, by incorporating entities in other areas while taking into account more viewpoints from end users, another research work will surely bring more insights enabling a fair generalization of findings and, thus, a comparison between firms in cities with those in rural areas.

In the current globalized world, organizations are doomed to interact, exchange information, compete or merge with others more than ever, for a better global positioning. Changes are all the more impressive as organizations connected to the same network will not necessarily react in the same way, because of specific factors such as culture and geographic situation. It may look interesting to deeply investigate the impact of such specific factors in further research.

With the rapid growth of ITs, SMEs in Cameroon will significantly gain net benefits if they use it to enhance their strategy, boost their productivity, obtain accurate information or innovate. In Cameroon like in other developing countries, the adoption of ITs (including HRIS) represents a major challenge because of economic and infrastructural constraints [24].

In addition, they are sustainable indicators for managers willing to implement the HRIS in their industry. The results revealed that the specific groups of Age and Education are significantly different for the relationship Adoption Intention → Use. So, managers can create segmentation in their firm during the phase of implementation, so as to apply a group policy for specific-groups that are significantly different. It is commonplace that HRIS will also significantly help managers to analyze not only the perceived costs of a modern system, but also the competitive pressure from the surrounding environment when it comes to gaining strategic business advantage. The internal social influence has a positive effect on the Adoption Intention of the HRIS. Besides, managers are expected to build on HRIS to be able to develop a strategy for increased cohesion between the social corps, because the more people interact and exchange information in an organization, the more the organization gains in both knowledge accumulation and maturity.

6   Conclusion

This research work has extended the understanding of HRIS adoption by testing the phenomenon in a developing economy. It is obvious that organizations can benefit from HRIS only if this system is effectively adopted and used by the adopters. Such adoption and use will involve the engagement of all stakeholders within the organization's chain, from the end users to the managers. The aim of this study was to identify critical factors that can influence the adoption of HRIS within our context. The review of the literature has already acknowledged that several factors do influence the HRIS adoption at different levels and contexts. For such factors, including factors of UTAUT, it was showed that performance expectancy and internal social influence produced positive effects on the intention to adopt HRIS, and that age and education, have significant group-specific difference in the relationship between Adoption Intention and Use. By contrast, there is no significant difference between gender groups. Using UTAUT in our model, our study has confirmed—and sometimes denied—many of the findings developed in the extant literature; better still, it has once more demonstrated that UTAUT is one of the predictive models for IT adoption.

References

1. Wei, S., Feng, A.: Research on applications on human resource information system in SMEs. In: 2nd International Conference on Science and Social Research (ICSSR), pp. 804–807. Atlantis Press, Beijing (2013)
2. Storhaye, P.: Le SIRH: Enjeux, Facteurs de Succès, Perspectives. DUNOD, Paris, p. 247 (2013)
3. Beadles II, N.A., Lowery, C.M., Johns, K.: the impact of human resource information systems: an exploratory study in the public sector. Commun. IIMA. **5**, 39–46 (2005)
4. Gupta, B.: Human resource information system (HRIS): important element of current scenario. IOSR J. Bus. Manage. **13**, 41–46 (2013)
5. Ponduri, S.B.: Quality of human resource information systems at commercial bank of Ethiopia (a case study of dessie district at dessie, Ethiopia. Int. J. Res. **4**, 31–41 (2016)
6. Nagendra, A., Deshpande, M.: Human resource information systems (HRIS) in HR planning and development in mid to large sized organizations. Procedia—Soc. Behav. Sci. **133**, 61–67 (2014)
7. DeSanctis, G.: Human resource information systems: a current assessment. MIS Q. **10**, 15–26 (1986)
8. Buzkan, H.: The role of human resource information system (HRIS) in organizations: a review of literature. Acad. J. Interdisc. Stud. **5**, 133–138 (2016)
9. Ngai, E., Wat, F.: Human resource information systems: a review and empirical analysis. Pers. Rev. **35**, 297–314 (2006)
10. Blount, Y., Castleman, T.: The curious case of missing employee in information systems research. In: 20th Australasian Conference on Information Systems, pp. 300–310, Monash University Australia, Melbourne (2009)
11. Ankrah, E., Sokro, E.: Intention and usage of human resource information systems among ghanaian human resource managers. Int. J. Bus. Manage. **11**, 241–248 (2016)
12. Noutsa, F.A., Kala, K.J.R., Fosso Wamba, S.: Acceptance and use of HRIS and influence on organizational performance of SMEs in a developing economy: the case of Cameroon. In: Rocha Á. et al. (eds.) Recent Advances in Information Systems and Technologies, AISC 2017. LNCS, vol. 569, pp. Springer, Porto Santo (2017). https://doi.org/10.1007/978-3-319-56535-4_57
13. Kemayou Yombia, S.M., Kala Kamdjoug, J.R., Fosso Wamba, S.: Les Facteurs Favorisant l'Acceptation et l'Utilisation des TIC en Entreprise: Cas de la CNPS. AIM, Lille (2016)

14. Hendrickson, A.: Human resource information systems: backbone technology of contemporary human resources. J. Labour Res. **24**, 381–394 (2003)
15. Chakraborty, A.R., Mansor, N.N.A.: Adoption of human resource information system: a theoretical analysis. In: 2nd International Conference on Leadership, Technology and Innovation Management. Istanbul (2013)
16. Parry, E.: The benefits of using technology in human resource management. In: Torres-Coronas, T., Arias-Oliva, M. (eds.) Encyclopedia of human resources information systems: challenges in e-HRM, vol. 1, pp. 110–116. IGI global, Cranfield (2010)
17. Khera, S.N., Gulati, M.K.: Human resource information system and its impact on human resource planning: a perceptual analysis of information technology companies. IOSR J. Bus. Manage. **3**, 6–13 (2012)
18. Aggarwal, N., Kappor, M.: Human resource information systems (HRIS)—its role and importance in business competitiveness. Gian Jyote e-J. **1** (2012)
19. Khan, A.R., Hasan, N., Rubel, M.: Factors affecting organizations adopting human resource information systems: a study in Bangladesh. J. Bus. Manage. **17**, 45–54 (2015)
20. Chowdhury, M.S.A., Yunus, M., Bhuiyan, F., Kabir, M.R.: Impact of human resources information system (HRIS) on the performance of firms: a study on some selected bangladeshi banks. In: 9th Asian Business Research Conference, Dhaka (2013)
21. Rahman, M.A., Qi, X., Jinnah, M.S.: Factors affecting the adoption of HRIS by the Bangladeshi banking and financial sector. Cogent Bus. Manage. **3**, 1–10 (2016)
22. Altarawneh, I., Al-Shqairat, Z.: Human resource information systems in Jordanian universities. Int. J. Bus. Manage. **5**, 113–127 (2010)
23. Davarpanah, A., Mohamed, N.: Human resource information systems (HRIS) success factors in a public higher education institution context. In: 3rd International Conference on Research and Innovation in Information Systems, Kuala Lumpur (2013)
24. Alam, M.G.R., Masum, A.K.M., Beh, L.-S., Hong, C.S.: Critical factors influencing decision to adopt HRIS in hospitals. PLoS ONE **11**, 1–22 (2016)
25. Mamun, M.A.A., Islam, M.S.: Perception of management on outcomes of human resource information system (HRIS). Int. J. Bus. Soc. Res. **6**, 29–37 (2016)
26. Bal, Y., Bozkurt S., Ertemsir, E.: The importance of using human resources information systems (HRIS) and a research on determining the success of HRIS. In: International Conference (2012)
27. Haines, V.H., Petit, A.: Conditions for successful human resources information systems. Hum. Resour. Manage. **36**, 261–275 (1997)
28. Society for Human Resource Management. https://www.shrm.org
29. Venkatesh, V., Morris, M.G., Davis, G.B., Davis, F.D.: User acceptance of information technology: toward a unified view. MIS Q. **27**, 425–478 (2003)
30. Venkatesk, V., Thong, J.Y.L., Xu, X.: Consumer acceptance and use of information technology: extending the unified theory of acceptance and use of technology. MIS Q. **36**, 157–178 (2012)
31. Al-Khowaiter, W.A.A., Dwivedi, Y.K., Williams, M.D.: Examining the role of social influence, usefulness and ease of use for determining the mandatory use of a human resource information system in the context of Saudi Ministries. Int. J. Electron. Gov. Res. (IJEGR) **11**, 24–42 (2015)
32. SmartPLS 3. http://www.smartpls.de
33. Chin, W.W., Marcolin, B.L., Newsted, P.R.: A partial least squares latent variable modeling approach for measuring interaction effects: results from a monte carlo simulation study and an electronic-mail emotion/adoption study. Inf. Syst. Res. **14**, 189–217 (2003)
34. Hair, J.F., Hult, G.T.M., Ringle, C.M., Sarstedt, M.: A primer on partial least structural equation modeling (PLS-SEM), 2nd edn. Sage Publications, Thousand Oaks (2016)
35. Chin, W.W.: The partial least squares approach for structural equation modeling. In: Marcoulides, G.A. (ed.) Modern methods for business research, vol. 8, pp. 295–336. Lawrence Erlbaum Associates Publishers, Mahwah (1998)

36. Fornell, C., Cha, J.: Partial least squares. In: Bagozzi, R.P. (ed.) Advanced methods of marketing research, pp. 52–78. Blackwell, Cambridge (1994)
37. Sarstedt, M., Henseler, J., Ringle, C.M.: Multigroup analysis in partial least squares (PLS) path modeling: alternative methods and empirical results. In: Advances in International Marketing, pp. 195–218. Emerald, Bingley (2011)
38. Henseler, J., Ringle, C.M., Sinkovics, R.R.: The use of partial least squares path modeling in international marketing. In: Advances in International Marketing, pp. 277–320. Emerald, Bingley (2009)
39. Dečman, M.: Understanding technology acceptance of government information systems from employees' perspective. Int. J. Electron. Gov. Res. (IJEGR) 11, 69–88 (2015)
40. Harsono, I.L.D., Suryana, L.A.: Factors affecting the use behavior of social media using utaut 2 model. In: 1st Asia-Pacific Conference on Global Business, Economics, Finance and Social Sciences (AP14Singapore Conference), pp. 1–14. Globalbizresearch, Singapore (2014)

Part III
Technologies Influencing
Enterprise Modeling

Big Data at the Service of Universities: Towards a Change in the Organizational Structure and the Decision-Making Processes

Dina Sidani and May Sayegh

Abstract If the information is at the heart of economic intelligence and institutional power, the data are the essential elements to build knowledge for a decision making that might seem to be optimal in view of the opportunities and knowledge available at a given time. Today, with the explosion of mass data which are characterized by their diversity, their nature and their connections to other objects, Business Intelligence shows its limits. In a context where business competitiveness depends on the use of technology for processing the data to facilitate decision making, Big Data seems to be the right solution. Nowadays, the variety of data sources and the need for fast and real-time processing demand new methods of data storage and analysis. Big Data is a (R) evolution of technologies and decision-support approaches. It precisely allows refining the understanding of the situation and improving decision efficiency through prediction. The adoption of Big Data has profound implications in institutions. It is the organizational structure that is called into question, calling not only for new decision-making approaches but also and especially for new profiles. In the same context, there is a growing interest among institutions of higher education in taking advantage of Big Data to improve student performance, while reducing administrative work load. Higher educational institutions can benchmark their student, professor and curriculum performance against like universities, offering yet new insight into the potential for improvement. Through a qualitative study conducted in 6 universities, we will show how the adoption of Big Data will transform the organizational structure and the decision-making processes within the universities of Lebanon.

Keywords Big data · Data analysis · Structural (R) evolution · Organizational structure · Decision-making processes · Data scientist · University perspectives

D. Sidani (✉) · M. Sayegh
Faculty of Management, Saint-Joseph University, Beirut, Lebanon
e-mail: dina.sidani@usj.edu.lb

M. Sayegh
e-mail: may.merhejsayegh@usj.edu.lb

© Springer Nature Switzerland AG 2019
Y. Baghdadi and A. Harfouche (eds.), *ICT for a Better Life and a Better World*,
Lecture Notes in Information Systems and Organisation 30,
https://doi.org/10.1007/978-3-030-10737-6_19

1 Introduction

If the information is at the heart of economic intelligence and institutional power, the data are the essential elements to build knowledge for a decision making that might seem to be optimal in view of the opportunities and knowledge available at a given time.

Today, three words are highlighted by the decision-making model: "Data", "Information" and "Knowledge". The relation between these words is represented by the place of honor held by knowledge, to emphasize the fact that a lot of data are required to gain a knowledge. In parallel, the power lies in the good command of data use and linkage. More and more aware of the importance of data and of information, businesses are rushing to think about how to manage, enrich and analyze them in the most advantageous way [1].

Thus, with a Big Data project, businesses would face technological issues and, since an appropriate architecture needs to be set up, organizational issues as they decide about the strategy and the organization of the flows of data to be processed, as well as issues related to the decision-making processes.

Having defined the Big Data concept, we will show why and how its adoption within institutions is associated with an in-depth reorganization of the very structure of the organization in addition to its decision-making modes. Our paper aims to study the managerial perspectives arising from the adoption of Big Data within universities. Based on a qualitative research conducted in six (6) Lebanese universities, our study seeks to understand and consider the perceptions of the information specialists in light of the Big Data concept, and to explain why the adoption of such concept can modify the organizational structure and the decision-making processes within institutions.

2 From Business Intelligence to Big Data: Towards a (R) Evolution in Data Analysis

2.1 Business Intelligence

Business Intelligence (BI) is a technological process that analyzes relevant and usable information and data to help corporate managers, directors and other decision-makers to take more informed business decisions.

BI is about applying the decision-making process associated with the use of technologies to make it easy for institutions to make decisions. The fact that the ecosystem generates more and more data results in increasingly growing number of "datavores" among users.

The increased volume of data to be analyzed in a company follows what is called an exponential distribution, which make the institutions think about new forms of architectures not only in storage, but also in the analysis of those data.

2.1.1 Limits of BI

Let's consider the social networks which emerged as a result of the modern technological and technical revolutions, allowing for faster interactions with web pages. These social networks are playing a growing role in our professional and our social and personal lives, across the social media, taking multiples forms such as «Rich Site Summary» (RSS) flows, microblogs (Twitter), podcasts or even video sharing and involving different activities that combine technologies with social interactions [2].

In view of these new interactions, the members of such social networks have grown in number, and so did the data. This is where Big Data steps in, by structuring, linking up and analyzing the data of the different social and other networks, within a company, to control the flows of information, to enhance and stimulate the communication, to create communities and, above all, to analyze the tendencies.

However, so far, it has been so difficult, even impossible, to exploit this volume of data by use of the traditional BI techniques (Text Mining, Data Mining, Knowledge Data Discovery (KDD), On Line Analytical Process-OLAP...) without setting in place complicated and costly organizational and technological architectures and infrastructures which are adapted to such a large amount of data.

It is at this point that the limits of the traditional decision-making architectures of Business Intelligence are reached.

- A data warehouse of several terabytes is very complicated to maintain and to develop.
- The unstructured data have never been handled by the BI technologies, which are mainly based on structured data that were hitherto deemed inadequate to make decisions.
- The implementation of new uses is not possible: work on unstructured data, new sources ignored by the data warehouses such as the sensor or social media data, massive amounts of data that need to be handled and integrated in the company's information system, integration of predictive algorithms becoming available to everyone...

The traditional databases are losing ground to diversified and less and less structured data.

2.1.2 New Technological Era: Big Data Stimulating BI

Today, BI is reinventing itself in this time of technological turmoil. Business intelligence has always been considered as an element apart from the company's information system. The Big Data technologies help explore new possibilities that would revolutionize the business intelligence. Big Data is a phenomenon that came out with the emergence of bulky data that the traditional techniques were not capable of handling. The Big Data early projects are those of the information research actors on the "web search engines" like Google and Yahoo. Effectively, those actors have encountered problems related to the scalability (scaling up) of the systems and the time to respond to the users' demands. Very quickly, other actors, like Amazon and Facebook, followed suit. For many industrial actors, Big Data has become an unavoidable trend, given its contribution in terms of data storage, processing and analysis. The data sets are so large that new technical and scientific tools are required to understand and take advantage of them. This flood of data involves deep issues on their collecting, their interpretation and particularly their analysis.

2.2 Definition of Big Data

Big Data basically refers to two concepts: data storage and data analysis.

2.2.1 Data Storage

«Big Data» alludes to technologies, processes and techniques allowing an organization to create, handle and manage large-scale data [3] and to extract new knowledge so as to create economic value. In literature, the concept of Big Data is defined through the 4 V theory [4]: Volume, Variety, Velocity and Veracity to which some authors added other V such as Value.

- *Volume*: The volume is the mass of collected data as well as the flow of data that continuously originate and rapidly grow from petaoctet to exaoctet.
- *Variety*: Those flows are varied and stem from shape-shifting sources—internal corporate data (Customer Relationship Management, internal information system…), external data (social media, mails, mobile terminals …), structured data (documents, images…) and/or unstructured data (tweets, GPS data, sensors…). They are also difficult to handle with the data processing traditional tools.
- *Velocity*: The velocity indicates the speed with which the data are simultaneously processed.
- *Veracity*: The veracity refers to issues of confidence and of uncertainty as to the data and the results of the analysis of such data.

So, one can speak of "Big Data" once the volumes to be handled reach bulky sizes: Peta (web), Terra, Exa, Zettaoctets … and once the existing tools fail to handle the exploitation and the analysis of those data.

2.2.2 Data Analysis

A Big Data project is of real importance in that it combines heterogeneous data in real time and creates possible combinations and cross-referencing. This helps refine the knowledge of the situation, on one hand, and provide knowledge that has been up to now inaccessible and take advantage of it, on the other hand. This falls more generally within an evolution of the decision-support technologics and tools (Business Intclligence).

While the classic decision support tools referring to Big Intelligence are characterized by a slow processing time, Big Data handles the masses of bulky data more simply and less costly [5].

With various sources and a swift data processing, the understanding of the situation is particularly refined and the decision efficiency is enhanced through prediction.

3 Managerial Perspectives

The Big Data phenomenon gives rise to and is associated with new technological and organizational issues that require a redefinition not only of the data structures, but also and above all, the way in which such data will be analysed. With a Big Data project, businesses would face technological issues since an appropriate architecture needs to be set up.

Today, the data management systems, deployed in most of the companies, are unable to handle all those flows. The technological infrastructure and the technical architecture must be reconsidered to fit. In addition to this technological issue, there is an organizational challenge to decide about the strategy and how to organize the nature and the flows of the data to be processed as well as about the assignment of a team that would call into question the decision-making modes and processes.

3.1 New Infrastructure and New Organization...

3.1.1 Technological Issues: What Tools and Techniques to Use to Ensure Data Processing?

The storage, transmission, processing and visualization tools will be affected by the bulky size of data. On a small scale, from the Teraoctet order, data can be stored on hard disks. But in the case of Big Data, the data volumes might exceed the Petaoctet, and thus, data are stored in specialized sites, the Datacentres.

3.1.2 Organizational Issues: What Data to Process? How to Organize the Flow?

The identification of the most relevant data which constitute only a small percentage of the quantity of data the company has is one of the major organizational issues relating to the deployment of the Big Data strategy. Due to the multiplicity of the data sources, in order to make good use of such massive data and extract a strategic value from them, there is a double challenge:

- To set up a structure that allows the classification of those data, rank them according to analytical priorities and choose the combinations and cross-references to do in order to extract a strategic value.
- To assign a qualified team, focused on the acquisition of knowledge, and who can transform information into knowledge. To achieve this, it becomes necessary to knock down the partitioning walls that create silos within the company.

"Big Data is one of the transformative elements of the company; it is interdisciplinary and concerns all professions. In this sense, Big Data is not an Information System (SI) project; rather, it is a new way of thinking about the information and understanding it. It is more of a cultural and technological revolution than a new SI subject." [6]. This is not about modifying the information but about analysing it without any risk of breach of integrity. The usual opposition between operational and IT teams is going to give way to a new dynamic:

«Operational teams + IT teams = Innovative Capability» [6].

3.2 New Skills Required

3.2.1 Interdisciplinary Skills...

A Big Data project requires a good approach of the data governance as well as new specialized skills not only in the handling of large-scale data, but also and above all in their analysis.

Besides the technical and technological skills which help smartly link up selected data among a mass of data, those "Data Scientists" must also have operational skills that allow them to get connected with the company's global strategy with a view to helping make better decisions. They should be abreast of both the technical and the managerial dimensions of the data so as to cross-reference data in a creative way. In other words, those actors must be skilful in mathematics (for the mastery of statistics), in information technology (for a good exploration of the virtual machines and of the servers) and in strategic consulting to be able to give meaning to raw data and to identify the powerful indicators for the General Management.

3.2.2 For Better Decisions Making

Traditionally, the final decision is generally made by the famous Highest Paid Person's Opinion (HIPPO). On one hand, the Big Data techniques reconsider the company's decision-making modalities. Henceforth, the deciders are going to make the best use of their skills to set clear objectives and ask good questions, instead of seeking to multiply the data sources [7]. On the other hand, the exploitation of Big Data needs new skills, based on the good command of both the technical features of the Big Data processing environments and the necessary data sets (which are generally unstructured). This presupposes a better organization and a better use of the information those "Data Scientists" have. The question here is about the profile of the actors who are in charge of such governance. New functions as Information Governance Officers appear in companies, requiring a training on how to handle and analyses data, as well as on new decision-making approaches, to avoid deviating toward automated decision-making processes.

## 4	Big Data Perspectives in Universities

Though still a niche, Big Data is thriving within the education field. The digital revolution is deeply transforming the education world; the developments are very often revolutionary, with respect to both the teaching and the learning methods… Reports are being issued by governments about the potential of Big Data in the education field (Consultation report by the US Office of Educational Technology, Department of Education, 2012).

Big Data in Universities: A Tool for a Strategic Decision-making Approach.

In order to maintain a competitive edge in the most rapidly evolving markets, like any institution, universities need not only to have the necessary data to fit in their environment, but also to make forecasts and anticipate the demand. At universities, this cult of data,—«Data is King»—is increasingly becoming a must in view of the profusion and the free access to data, as well as the explosion of social media. Effectively, Big Data would serve as a lever for universities in terms of the use of data for internal purposes and of the analytics opportunities for a better decision-making approach in a competitive context.

The issues related to the adoption of Big Data are of two types: material issues and human issues. The material issues concern the storage and the distribution of a mass of data as well as the possibility of accessing them in real time, which involves a specific and suitable technology. However, as far as the human issue is concerned, the expertise is essential to give meaning to those data from a strategic point of view. It is not the software that constitutes the keystone of Big Data, but rather the expertise and the understanding of the use of such software.

There is no question that Big Data needs Specialists to build and develop the architecture of the data, link them up and analyse them. The challenge is to extract value from those data by linking up, in a relevant way, data that are carefully drawn from the data mass.

4.1   Overview of the Research Methodology

Our specific research purpose will be taken into consideration through a qualitative methodology based on the nature of the data and a pursuit of regularities through the content analysis. By favouring a qualitative methodology, we address the following exploratory issue: Our paper's aim is to study, analyse and understand the perceptions of the stakeholders about the concept of Big Data in the academic community. In our study, we follow an inductive approach that consists of producing the understanding of the facts by relying on the perspective gained from references to the collected theoretical elements and from our empirical study.

Trying to understand the perceptions of stakeholders who deal with data and information system will allows us to consider exploring in depth a program, an event, an activity, a process or a concept. This method appears to be appropriate for our research because it focuses on the stakeholders' beliefs and concerns; it allows us to understand the overall context of ICT in the specific area of using Big Data in the universities of Lebanon. This method is most often used by researchers seeking to better understand the context.

Our empirical field constitutes of six interviews with six information systems specialists from the six top universities in Lebanon: AUB, St. Joseph University, Lebanese University, LAU, AUST, and CNAM. According to Vernette and Giannelonni [8], the semi-directive interview is the best suited for our study, insofar as it allows grasping and understanding the perceptions regarding the concept of the study.

4.1.1   Choice of the Field

The target of our empirical study was chosen according to the following criteria:

- The IS specialists interviewed are from the six top universities in Lebanon.
- Our source of information is mainly based on the perceptions expressed by the directors and middle managers of IS Departments in universities.
- Those IS specialists head the IS department in their university or at least hold an important position in this domain.
- Most of them have more than 6 years of service in their position.
- Those specialists experienced and adopted unavoidable technological changes that have occurred in the last few years.

This study aims to draw the perceptions of the actors interviewed concerning the information system in the universities of Lebanon. Our main goal is to better understand the relationship between the use of data and the decisional process or decision making. We explore the purpose of collecting and analysing Data. Garreau [9], based on Strauss and Corbin [10], research suggests three types of coding that aim to: identify potentially relevant categories (open coding), connect them (axial coding) and select those that best explain the phenomenon studied (selective coding).

Based on the data collected, we can identify the relevant categories using the open coding which allows detecting the interesting elements in the data. Then, we use the axial coding through which we can link the data together to address the selective coding of selected items from our theoretical construct. Applying the method of Garreau [9] cited above, we have conducted an analysis of the interviews, while going over the main themes or variables based on the organizational and managerial implications and perspectives related to the use of Big Data in universities, especially terms of decision making processes.

We have indicated the key ideas in order to identify the patterns adopted within the organizational structures in terms of organizational structure and decision-making processes as a result of the use of Big Data.

4.1.2 Data Collecting Source and Method

The semi-directive interviews were conducted face to face with six IS specialists from the six top Lebanese universities. Each interview lasted between 45 min and 1 h and the data were gathered over one and a half months.

We prepared an interview guide by relying on the literature. The conducted interviews are structured in two topics: the first aiming to understand and analyse the information system as it is, its use and the way of collecting and analysing the data in the organizational structure; the second being related to the perception of the decision-making process arising from the use of the Information Systems in universities, as shown in Table 1.

Table 1 Interview analysis

	Data sources	Purposes of collecting data	Organizational structure: collecting storing, analyzing	Decision making
1	Logs from websites: time spent on website, number of visits, Insights of social media Emails, class management systems, feedback, student course evaluations	Benchmarking programs to other programs Tracking students' performance Understanding the students' preferences and evolution Comparing performances Recruiting convenient students Aligning students with the appropriate major Measuring students' performance	Department responsible for collecting, storing and analyzing data Software: excel, R, SPSS	Results are reviewed by the person who conducts the analysis The analyst reports to the rector and formulates recommendations

(continued)

Table 1 (continued)

	Data sources	Purposes of collecting data	Organizational structure: collecting storing, analyzing	Decision making
		Identifying the risks for students Analyzing the teaching effectiveness		
2	University's Information System	Data are used to a better decision making and all the above.	Using business Intelligence A team is responsible for collecting data about recruitment and reports to the president; otherwise, each department is responsible for collecting its own Data and reports to the head of the department who in turn reports to the president	People in charge: in this case, the rector and the deans who ask, in coordination with the IT specialist, that some data be cross-referenced in order to understand or analyze tendencies in terms of headcount, the students, the candidates' profiles, the geographic localization, ...
3	Logs, insights, online surveys	Benchmarking at the financial, marketing, social and environment levels Results used by heads of departments	No such system to collect Data, only Excel to collect and analyze Data such as statistical studies, SQI and Server Data bases	IT Analysts whose function is to link up in a relevant way the data which are carefully selected from the data mass The objective is to have better decision—making procedures which will lead to better decisions
4	ERP, internet, or public requests	Taking strategic decisions, data transferred to rector, vice rector and deans	ERP, IT Department, platforms, Excel, SPSS...	Report → analytics, Decision → proposition to University board → Board
5	Logs, insights, information system, social media	Being aware of the market evolution in terms also of benchmarking in order to adapt our education to the students' requirements Taking strategic decisions, data transferred to rector, vice rector and deans	Ad-hoc department to collect data. applications used through Hootsuite and Tweetdeck. Tracking followers through Insta follow, in addition to excel sheets	Aligning communication strategy with needs and visions Identifying indicators allowing to give meaning to raw data and to use them to develop the strategy Communications to the rector and the deans

4.2 Organizational Issues

4.2.1 Modification of the Organizational Structure...

Our interviews highlight the importance of having a maximum amount of information from diverse sources. The major issue is to know how to cross-reference the data in an intelligent way to extract a strategic value.

The persons interviewed admit that the days of accepting students into colleges and universities based primarily on standardized test scores, high school grade point averages (GPAs) and extracurricular involvement are on the decline. University admissions officers are relying more on data collecting to decide rapidly and actively on the enrolments. Those decisions are based on a wealth of new available data and predictive modelling and yield multiple long-term benefits, including enhanced student retention. They are using Data for the same purpose without using Big Data utilities. The IS specialists interviewed underline the importance of deciding or selecting the nature of data to be processed or to be linked up in order to know later how to formulate recommendations at the Top Management, in this case the Rector, the Deans and the Directors of institutions.

When it comes to the organizational structure, the data are collected and stored within a department and then organized or linked together for analysis at the request of the decision makers. The data are stored according to the department, very often according to the topic and are used by those in charge of such departments. The challenge would be to set up a structure that allows collecting all these data coming from largely diversified sources, classify them, rank them by analytical priorities and choose the combinations and the cross-referencing to do in order to extract a strategic value. This new organizational structure, characterized by the diversity of sources and ensuring the collection and the classification of data, requires transversal work teams within the different departments of the institution as well as the elimination of the frontiers between IS specialists and decision-makers.

4.2.2 For New «Scientific Decision-Making» Professions: Data Architects and Scientists

The adoption of Big Data will not only result in a reorganization of the structures; it will also give rise to new collaboration forms. Effectively, innovation centres with transversal teams must be created and run by strategic decision-makers (Vice-rectors, Deans, Officers...) and IS managers pulling together to merge their skills.

Regarding the decision-making processes, the technological skills must go hand in hand with a relevant analysis of the data linked up to extract a knowledge represented in information that may be used in the strategic decisions. So, the keystone in the handling of data is going to draw on the expertise and the relevance of giving meaning to those linked data so as to extract information useful for the institution strategy. At this point, it would be suitable as well for the data specialists or scientists to be also able to read and analyse the raw data, to interpret them and even to develop strategic recommendations.

The challenge would be to analyse the information with no risk of breach of integrity, which requires an in-depth change in the decision-making processes, based both on data handling and analysis techniques and on professional skills.

5 Conclusion

Today, there is no clear and well-defined strategy that can guarantee a successful deployment, and above all, governance of a Big Data project. To create value in a company, it is not enough to deploy an appropriate infrastructure and to invest in advanced data processing technologies. The research of Karoui et al. [7] show that the integration of data in the culture of an organization requires a structural and organizational adjustment based on new collaboration forms privileging transversal structures through teams who would have their skills merged for the only purpose of transforming information into knowledge. Here, to avoid the trap of the automatization of the decision-making processes, it is essential to seek a "Data Scientist", not only trained on the technical dimension of data handling and analytics, but also aware of the managerial dimension of data, in order to have a strategic vision in the intelligent cross-referencing of data.

In this technological context submerged by a mass of data and privileging a personalized marketing (Era of the Customer Relationship Management), the adoption of Bid Data constitutes a valuable asset in favour of the academic performance in terms of:

- Targeted recruitment according to the geographic areas making up the strongest potential for admissions;
- Attraction of valuable candidates for the institutions;
- Creation of the profile of the recruited candidates;
- Retention of the best students;
- Follow-up on the progress of each of its students with alerts to be addressed should those face academic problems.

With reference to the above, universities must install the convenient architectural structure to analyse data. To transform data into knowledge, the IS teams must work with the decision makers for an optimal decision making.

In this regard, giving a strategic meaning to data entails a team work between IS managers and strategists within the organization. Thus, it is going to be a real (R) evolution in the organizational structure of universities in the light of a new strategic decision support approach resulting from the adoption of Big Data.

The decision-making process and power are in the hands of the IT Scientist—a new job profile which, besides the technological skills, must have professional skills to link together the information drawn from the data cross-referenced and the corporate global strategy so as to make optimal decisions. The cult of the data involves not only data at the service of the decision makers but also data which are analysed and transformed into information to be used by the decision makers themselves.

How to enhance the transversal structures between IS teams and professional teams for a new data scientist profession within the universities where the data are always transmitted strategically for decision-making falling within the scope of the Top Management?

Questionnaire

Dear Madam, Dear Sir,

In order to understand the importance of data storage and data analysis in universities, we are leading a survey about these two concepts. We would be grateful if you can give us 30 (thirty) min of your time to answer the following questions.

1. What is the role of information/data nowadays, especially in universities?
2. How do you collect information/data about your students at the university?
3. How do you collect information about other universities in order to rank yourself (Third party data)?
4. How do you manage the storage of those collected information?
5. Who is in charge of collecting data? One person or more? Or a team? What is the place of such person(s)/team within the organizational structure?
6. What software do you use in order to analyse the collected data?
7. Who analyses the data? What position does he (she) hold within the organizational structure?
8. Why do you search for data? And why do you analyse them? What is the purpose of collecting and analysing data?
9. After analysing the data, to whom do you communicate the results? Why this person or group exactly? What is his (their) position within the structure?
10. Who uses information related to data analysis? Which institution or department? After obtaining information about data analysis, what is the next step?
11. Can you describe the decision-making process following the data analysis?
12. Are data collectors different from data analysers who also differ from decision makers? If not, why should they be the same or at least working together?
13. What are the budget and resources allocated to collect, store and analyse data in your institution?
14. What do you know about Big Data?

References

1. Monino, J.L.: Big Data, Open Data et valorisation des données, Research network on innovation. Working papers, N° 48 (2015)
2. Power, D., et Phillips-Wren, G.: Impact of social media and web 2.0 on decision-making. J. Decis. Syst. **20**(3), 249–261 (2011)
3. Hopkins, B., Evelson, B.: Expand your Digital Horizon with Big Data, For CIOs, Forrester (2011)
4. Sicular, S.: Gartner's big data definition consists of three parts, not to be confused with three "V"s (2013)
5. Brasseur, C.: Enjeux et usages du Big Data, Editions Hermès (2013)
6. Cigref: Big Data—La vision des entreprises: opportunités et enjeux, October 2013. http://www.cigref.fr/big-data-vision-grandes-entreprises
7. Karoui, M., Davauchelle, G. et Dudezert, A.: Big data: Mise en perspective et enjeux pour les entreprises. Inf. Syst. Eng. (2014)
8. Vernette E., Giannelloni J.-L.: Etudes de marché, Paris, Vuibert, pp. 213–220 (2001)
9. Garreau, L. (2010) La construction du sens. Comment accéder à l'opérationnalisation d'un concept complexe au travers de la théorie enracinée? Revue Internationale de Psychosociologie, vol. 16
10. Strauss, A., et Corbin, J.: Basics of Qualitative Research: Grounded Theory Procedures and Techniques, Thousand Oaks: Sage (1990)

Online Consumer Reviews in the Hotel Sector: Why and How to Answer?

T. Pekarskaia Dauxert

Abstract This research aims to analyze the practices of the online review management by hotels. Little research has been done so far on the responses to online reviews by the hotels and on their impact on actual and potential clients. Expert face-to-face interviews have been realized with hospitality and social media professionals in France in 2015–2016, completed by an analysis of two online review web sites (TripAdvisor and Booking.com). The results show differences existing in the online review responding practices: from a simple monitoring without response to a regular policy of response to all reviews. Several factors could explain these differences, such as belonging to a hotel chain, hotel category, financial and human resources dedicated to customer service, or the responsibilities of the staff. The results could help the hotel managers in their practice of answering the online reviews and any other organization dealing with customer reviews.

Keywords Hotel · Online review · Organizational response · Service marketing · TripAdvisor

1 Introduction

As a major source of the electronic word-of-mouth (eWOM), Internet has transformed the way of searching for products and services by individuals [1–3].

Among the eWOM forms, the online consumer reviews have a particularly important impact on the search of information, the evaluation and the decision-making of the consumers in the field of tourism and hospitality [4–8].

Several reasons could explain the popularity and the impact of the web sites with user-generated content (UGC) among consumers. One could mention the ubiquity of the web, the ease and the anonymity to access online consumer reviews web

T. Pekarskaia Dauxert (✉)
PRISM, Université Paris 1 Panthéon-Sorbonne, 17 Rue de La Sorbonne,
75005 Paris, France
e-mail: tatiana.dauxert@gmail.com

© Springer Nature Switzerland AG 2019
Y. Baghdadi and A. Harfouche (eds.), *ICT for a Better Life and a Better World*,
Lecture Notes in Information Systems and Organisation 30,
https://doi.org/10.1007/978-3-030-10737-6_20

sites, and also the availability of positive and negative evaluations of tourist and hotel products and services posted by a large number of consumers [9]. The information on these sites is generally provided by the customers that have had a recent and direct experience with a product or a service. This information can take different forms, such as aggregated ratings or detailed stories on individual experiences [10]. The trust in these online reviews is quite high, with about 70% of consumers indicating that they do trust this type of communication [11].

Tourist and hotel products and services are considered to be «experiential». With no previous experience of their own, potential customers tend to consider other customers' evaluations a reliable basis for preparing their future purchase decisions [10, 12]. Thus, online consumer reviews are considered by consumers to be rapid and practical means for evaluating and comparing tourist and hotel products and services, means that reduces risks which are potentially associated with the buying act [7]. However, according to some studies, online reviews could have a more important role for information and knowledge sharing, rather than for a direct influence on purchase decisions [12–14].

The French hotel market is chosen as the object of our study for several reasons. France is the first tourist destination in the world [15], and Paris is still one of the favorite tourist destinations, despite a certain decrease of tourist attendance after recent terrorist attacks. Practices of online review management in different types of Parisian hotels (chain, franchised or independent three to five star hotels,) have a great interest for our research. Besides, as far as we know, few research articles have treated the French hotel market so far [16]. So it seemed to us that it would be interesting and useful to explore the practices of online review management in the French hotel market, to see whether they are similar to or different from those that have been analyzed in the existing literature on the hotel market in other countries (such as the USA or China).

The results of our study show a number of factors that influence the online review management by hoteliers. Among these results, there are the financial and human resources dedicated to customer service, and in particular to the online review management, general management policy in this field, belonging to a hotel chain with a deliberate and specified online review management strategy, and also the responsibilities of the staff in charge of the customer service.

2   Literature Review

Through reading online reviews, consumers can obtain purchase-related information (e.g. price equity), learn about the actual consumption of a product and observe the buying behavior of their reference groups [17]. Online reviews are valuable in purchase decision making because they help shoppers glean unique information over and above that provided by sellers [18]. While sellers typically supply information such as product attributes, technical specifications and performance, online reviews are often framed around users' perspectives and provide information about actual product usage [19]. Online reviews may also reveal information that firms would hesitate to mention or omit due to space constraints in traditional marketing media. Online reviews can have a positive or negative valence. In any customer opinion platform one can find positive and negative online reviews, and they have been shown to be separate constructs demonstrating discriminant validity [20]. Evaluations can be viewed during a certain period of time, often for a very long time. Research has shown that they could have a considerable impact on the organizational e-reputation, including tourist and hotel properties [21, 22], and also on operational performance [23]. While positive reviews tend to increase prospective customers' anticipation of benefits, negative ones induce expectation of risks [19]. According to some researchers, negative online reviews occur three times less than positive reviews [24, 25] but customers tend to be more affected by the negative ones [19]. One of the possible explanations is that potential customers may consider negative online reviews to be more diagnostic and informative than positive ones because information about product benefits is usually already available as part of a product's marketing efforts (e.g. in advertisements and product description) [26].

In order to avoid eventual negative effects that unsatisfied customer experiences could have on a wide web audience, many organizations designated one or several representatives to monitor and to intervene, when necessary, in the online discussions [27]. These practices are known as "webcare", or "the act of engaging in online interactions with (complaining) consumers, by actively searching the web to address consumer feedback (e.g., questions, concerns and complaints)" [28]. Webcare addresses consumers that post comments (especially negative ones) in a digital environment. But it also addresses large audience that could read these comments. So the webcare concerns multiple organizational objectives: customer care, marketing and also public relations [27].

Thus, it becomes more and more important for firms in different sectors, including tourism and hospitality business, to monitor and to manage the electronic word-of-mouth (eWOM). One of the main questions one could ask is to know how the response from businesses to the customers' comments could improve the consumer attitudes towards these businesses, hotels in particular. How quick and in what way should a firm, or should it not, answer consumer comments?

On the one hand, some studies on hotel responses strategies to negative online reviews have already been realized [29–31]. According to some researchers, an organization could minimize critics by leaving without answer negative events [32]. Response could, under certain conditions, have a negative effect on buying customer intentions [30] and on hotel performance [33].

On the other hand, in their research, Wei et al. [34] insist on the necessity for hotels to search and to answer comments that have been posted by consumers. They also call for more research in this area, especially concerning ambivalent consumer reviews, non–student samples and various dimensions of management responses such as the tone of the responses or the sources' characteristics. According to the research of Chan and Guillet [35], «by leaving negative comments of its customers without an answer, a firm could find itself in an unfavorable situation and loose its existing or potential clients». A study conducted by Leung et al. [36] encourages managers to answer online consumer reviews, especially negative ones, and to explain why the problem has appeared. These authors also call for further research on the efficiency of the organizational response.

Some authors proposed dedicated typologies of responses [7, 29], and other suggested strategies for those responses [31], while some other researchers analyzed different typical components of the hoteliers' responses [37]. So our research aims to follow these studies. In particular, we analyze whether the typology of strategies of Park and Allen [31] and the "triple "A" typology of response elements of Sparks et al. [7] apply to the studied sector.

Park and Allen [31] proposed a typology of frequent/infrequent responders in upscale and luxury hotels in the USA, based on the frequency of responses of the hotels but also on the perception of online reviews by the management and the internal communication and the global strategy of the hotel management. The "triple "A"" typology of Sparks et al. [7] includes acknowledge, account and action.

Thus, it seems interesting to us to study online consumer reviews management practices and the response strategies of the hotels, to analyze and to compare these findings with those analyzed in the existing research and to find similarities or differences.

The research question is then: what strategies of online consumer reviews management are used in the French hotel market, and what are the factors that influence these strategies?

3 Method

To explore our subject and to find elements useful to answer the research questions, two qualitative methods have been used.

First, in-depth semi-structured face-to-face interviews with hotel experts (3–5 star hotels in Paris) and marketing/communication/social media experts (27 interviews). These interviews have been registered and fully transcripted. A thematic content analysis has been realized.

Second, an analysis of two online consumer review web sites (TripAdvisor and Booking.com, 3, 4 and 5 star hotels in Paris and Paris' region IDF that answer their reviews). We mostly registered and analyzed the online reviews and responses to these reviews (when available) from the hotels whose management accepted a face-to-face interview, to compare the interviews' content to real practices of these hotels on online consumer review web sites. The NVivo 11 software has been used to collect information, as it seems to us to be particularly adapted to collect social media content.

4 Results

According to our findings, we confirmed the main elements of the existing typologies of response elements [7] and of response strategies [31].

An important number of online consumer reviews (56%) that we have analyzed contains the three main elements proposed by Sparks et al. [7]: acknowledge, account and action.

Response strategies by Park and Allen [31] are also similar to some hotels of our sample, according to the results of our interviews. We have found frequent and infrequent responders, and we observe different perceptions of the consumer reviews by the management: they are considered to be mostly falsified and not reflecting the reality (3 respondents) but also perceived as a real source of value for the property that can help providing service of a better quality (12 respondents).

We have also found several factors that influence the response strategies of the hotels, such as:

- The general hotel group or chain policy regarding the response to online reviews (for hotels belonging to hotel groups or chains).
- The policy of the hotel general manager towards the response to online reviews.
- The financial and human resources dedicated to response to online reviews.
- The responsibilities of the manager or of the employee in charge of responding (whether answering the reviews is his/her priority or just one of his/her function among other responsibilities).
- The emergency of the complaints.
- The language of the online reviews and the ease or difficulties to find a qualified employee able to answer these reviews (especially in small/budget hotels and for rare languages).

Some hotels (especially 3 star ones in our sample) lack resources, financial, human or both of them, necessary to develop a social media policy and to provide a regular monitoring and an efficient management of online consumer comments. In some cases, front office or customer service managers read online reviews on their hotels only from time to time, irregularly, and answer randomly and rather to negative and very negative reviews (as in some 3 star hotels in our sample).

Some hotels explain this behavior by inertia of the general management, a lack of financial and human resources and an insufficiently dynamic hierarchical structure. The latter does not allow, for example, to quickly adapt to constantly changing market needs and to hire staff with competencies in social media management, especially in online review management, or to plan an appropriate training for the hotel staff: "we are supposed to answer online reviews but I do it as I can, as I feel from the "real" practice (...). They [the managers] never offered me an appropriate training... they do not have money for this" (interview 12).

On the other hand, online review management practices can differ even within the same hotel chain (for example hotels belonging to a hotel chain or franchised hotels in France). Thus, in 3 star franchised hotels, the staff seems to be more independent than in the hotels belonging to the hotel chains and more upscale hotels. For example, in one of the franchised hotels in our interview sample, the manager in charge to answer online reviews is also conference & events sales executive, so he has many responsibilities and often lacks of time to regularly answer online reviews. At the same time, he is not obliged to submit any report about his activity regarding online reviews to the general manager, "unless some very negative, even dangerous" reviews (interview 16). Normally, the general manager trusts his sales executive, so the latter says he "organizes his work as [he] can" (interview 16).

As for the hotels belonging to international hotel chains or to private groups (some 3 star but especially 4 and 5 star hotels), these properties have a more developed customer relation service that is much more active in responding online reviews. Most of the customer service managers in these hotels find that it is very important to respond all online reviews, both negative and positive, to show their care to their guests. They have to regularly report to their general management on their activities of online reviews and comments management. They consider the efforts of personalization of the responses to be their priority, especially in responding to negative comments, and they set as their main purpose to "transform every unsatisfied guest into a loyal guest" (interview 14).

The personalization can take different forms and can concern different elements. Most experts talked, for example, about mentioning the name (first and/or last name) of the guest or his/her nickname (on the online review web sites) (interviews 5, 10, 12). Some of them think that it is important to express empathy in the answer to a review (showing to the guest that the respondent understands what he/she felt, as if the respondent tried to put him(her-)self on the place of the guest). Paraphrasing the guest's review is also important, according to some interviewed experts. As in the case of empathy, paraphrase is supposed to show the hotel's consideration to the authors of the reviews (to show that the reviews are read carefully by the hotel staff and the hotel really cares about the service quality). Some hoteliers also provide their direct email in the answer to comments, in order to invite the author of the review to contact directly this manager in order to have a more personalized response or treatment. According to some managers, providing a direct email could also be considered as a blurred "promise" of an eventual compensation (for example, a discount or an upgrading or a supplementary service during the next stay of the guest). As for the voice of the answer, some managers prefer to respond using an official voice, but some others try to adapt their voice to the review tone. It means that if the review is written in rather conversational voice, the response will follow it and adopt the "conversational human voice".

The emergency of the claims is also important, as hoteliers care about the e-reputation of their hotels and try to avoid the negative word-of-mouth as much as possible. So most of the interviewed experts (23 interviews) talked about very urgent problems that need to be solved immediately or as soon as possible, and the authors of such reviews should be contacted as soon as possible too. According to some experts, there are unfortunately some false reviews or reviews reporting inexistent problems that are very difficult to eliminate from independent online review web sites (such as TripAdvisor). Some experts talked about cases of thefts (interviews 9, 10 and 14): when the guests reported a theft on TripAdvisor or Booking.com, while the hotels made all possible investigations and couldn't find any elements of proof of such thefts. Even if in such cases the hotel managers try to contact the guests immediately to resolve the problem directly with them, the negative review left in an online review website can still remain online for a long time. It is quite difficult for hotels, in the opinion of some experts, to prove that the problem is false and to delete such reviews, as the web sites like TripAdvisor are very strict on the transparency of reviews and the rights of their authors of reviews to express their point of view.

The language of the review is also an important factor for the response strategies. In fact, some hoteliers prefer to answer all or almost all online reviews, so they answer themselves in languages they are proficient in. But as for online reviews in languages they don't speak, the managers or employees have to ask help to their colleagues (if some of them are proficient in these languages). This aspect could make the response less quick and sometimes less efficient. Some managers prefer to translate the reviews that they can't understand and their answers to these reviews, with the automatic translating software available online. "Of course, this translation is far from being perfect but at least I can understand most of the reviews and I can answer the guests who have written them, even if my answer is not perfect. (…) This is to show our respect and consideration for guests who dedicated time to write a review on our hotel" (interview 10). It is even more difficult with reviews in less popular languages (for example, non-European languages, such as Chinese, Japanese, Russian…), especially for some 3 star hotels that lack of multilingual staff. In this case, some managers prefer to answer in English (after an automatic translation on the web), and some others prefer not to answer at all, as they are not sure to be able to write a correct and suitable response with the only help of an automatic translation program.

5 Theoretical and Managerial Implications

This study aims to contribute to fill in some theoretical gaps in the understanding of practices in terms of online consumer reviews management, for example, by distinguishing several types of hotels (belonging to a hotel chain, franchised, independent) and their influence on the response to online reviews strategy. We have found similarities with the typology of frequent/infrequent responders of Park and Allen [31]. Our research aims to better understand and to conceptualize different components of hotel responses to online reviews, following and confirming the 'triple "A" typology of Sparks et al. [7]. The main objective of our research is to identify the components that are able to influence attitudes and repeat purchase intentions of consumers that posted an online review and got a response.

Thanks to this research, we have also formulated practical recommendations on the structure and different elements of response, as well as on their influence on consumers. These recommendations include, *inter alia*, personalization of the responses, presence of empathy and paraphrase elements, apologizing, and confirmation of the actions aimed to avoid the claimed problems in the future or the promise to take these actions. These recommendations could certainly be useful for hotel managers and also for any organization dealing with the online review management.

6 Future Work

As for the limitations of this study, several constraints related to interviews, especially access to experts, time and budget, have not let us realize a more exhaustive research yet. We also chose a limited sample of hotels, in one country (France) and in the capital (Paris).

As for the further research, it seems to be interesting to study these phenomena in other countries and/or other sectors, with an eventually larger sample of organizations. It would be also useful to use other methods than expert interviews.

In the future, we plan to analyze the different variables of the hotel responses to online reviews (like the style, the source of response or the content details of the response) and their influence on the individuals who are the authors of these reviews. Our future aim is to understand how responses to online consumer reviews influence the attitudes and repeat purchase intentions of the consumers who are the authors of these reviews. We propose to analyze the influence of different variables of hotel responses (such as timeliness, source of response, empathy, paraphrase of the review components, personalization of the answer message, etc.) on the attitudes and repeat purchase intentions of the consumers who posted the reviews.

Besides, an important number of research articles on responses to online consumer reviews have been realized on student samples. To have more robust results, we will submit an online questionnaire to individuals that posted an online review on a hotel, after a stay in this hotel, and got a response from it. The customer database from some hotels in Paris will be used, and we will also contact the review authors on TripAdvisor, since this website has the option that enables any registered individual to contact directly (by private or by public message) the visitors who posted reviews.

7 Conclusion

The available body of research has emphasized the importance of online consumer reviews for the e-reputation management of organizations and for their operational performance in different sectors, especially in tourism and hospitality. Responses to the reviews, especially to the negative ones, within the appropriate environment (online review sites, social media...) constitute an important feature of the online review management. At present, little research has been dedicated to the influence of the responses to online reviews on the authors of these reviews and on the observing public.

Our research aims to enrich the existing literature on this topic and to bring complementary elements of comprehension of different ways to manage the online consumer reviews in French hotels. Several factors have been found that could influence the policy of review management, among them financial and human resources, global strategy of the general management, as well as the responsibilities of the staff related to online review management, the emergency of the claims and the language of the online reviews and of the response to these reviews.

References

1. Belvaux, B., Marteaux, S.: Les recommandations d'internautes comme source d'information: quel impact sur les entrées des films au cinéma? Recherche et Applications en Marketing **22** (3), 65–82 (2007)
2. King, R.A., Racherla, P., Bush, V.D.: What we know and don't know about online word-of-mouth: a review and synthesis of the literature. J. Interact. Mark. **28**(3), 167–183 (2014)
3. Serra Cantallops, A., Salvi, F.: New consumer behavior: a review of research on eWOM and hotels. Int. J. Hospitality Manage. **36**, 41–51 (2014)
4. Browning, V., So, K.K.F., Sparks, B.A.: The influence of online reviews on consumers' attributions of service quality and control for service standards in hotels. J. Travel Tourism Mark. **30**(1–2), 23–40 (2013)
5. Hudson, S., Thal, K.: The impact of social media on the consumer decision process: implications for tourism marketing. J. Travel Tour. Mark. **30**(1–2), 156–160 (2013)
6. Electronic word-of-mouth in hospitality and tourism management: Litvin, S. W., R. E. Goldsmith, Pan, B. Tour. Manag. **29**, 458–468 (2008)
7. Sparks, B., So, K., Bradley, G.: Responding to negative online reviews: The effects of hotel responses on customer inferences of trust and concern. Tour. Manag. **53**, 74–85 (2016)
8. Xiang, Z., Gretzel, U.: Role of social media in online travel information search. Tour. Manag. **31**(2), 179–188 (2010)
9. Buhalis, D., Law, R.: Progress in information technology and tourism management: 20 years on and 10 years after the Internet: the state of eTourism research. Tour. Manag. **29**(4), 609–623 (2008)
10. Flanagin, A.J., Metzger, M.J.: Trusting expert-versus user-generated ratings online: the role of information volume, valence, and consumer characteristics. Comput. Hum. Behav. **29**(4), 1626–1634 (2013)
11. Nielsen AC: Nielsen: global consumers' trust in 'earned' advertising grows in Importance, http://www.nielsen.com/us/en/press-room/2012/nielsen-global-consumers-trust-in-earned-advertising-grows.html (2012) (Accessed 10 Oct 2016)
12. Vermeulen, I.E., Seegers, D.: Tried and tested: the impact of online hotel reviews on consumer consideration. Tour. Manag. **30**, 123–127 (2009)
13. Duan, W., Gu, B., Whinston, A.B.: The dynamics of online word-of-mouth an product sales: an empirical investigation of the movie industry. J. Retail. **84**(2), 233–245 (2008)
14. Luca, M.: Reviews, reputation, and revenue: the case of Yelp.com. Harvard Business School NOM Unit Working Paper, 12–016 (2011)
15. UNWTO Tourism Highlights: 2017 Edition (2017)

16. Beauvisage, T., Beuscart, J.S., Cardon, V., Mellet, K., Trespeuch, M.: Notes et avis des consommateurs sur le web. Réseaux **1**, 131–161 (2013)
17. Hennig-Thurau, T., Walsh, G.: Electronic word-of-mouth: motives for and consequences of reading customer articulations on the internet. Int. J. Electron. Commer. **8**(2), 51–74 (2003)
18. Pee, L.G.: Negative online consumer reviews: can the impact be mitigated? Int. J. Mark. Res. **58**(4), 545–568 (2016)
19. Lee, J., Park, D.-H., Han, I.: The effect of negative online consumer reviews on product attitude: an information processing view. Electron. Commer. Res. Appl. **7**(3), 341–352 (2008)
20. Goyette, I., Ricard, L., Bergeron, J., Marticotte, F.: E-wom scale: word-of-mouth measurement scale for e-services context. Can. J. Adm. Sci. **27**(1), 5–23 (2010)
21. Hennig-Thurau, T., Gwinner, K.P., Walsh, G., Gremler, D.D.: Electronic word-of-mouth via consumer-opinion platforms: what motivates consumers to articulate themselves on the Internet? J. Interact. Mark. **18**(1), 38–52 (2004)
22. Hennig-Thurau, T., Hofacker, Ch. F., Bloching, B.: Marketing the pinball way: understanding how social media change the generation of value for consumers and companies. J. Interact. Mark. (Mergent, Inc.) **27**(4), 237–241 (2013)
23. Ye, Q., Law, R., Gu, B.: The impact of online user reviews on hotel room sales. Int. J. Hospitality Manage. **28**(1), 180–182 (2009)
24. Ha, H.-Y.: The effects of consumer risk perception on pre-purchase information in online auctions: brand, word-of-mouth, and customized information. J. Comput.-Mediated Commun. **8**, 1 (2002)
25. East, R., Hammond, K., Wright, M.: The relative incidence of positive and negative word of mouth: a multi-category study. Int. J. Res. Mark. **24**(2), 175–184 (2007)
26. Lee, M., Rodgers, S., Kim, M.: Effects of valence and extremity of e-wom on attitude towards the brand and website. J. Current Issues Res. Advertising **31**(2), 1–11 (2009)
27. Van Noort, G., Willemsen, L., Kerkhof, P., Verhoeven, J.: Webcare as an integrative tool for customer care, reputation management, and online marketing: a literature review. In: Kitchen, Philip J., Uzunoglu, Ebru (eds.) Integrated communications in the post-modern era, pp. 77–99. Basingstoke (UK), Palgrave-Macmilla (2014)
28. Van Noort, G., Willemsen, L.M.: Online damage control: the effects of proactive versus reactive webcare interventions in consumer-generated and brand-generated platforms. J. Interact. Mark. **26**(3), 131–140 (2012)
29. Levy, S.E., Duan, W., Boo, S.: An analysis of one-star online reviews and responses in the Washington, DC, lodging market. Cornell Hospitality Quart. **54**(1), 49–63 (2013)
30. Mauri, A.G., Minazzi, R.: Web reviews influence on expectations and purchasing intentions of hotel potential customers. Int. J. Hospitality Manag. **34**, 99–107 (2013)
31. Park, S.-Y., Allen, J.P.: Responding to online reviews problem solving and engagement in hotels. Cornell Hospitality Quart. **54**(1), 64–73 (2013)
32. McLaughun, M.L., Cody, M.J., O'Hair, H.: The management of failure events: some contextual determinants of accounting behavior. Human Commun. Res. **9**(3), 208–224 (1983)
33. Xie, K.L., Zhang, Z., Zhang, Z.: The business value of online consumer reviews and management response to hotel performance. Int. J. Hospitality Manag. **43**, 1–1 (2014)
34. Wei, W., Miao, L., Huang, Z.J.: Customer engagement behaviors and hotel responses. Int. J. Hospitality Manag. **33**, 316–330 (2013)
35. Chan, N.L., Guillet, B.D.: Investigation of social media marketing: how does the hotel industry in Hong Kong perform in marketing on social media websites? J. Travel Tour. Mark. **28**(4), 345–368 (2011)
36. Leung, D., Law, R., van Hoof, H., Buhalis, D.: Social media in tourism and hospitality: a literature review. J. Travel and Tourism Mark. **30**(1–2), 3–22 (2013)
37. Zhang, Y., Vasquez, C.: Hotels' responses to online reviews: managing consumer dissatisfaction. Discourse, Context & Media **6**, 54–64 (2014)

Evaluating the Performance of IT Governance in Service-Oriented Enterprises

Morteza Alaeddini and Seyed Alireza Hashemi

Abstract IT governance (ITG) has been defined as specifying the decision rights and accountability framework to encourage desirable behavior in use of IT. Due to growing the new concept "service-orientation" and its entrance to business terms, it is necessary to change the theory and mechanisms of implementation of ITG. Regardless of the need to a foundation for managing services and reforming mechanisms to govern IT as one of the most important enablers of business, organizational movements to service-orientation will be faced with serious challenges. The relationship between the ITG and service-oriented architecture (SOA) is discussable from two aspects: first, the role of an effective ITG in deploying SOA throughout the organization and second, necessary reforms in the traditional ITG methods in a service-oriented enterprise (SOE). In this paper, we have a particular focus on the second aspect to propose an evaluation framework for assessing ITG in SOEs.

Keywords IT governance (ITG) · Service-oriented architecture (SOA) ·
Service-oriented enterprise (SOE) · COBIT

1 Introduction

IT governance is known as an aspect of a broad framework of enterprise governance [1] and is defined as "specifying the decision rights and accountability framework to encourage desirable behavior in the use of IT" [2]. In this era, it is necessary that we think about the methods to create and effectively establish IT governance responsibilities in the new shape of organizations, i.e., "service-oriented enterprises" (SOEs).

M. Alaeddini (✉) · S. A. Hashemi
Department of Computer Engineering and Information Technology,
Amirkabir University of Technology, 424 Hafez Ave, 15875-4413 Tehran, Iran
e-mail: m.alaeddini@aut.ac.ir

S. A. Hashemi
e-mail: sa.hashemi@aut.ac.ir

© Springer Nature Switzerland AG 2019   323
Y. Baghdadi and A. Harfouche (eds.), *ICT for a Better Life and a Better World*,
Lecture Notes in Information Systems and Organisation 30,
https://doi.org/10.1007/978-3-030-10737-6_21

Unlike SOA governance, which is an extension of ITG with the focus on the lifecycle of services to ensure the business value of SOA [3–5], our research is focused on the common ITG frameworks (e.g. COBIT [6] and ITIL [7, 8]). Our motivation is to implement and deploy traditional frameworks in SOEs and codify a method for assessing the performance of these frameworks, although there is no direct suggestion that they can support SOA.

Regarding challenges with which organizations must contend before they can begin the realization of the benefits of SOA (e.g. need an SOA strategy, establish an SOA business case, provide an SOA reference model and create SOA enterprise architecture [9]) and due to this fact that SOA has become the most critical IT trend of the recent years [9], it is necessary to consider many aspects of this approach and especially the mechanisms to make IT decisions in SOEs. For this reason, we have begun a chain of studies in the fields of creating a method to assess the performance of ITG based on SOA literature and evaluating the performance of current ITG frameworks in SOEs, since several years ago.

This paper explains a part of our studies about assessing the implementation of COBIT in an Iranian SOE. The paper aims at presenting the assessment method and its application in the case company for two times: once to assess the current situation of ITG in the firm and determine its necessary improvements, and another time, to evaluate the performance of the reformed framework. After explaining our motives on this topic due to the challenges in SOEs, and reviewing the history of related researches, we present the theory and the method of performance evaluation based on COBIT. The results of our study in the case company are also discussed in this paper. Finally, the paper ends with presenting some concluding remarks.

2 Literature Review

2.1 IT Governance

According to research results obtained by scholars, "alignment via governance" is one of the approaches to align business and IT [10]. Expected alignment can be achieved through formalization and institutionalization of strategic IT decision making and monitoring procedures in organizations [11]. ITG is the responsibility of executives and the board of directors [12] and consists of the leadership, organizational structures and processes to ensure that the enterprise's IT sustains and extends the organization's strategies and objectives [6]. Scholars have divided it into two major threads: IT service management and business performance management [10]. Two main approaches embraced by industry in this domain include an ITG framework such as COBIT and a set of IT service management best practices like ITIL [7].

2.2 COBIT

One of the basic needs of every enterprise is to acquire and use a framework to control IT. A suitable and efficient control framework needs to serve a variety of internal and external stakeholders [6]. The COBIT framework that is used for worldwide endorsement by various organizations addresses the right management practices for security and control in IT [13]. The main characteristics of COBIT, which introduce it as an applicable framework for ITG, are consisted of being business-focused, process-oriented, control-based and measurement-driven [6].

2.3 Service-Oriented Enterprise (SOE)

The concept of service is widely used in both IT and business science [14], but the usage and definition of the concept differ considerably in these areas. This difference can be generalized to the definition of SOE. from an IT perspective, SOE is a model to architect software and IT infrastructure, but from a business perspective, the concept of SOE should also cover the componentization of business functions into services so that re-composition using business processes will result in various business functions [15]. In this viewpoint, the focus of organizations is on providing superior services to their customers [16]. Based on the definition by federal enterprise architecture (FEA), an SOE includes the business, management, and operational processes, procedures, and policies to support a service model [17]. Literature shows that the business processes of an SOE are managed as some services in a service-oriented architecture. The alignment of these processes and services with SOE's business strategy is also monitored [18, 19]. Table 1 shows the SOE concerns about ITG in the form of some keywords.

3 Theory and Method

3.1 Research Methodology

As explained above, to move to service-orientation and to align business with IT services, SOEs have to create new mechanisms for their ITG as well as to provide an infrastructure to manage their services. The first step is to identify the required criteria to establish an ITG framework in this type of organizations to align IT with a service-based business model and to evaluate the performance of this framework.

Regarding considerations of service-orientation (Table 1) and based on the current methods of performance evaluation of ITG frameworks [34, 35], a qualitative approach in an actual environment is applied in this research to profoundly

Table 1 The keywords of service-orientation

No.	Keyword	Resource(s)
1	Service quality	[20–28]
2	Service level	[2, 10, 20–22, 26, 28–30]
3	Service management	[20–22, 31]
4	Service cost	[2, 20–22, 30]
5	Service continuity	[20–22, 30]
6	Service availability	[20–22, 30]
7	Service infrastructure	[31]
8	Service security	[23–28, 31]
9	Service innovation	[10, 26, 28, 29, 31]
10	Service configuration	[20–22, 30]
11	Service change	[20–22, 30]
12	Service provider	[10, 21, 26, 28, 29]
13	Service consumer	[10, 21, 26, 28, 29]
14	Service/solution development	[32]
15	Service/solution deployment	[32]
16	Service delivery/support	[32]
17	Data/knowledge management	[20–22]
18	IT measure	[20–22, 33–35]
19	Incident/problem	[20–22, 30]
20	Accountability level	[32]
21	Business process	[31]
22	Project/risk management	[2, 23–28]
23	Investment	[31]
24	Roles and responsibilities	[31]

look over the problem and to obtain the reliable results. Furthermore, due to how/ why nature of research questions, little control over events, and focus on a contemporary phenomenon within some real-life context [36], a case study is preferred as the methodology of research. The questionnaire, interview, direct observation, and document reviewing are four sources of evidence, which are used in this qualitative research to understand the performance of ITG in the unit of analysis.

Therefore, after discovering the governmental policies and commands related to IT usage in the public sector and ensuring that all of them are adjustable by COBIT, we understood metrics of performance evaluation and defined the method of assessment. Furthermore, we performed analyzing the collected data by different tools and techniques and indicated some improvement points to enhance the performance of ITG in the unit of analysis. After all, we reassessed the proposed ITG framework, which is developed, based on COBIT and compared results of both experiments together.

3.2   Performance Evaluation Method

In this research, a new method of performance evaluation is codified by consolidating some previous methods [34, 35] and looking at SOE expectations of ITG (Table 1). Pillars of this method are found on internal metrics (IM), which are related to the components of COBIT, and external metrics (EM), which are related to the results of establishing COBIT, to cover the mentioned SOE concerns.

Internal metrics include the maturity of IT processes of COBIT. These processes can support all keywords except 1, 3, 6, 16, and 21. External metrics also are composed of:

- EM_1: the importance of outcomes of ITG; including the importance of cost-effective use of IT and effective use of IT for growth, asset utilization, and business flexibility, on a scale from not important (1) to very important (5) [34, 35]. These metrics can cover keywords 4, 17, 21 and 23;
- EM_2: influence of the ITG in the business; involving the impact on cost-effective use of IT and effective use of IT for growth, asset utilization, and business flexibility, on a scale from not successful (1) to very successful (5) [34, 35]. These metrics can cover keywords 4, 17, 21 and 23;
- EM_3: business/IT alignment; comprising the small extent (1), large extent (3), and complete (5) alignment of IT services with business [35], which can cover keywords 19 and 21;
- EM_4: up-to-dating of IT services; containing up-to-dating a few (1), most (3), and all (5) IT services [35], which can cover keywords 9 and 16;
- EM_5: complying IT with agreed-upon service levels; including complying with a few (1), most (3), and all (5) offered services [35], which can cover keyword 2;
- EM_6: extent of IT service interrupts effect on critical business operations; involving daily (1), weekly (2), monthly (3), yearly (4), and never (5) over the past year [35], which can cover keywords 1 and 21;
- EM_7: performing IT projects on-time, on-budget and according to business quality standards; comprising 0–25% (1), 25–50% (2), 50–75% (3), 75–100% (4), and the whole (5) of IT projects [35], which can cover keyword 22;
- EM_8: extent of installation/upgrade of hardware and software; including 0–25% (1), 25–50% (2), 50–75% (3), 75–100% (4), and the whole (5) of hardware and software are corrected the first by IT department [35], which can cover keywords 5 and 11; and
- EM_9: availability of IT services; involving irregular (1), at the working time (3), and at 24*7 (5) availability of IT services [35], which can cover keyword 6.

Due to these metrics and regarding the methods of calculating the performance of ITG [34, 35], the score of performance as the arithmetic average of the final scores of internal and external metrics has to be calculated as formula (1). In this equation, IM_i is the maturity level of each 34 COBIT processes, and EM_j is the performance score of each nine external metrics.

$$Score = \frac{1}{2}\left(\frac{\sum_{i=1}^{34} IM_i}{34} + \frac{\sum_{j=1}^{9} EM_j}{9}\right) \qquad (1)$$

Primarily, a questionnaire was provided and used to measure these metrics. The collected data was also validated by other applied sources of evidence. IT department of the company was selected as the unit of analysis because:

- The management style of organizational units and the relationships between them were set in the form of shared service centers [37], where high coordination costs, using common assets, efforts of reducing the complexity of services, and high operational risks are observed;
- Members of the IT department were familiar with the concepts of ITG and COBIT; and
- A strict protocol was sealed in the form of a legal contract between the case company and us to study the case.

3.3 Case Brief

The company in the case was founded in Iran in 2005 as an electricity grid management company. Due to being the interface between the electricity market actors such as power generation, transmission, and distribution firms, the company has a multilateral role in the field of high-level management of the electricity grid in Iran.

Conducting and monitoring utilization of production and transmission of the national network; providing open access to the network for governmental and non-governmental applicants; preparing the conditions for competitive transactions, establishing, operating, and developing power market and stocks; as well as adopting effective policies and operating necessary measures in order to ensure power supply are the main objectives and responsibilities of the company.

4 Data, Test, and Results

Four sources of evidence, which were utilized in this study, are explained in Table 2.

Results of using the mentioned four sources of evidence in the case company are shown here. Final analyses were performed based on data collected using these tools. The data gathered via each source was checked and validated by data collected via other sources. Results of applying these tools are shown in Table 3. As mentioned above, we have gathered data twice: once at the time of beginning the study to assess the ITG in the company and again two years later, where some additional frameworks such as ITIL were utilized by IT department for covering

Table 2 Four sources of evidence in the study

Technique	Description
Questionnaire	We provided a closed questionnaire and ran it twice to be responded by IT managers and staff
Interview	We had two meetings with IT managers and staff to validate the data gathered through the questionnaires
Observation	We assessed the validity and reliability of the data through direct observation in the company during the research period
Documents	Reviewing the company's managerial and technical documents in the field of IT was a unique tool to check the validity and reliability of the data gathered through the questionnaires and interviews

Table 3 Results of performance assessment of ITG in the case company

Code	Title	Score	
		Y0	Y2
IM_{PO1}	Define a strategic IT Plan	1	4
IM_{PO2}	Define the Information Architecture	1	4
IM_{PO3}	Determine Technological Direction	2	4
IM_{PO4}	Define the IT Processes, Organization, and Relationships	3	4
IM_{PO5}	Manage the IT Investment	2	3
IM_{PO6}	Communicate Management Aims and Direction	1	3
IM_{PO7}	Manage IT Human Resources	3	3
IM_{PO8}	Manage Quality	2	3
IM_{PO9}	Assess and Manage IT Risks	1	3
IM_{PO10}	Manage Projects	2	4
IM_{AI1}	Identify Automated Solutions	3	4
IM_{AI2}	Acquire and Maintain Application Software	2	3
IM_{AI3}	Acquire and Maintain Technology Infrastructure	3	3
IM_{AI4}	Enable Operation and Use	2	2
IM_{AI5}	Procure IT Resources	3	4
IM_{AI6}	Manage Changes	1	3
IM_{AI7}	Install and Accredit Solutions and Changes	1	3
IM_{DS1}	Define and Manage Service Levels	2	4
IM_{DS2}	Manage Third-party Services	1	3
IM_{DS3}	Manage Performance and Capacity	1	3
IM_{DS4}	Ensure Continuous Service	3	3
IM_{DS5}	Ensure Systems Security	2	3
IM_{DS6}	Identify and Allocate Costs	1	3
IM_{DS7}	Educate and Train Users	2	2
IM_{DS8}	Manage Service Desk and Incidents	1	3
IM_{DS9}	Manage the Configuration	1	3

(continued)

Table 3 (continued)

Code	Title	Score	
		Y0	Y2
IM_{DS10}	Manage Problems	2	3
IM_{DS11}	Manage Data	2	3
IM_{DS12}	Manage the Physical Environment	3	3
IM_{DS13}	Manage Operations	3	3
IM_{ME1}	Monitor and Evaluate IT Performance	2	3
IM_{ME2}	Monitor and Evaluate Internal Control	1	3
IM_{ME3}	Ensure Compliance with External Requirements	2	2
IM_{ME4}	Provide IT Governance	1	3
$EM_{1.1}$	Importance of Cost-Effective Use of IT	4	4
$EM_{1.2}$	Importance of Effective Use of IT for Growth	1	3
$EM_{1.3}$	Importance of Effective Use of IT for Asset Utilization	2	3
$EM_{1.4}$	Importance of Effective Use of IT for Business Flexibility	2	4
$EM_{2.1}$	Impact on Cost-Effective Use of IT	1	4
$EM_{2.2}$	Impact on Effective Use of IT for Growth	1	4
$EM_{2.3}$	Impact on Effective Use of IT for Asset Utilization	1	4
$EM_{2.4}$	Impact on Effective Use of IT for Business Flexibility	2	5
EM_3	Business/IT Alignment	3	5
EM_4	Up-to-dating of IT Services	1	1
EM_5	Complying IT with Agreed-upon Service Levels	1	5
EM_6	The Extent of IT Service Interrupts on Critical Business Operations	3	4
EM_7	Performing IT Projects On-time, On-budget and According to Business Quality Standards	4	4
EM_8	The Extent of Installation/Upgrade of Hardware and Software	1	4
EM_9	Availability of IT Services	3	5

treatments identified through the prior assessment, to evaluate the efficiency of the proposed framework and to determine the effect of reforms.

Due to these results and by using formula (1), the final score of both states can be calculated as below:

$$Score_{COBIT} = \frac{1}{2}\left(\frac{63}{34} + \frac{\frac{9}{4} + \frac{5}{4} + 16}{9}\right) = 2.01 \tag{2}$$

$$Score_{COBIT-SOE} = \frac{1}{2}\left(\frac{107}{34} + \frac{\frac{14}{4} + \frac{17}{4} + 28}{9}\right) = 3.56 \tag{3}$$

From Table 3, the simple averages of the values $EM_{1.1}$–$EM_{1.4}$ and $EM_{2.1}$–$EM_{2.4}$ are utilized to calculate EM_1 and EM_2. As shown in formulas (2) and (3), the proposed framework, which was made by reforming COBIT, is more efficient than

(a)   **(b)**

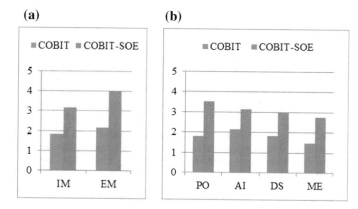

Fig. 1 Comparing performance increasing in **a** internal and external metrics, and **b** process domains of COBIT

its current form. Our study shows that the increase of performance in external metrics is a little more than efficiency in internal metrics (83% growth in comparison with 70%). This effect is not also similar in four process domains of COBIT. The highest performance is observed in the domain "plan and organize" (with 94% growth), and the lowest one is in the domain "acquire and implement" (with 47% growth). These comparisons are shown in Fig. 1.

5 Conclusion

In this paper, after reviewing the literature of ITG, service-orientation and SOE concerns, we presented a method for assessing the performance of ITG based on both of the existing methods and some performed analyses. After that, we assessed the performance of ITG in an actual environment by using the results of applying different data collection methods. This assessment was performed two times, and finally, the results of these assessments were compared and analyzed. Results show that the intensification of the score in external metrics is more enormous than internals. Furthermore, the processes of PO domain are the most affected processes in comparison with other process domains of COBIT, and the processes of the AI domain are the least.

The primary constraint of this research is related to the validation of results in the case company, which are probably not attainable in other organizations. Performance evaluation is also limited to a study in the IT department of the firm, and complementary studies are not performed in other organizational units or other periods.

6 Future Work

However, because of the novelties of this research, it would be used for future researches in this domain. Preparing a customized ITG framework for SOEs, organizing a service-oriented IT department, as well as managing business performance in this type of organizations are some potential fields to further research.

Acknowledgements The authors would like to express appreciation to Mr. Yazdian and Mrs. Fasihi, the related staff of this research in the case company for their time and support for this study. The authors would also like to thank Mr. Karami, CEO of Golsoft Co., for his feedback and help throughout this work.

References

1. Hardy, G.: Using IT governance and COBIT to deliver value with IT and respond to legal, regulatory and compliance challenges. Information Security Technical Report **11**, 55–61 (2006)
2. Weill, P., Ross, J.W.: IT Governance—How Top Performers Manage IT Decision Rights for Superior Results, 1st edn. Harvard Business School Press, Boston, Massachusettes, USA (2004)
3. Hosseinzadeh, B.: SOA Governance. 2008, IBM Corporation presentation
4. Kavianpour, M.: SOA and Large Scale and Complex Enterprise Transformation. ICSOC **2007**, 530–545 (2007)
5. Woolf, B.: Exploring IBM SOA Technology & Practice—How to Plan, Build, and Manage a Service Oriented Architecture in the Real World. Maximum Press, Canada (2008)
6. ITGI: Control Objectives for Information and related Technology (COBIT). Ver 4.1 (2007)
7. ITIL: The Information Technology Infrastructure Library (v3). http://www.itilfoundations.com
8. OGC: Official Introduction to the ITIL Service Lifecycle. London: TSO (2007)
9. Marks, E.A., Carlson, B., Nadler, D., Snyder, V.R.: Service-Oriented Architecture Governance for the Services Driven Enterprise. Wiley, New Jersey, USA (2008)
10. Chen, H.M.: towards service engineering: service orientation and business-IT alignment. In: 41st Hawaii International Conference on System Sciences (HICSS) (2008)
11. Haes, S.D., Grembergen, W.V.: Analysing the relationship between it governance and business/it alignment maturity. In: 41st Hawaii International Conference on System Sciences (HICSS), Hawaii Big Island (2008)
12. Robinson, N.: IT excellence starts with governance. J. Investment Compliance **6**, 45–49 (2005)
13. Misra, S.C., Kumar, V., Kumar, U.: A strategic modeling technique for information security risk assessment. Inf Manag Comput. Secur. **15**, 64–77 (2007)
14. Quartel, D.A.C., Steen, M.W.A., Pokraev, S., Sinderen, M.J.V.: COSMO: A conceptual framework for service modelling and refinement. Inf Syst. Frontiers **9**, 225–244 (2007)
15. Huang, Y., Kumaran, S., Chung, J.Y.: A model-driven framework for enterprise service management. IseB **3**, 201–217 (2005)
16. Nayak, N., Linehan, M., Nigam, A., Marston, D.: Core business architecture for a service-oriented enterprise. IBM Syst. J. **46**, 723–742 (2007)
17. CIO Council: A Practical guide to federal service oriented architecture. Version 1.1 (2008)
18. Khoshafian, S.: Service Oriented Enterprises. Auerbach Publications, USA (2007)

19. Lawler, J.P., Howell-Barber, H.: Service Oriented Architecture: SOA Strategy, Methodology, and Technology. Auerbach Publications, USA (2008)
20. Keel, A.J., Orr, M.A., Hernandez, R.R., Patrocinio, E.A., Bouchard, J.: From a technology-oriented to a service-oriented approach to IT management. IBM Syst. J. **46**, 549–564 (2007)
21. Lindstrom, A., Johnson, E., Ekstedt, M., Simonsson, M.: A survey on CIO concerns—do enterprise architecture frameworks support them? Inf. Syst. Front. **8**, 81–90 (2006)
22. Hochstein, A., Zarnekow, R., Brenner, W.: Evaluation of service-oriented IT management in practice. In: International Conference on Services Systems and Services Management (ICSSSM), pp. 80–84, Chongqing, China (2005)
23. Mansukhani, M.: Service Oriented Architecture White Paper. Hewlett-Packard Development Company, L.P., White Paper (2005)
24. Bieberstein, N., Bose, S., Walker, L., Lynch, A.: Impact of service-oriented architecture on enterprise systems, organizational structures, and individuals. IBM Systems Journal **44**, 691–708 (2005)
25. Alencar, P., Weigand, H.: Challenges in predictive self-adaptation of service bundles. In: International Conference on Web Intelligence and Intelligent Agent Technology, pp. 457–461 (2009)
26. Knippel, R.: Service Oriented enterprise architecture. IT-University of Copenhagen, Master thesis (2005)
27. Balasubramaniam, S., Lewis, G.A., Morris, E., Simanta, S., Smith, D.B.: Challenges for assuring quality of service in a service-oriented environment. In: ICSE'09 Workshop, pp. 103–106, Vancouver, Canada (2009)
28. Demirkan, H., Kauffman, R.J., Vayghan, J.A., Fill, H.G., Karagiannis, D., Maglio, P.P.: Service-oriented technology and management: perspectives on research and practice for the coming decade. Electron. Commer. Res. Appl. **7**, 356–376 (2008)
29. Cai, H., Chung, J.Y., Su, H.: Relooking at services science and services innovation. SOCA **2**, 1–14 (2008)
30. Jin, K., Ray, P.: Business-oriented development methodology for IT service management. In: 41st Hawaii International Conference on System Sciences, pp. 1–10, Hawaii Big Island (2008)
31. Schröpfer, C., Schönherr, M.: Introducing a method to derive an enterprise-specific SOA operating model. In: 12th International IEEE Enterprise Distributed Object Computing Conference, pp. 235–244, Munich, Germany (2008)
32. Ernest, M., Nisavic, J.M.: Adding value to the IT organization with the component business model. IBM Syst. J. **46**, 387–403 (2007)
33. Ali, S., Green, P.: Effective information technology (IT) governance mechanisms: an IT outsourcing perspective. Information Systems Frontiers (2009)
34. Weill, P., Ross, J.W.: IT governance on one page. center for information systems research (CISR) in MIT sloan school of management, Cambridge, Massachusetts, Working Paper CISR WP No. 349 (2004)
35. Simonsson, M. Johnson, P.: The IT Organization modeling and assessment tool: correlating IT governance maturity with the effect of IT. In: 41st Hawaii International Conference on System Sciences, Hawaii Big Island, USA (2008)
36. Yin, R.K.: Case study research design and methods, 3rd edn. Sage, Thousand Oaks, CA (2003)
37. Janssen., M., Joha, A.: Emerging shared service organizations and the service-oriented enterprise: Critical management issues. Strateg. Outsourcing: An Int. J. **1**, 35–49 (2008)

New Market Creation for Technological Breakthroughs: Commercial Drones and the Disruption of the Emergency Market

Federico Carli, Maria Elena Manzotti and Hugo Savoini

Abstract The emergency response market is considered as the most far from warfare, in which drones were incepted. The multicase study research focusing on three NGOs operating to save the lives of migrants in distress at sea in the Mediterranean area showed that emergency is indeed a market suitable for disruption. Moreover, being a not for profit field, the disruption by commercial drones follows a different path than other civilian markets. Commercial drones will likely spread among civilian markets and disrupt several of them, including emergency.

Keywords Drones · Emergency · Disruption

1 Introduction

The purpose of this study is to provide an in depth picture of commercial drones as a breakthrough innovation and to gather whether they are to disrupt the emergency market among the several new applications currently being incepted for their technology. Although there are many theoretical contributions dealing with radical innovations and new market creation techniques, none focuses on drones and the disruption patterns of not for profit markets. Moreover, as of today, heated discussions coming from ethical, privacy and safety concerns revolve around the deployment of drones into civilian markets. The objective of this paper is to provide

F. Carli (✉)
Università Telematica Internazionale UNINETTUNO, Corso Vittorio
Emanuele II 39, 00186 Rome, Italy
e-mail: federico.carli@gmail.com

M. E. Manzotti
LUISS Guido Carli, Viale Pola 12, 00198 Rome, Italy
e-mail: mariaelena.manzotti@gmail.com

H. Savoini
Associazione di Cultura Economica e Politica Guido Carli,
Via Cappuccio 13, 20123 Milan, Italy
e-mail: hugosurfer@hotmail.it

© Springer Nature Switzerland AG 2019
Y. Baghdadi and A. Harfouche (eds.), *ICT for a Better Life and a Better World*,
Lecture Notes in Information Systems and Organisation 30,
https://doi.org/10.1007/978-3-030-10737-6_22

335

a framework for drones' penetration of the emergency field and to gather if they will represent an actual disruption or just a fade. In order to achieve the latter, an overall picture of C-RPAS and their technological development in the emergency market as a potentially profitable field are provided. Afterward, the case study and relating methodology are presented. The selected cases focus on three NGOs operating within the Mediterranean Sea to save the lives of migrants trying to make the crossing from Libya and Syria to Europe. While Migrants Offshore Aid Station deploys two camcopters into its humanitarian operations, Sea-Watch and SOS Méditerranée do not. Additionally, the experiment made by the leading drones manufacturing company DJI to teach European rescuers how to pilot C-RPAS is analysed. Lastly, a cross-case analysis is performed to ultimately uncover the future of commercial drones into the emergency market.

2   Drones as Technological Breakthroughs

According to the International Civil Aviation Organization (Cir. 328, 2011), Remotely Piloted Aircraft Systems (RPAS) include an aircraft and its associated elements that are operated with no pilot on board from a nearby station. They are commonly known as "drones", which stands for Dynamic Remotely Operated Navigation Equipment [1] and encompasses all kinds of RPAS. Albeit their inception is rooted into the military industry where drones have disrupted warfare, their fast-paced technological development has led to the creation of new commercial applications.

R&D activities started indeed during World Wars I and II with two major UK drone programs—Larynx and Ram—that were developed for air war in response to German radio-controlled bombing [2]. During the Cold War, drone new product development (NPD) was restored for intelligence, surveillance and reconnaissance activities in the US since it allowed larger geographical range and better technological performances. However, it was during the Kosovo War that the deployment of RPAs really took off through the development of Predator and Global Hawk drone programs. Afterwards, Unmanned Aerial Vehicles (UAV) were used in the Afghanistan, Iraq and Yemen's strikes, at which point surveillance and targeting activities started to converge with a strive for making drones more automated [3]. The very shift to civilian applications occurred in 2005, when the rescue effort following Hurricane Katrina saw the deployment of military drones in the US to look for survivors. A year later, the Federal Aviation Administration (FAA) authorized Predators military drones to fly over civilian skies and, from then on, commercial drones have started emerging worldwide [4].

Size is the base on which to pinpoint different categories of drones: [5]

- *Large drones*: 150 kg or more;
- *Mini-drones*: between 20 and 150 kg;

- *Micro-drones*: between 0.1 and 7 kg;
- *Nano-drones*: less than 0.1 kg.

Depending on size, other two important attributes of RPAS vary: the range of flight (from few feet around the operator to over 17,000 miles) and the flight altitude (from few feet to a maximum of 65,000 ft.).

In comparison to their military counterparts, commercial drones are smaller and cheaper. As of today, most of them have a similar design that includes "*a micro-controller with four to eight motors and propellers, a radio receiver, electronic speed control and a battery built on a light plastic or metal frame*". Additionally, GPS devices can be used to navigate and sensors, cameras and gimbals can be added to increase stability, for aerial imagery and for image stability. On the quality of sensors and data and control feeds depend the primary functions of drones: control, navigation and operation. Remote feeds, in turn, depend on the communication facilities (like the GPS device) that are to be found on board and that affect the drone's usability. The operational functions such as load carrying primarily depend on the available payload (affected in turn by size and engineering power), the duration of the flight (related to the available power-source) and the environment (for instance altitude). Additionally, dealing with the majority of RPAS technology, control, navigation and operations are performed by different people, so that to fly one drone at least three people are required.

When it comes to the development of commercial remotely piloted aircraft systems (C-RPAS), leading companies such as DJI, 3DRobotics invite communities of enthusiast to participate in the development process of their open source hardware and software projects. This sharing of ideas across open platforms brings along an open source attitude to innovation [6]. Moreover, the NPD process of drones is parallel to the one of other emerging technologies, like 3D printers, computing, sensors and robotics, from which they inherit both opportunities and setbacks. This feature of RPAS' technology is called technological convergence and has recently lead small drones to reach the performance standards of manned aircraft. While large military remotely piloted aircraft systems (M-RPAS) are still expensive to maintain and control, though, the emergence of high power density batteries, miniaturized equipment, wireless network devices and the consequent increasing production volumes have led to lower costs for C-RPAS [7]. Their purchase price is between $100 and $10,000 and the average cost per hour of flight is about $25.

The technological progress in aircraft technology follows two main trajectories—civil and military—with major improvements in power, range and speed along both [8]. Concerning the military trajectory, it is approaching a ceiling because of its paradigm boundaries. On the one hand, in fact, no matter how many improvements are made, human limitations hinder the technological performance (like night view or longer-range precision in attacks). On the other hand, going beyond the paradigm to further improve the technology puts pilots' safety in jeopardy. Therefore, drones are a major technological breakthrough in that they entail a paradigm shift from having a pilot on board the aircraft to flying without one. Since drones essentially are flying robots [9] it can be said that they represent a major technological breakthrough in Robotics as well, shifting paradigm from land robots to flying ones.

The shift implies new perspectives and progress path to follow basing on an entirely new body of knowledge. RPAs are indeed disrupting warfare in that they alter who fights wars from humans to machines. Commercial drones are to be considered as another technological breakthrough coming from a shift in trajectory from military to civil within the new unmanned aircraft systems (UAS) paradigm. The reduction in size, in fact, leads to the creation of new markets beside the military one and to new directions of technical change.

Thanks to the open source development allowing for a core technological base that can be altered and the subsequent lower costs, several niche applications for UAVs are now financially viable worldwide. An estimate by the Teal Group predicts for annual sales of drones *"to double from $5.2 billion to $11.6 billion by 2023"*. R&D expenditure and procurement will reach $89 billion in the next ten years [10]. The civilian market is indeed broader compared to the military one, so that it holds a huge potential which is still quite untapped [11]. As of today, the primary commercial application areas for RPAS are agriculture, delivery, hobby, photography, journalism, law enforcement and emergency services.

Despite the different applications that are still popping up for C-RPAS, several factors are hampering the adoption of drones. The most relevant one is perhaps regulation as it differs between M-RPAS and C-RPAS and, concerning the latter, technology has definitely outpaced the regulatory process since there is no clear regulatory process to follow. Safety and privacy are also major concerns. While the privacy issue is linked to the regulatory one, small mistakes in flying drones could lead to great damage and harm civilians' health. Besides the risk connected to poor communications channels of UAVs and the chance that they could be hijacked by fake GPS signals, there is also the issue of carrying payload concerning the logistical challenges of drone delivery. Lastly, the connection of RPAS to warfare attracts tough opposition on their spreading to commercial markets.

3   The Emergency Market

The term humanitarian assistance refers to aid and action designed to save lives, alleviate suffering, and maintain and protect human dignity during and in the aftermath of emergencies [12].

The global emergency response market is expected to grow from $80.10 billion in 2015 to $101.33 billion by 2020, with a compound annual growth rate of 4, 8% during the period 2015–2020. This is due for the largest part to the advancement in technology connected to this field.

Although the emergency market can be seen as diametrically opposite to the one in which UAVs were incepted, that is to say for war, they are actually strictly entangled. In fact, the most valuable attributes of drones in military are essentially the same for emergency activities. Drones might in fact be deployed for providing data about emergencies and for humanitarian relief, thus participating directly in human relief operations. Additionally, their precision in delivering attacks can be used for human targeting, again helping in saving lives.

This technology transfer from military to emergency is due to the development process of drones, but also to the interaction of different stakeholders, namely developers and politicians aiming to gain legitimacy for the UAVs industry against oppositions. In other words, it is the result of both exploration and effectuation.

Mosterman et al. argue that the deployment of C-RPAS into humanitarian activities is difficult due to the peculiar nature of emergencies' needs such as availability, responsiveness, agility, transparency and interactivity. However, new developments in communication networks and wireless and crash-avoidance technology are helping in better exercising guidance and control tasks. As a consequence, it can be said that although the technology of C-RPAS is not mature, its development paths may be a premise for *"more efficient and less costly emergency response and relief"* [13].

A report funded by the *European Commission's Humanitarian Aid and Civil Protection Department* demonstrates that RPAS is a truly valuable technology within the emergency field. The report, made of 14 case studies centred on the actual deployment of drones within different emergency instances, provides an overview of the possible applications for RPAS within the global emergency market. Among the cases, a successful project has been implemented in Africa to develop exposure maps and model flood risks in Dar es Salaam by deploying drones. Another case focuses on Médecins Sans Frontières, which has been the first humanitarian organization to test the use of delivery drones to overcome the limited access to healthcare diagnostics due to severe logistical constraints in Papua New Guinea. Lastly, the introduction of a drone within the Greater Manchester Fire and Rescue Service's emergency response toolkit has led to a huge success and also appeared to be motivating other fire departments across the United Kingdom to do the same. The other 11 cases support as well the evidence that the deployment of drones within different emergency instances has been fundamental in carrying out the organizations' daily operations.

In addition to this, the authors of the report have conducted a comprehensive survey among 200 disaster people working in 61 different countries in order to gather how humanitarian professionals view drones: the 60% of them answered that they are favorable to the use of drones in humanitarian activities. The report identifies four major applications for drones in the emergency sector: mapping, search and rescue, monitoring, and cargo delivery.

Mapping is the most common and most popular drone application to date. Lightweight, consumer-friendly designs and automated workflows make this technology accessible even to non-technical users. Mapping drones are used to make accurate, two-dimensional maps, elevation models, and 3D models of terrain.

Interest is building in the use of drones to assist in search and rescue (SAR), particularly when drones can be equipped with infrared or other specialized cameras. Deployment of drones in SAR aims in particular at increasing observational awareness of ground teams to improve safety, as well as aiding in locating missing people.

Using drones for real-time information presents additional opportunities that have not yet been sufficiently explored in the field. Small drones have streamed live video mostly in tactical situations to provide an understanding about potential road blockages or to quickly assess structures and infrastructure. Within the humanitarian community, however, there is much interest in functions that would allow the assessment and monitoring of large areas.

The delivery of cargo with drones is a rapidly emerging field that may offer the option to transport small items with high frequency, thus complementing traditional means. One third of the world's population lacks regular access to essential medicines. The causes include poor infrastructure in developing countries, complex logistics and lack of money. Poor last mile delivery logistics is the critical constraint preventing medical supplies from reaching these areas, and causes 40% of vaccines supplied to parts of the underdeveloped world to expire before they can be administered. [14]

Yet, it is still unclear if the deployment of C-RPAS in this field will be an actual disruption or just a fade. Notwithstanding the several advantages like speed, efficiency and safety, regulation, ethical and privacy issue are still barriers to the adoption of drones. Furthermore, the underlying technology of UAVs still need improvements and thus represents a barrier in itself.

4   The Case Study Research

The use of drones in the emergency market is indeed at its embryonic stage, both technologically speaking and as a concept. Subsequently, the best way to assess their disruptive potential is exploring and comparing emergency activities that actually use RPAS technology. To this extent, a case study among different non-governmental organizations (NGOs) has been chosen as a research strategy in order to gather the likelihood of drones' adoption and consequent disruption of the emergency industry.

Given that no single case is representative or relevant enough to formulate a general theory, a multiple case study approach has been used. Each case study is analysed as a stand-alone entity at first instance and afterwards related to the others in order to gather differences and similarities.

The quintain of this research is the deployment of drones by NGOs in their surveillance, rescue and first aid activities. The foreshadow problem is that few companies within the emergency market actually deploy C-RPAS, therefore it is uncertain whether they will cause a disruption. The following research questions have been addressed:

- How emergency activities are currently carried out by each NGO?
- What are the similarities in their needs?
- Is emergency a potentially profitable market for C-RPAS?
- How can C-RPAS be actually deployed within the emergency market?

Since humanitarian activities are broad in nature and geographic scope, the research focuses on surveillance, rescue and first aid at sea in the Central Mediterranean area.

Nowadays, Libya and Syria are among the most violent places in the world, so that migrants undertake journeys on small vessels to escape poverty, violence and wars. According to the archives of La Stampa, 2015 has been the year with more deaths as 3771 migrants have perished in the Central Mediterranean Sea. Hence, the government and several NGOs are acting to fill the absence of large-scale humanitarian operations and save the lives of refugees. Among the others, Migrant Offshore Aid Station [15] Sea-Watch [16] and SOS Méditerranée [17] have been chosen to develop the case studies. Besides the multiple case studies, evidences have been gathered from an experiment held in Europe by the Chinese company DJI [18] starting in May 2016 to train European emergency workers to pilot C-RPAS for rescue missions. The experiment has the purpose of promoting the integration of drones into humanitarian operations. Background information about the companies involved in the sample has been gathered from documentary sources such as newspapers, newsletters and their websites, blogs and Social Media channels. Additionally, European regulatory frameworks as well as country news media relating to refugees issue have been reviewed to gain further understanding of the environment of the research. For what concerns the DJI experiment, technical journals, YouTube videos, annual reports and local newspapers are the main sources of data collection.

The cases have been compared in pairs looking for differences within the most similar ones and for similarities within the most distant ones.

By comparing the companies' fundamental data shown in Table 1 it is possible to make some preliminary observations:

- The relative size of the concerned NGOs ranges from small to large and the largest one is also the one with less months of activity;
- While all deploy a ship, MOAS also leases two camcopters and SW is about to launch its aerial surveillance;
- On average and notwithstanding neither the number of missions nor the months of inactivity, MOAS and SOS Méditerranée have saved so far a number of lives per month that is close. SW have averagely saved half of the refugees of the other two on a monthly basis;
- Sea-Watch 2 has half the capacity of crewmembers and refugees of the Aquarius and can host 5 crewmembers and 50 migrants less than the Phoenix. The Phoenix can host 200 less migrants and 7 less crewmembers on board than the Aquarius;
- All NGOs have currently four active cooperation.

The estimated monthly operating costs of MOAS are almost twice as much the ones of SOS Méditerranée.

Table 1 Fundamental data. *Source* Personal elaboration

Company	MOAS	SW	SOS Méditerranée
Relative size	Medium	Small	Large
Mission	"No one deserves to die at sea"	"Saving lives, testify ad find imitators"	"Saving human lives, protecting and assisting, raising public awareness"
Months of activity	23	12	6
Number of lives saved	25,000	5600	5600
Equipment	One ship, two speedboats, two drones	One ship, two speedboats, one aircraft	One ship
Ship	Phoenix (40 m)	Sea Watch 2 (33 m)	MS Aquarius (77 m)
Capacity	20 crew people, 300 migrants	15 crew people, 250 migrants	27 crew people, 500 migrants
Cooperation	MRCC, Doctors without borders, Schiebel, Emergency	Watch The Med, Human Rights at Sea, HPI, MRCC	MRCC, Doctors Without Borders, Doctors of the World, Human Rights at Sea
Operative base	Malta	Lampedusa	Palermo
Estimated monthly operating costs	$600,000	n.a.	$372,000

Going back to the research questions:

Q1: How emergency activities are currently carried out by each NGO? MOAS, SW and SOS Méditerranée carry out their emergency activities following the same schedule but deploying different technologies when it comes to surveillance tasks. More specifically, MOAS leases two drones, SW has partnered with HPI to launch its aerial surveillance through the use of a microlight airplane and SOS Méditerranée relies on binoculars and human sight. The deployment of different technologies has led to different performances. If the number of lives saved per month is taken into account as a fundamental key performance indicator, as of today MOAS is the better performing company. Although Sea-Watch Air is expected to increase the performance of SW, the disrupting attributes of MOAS's camcopters are likely to outpace the ones of the microlight airplane. In other words, MOAS is expected to maintain the best performance because its emergency activities are not paused or terminated due to bad weather or dangerous conditions thanks to the absence of a pilot on board its vehicles, as shown in Table 2. The absence of a pilot aboard also removes other human limitations such as poor night view, which still concerns the pilot of an aircraft. Moreover, C-RPAS bring along the same advantages as SW's microlight airplane in that they allow speed and broader geographical scope and consequent savings in time and efforts. Furthermore, while MOAS holds a no deaths record, the

Table 2 Comparison between aircraft and drone technologies in emergency. *Source* Personal elaboration

		Microlight airplane	Camcopter
Similarities	Time to patrol the area	Less	Less
	Patrolling area	Wider	Wider
	Precision in pinpointing locations	Enhanced	Enhanced
	Communication	With MRCC	With MRCC
Differences	Pilot	One	Three
	Termination due to weather	Yes	No
	Human limitations	Yes	No
	Cost	$35,000–$100,000	$2.75 million

crew of SOS Méditerranée does not. Albeit the fact that specific circumstances have to be taken into account and for this reason it is not possible to state that it is entirely due to the deployment of drones, it can be assumed that at least part of the difference in their deaths record might come from the deployment of drones. The psychological challenges faced by the Aquarius crew could also be overcome by using UAVs, which are estranged from emotional components and the need to rest. The same evidence is presented by the DJI experiment, which demonstrates drones' potential of helping commanders in accelerating the decision-making process by providing detailed information in advance dealing with the situation they are about to face.

Q2: What are the similarities in the NGOs' needs? Recurring needs within the three organizations are raising public awareness with regard to the dying migrants' issue in order to increase their donations' volume and be ultimately able to save more lives and being more efficient in their rescue operations. With the shared main objective of saving lives, donations and technology are the two enabling factors concerning a better performance. To be more efficient, in fact, NGOs need to save time, efforts and costs. The deployment of drones has proved to serve the latter need as it allows less time-consuming operations, more precise data to be obtained in advance and the ability to patrol a wider area of sea. However, efficiency is somehow conflicting with the need for increasing availability of funds because the cost of drones' deployment is higher when compared to the one of other less efficient technologies like binoculars or airplanes. While a microlight airplane has a market price of $100,000 at most, MOAS's camcopters together costs $5,5 million. The DJI's Phantom and Inspire drones are far cheaper: together with the M100 platform they cost averagely $5000 each, which is less than the minimum market price for microlight airplanes (i.e. $35,000). However, alongside the difference in price comes the difference in performances. While Schiebel camcopters can fly for six hours and have a flight range of 200 km, DJI's ones have a flight time of half an hour and a flight range of 5 km. Furthermore, Schiebel drones have no reported difficulties neither in communicating with the emergency IT systems nor in flying in bad weather conditions as DJI's ones. In addition to this, only one pilot is needed for flying the microlight airplane, while to control the camcopters at least three people are required. As the technology development goes further, increased autonomy and easiness in control are expected to reduce both the number of pilots and the need for training. Cooperation with C-RPAS' manufacturers aiming at gaining legitimacy will drive down the costs of deployment and increase interest towards the emerging technology as well. Experimentations with the objective of integrating drones into humanitarian operations will both educate rescuers and raise awareness towards the potentially invaluable benefits of deployment, this way possibly increasing also the volume of donations to lead users NGOs. In turn, incremental innovations and increased deployment will drive down the production costs and thus the market price of camcopters. Eventually, C-RPAS will drive down NGOs' operating costs in the long term thanks to the increase in efficiency that they bring along.

Q3: Is emergency a potentially profitable market for C-RPAS? Emergency is indeed a potentially profitable field for the deployment of drones, even though it might not be the most profitable one amongst all civilian markets. The interests in saving more lives, gaining legitimacy thanks to the positive associations with humanitarian operations and spreading the overall use of drones by overcoming oppositions are motivating stakeholders to contribute in the development of drones and penetration of the emergency market. The expected growth rate indeed equals 4.8% per year. However, the prospect of cooperating with NGOs hinders the potential profit. The gains are thus mostly in the long run than in the short run profits and probably more strategically than monetary. Furthermore, the uncertainty connected to regulations may represent a great limitation to profitability and success in commercialization and deployment of C-RPAS. Again, experimentation aiming at showing the benefits of drones' integration into rescue activities and technological development can reduce oppositions by reducing the concerns over privacy and safety. Reducing opposition will in turn reduce the need for a restricting regulation, this way eliminating uncertainty to the latter extent.

Q4: How can C-RPAS be deployed within the emergency market? As claimed by MOAS, SOS Méditerranée and pilots involved in the DJI experiment, the most beneficial deployment of drones into emergency response is surveillance and real-time intelligence thanks to the attribute of precision in targeting and data gathering. Moreover, as the technological development progress, commercial drones may be able to lift heavier payloads in the near future, thus performing relief as well.

5   Conclusion

This paper is about new commercial applications for drones. More specifically, the research focuses on the emergency response market that at first glance is considered as the most far from warfare, in which drones were incepted. In recent days, discussions revolving around privacy, regulatory and safety concerns on commercial drones are as acute as ever. Since there is a lack of literature concerning this topic, the study aims at building a theory to the latter regard: are commercial drones actually about to disrupt civilian markets? Is emergency among them? The multicase study research strategy has been selected as a methodology because the data are mostly qualitative and there is no control over the involved actors' behaviour. Three NGOs operating to save the lives of migrants in distress at sea in the Mediterranean have been selected as a sample because heating discussions are affecting also this issue and rescuers might be lead users for drones' technology. Additionally, the contributions were drawn from an experiment made by DJI to teach rescuers how to fly drones. The empirical results coming from the cross-case analysis showed that emergency is indeed a market suitable for disruption. Moreover, being a not for profit field, the disruption by commercial drones follows a different path than other civilian markets. It can be concluded that commercial drones will spread among civilian markets and disrupt several of them, including emergency.

References

1. Parihar, P., Bhawsar, P., Hargod, P.: Design & development analysis of quadcopter. Int. J. Adv. Comput. Technol. **5**(6), 2128–2133 (2016)
2. Farquharson, J.: Britain and the flying bomb: the research programme between the two World Wars. War in History, **133**, 363–379 (2016)
3. Kindervater, K.H: The emergence of lethal surveillance: watching and killing in the history of drone technology. Secur. Dialogue, **47**(3), 223–238 (2016)
4. Rao, B., Gopi, A.G., Maione, R.: The societal impact of commercial drones. Technol. Soc. **45**, 83–90 (2016)
5. Clarke, R.: Understanding the drone epidemic. Comput. Law and Secur. Rev. **30**(3), 230–246 (2014)
6. Boucher, P.: Domesticating the drone: management strategies for unmanned aircraft in society. Making Society through Science and Technology, A Matter of Design (2014)
7. Chao, H, Cao, Y., Chen, Y.: Autopilots for small unmanned aerial vehicles: a survey. Int. J. Control, Autom. Syst., **8**(1), 36–44 (2010)
8. Dosi, G.: Sources, procedures, and microeconomic effects of innovation. J. Econ. Lit. **26**(3), 1120–1171 (1988)
9. Clarke, R.: What drones inherit from their ancestors. Comput. Law and Secur. Rev. **30**(3), 247–262 (2014)
10. Boyle, M.J.: The race for drones. Orbis. **59**(1), 76–94 (2015)
11. Antebi, L.: Changing trends in unmanned aerial vehicles: new challenges for states, armies and security industries. Mil. Strateg. Aff. **6**(2), 21–36 (2014)
12. Sandvik, K.B., Lohne, K.: The rise of the humanitarian drone: giving content to an emerging concept. Millennium: J. Int. Stud. **43**(1), 145–164 (2014)
13. Mosterman, P.J., Sanabria, D.E., Bilgin, E., Zhang, K., Zander, J.: Automating humanitarian missions with a heterogeneous fleet of vehicles. Annu. Rev. Control, **38**(2), 259–270 (2014)
14. Soesilo, D., Meier, P., Lessard-Fontaine, A., Du Plessis, J., Stuhlberger, C., Fabbroni, V.: Drones in Humanitarian Action. Indipendent report, Swiss Foundation for Mine Action (FSD) (2017)
15. Migrant Offshore Aid Station, https://www.moas.eu/
16. Sea-Watch, https://sea-watch.org/
17. SOS Méditerranée, sosmediterranee.org
18. DJI, https://www.dji.com/

Enterprise Architecture: A Pillar in an Integrated Framework to Measure the Internal Control Effectiveness in the Oil & Gas Sector

Mohamed Akoum and Véronique Blum

Abstract Enterprise Architecture (EA) has always been considered as a bridge linking the technical domain of an organization with its core business. EA has evolved from information system architecture predominant in IT to a business tool. This paper proposes using the methods put forward by this practice to gain operational insight into the Oil & Gas industry. We used Zachman EA framework as one of four pillars of an integrated framework to measure the Internal Control Effectiveness of Petroleum companies. Following the Evidence-Based Management (EBM) methodology, we create a new tool by applying the methodical thinking of EA on COSO's Internal Control framework. The outcome is an integrated framework named ICEMF (Internal Control Effectiveness Measurement Framework).

Keywords Internal control · Enterprise architecture · COSO · Corporate governance · Petroleum · Performance rating

1 Introduction

Corporate Governance has reaped significant focus towards the last decade of the 20th Century following the highly publicized corporate failures in many developed countries, leading to great economic turmoil [1]. Ripples of this recession were sensed all across the globe in either a big or small way. The fragility of corporate governance was deemed a major factor that lead to the insolvency of some corporates and to serious financial struggles of others [2].

In the US, public outcry over accountability and responsibility in corporate behaviour was intensified with scandals like Enron (US Power giant),

M. Akoum (✉)
Grenoble Ecole de Management, 12, rue Pierre Sémard, 38000 Grenoble, France
e-mail: Mohamad.akoum@grenoble-em.com

V. Blum
Université Grenoble Alpes, 2 Place Doyen Gosse, 38000 Grenoble, France
e-mail: veronique.blum-garier@iut2.upmf-grenoble.fr

© Springer Nature Switzerland AG 2019
Y. Baghdadi and A. Harfouche (eds.), *ICT for a Better Life and a Better World*,
Lecture Notes in Information Systems and Organisation 30,
https://doi.org/10.1007/978-3-030-10737-6_23

347

WorldCom and many others [3]. This coerced the US Congress to introduce the 'Sarbanes-Oxley Act' in 2002 imposing controls and regulatory requirements on publicly traded companies [4]. Publicized prosecutions against corporate leaders followed which led to the decline of many corporates [5]. The objective of soft laws such as the 'Code of Best Practices' and 'Regulatory Acts' in UK and US was to impose operational sanctity and financial transparency on the corporates aiming at restoring the public confidence in capital markets and ensuring their on-going vitality [6]. All these speak of the significance of a responsible Corporate Governance in enterprises, and its importance in sustaining the national economies, the world financial order but also the environment and society.

The key enterprise risks in the Oil & Gas businesses are raised by work related accidents [7]. Accidents in the Oil & Gas sector are highly publicized failures and usually have very high impact on People, Environment, Assets, Reputation and Liability (PEARL) of the organization, leading to huge financial losses on the company and even challenging its existence. One example of high profile high-risk incident happened in 2010, the Macondo Blowout in the Gulf of Mexico (BP Oil Spill—2010) is still not a forgotten story. The explosion and sinking of the 'Deepwater Horizon' oil rig claimed 11 lives, a sea-floor oil gusher flowed for 87 days discharging some 4.9 million barrels of crude Oil in the sea, and the company reputation was severely tarnished in addition to the exorbitant financial losses [8]. The Macondo incident is just one of many unfortunate incidents that happened across the globe in the Oil & Gas history [9]. Other weaknesses in internal control have been examined in the literature, however researchers have demonstrated more interest in their impact on communication than on the causality analysis or moreover, on the tools likely to support a better identification of causes. Cho [10] analysed the communication around the environmental disaster created by the Erika oil spill and the case of the industrial AZF accident. Beelitz and Merkl-Davies [11] examined the same issue of legitimation restoration after a nuclear incident in a German power plant. Barros [12] has examined the way in which the Internet site of a petroleum company could support its remoteness to corruption allegations. Energy sector appears to be sensitive to such Internal Control issues, while being subject to observers' scrutiny (see for example).

Such incidents and their impact on long-term reputation and operations suggest that the Corporate Governance in Oil & Gas companies should look beyond managing and monitoring governance bodies and organizing and maintaining books of records. An Oil & Gas organization, even with the most efficient financial controls in place still has other key operational areas (Internal Controls) that need to be effectively controlled for ensuring proper governance, management of enterprise risk and assuring shareholders' interest as stated by BP CEO himself "Our operations failed to meet our own standards and the requirements of the law" [13]. This raises the issue of the efficiency of existing and recommended by soft law disciplinary processes. Arguably, existing internal control methods can be questioned and may be assumed insufficient in preventing such high impact incidents from happening. It then becomes crucial to understand whether failures can be explained by lack of controls, poor acuteness of governance principles or the absence of a hard law kind of regulation.

Possibly, the described un-circumvented events are associated with a very low frequency and belong to the black swan kind [14], which cannot be prevented by processes addressing and assuming a normal operational functioning of the company and its business units. Such situation can even worsen when proxy advisors or investors impose their *One-size-fits-all* model of Governance practices. It follows that existing IC procedures may very efficiently capture recurrent and thinkable events, but still ignore high impact and menial frequency losses. This implies that IC methodology be revised to address not only *Mediocristan*—where recurrence occurs—but also *Extremistan*—where high impact ruining events happen—operational states. Indeed, what previous incidents share is a defaulting operational and procedural security. Thus, we raise the following Research Question: Can the Internal Control Effectiveness of Upstream Oil & Gas organizations be measured and improved for early detection of potential and possible yet improbable failures?

The previously cited alarming facts nurture the need for gaining better operational insight, spreading functional awareness, and evaluating the effectiveness of Operational Internal Controls to achieve more effective and responsible governance in Oil & Gas companies [15]. Gaining operational insight, as simple as it might appear proves in reality to be highly complex and convoluted. The problem becomes even more difficult when compounded with the widespread impact of the Health, Safety and Environment (HSE) concerns across all areas of an Oil & Gas operation mostly performed by contractors and sub-contractors. Operational insight for effective governance in Oil & Gas businesses requires careful consideration of the following factors, among others: (i) qualifying internal controls contextual to organizations, (ii) scoping the controls to their application areas, (iii) defining regulatory compliance requirements, and (iv) identifying embedded controls in the business processes and automated systems. This shows an imminent need for a framework to measure the actual effectiveness of the Internal Controls in order to give external and internal stakeholders (Management, Shareholders, Credit Rating Agencies, Investors, Regulators/Government, Public, last but not least the Employees) an indicator of the soundness of their companies' operations.

Our literature review confirms the lack of an existing comprehensive tool, framework, methodology, or any other means to measure the effectiveness of Operational Internal Controls in the Oil & Gas sector. Masli et al. [16] state "Despite the importance of meeting the SOX internal control requirements, we know of few studies that investigate the specific strategies used by companies to monitor and assure the effectiveness of internal controls", although this requirement is required by the section 404 of the SOX law. Moreover, other actors, such as Credit Rating Agencies who rate companies and organizations based on their adherence to the Corporate Governance principles and on their financial stability & strength may not sufficiently consider the effectiveness of Operational Internal Controls in place within the assessed organizations. Thus, one might find a very highly rated company with poor or inadequate Operational Internal Controls, which may mislead potential investors and other stakeholders. Some observers have expressed harsh critics about the Financial Internal Controls criteria used by rating agencies, especially after the Enron scandal "We examine whether commercially available corporate governance rankings provide useful information for share-holders. Our results suggest that they do not" [17]. In brief, as narrated by Al-Zwyalif [18] Corporate Governance and Internal Control should go hand-by-hand for the interest of the organization and its network of stakeholders "Good Corporate Governance cannot exist without Internal Control. The internal control system is essential to achieve sound Corporate Governance".

This research proposes a comprehensive integrated framework for measuring the Effectiveness of Internal Controls in the upstream Oil & Gas industry. The proposed Internal Control Effectiveness Measurement Framework (ICEMF) constitutes a major first breakthrough in measuring and quantifying the posture of the Operational Internal Controls applied in the upstream Oil & Gas sector. The derived Index should be useful to many internal and external stakeholders in their strategic, tactical, financial, sustainable and operational decision-making process.

The rest of the paper is organized as follows: Sect. 2 describes our methodology and the components of the proposed framework and their relationships; Sect. 3 explains the measurement method and its related algorithms; Sect. 4 highlights the ICEMF utilization domains and Sect. 5 concludes and proposes the future research way forward.

2   An Operational Framework: The Internal Control Effectiveness Measurement Framework and Its Components (ICEMF)

Our contribution relies on the suggested integration of COSO Internal Control framework with three other components. We defend the idea that their combination can fulfil the needs relative to Internal Control Effectiveness Measurement. Our proposed framework is composed of four (4) pillars which will be successively introduced in the present section: (A) The COSO Internal Control Integrated Framework, (B) A Balanced Scorecard Performance Management Framework, (C) Energetics E&P Business Process Reference Model, and (D) The Zachman Enterprise Architecture Framework.

2.1   Research Methodology

The evidence mentioned in the introduction calls for a more exhaustive comprehension of risks. They also suggest a deficiency in the existing tools related to the Internal Control measurement capability. We use a methodology of

Evidence-Based Management (EBM) in order to understand the way in which existing tools could support some improvement. Indeed, many existing tools from industrial ones (see for example the Jacquard machine) to control tools have resulted from the acute combination of previously existing tools "In the two previous lectures my chief aim has been to point out the traditional continuity of the art of weaving and to show that all real advances in it have been made by bringing new ideas to bear on old principles. This method of advance is common not only to the textile but to all the arts of life" [19]. This approach similar to that of Grounded Theory is a supported research practice in Management Control and is mainly meant to elaborate theoretical knowledge from rigorous observations of collected facts. An acute analysis is next expected to enhance the effectiveness and efficiency of managerial decision-making [20].

From an epistemological perspective, our work produces a research question addressing the link and the articulation of methodological objects; this should allow the discovery of new methodological and empirical objects [21, 22]. Amongst those, new methodological approaches are expected to improve the performance measurement, suggest a new methodology of analysis or provide a novel decision making tool. This is indeed our purpose as we aim at building a tool to measure the effectiveness of Internal Controls in the specific Oil & Gas sector. As Internal Control is by itself a measurement function, our proposal is to render the remaining risk by proceeding to an "evaluation of evaluation", which could implicitly simultaneously assess the effectiveness of a regulation. To our knowledge literature has broadly addressed measurement issues with the aim of producing a new constructed tool. The present contribution shares the same approach. To do so, we borrow Lazarsfeld's process [23] process acknowledged as scientifically acceptable: the first operational step usually consists of identifying relevant concepts. Next, those are deconstructed in such a way that they can reveal their inner dimensions. In our case, this work is conducted through the analysis of the selected aggregated tools (Sect. 2.2). In the second step, we connected the four components and constructed a new framework. The third step is fulfilled when the measurement tool is assessed, gaining the status of indicator. Action-research will next stem from our initial proposal that is the topic of the present article. In that sense, we hope to reveal constituents of reality, but moreover, to solve concrete problems faced by practitioners. Though our stance is humble, we hope that this action research can help if not to change reality, at least to identify new paths to allow future changes.

Our analysis first focuses on the Internal Control frameworks which lack a comprehensive measurement tool to support the existing complex practices in the Oil & Gas industry. Also, the lack of an Internal Control measurement tool was deemed to undermine the genuineness of the credit agencies' ratings (BP was highly rated just before the Deepwater Horizon accident). These evidences collected from the ground by practitioners, observers and researchers paved the way for a new enhanced theory aimed at introducing an enhanced method for managing and measuring the Internal Controls [24] and by that, measure the efficiency of the existing regulation.

As narrated by Kaplan, "this situation leaves academic management accounting researchers who are interested in actual practice with three choices for their research programs: (1) find areas of study where widespread adoption has already occurred so that normal science methods can be productively employed to study "what-is"; (2) engage in case study and longitudinal research methods to study "what's new," areas where adoption is underway; and (3) study areas where no adoption exists. In this third alternative, successful change or adoption is either so slow or unlikely that academics engage in action and intervention research to create something that did not exist before" [25]. Kaplan used the same EBM method to develop a new balanced manner to measure the organization performance after observing an un-balanced weight between financial and operational performances [26]. Not without irony, his balanced scorecard is actually a component of the proposed research.

A quick glance at the literature clearly shows that researchers have widely used a similar approach to combine or integrate existing methods or framework in view of proposing a new, more comprehensive, better or perhaps a different way of addressing a subject of interest. A simple query about "combined framework" in any scholar library search engine gives an impressive number of publications that mobilized this method to conduct their research. Our approach in this research is not different. We clearly identified the business interfaces between the various components and welded them with technical links so to provide an integrated framework capable of measuring the internal control effectiveness in a very detailed manner. The outcome could serve as an Index that is as accurate as the company's financial statements to jointly provide better corporate governance rating of an Oil & Gas organization, in an approach addressing corporate governance acuteness to the given firm.

2.2 ICEMF Components

Our contribution comes from the conceptualization of such an integrated model that combines the relevant components thought for each specific tool in its specific domain. The choice of a framework/component over another (e.g. Balanced-Scorecard vs. another Performance Management tool) is less critical since it can be substituted by practitioners. Nevertheless, our selection is based on the widespread usage and maturity of these frameworks and reference models, which strengthened the functionality of our integrated proposed framework.

2.2.1 The COSO Internal Control Integrated Framework

The COSO (the Committee of Sponsoring Organizations of the Treadway Commission) is a well-known Internal Control framework that provides the foundation of a sound Internal Controls culture and practice in any organization. COSO believes this framework will enable organizations to effectively and efficiently develop and maintain systems of internal control that can enhance the likelihood of achieving the entity's objectives and adapt to changes in the business and operating environments. COSO's five Internal Controls Components (Control Environment, Risk Assessment, Control Activities, Information & Communication and Monitoring Activities) are divided into seventeen (17) guiding principles. Those principles are in turn supported by eighty one (81) Control Attributes [27]. Practically, those principles/attributes are assigned to the organization's business objectives to assess whether the control element (Component/ principle/attribute) is present or absent and whether it is functioning or malfunctioning.

2.2.2 The Balanced Scorecard Performance Management Framework

The balanced scorecard is a strategic planning and management system and a performance measurement framework that adds strategic non-financial performance measures to traditional financial metrics to give managers and executives a more 'balanced' view of organizational performance.

Having well defined objectives is a prerequisite for any COSO framework implementation—Hence the rationale for integrating the Performance Management framework with COSO framework. In addition to enforcing COSO's requirements, this integration allows the measurement of the Internal Controls associated with all the Balanced Scorecards sub-elements (Objectives, Strategies, Affiliates, Projects, KPI, locations, division, etc.) or any combination of the above.

2.2.3 ENERGISTICS E&P Business Process Reference Model

Energetics is an international association devoted to developing, supporting, evolving, and promoting open standards for the scientific, engineering, and operations aspects of the Oil & Gas Exploration and Production (E&P) industry. Energistics E&P Business Process Reference Model is one of the standards which describes the business processes that are commonly required to run the upstream Oil & Gas operations throughout the five stages of the asset (hydrocarbon reservoirs) life cycle. The five stages are: Exploration, Appraisal, Development, Production and Abandonment. Each of these major processes are divided into sub-processes which in turn are sub-divided down to the day-to-day activities of an Oil & Gas operation [28].

2.2.4 Zachman Enterprise Architecture Framework

The Zachman Framework is enterprise ontology and is a fundamental structure for Enterprise Architecture which provides a formal and structured way of viewing and defining an entity, enterprise, task or any other object. The ontology is a two dimensional classification schema (6 × 6) that reflects the intersection between two historical classifications: interrogatives and transformative.

Zachman framework is used to view any task of Energistics Business Process Model from a multi-dimensional perspective in order to assess the status of compliance with COSO Internal Control Framework and accordingly give the right assessment in terms of weight and eventual score.

2.2.5 The Combination of the Four Components (A, B, C & D) into the Internal Control Effectiveness Measurement Framework

The COSO framework states the following: "The quality and suitability of objectives established are pre-condition to Internal Control". To comply with this COSO obligation, we use the Performance Management framework (Balanced Scorecard) that embodies the company's SMARTly defined Objectives against which COSO Internal Controls elements shall be measured. These Objectives are attained through a series of business processes aimed at achieving the corporate objectives in an effective manner. We therefore use Energetics Business Process Reference Model which contains all the required business processes and their related tasks and activities. COSO's Internal Control elements (Components, Principles and Attributes) are then mapped against the control activities and tasks associated with Energistics business processes of the selected balanced scorecard objectives. Next, we use Zachman Enterprise Architecture framework to weigh and score each control element using Zachman 6 × 6 multidimensional perspective matrix [29]. Depending on the results of Zachman questions and views, a precise score is given to the task and hence to the control element assuring a minimum subjectivity and maximum objectivity.

Finally, the Internal Control effectiveness scores are aggregated in a Bottom-Up approach from the business activities (tasks), to the business processes, to the objectives, to the business area, and then to the company as a whole. Figure 1 illustrates the four pillars naturally joined to form the Internal Control Effectiveness Measurement Framework (ICEMF) business entity model. The four pillars of our proposed framework do indeed complement each other in a seamless logical flow. Each component addresses a business aspect of the process of identifying, mapping, and assessing the control activities, which are to be measured. The scoring method of the following sections will describe how the data (weights and scores) is being calculated using the proposed algorithms. Table 1 illustrates the aspects of COSO framework, which will be addressed in the subject research.

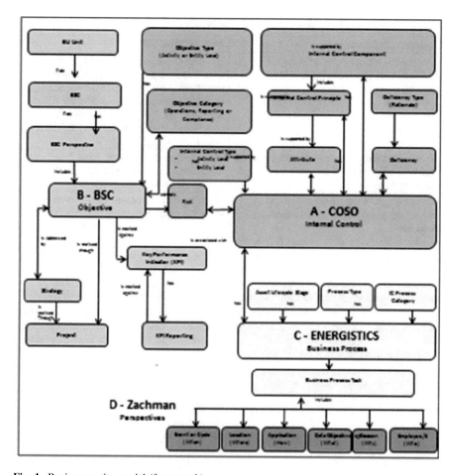

Fig. 1 Business entity model (framework)

3 ICEMF Concept Description

The proposed Internal Control Effectiveness Measurement Framework (ICEMF) is composed of a Business Entity Model and a Measurement Method illustrated respectively in Figs. 1 and 2. The Method is supported by a series of algorithms, flowcharts and calculation matrices to calculate the effectiveness Index.

3.1 ICEMF Business Diagram

Illustrated in Fig. 1, ICEMF allows the measurement of the Internal Controls Effectiveness of a particular Business Objective or a set of Objectives, a particular

Table 1 COSO main highlights and research requirements

Coso main highlight	Research requirements
The quality and suitability of objectives established are pre-condition to internal control	The COSO framework should be tightly related to a proper objectives setting and Performance Management Framework (e.g. balanced scorecard) where company's objectives are SMART-ly (specific, measurable, achievable, realistic, and time bound) articulated
To have an effective system of internal control each of the five components must be Present and work together	There proposed framework needs to identify the presence/absence of COSO controls and to measure their inter-relationships
Determining whether an overall system of Internal control is effective is a *subjective judgement*	Zachman framework will greatly support in removing (minimizing) the subjectivity related to humans' roles in assessing the applied controls
Assessing whether the system of internal control is effective means determining to what extent the principles/attributes associated with each component are present and functioning	The proposed framework needs to measure the two aspects: (1) the presence [implantation, design, set-up] and (2) the functioning [implementation, operational effectiveness]
When a principle is deemed not to be present or functioning, an internal control deficiency exists. (COSO suggests classifying such deficiencies as major and minor non-conformities)	The proposed framework needs to identify the deficiencies, weigh them and consider them in the overall internal control effectiveness score
Multiple minor non-conformities when considered collectively may result in a determination that a major non-conformity exists	The proposed framework needs to cover all company's objectives, associated risks, IC and the underlying processes in order not to miss any unnoticed weaknesses in the applied controls. Energistics standard grandly support this effort
Certain external parties, such as external auditors and regulators, are not part of the system of internal control and cannot be relied upon to detect and assess deficiencies	There is a need to have a holistic view of the entire operations and underlying activities for proper assessment of the IC status without the need to have an external eye (auditors). Such a holistic multiperspective view can be provided by an enterprise architecture framework such as Zachman)
There are two sets of internal controls: 1-entity level: control environment, information & communication and monitoring activities 2-activity level: risk assessment & control activities	The proposed framework needs to differentiate between the two sets of controls while calculating the internal controls effectiveness

Project or a set of Projects, a Business Unit or a set of Business Units (branches, affiliates, subsidiaries, etc.), and the entirety of Internal Controls within the organization.

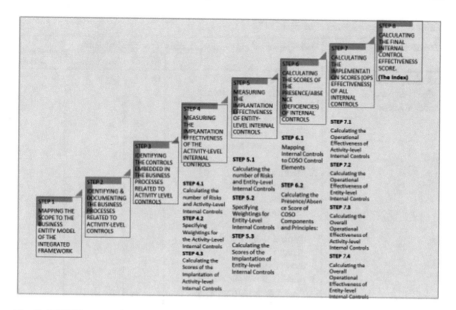

Fig. 2 ICEMF measurement method

The model encompasses predefined relationships (primary and secondary) linking the various components of the framework enabling this extended flexibility. e.g. once an Internal Control weakness is identified (Zachman assessment stage), it is possible to go backwards using the entities' inter-relationships and track all objectives, KPIs, projects and business units where this 'weak' Control is being used in any of the related business processes in order to take the right corrective action. Also, during the application of any 'Change Management' program, be it organizational, functional, business expansion or downsizing, restructuring, merging or splitting, ICEMF allows to measure the impact of the change on the Internal Control establishment. The below Table 2 describes how various business scenarios can be managed using ICEMF through a series of steps. It also shows the order of using the four ICEMF components and the inner fringes.

3.2 ICEMF Method

Illustrated in Fig. 2, the Internal Controls Effectiveness Measurement Method is composed of eight (8) steps. Step one (1) to three (3) sets the environment and the business scope to be covered (area to be measured) while step four (4) to eight (8) do the actual calculation of the Internal Control Implantation and Implementation effectiveness scores as well as the identification of the control deficiencies using predefined formulas and supported by mathematical algorithms.

Table 2 Business scenarios using ICEFM

Scenario	Description	ICEMF process flow (order)			
		BScd	COSO	Energistics	Zackman
Measure the IC effectiveness of a specific scope	1. Define the scope of IC to be measured within the organization such as objectives related to projects, divisions, affiliates, corporate, etc. 2. Identify the risks associated to these objectives and accordingly map COSO's Internal Control elements meant to address those risks 3. Identify the business processes required to be run in order to attain the subject objectives and identify the activity level controls and entity level controls associated to these business processes 4. Use Zachman to weigh the Implantation and Implementation effectiveness of these controls	❶	❷	❸	❹
Measure the IC effectiveness of a set of COSO controls	1. Identify a set of controls to be measured from COSO's predefined Control Elements 2. Identify the business processes associated with these controls 3. Measure the effectiveness of the internal controls using Zachman framework 4. (optional) identify the list of objectives impacted by the identified business process	④	❶	❷	❸

(continued)

Table 2 (continued)

Scenario	Description	ICEMF process flow (order)			
		BScd	COSO	Energistics	Zackman
Relate identified IC weaknesses to business objectives	1. Identify weaknesses in one or more IC(s) relative to an entity or a business process level 2. Identify the business processes impacted by these control elements 3. Identify COSO's components and the risks associated with these controls 4. Relate the business objectives impacted by the identified IC weakness	❹	❸	❷	❶
Improve the performance of objectives impacted by specific low-performing business process	1. Identify a non-satisfactory (low performance) business process 2. Relate the COSO internal controls elements associated with the business process 3. Measure the IC effectiveness using Zachman (in view of fixing any Implantation or Implementation issue which will lead to improving the performance of the process) 4. Relate and measure the performance improvement of objectives that are impacted by the subject business process	❹	❷	❶	❸

Step eight (8) of the ICEMF calculation method consists of calculating the final Internal Control Effectiveness Score (The Index): Let:

A(i): Activity-Level Implantation Score for Objective i
B(i): Activity-Level Implementation Score for Objective i
C(i): Entity-Level Implantation Score for Objective i
D(i): Entity-Level Implementation Score for Objective i
NB: Total Number of Objectives
SO(i): Internal Control Effectiveness Score for objective i
SO(i) = AVG[(B(i) * A(i)), D(i) * C(i))]
Provisional Internal Control Overall Score = $\sum_{i=1}^{NB} SO(i)/NB$
However, two additional factors shall be considered in the overall score:

1. Deficiency factor (m)
2. Internal Control 'Working Together' factor (n)

Internal Control Effectiveness Index = $m * n * \sum_{i=1}^{NB} SO(i)/NB$

The final Internal Control score takes into consideration all aspects of COSO framework and provides an accurate indication as to what extent the company's Internal Controls are being effective.

Remark: This formula assumes that all objectives have the same importance. The case where the organization has different weights per objective was also handled part of ICEMF Index calculation.

4 ICEMF Utilization

Different stakeholders can use the proposed framework for multiple purposes:

Management: To ensure proper delivery of the company's objectives and proper controls in place.

Shareholders: Get the necessary assurance that the company is being managed and controlled effectively and that the corporate business strategy has better chances of being achieved.

Investors: For individuals, banks/ borrowers, investment funds or any other potential investor, this framework sheds the light on the company's internal operations allowing a better visibility into the company's daily transactions as well as its major corporate objectives. It also provides insights on the risks and the associated Internal Controls management. Thus, a better decision would then be made on whether to invest or not, and on the share value as well.

Internal Auditors: Internal audit is an internal powerful tool based on the company's corporate governance structure. The ICEMF Index can indeed shape up the role of Internal Audit by focusing on the critical objectives which have Internal Control concerns; on the Internal Control deficiencies; Supporting Management and Board of Directors (BoD) in assessing the severity of the identified deficiencies and recommending the appropriate remedies; Reviewing the latest Internal Controls ratings and accordingly set the yearly audit plan priorities; Review the risks associated with the entity objectives and the related Internal Controls and accordingly decide on the course of actions and recommendations.

External Auditors: Similar to Internal Audit, the external Auditors would benefit from the same advantages listed above. In addition, external auditors might be called upon by companies interested in acquiring or merging with the organization in order to get a better insight about the non-financial corporate governance (Internal Control) stature, the Risk Management practices and the likelihood of achieving the corporate objectives.

Government: Would also use the External Auditors to measure the companies' performances in terms of implementing the right internal Controls which go alongside the laws and regulations in place.

Employees: Last but definitely not least, the employees are the most affected by any Internal Control deficiency. As stated in the literature review, the outcome of any failure due to non-presence or malfunctioning Internal Control is usually catastrophic in terms of human casualties. Involving the employees in enhancing the Internal Control Index based on the proposed framework would un-doubtfully be very beneficial.

Other stakeholders are of course concerned with the measurement of the effectiveness of processes. This includes at the first place the citizen of the world, especially when the reduction of harm to the planet is concerned. The representatives of the civil society, under the form of NGOs fall in that category. Consumers whom will consume more sustainable goods or at least increase their awareness will be able to shift to substitutes, consume in the knowledge of the consequence or consume the best possible goods in one category, and likely with more information on their sustainability performance. Funds providers whom will be better informed and whose values could converge will also appreciate the complementary information, and possibly will be able to define collaterals accordingly. Suppliers may enjoy better information about the becoming of their sales. Regulators, institutions will also gain in the understanding of the effect of regulation and their disciplinary contents.

5 Conclusion and Future Direction

We propose and test in a case study a framework measuring the status of Internal Controls in the organization. ICEMF is designed to identify the existing Internal Control related to a specific company Objective and Control Deficiencies Rate (measure) the effectiveness of identified Internal Controls and finally, it allows to calculate an overall Internal Control Effectiveness Index of the entire organization or a function. Accordingly, the company management and stakeholders shall decide on an appropriate course of actions to adjust controls. The researched ICEMF Index could forcefully measure and improve the Internal Control Effectiveness and consequently allow early detection of potential and possible yet improbable failures.

The focus of the research was mainly on the Oil & Gas sector. This is because of the use of Energetics as a Standard Business Process Model for the Industry. Though not tested here, and this is a limit of our work, ICEMF could be applicable to all businesses and industries. Although ICEMF is believed improve the measure of the Internal Controls effectiveness in the Oil & Gas Industry, it remains nevertheless a first step in a series of further improvement and research to come. The development of a method to calculate the degree of dependence/relationships between the various COSO elements to score the 'Working Together' factor as a COSO requirement is a tool enhancement possibility. The definition of a research model based on empirical analysis to help in deciding when minor deficiencies constitute a major concern is another one.

References

1. Mishra, A.S., Bhattacharya, S.: The Linkage between financial crisis and corporate governance: a literature review. The IUP Journal of Corporate Governance X 3, 71–84 (2011)
2. Isaksson, M., Kirkpatrick, G.: Corporate governance: lessons from the financial crisis. OECD Observer 2009/1(273), 11–12 (2009). https://doi.org/10.1787/fmt-v2009-art3-en
3. Brickey, K.F.: From enron to worldcom and beyond : life and crime after sarbanes-oxley. Wash. Univ. Law Rev. 81(2) (2003)
4. Blum, V., Girard, R.: Les Risques Liés À La Diffusion Des Innovations Pétrolières: Du Relâchement Prudentiel À La Porosité Du Due Process. In: Guillon, B. (ed.) Pour Une Politique Du Risque, Comprendre et Agir. L'Harmattan, Paris (2014)
5. Cohan, J.A.: 'I Didn' T know' and 'I Was Only Doing My Job': Has Corporate Governance Careened Out of Control? A Case Study of Enron's Information Myopia. J. Bus. Ethics 40(3), 275–299 (2002)
6. Oxley, M.R.: Rep. michael oxley cites restoration of investor confidence as the legacy of the sarbanes-oxley act. Michigan Banker, 16(6), 95 (2004)
7. Lee, T.: Research in internal control in the extractive industries: corporate govern. Petrol. Acc. Financ. Manag. J. 26(1), 27–54 (2007)
8. Lin-Hi, N., Blumberg, I.: The relationship between corporate governance, global governance, and sustainable profits: lessons learned from BP. Corp. Gov. 11(5), 571–584 (2011). https://doi.org/10.1108/14720701111176984
9. Blanchard, J., Dobson J., Angus, A.: Preventing major accidents in the oil and gas industry. RPS Energy, no. May (2010)
10. Cho, C.H.: Legitimation strategies used in response to environmental disaster: a french case study of total SA's Erika and AZF Incidents. Eur Account. Rev. 18(1), 33–62 (2009). https://doi.org/10.1080/09638180802579616
11. Beelitz, A., Merkl-Davies, D.M.: Using discourse to restore organisational legitimacy: 'CEO-Speak' after an incident in a german nuclear power plant. J. Bus. Ethics 108(1), 101–120 (2012). https://doi.org/10.1007/s10551-011-1065-9
12. Barros, M.: Tools of legitimacy: the case of the petrobras corporate blog. Organ. Stud. 35(8), 1211–1230 (2014). https://doi.org/10.1177/0170840614530914
13. Steinberg, By Richard M.: How Did BP's Risk management lead to failure?" Compliance week, no. August: 40–42 (2010)
14. Taleb, N.N.: The Black Swan : The Impact of the Highly Improbable. Penguin Books Ltd. (2007)

15. Williams, B.: Oil industry adapting to evolving new paradigm on corporate governance, accountability. Oil Gas J. **100**(44), 20–32 (2002)
16. Masli, A., Peters, G.F., Richardson, V.J., Sanchez, J.M.: Examining the potential benefits of internal control monitoring technology. Acc. Rev. **85**(3), 1001–1034 (2010). https://doi.org/10.2308/accr.2010.85.3.1001
17. Daines, R.M., Gow, I.D., Larcker, D.F.: Rating the ratings: how good are commercial governance ratings? J. Financ. Econ. **98**(3), 439–461 (2010). https://doi.org/10.1016/j.jfineco.2010.06.005
18. Al-Zwyalif, I.M.: The role of internal control in enhancing corporate governance: evidence from jordan. Int. J. Bus. Manag. **10**(7), 57–66 (2015). https://doi.org/10.5539/ijbm.v10n7p57
19. Hooper, L.: The Loom and Spindle: Past, Present, and Future. Annual Report Smithsonion Institution, pp. 629–79 (1914)
20. Cappelletti, L.: La Recherche-Intervention: Quels Usages En Controle De Gestion ?" Congrès de l'Association Francophone de Comptabilité (AFC), pp. 1–25 (2010)
21. Allard-Poesi, F., Perret, V.: La Recherche-Action. Une Approche Qualitative. e-theque, Conduire Un Projet de Recherche (2004)
22. Allard-Poesi, F., Maréchal, G.: Construction de L'objet de La Recherche. In: Méthodes de Recherche En Management, pp. 34–57 (2007)
23. Angot, J., Milano P.: Comment Lier Concepts et Données. In: Thiétart R.A. (ed.) Méthodes de Recherche En Management, pp. 173–91. Dunod, 3{è}me {é}dition (col. Gestion Sup.)— ISBN 2–10-050828-8 (2007)
24. Joannides, V., Berland, N.: Grounded Theory: Quels Usages Dans Les Recherches En Contrôle de Gestion? COMPTABILITÉ—CONTRÔLE—AUDIT Numéro thé: pp. 141–63 (2008)
25. Kaplan, R.: Research opportunities in management accounting. J. Manag. Acc. Res. **5**, 1 (1993)
26. Balanced Scorecard Institute.: How a balanced scorecard can help your organization. Balanced Scorecard Institute Journal (2000)
27. PriceWaterhouseCooper.: COSO Internal Control—Integrated Framework (2012)
28. Energistics.: Energistics E&P business process reference model (2012)
29. Zachman, J.A.: The Zachman framework for enterprise architecture, primer for enterprise engineering and manufacturing. CA Magazine **128**(9), 15 (2003). https://doi.org/10.1109/CSIE.2009.478

Ontology for Enterprise Interactions: Extended and Virtual Enterprises

F. Al Hadidi and Y. Baghdadi

Abstract The interaction concept has been given much importance in computer science and information systems. The interactions happen at different levels and in different situations. Interactions involve actors that act in re-action to one other action. The enterprise, as an actor, needs to implement interactions. Indeed, the knowledge emerging from interactions is greater than the sum of the involved actor's knowledge. Traditionally, interactions are implemented on a case-by-case basis without managed view, which yields costly integration architectures, because they do not consider the semantic aspect of the interactions. Ontology is the solution for the semantic problem, which provides a smooth integration. This paper aims at building Ontology for enterprise interactions, specifically Extended Enterprise (EE) and Virtual Enterprise (VE), whereby an EE is a kind of collaboration between loosely coupled enterprises that combine their economic output to provide product/service offerings. An EV is a temporary relationship between distributed enterprises, competitors, and partners which access each other market.

Keywords Interaction · Semantic integration · Ontology for enterprise

1 Introduction

In the last decades, the concept of interaction has evolved and has been given much importance in many computer science areas, including: databases, distributed systems, and artificial intelligence, as the knowledge emerging from interactions is greater than the sum of actor's knowledge. Interactions involve actors that act in re-action to one-other action [1, 2].

F. Al Hadidi (✉) · Y. Baghdadi
Department of Computer Science, Sultan Qaboos University, Muscat, Oman
e-mail: m100050@student.squ.edu.om

Y. Baghdadi
e-mail: ybaghdadi@squ.edu.om

© Springer Nature Switzerland AG 2019
Y. Baghdadi and A. Harfouche (eds.), *ICT for a Better Life and a Better World*,
Lecture Notes in Information Systems and Organisation 30,
https://doi.org/10.1007/978-3-030-10737-6_24

The enterprise, as an actor, needs to implement interactions for different purposes, in different situations, and at different levels. The most significant purpose is realizing the required integration architectures that add great value to the enterprise. Indeed, an enterprise needs to involve and promote interactions in its environment (e.g. customers, partners, suppliers, regulatory authorities, or even competitors) as well as employees, specially that: (i) the performance of an enterprise depends on how its parts interact, not on how they act taken separately [3], (ii) collaborative efforts of networked users and services usually lead to better output [4–7].

Traditionally, interactions are implemented from a technology perspective on a case-by-case basis without a comprehensive managed view, which yields brittle and costly integration architectures. Indeed, most of the integration for intra- and inter-organizational Business Processes (BPs) has been driven by advances in technology [8–11] and realized, on a case-by-case basis, by using adapters, wrappers, object oriented middleware such as CORBA, DCOM, or EJB, which has resulted in the well-known N*(N-1) integration problem [12].

In the other hand, Enterprise Architecture (EA) has been used as a key approach to grasp the elements and relations in the enterprise environment and to describe them [13]. It acts as an enterprise blueprint that builds the units of an enterprise, such as business processes, organizations, data, and information technologies.

Ontology has been introduced as a technical solution for the semantic problem. It is considered as a way to share knowledge. Consequently, many research efforts have been conducted to employ ontology to facilitate the process of sharing knowledge among actors and providing smooth integration.

This research aims at presenting a comprehensive framework for two types of enterprise collaborations by using ontology for interactions to facilitate their modeling, engineering, and management. These collaboration types are Extended Enterprise (EE) and Virtual Enterprise (VE). The choice of these two types of collaborations is twofold: (i) to show the efficiency of ontology in providing the required semantics and to infer, share, and reuse knowledge and (ii) to show how to improve collaborations.

2   Ontology

Ontology in the philosophy is an explanation and a systemic answer of the question what are the concepts in the domain? [14, 15]. However, this is an informal definition because it opens the door for several questions like what we can do with these concepts. What are the relations between them? What these concepts form? However, employing Ontology in a specific domain that has some constraints will force Ontology to be a formal. Enterprise is an example of a domain to implement a formal Ontology.

2.1   Definitions

There are many definitions of Ontology as a science exported from philosophy. All these definitions are around Gruber definition [16] who stated that "Ontology is an explicit specification of a conceptualization". Conceptualization, according to Genesereth and Nilsson [17], is defined as "the objects, concepts and other entities that are assumed to exist in some area of interest and their inter-relationships." After that, Borst [18] defined Ontology as "a formal specification of a shared conceptualization." however, the most used definition was introduced in 1998 by Studer and his colleagues, they stated that "An Ontology is a formal, explicit specification of a shared conceptualization." [19].

Ontology invaded most of the computer science fields, however the artificial intelligent is in the front. Moreover, it is applied in the information organization, natural language processing, information retrieval for designing thesaurus, knowledge representation, knowledge acquisition, e-commerce, intelligent integration information, semantic web, knowledge engineering, database for designing XML schema, linked-data for designing a model represented in OWL and software engineering [14, 20, 21].

2.2   Ontology for Enterprise

Ontology for enterprise helps to share common understanding of the structure of information among people or software agents. It establishes a consistent and a stable platform of enterprises domain information among different web sites and applications. This enterprise domain information specifies concepts of the enterprises domain, relationships between concepts and properties and axioms of the specified domain. Consequently, the transformation of unorganized domain of enterprise information to a shared and stable Ontology would actually support agents through easy extraction of information. After that, this information can be used to answer user queries or as input data to other applications. Generally, constructing Ontology through alignment, mapping or integrating several existing ontologies either of the same domain or different domains would enable reuse of domain knowledge. Hence, the most important advantage of Ontology is saving time and effort [22].

3   Ontology and Enterprise Architecture (EAs)

There are many enterprise architectures. Some of them are considered as Ontology and some of them are not.

Zachman created a framework called Zachman framework to define information system architecture [23]. He developed his framework based on rationalizing the various architectural concepts and specifications, thus many factors can be achieved: (i) clear professional communications, (ii) an improvement and an integration of development methodologies and tools, and (iii) establishment credibility and confidence in the investment of systems resources. Zachman framework is estimated as a standard Enterprise Architecture that every enterprise can use to build its architecture [24]. However, it is poor in providing a detailed model of enterprise's components and relations among them. Moreover, it does not provide a concrete implementing method. It systematically describes the enterprise components. The authors suggest that the failed integration is resulted from the bad communication among human, systems or human and systems. Therefore, they have built three composed levels of ontologies. The first level is ontology of business terms, the second level for ontology of enterprise architecture components, and the third level for ontology of relationships among enterprise architecture components.

OntoSTEP is a step toward developing a semantically enriched product models [25]. This ontology model relays on how to represent (STEP) the STandard for Exchange of Product data model. A STEP is a schema developed by (ISO) the International Organization for Standardization to enable the exchange of product data throughout a product's lifecycle. In addition, OntoSTEP implements an automatic translation of instances and EXPRESS schema. EXPRESS schema is a language was developed for representing product models and providing support to describe the information required for designing, building, and maintaining product.

In [26], a framework of ontology mapping based on an intelligent agent search for product information has been proposed. The main goal of this framework pours in customer's intent to enhance some issues related to online sites of product shopping such as Amazon.com and Buy.com.

Panetto et al. [27] formalized a product ontology (ONTO-PDM) based on knowledge embedded into eight existing IEC 62264 models (Product Definition, Material, Equipment, Personnel, Process Segment, Production Schedule, Production Capability, and Production Performance). Each model is extended by STEP PDM concepts, manufacturing constraints, and mapping rules. They refer to IEC 62264 and ISO 10303 particularly STEP PDM as a standard for product technical. IEC 62264 specifies a set of reference models for information exchange between business applications and manufacturing control applications. However, a STEP PDM Schema deals with typical product-related information, including geometry, engineering drawings, project plans, part files, assembly diagrams, product specifications, numerical control machine-tool programs, analysis results, correspondence, and bills of material, engineering change orders, etc.

4 Types of Collaborations

Within the continuum of enterprise networks, there are three types of collaborations that can form a component of an enterprise network. These types are as shown in Fig. 1:

- Supply Chain (SC)
- Extended Enterprise (EE)
- Virtual Enterprise (VE)
- Integrated Enterprise (IE).

4.1 Supply Chain (SC)

Supply chain is a series of business activities that begin with "start Activity" and end with "End Activity" in order to submit the final product to the extended customers. The concept of supply chain evolved long before the advent of ICT [28]. During the implementation of any supply chain in the field, there are a set of requirements that must be achieved. These requirements include:

- The involved partner in the supply chain has to understand and accept the role of the other partners.
- Different business processes such as marketing, purchasing, sales, production, and planning have to establish an effective communication chain between them.
- Each enterprise must adapt dynamically to the continuous change of other enterprises in the supply chain.

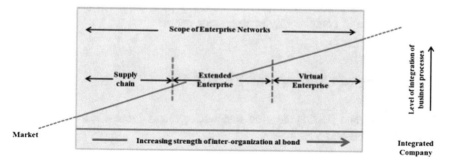

Fig. 1 Types of collaborations. (*Source* Jagdev and Thoben [28])

4.2   Extended Enterprise (EE)

The concept of Extended Enterprise is used recently in the business field to represent the high level of cooperation between different organizations. Extended Enterprise is used whenever referring to any new style of manufacturing. The baseline of EE is two or more enterprises that wish to extend their activities to other enterprise in order to increase their competitiveness and enhance their existing capabilities. An example of EE is the collaboration between existing organizations. Each of them provides one or more services such as financial service, transportation service, or any form of distribution services [29].

4.3   Virtual Enterprise (VE)

VE is a flat management and low overhead of temporary and independent nodes that form an electronic communication network of companies, competitors and partners. These nodes are all comprise "owner", ready to access each other market and apply flexible integration over ICT technologies. Even they are geographically distributed with temporarily relationships [29].

4.4   Integrated Enterprise (IE)

The development of integration among EE and VE collaborations leads to another type of collaboration which is called Enterprise Integration (IE) [28]. IE comes over hiding the means of extend and virtual to a one type of collaboration based essentially on integration. The level of successful integration can be seen through the high degree of compatibility between enterprises.

5   Building of Ontology for EE and VE

We use Noy and McGuinness as methodology and Protégé as tool to build Ontology for EE and VE.

5.1 Noy and McGuinness Methodology for Building the New Ontology

In order to insure successful methodology of Ontology development, Noy and McGuinness [22] proposed seven-step approach to organize the way of building Ontology. Figure 2 represents these steps.

Step 1: Domain and scope of the Ontology

In this step, a few questions should be answered before starting building Ontology.

- What is the domain that the proposed Ontology will cover?
- What will the Ontology be used for?
- What questions will the Ontology provide answers to?

– What is the basic information that reveals the commonalities and differences between EE and VE?
– What is the new knowledge that can be inferred over this Ontology?

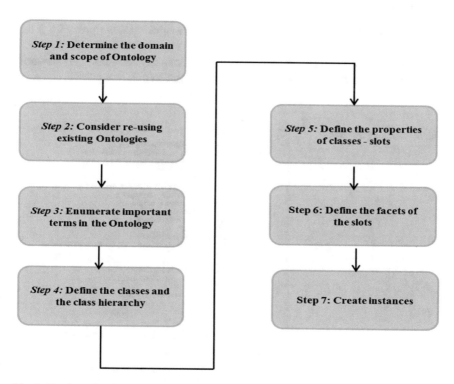

Fig. 2 Ontology development approach (based on Noy and McGuinness [22])

Step 2: Consider reusing existing ontologies

We prefer to build new Ontology based on some existing ontologies, because we found it more reflective and expressive to build new Ontology carrying our goal.

Step 3: Enumerate important terms in the Ontology

In this stage, the adopted terms or concepts extracted from the literature of many papers that touched on enterprises design and Ontology were listed. The focus of building this Ontology couched in three important concepts: framework, enterprise features, and interaction. To build the framework concept, we relied on some papers such as [30] "Concepts for Modeling Enterprise Architectures", [31] "Extended enterprise modeling language", [32] "Customer Focused Business Processes in Virtual Enterprises", and [33] "Tools for enterprises collaboration in virtual enterprises.

The terms under the concept enterprise features distinguish between extended enterprise and virtual enterprise. However, the third term interaction has been used to set the inferences that result from (i) framework concept and its relations, and (ii) the enterprise features concept and its relations.

Step 4: Define the classes and the class hierarchy

For the collection of classes obtained from the previous step, we post Fig. 3 that shows the classes hierarchy of some defined terms. For instance, the term "Framework" is a first level class that has an "Actor" as a subclass. "Framework" and "Actor" are terms that were enumerated through step 3.

Fig. 3 Ontology hierarchy

Step 5: Define the properties of classes—slots

Since we used Protégé 2000 to implement the Ontology, we have created two types of properties: (1) object properties to relate individuals with each other, and (2) data properties to relate individuals with literals. These properties comprise relations between the classes in the Ontology. Regarding the object properties, the Ontology has defined 27 properties and 11 inverse properties, while it has only defined one data property, which is the rate. Table 1 depicts the object properties in the middle column.

Table 1 Ontology facets

Domain is a class (C_i)	Object property is a relation (R)	Range is a class (C_j)
Application	applicabilitySupport	ContractType
Thing	Are	TriggerType
TriggerType	areFiredFor	Operations
ActorRole	beExpertIn	ActorExperience
CollaborationFeatures	hasActor	ActorName
ActorName	hasActorExperience	ActorExperience
ActorName	hasActorRole	ActorRole
CollaborationFeatures	hasClosedProcess	CloserProcesses
CollaborationFeatures	hasDepartment	Department
CollaborationFeatures	hasExample	ExampleOfCollaboration
Product	hasInfo	InfoProduct
Product	hasInformationRepresentation	InformationRepresentation
CollaborationFeatures	hasLayer	Layers
CollaborationFeatures	hasOrganizationType	OrganizationBased
CollaborationFeatures	hasProblem	Problems
ProcessName	hasProcessActivity	ProcessActivity
Product	hasService	Service
CollaborationFeatures	hasStrength	
	hasEEStrength	LongTerm
	hasVEStrength	Reduction
Product	hasTechnicalInfrastructure	TechnicalInfrastructure
CollaborationFeatures	hasTechnologyNature	ICTNature
CollaborationFeatures	hasVEDvantage	VEAdvantage
Trigger	interrupt	ProcessName
Thing	LocatedIn	Location
CollaborationFeatures	Produce	Location
TechnicalInfrastructure	technicallySupport	Application

Step 6: Define the facets of the slots

The triplet subject, predicate, and object is reflected in the Ontology as domain, property, and range respectively. Domain and range are classes, whereas property is a relationship or a verb that links classes. Ci denotes domain, R denotes property or relation, and Cj denotes range. This triplet is represented as {Ci, R, Cj}. The facets of the slot are defined when the domain, range, and value type of the slots or properties are defined. Most of the value types of our Ontology are instances of the proposed range. An example of the facet is (ActorName, hasActorRole, ActorRole), Table 1 depicts the facets.

Step 7: Create instances

The following figure depicts some instances of EE and VE Ontology. Figure 4 shows "Location" instances. Location is a class whereas the countries are its individuals. In addition, instances can be classes.

5.2 Adding Restrictions to the Ontology

Yet the Ontology is just a hierarchy of classes. In this section we are explaining some of the OWL restrictions that have been added to the Ontology.

The purpose of restrictions is to set the rules that restrict the ontology in order to get good inferences. Protégé 2000 has been used to build the Ontology and also to add restrictions. The most important restrictions are: Some and Only. Some means at least one value from the range of possible values. Only means that the allowed values are only from the specified filler or range. In addition, we use Pellet as a plug-in tool in Protégé to check the consistency of the Ontology.

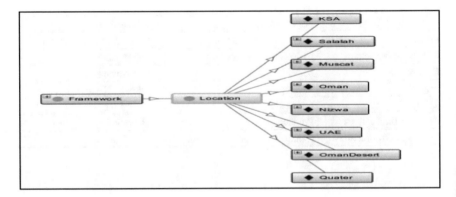

Fig. 4 "Location" instances

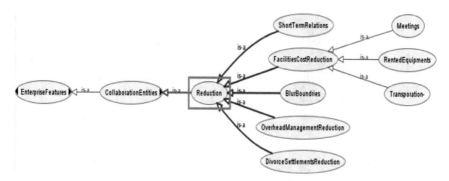

Fig. 5 Hierarchy of "Reduction" class

The following designed example aims to set the strength factors of VE. When the ontology is used to infer new knowledge, the strength factors will be inferred as a subclass of "VirtualEnterprise" class.

First, we build a "Reduction" class to have the strength factors as subclasses. For example, "ShortTermRelations" is a sub class of "Reduction" and it is one of the strength factors of VE as shown in Fig. 5.

Then, we define a "VirtualEnterpriseStrength" class through "hasStrength" property, "Some" restriction and the closer axiom using "Only" and union relation "or", as show in Fig. 6. We aim to add the strength factors of VE under the class "VirtualEnterprisestrength" through some restrictions.

Finally, we define "VirtualEnterprise" through "hasStrength" property, "Some" restriction and the range "Rediction", as shown in Fig. 7. The result will be (VirtualEnterprise hasStrength some Redution). In fact, "VirtualEnterprise" class will grab all subclasses of the class "Reduction'".

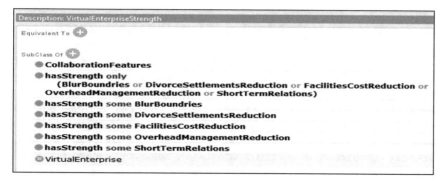

Fig. 6 Description view of "VirtualEnterprisestrength" class

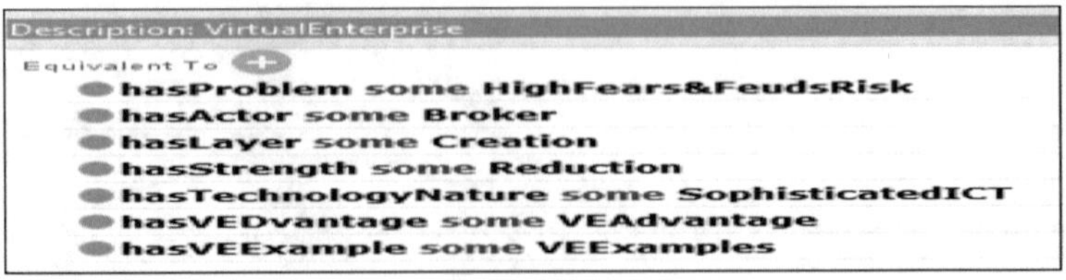

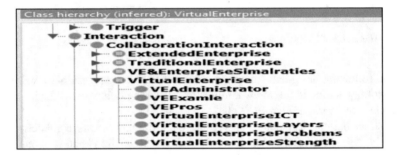

Fig. 7 'hasStrength some Reduction' in description view of 'VirtualEnterprise'

Fig. 8 "VirtualEnterpriseStrength" as subclass of "VirtualEnterprise" in inferred view

We design "VirtualEnterprise" class without any subclasses. However, after using the inferred feature in Protégé 2000, we will get some information about VE. One of this information is the strength factors of it. Figure 8 depicts the inference result when "VirtualEnterpriseStrength" acts as a subclass of "VirtualEnterprise".

6   Research Findings

The domain of enterprise collaborations (EE and VE) contains a wide range of entities and relationships among them. All these entities and relationships comprise the existing knowledge. Beside the existing knowledge there is a new knowledge that can be inferred through the interactions among domain entities. Existing knowledge and new knowledge can be semantically represented in a useful way using Ontology. In this research, for instance: actors, processes, activities, products, resources, services, and relationships comprise the domain of enterprise collaborations (EE and VE). However, the existing knowledge is represented through the hierarchy construction of domain entities and relationships. Whereas the new knowledge has been resulted after adding restrictions to the domain. An example of new knowledge is the representation of the properties of EE and VE as Fig. 9 shows. This figure depicts the Ontology after using a tool in Protégé to reason it.

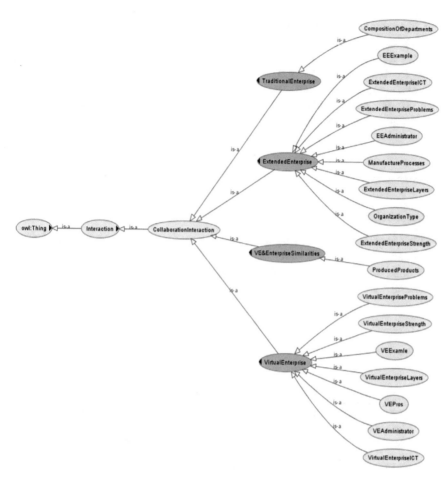

Fig. 9 EE and VE ontology after reasoning

Hence, the research findings are:

- A semantic representation of EE and VE properties
- A semantic representation of the differences and similarities of EE and VE
- A semantic representation of knowledge related to traditional collaboration.

7 Conclusion

Ontology is a formal, explicit specification of a shared conceptualization. Noticeably, the state of the art of enterprise architecture indicates the need for automated framework and a facilitator to a reliable integration that semantically sounds.

Consequently, we have built a new domain Ontology for two types of enterprise collaborations: Extended Enterprise and Virtual Enterprise.

The resulted Ontology has the same benefits of any Ontology in the sense that it helps to share knowledge and ease integration. This ontology has substantially provided a useful framework that acts as a common general framework for EE and VE. This framework adds value for integration and acts as a machine readable text that distinguishes between the two types of collaborations: EE and VE.

8 Future Work

The research has the following possible directions:

- Consider better relations between concepts because of the scarceness of mentioned relations in the literature.
- Extend the developed Ontology to other types of interactions (e.g. IoT and Social Interactions).

References

1. Giddens, A.: The constitution of society: outline of the theory of structuration. Cognit. Ther. Res. **12**, 448 (1984)
2. Hendrickx H.H.M.: Governance in the Practice of the Chief Information Officers. Tilburg University (2007)
3. Ackoff, R.L.: Re-crating the Corporation: A Design of Organizations for the 21st Century. Oxford University Press (1999)
4. Cai, J.: A social interaction analysis methodology for improving e-collaboration over the internet. Electron. Commer. Res. Appl. **4**, 85–99 (2005)
5. Chen, D.N., Liang, T.P.: Knowledge evolution strategies and organizational performance: a strategic fit analysis. Electron. Commer. Res. Appl. **10**, 75–84 (2011)
6. Smith-David, J., Wan, B., Westland, J.C.: Introduction to special issue: social networks and web 2.0. Electron. Commer. Res. Appl. **9**, 3–5 (2010)
7. Baghdadi, Y.: A framework for social commerce design. Inf. Syst. **60**, 95–113 (2016)
8. De Michelis, G. et al.: Cooperative information systems: a manifesto. Coop. Inf. Syst. Trends Dir. 315–165 (1997)
9. Medjahed, B., Benatallah, B., Bouguettaya, A., Ngu, A.H., Elmagarmid, A.K.: Business-to-business interactions: issues and enabling technologies. VLDB J.—Int. J. Very Large Data Bases **12**, 59–85 (2003)
10. Jung, J., Kim, H., Kang, S.H.: Standards-based approaches to B2B workflow integration. Comput. Ind. Eng. **51**, 321–334 (2006)
11. Baghdadi, Y., Al-Bulushi, W.: A guidance process to modernize legacy applications for SOA. Ser. Oriented Comput. App. **9**, 41–58 (2015)
12. Baghdadi, Y.: Architecture for deploying e-business: business processes, web services-based business interactions manager, and information systems. Int. J. Electron. Bus. **4**, 19–38 (2006)
13. Harmon, P.: Developing an enterprise architecture. Bus. Process Trends 1–15 (2002)

14. Corcho, O., Fern, M.: Methodologies, tools and languages for building ontologies. Where is their meeting point? **46**, 41–64 (2003)
15. Guarino, N., Oberle, D., Staab, S.: What is an Ontology? Handbook on ontologies 1–17 (2009)
16. Guarino, N., Poli, R.: Toward principles for the design of ontologies used for knowledge sharing. In: Formal Ontology in Conceptual Analysis and Knowledge Representation (Substantial revision of paper presented at the International Workshop on Formal Ontology). Kluwer Academic Publishers, 1993
17. Michael R.G., Nils J.N.: logical Foundation of Artificial Intelligent, vol. 6. Morgan Kaufmann (1986)
18. Borst, W.N.: Construction of engineering ontologies for knowledge sharing and reuse (1997)
19. Studer, R., Benjamins, V.R., Fensel, D.: Knowledge engineering: principles and methods. Data Knowl. Eng. **25**, 161–197 (1998)
20. Subhashini, R.: A survey on ontology construction methodologies 1 (2011)
21. Roussey, C., Pinet, F., Kang, M.A., Corcho, O.: An introduction to ontologies and ontology engineering. In: Ontologies in Urban Development Projects, pp. 9–39 (2011) https://doi.org/10.1007/978-0-85729-724-2
22. Noy, N.F., McGuinness, D.L.: Ontology development 101: a guide to creating your first ontology 1–25 (2000)
23. Zachman, J.A.: A framework for information systems architecture **26** (1987)
24. Kang, D., Lee, J., Choi, S., Kim, K.: Expert systems with applications an ontology-based enterprise architecture. Expert Syst. Appl. **37**, 1456–1464 (2010)
25. Barbau, R., et al.: OntoSTEP: enriching product model data using ontologies. Comput. Des. **44**, 575–590 (2012)
26. Kim, W., Choi, D.W., Park, S.: Agent based intelligent search framework for product information using ontology mapping. J. Intell. Inf. Syst. **30**, 227–247 (2008)
27. Panetto, H., Dassisti, M., Tursi, A.: Advanced engineering informatics ONTO-PDM: product-driven ontology for product data management interoperability within manufacturing process environment. Adv. Eng. Informatics **26**, 334–348 (2012)
28. Jagdev, H.S., Thoben, K.-D.: Anatomy of enterprise collaborations. Prod. Plan. Control **12**, 437–451 (2001)
29. Browne, J., Zhang, J.: Extended and virtual enterprises-similarities and differences. Int. J. Agil. Manag. **1**, 30–36 (1999)
30. Jonkers, H., Lankhorst, M. & Van Buuren, R.: Concepts for modeling enterprise architectures. Int. J. Coop. Inf. Syst. **13**, 257–287 (2004)
31. Work, P.: 1. EEML—Extended enterprise modelling language
32. Jürgen, D., Ying, J., Hakan, K.: Customer focused business processes in virtual enterprises. Electronic Commerce Competence Center EC3 (2001)
33. Kumar, S.K.: Tools for enterprises collaboration in virtual enterprises (2013)

Technological Innovation: The Pathway to Entrepreneurs' Economic Advancement

Wesley Palmer

Abstract The purpose of this phenomenological study was to explore the meaning of human experiences relating to entrepreneurs in New York City who have not adopted adequate innovative technology. This research was based on Kaplan and Warren's entrepreneurship management theory. The first research question concerned the experiences and perspectives of entrepreneurs who have not adopted advanced operations technology to gain competitive advantage, and the second question concerned the ways entrepreneurs experience economic challenges using outdated business technology. Data were collected through unstructured face-to-face interviews with 20 entrepreneurs in New York City using snowball and purposive sampling. Data analysis involved developing the participants' experiences into themes. The findings revealed that 85% of participants did not have adequate and updated technological operations systems. This study may initiate a review of late adopters and promote the importance of technological change by encouraging entrepreneurs to build networks that share technological innovations in the entrepreneurial community.

Keywords Entrepreneurs · New York city · Technology · Innovation · Venture capitalist · Competitive advantage

1 Introduction

Access to business technology and the ability to acquire and use innovative systems to bolster economic activities are the hallmarks of entrepreneurs' advancement in New York State. Many entrepreneurs invest in high-technology office suites for their business enterprises [1, 2]. This research was necessary because of the integral role entrepreneurs play in New York State and in national economic development.

W. Palmer (✉)
Department of Business and Economics, York College,
City University of New York, Jamaica, New York, USA
e-mail: wpalmer@york.cuny.edu

© Springer Nature Switzerland AG 2019
Y. Baghdadi and A. Harfouche (eds.), *ICT for a Better Life and a Better World*,
Lecture Notes in Information Systems and Organisation 30,
https://doi.org/10.1007/978-3-030-10737-6_25

Small and new businesses helped create 4.25 million private sector jobs between 2009 and 2012 [3]. Entrepreneurial firms are the leading job creators and have created two of every three new jobs since the early 1990s.

This exploratory study involved evaluating entrepreneurs' experiences with existing resources such as website designers and computer network providers to gain insights into how effective their services are to entrepreneurs. The staff members at technology providers' firms offer technical advice and specialized skills that allow entrepreneurs to provide efficient service. Developers provide direct technical support to the entrepreneurial business community. After entrepreneurs buy a networking program for their business, they have access to highly trained technology providers who are able to walk them through the operating process, troubleshoot, and provide answers. Community banks offer small loans to entrepreneurs to help them fund their technological needs, although some entrepreneurs must self-fund due to the lack of business credit as well as poor personal credit [4]. Venture capitalists provide capital and management support to entrepreneurs, and as a result, many entrepreneurs have acquired advanced operations systems [4, 5]. These resources help to advance entrepreneurs' ventures, especially those who could not get bank loans to finance their business enterprises. The findings section of this paper includes remedies for the problems and the shortcomings of these resources. The Small Business Administration (SBA) promotes using technology through its mentor–protégé program, which is a bold attempt to encourage entrepreneurs to adapt to modern technology [6].

Businesses associated with the SBA mentor–protégé program are relatively small [6]. The businesses enlisted in the program receive mentoring, training, and technical assistance. Many of the businesses admitted in the program are family businesses that have a capital requirement of $5000–$75,000. Most of the businesses enjoyed initial success and have been in business for at least 5 years. The dynamics of their success would be an interesting study for future research.

1.1 Purpose

The purpose of this research was to provide information that would help entrepreneurs make valuable contributions to their communities by using innovative technology. The exploratory study involved searching for the meaning of the lived experiences of the studied phenomenon. A phenomenological methodology was selected because it allowed the author to express the universal essence of the lived experiences of the participants rather than present an explanation of the researched subject [7, 8].

1.2   Problem Statement

The problem is the lack of understanding about the lived experiences of entrepreneurs in New York who are reluctant to use technological systems to advance their economic potential. More than 50% of loan applications from entrepreneurs are rejected, although the federal government has sanctioned more than $30 billion for entrepreneurial ventures [9]. Staff at the SBA reported that banks used $26 billion of the funds earmarked for entrepreneurial ventures to fund their own obligations and only allotted $4 billion to entrepreneurs [9].

Researchers at the Federal Reserve Bank of New York reported that 37% of loan applications did not receive approval, 36% received partial approval, 42% were not eligible to apply, 29% felt discouraged, and only 13% received full approval [10]. Many leaders of financial institutions, established business leaders, and professional employees are reluctant to conduct business with small and fledgling entrepreneurial businesses because of the scale of their operations, the lack of stability, weaknesses in their financial positions, and inadequate social ties with established market players [11]. New York entrepreneurs have similar elements of weakness and inadequacy that prevent them from acquiring the technology and technical assistance that they desire.

1.3   Research Questions

The City of New York, as well as surrounding counties and towns, are home to a wide range of businesses that make important contributions to the national economy. Because of their important contributions, there should be a ready source of financial capital to fund technology and maintain their economic stability. Federal and state officials should treat entrepreneurship as an integral part of economic development, and policy makers should equip the SBA with adequate resources so that it can play a more active consulting role in New York City to reduce the number of ill-advised entrepreneurial ventures in the city. Entrepreneurs are leaders in modern technology [1, 12] who continue to set new standards and forge innovations. Entrepreneurial firms have been the largest employers in the United States since the 1990s [13], yet some entrepreneurs continue to struggle for financial resources to modernize their business technology. This phenomenological study of entrepreneurial technological experiences was guided by two research questions:

1. What are the experiences and perspectives of entrepreneurs who are unable to acquire adequate business technology for their business ventures?
2. In what ways do entrepreneurs experience operations inefficiency as a result of their inability to modern technological systems for their businesses?

2 Theoretical Framework

Central to this study was Kaplan and Warren's entrepreneurship management theory [14]. Foundational concepts of entrepreneurship management theory include web-based technology, network connectivity, mobile devices, and the success and failure of technological system adoption. Capital acquisition is the most essential consideration when establishing businesses, and without the acquisition of capital, entrepreneurs cannot establish their businesses with the right technology. Risk can hamper capital acquisition; thus, risk assessment plays an integral role in business analysis. Risk assessment includes examining two types of risk: (a) business risk, which is the uncertainty that a business will receive favorable market response and generate income, and (b) financial risk, which is the risk added through borrowing financial capital.

Risk assessment also includes critical credit components to determine the creditworthiness of a business. The success and failure of a business depend on its ability to obtain credit. These fundamental concepts served as the foundation for the research. Furthermore, financial management theory helps to explain the importance of business analysis, financial decisions, and their impact on businesses, including entrepreneurial businesses [14].

A wide range of social, academic, and business literature contains descriptions of the technological void that entrepreneurs experience. Scholars and practitioners have developed several conceptual arguments through an iterative process in an attempt to explain entrepreneurs' technological experiences. The literature reviewed presented several mixed findings with regard to entrepreneurs' technological adaptation. Some of the findings attributed entrepreneurs' technological void to lack of managerial skills, poorly conceived ventures, lack of entrepreneurial education, liability of newness, and inaccessibility of capital [11, 15–19]. This research was built on the premise that technology is the root of entrepreneurs' success.

This phenomenological study followed a framework for data collection, data analysis, and addressing the research questions. High risk tolerance seems to be the driving force behind the entrepreneurs in New York, who are determined to acquire business technology despite their inability to raise capital through traditional financial institutions [4, 20]. The efforts to provide service to their communities while making a livelihood have been challenging for many entrepreneurs, yet they continue to persevere with hope of finding success.

3 Literature Review

The literature review revealed that 50% of entrepreneurial businesses used high-technology connectivity [21]. Notwithstanding these successes, many entrepreneurial businesses still lag behind due to the lack of appropriate education, technical competence, professionalism, and administrative leadership. Although all types of training and educational support are available, many entrepreneurs do not have the resources to acquire them.

Whereas technical incompetence and other administrative inefficiencies affect entrepreneurs in some ways, the major challenge to technological adoption is the reluctance to change. The U.S. economy has a substantial amount of capital available for investment. Approximately $1.25 trillion is available for investment in various debt instruments that are waiting for opportunities to make equitable returns [22]. Despite the large pool of investment capital available, leaders of nascent and small firms continue to use outdated business systems, primarily due to the high cost of capital.

Capital available in August 2008 was $1.572 trillion, and by August 2009, the amount of capital available through commercial banks was $1.452 trillion, or a decline of $120 billion; nevertheless, there was no shortage of capital [23]. In addition, researchers at the SBA reported that the government sanctioned $30 billion dollars for small business enterprises during 2012. The conditions for entrepreneurs' access to the capital include high credit ratings, SBA loan guarantees, and marketable collaterals. Researchers at the Federal Reserve Bank of New York interviewed a small sample of 12% of entrepreneurs in New York and found that none of the participants received approval for credit to acquire updated business technology [24]. Entrepreneurs in New York State who were denied credit to acquire updated technological systems tended to use outdated systems and therefore provide inefficient services that negatively affect their economic output [24].

3.1 Gap in the Research

The gap in the research was the lack of knowledge about the lived experiences of entrepreneurs in New York State. No known business entity exists to provide entrepreneurs with subsidized technological assistance that would enhance their economic development. There also exists no formal plan to assist entrepreneurs with technological acquisition costs. Entrepreneurial businesses can be far more efficient if they have the right business technology [15, 25, 26].

3.2 Methodology

In this research, the researcher selected a large pool of potential participants through a referral process and then randomly selected the participants for the study from that pool using the purposive sampling method. To obtain a sample that provided the information necessary to understand the phenomenon, the researcher combined snowball with purposive sampling [27, 28].

The initial list of entrepreneurs from New York came from a random selection of individuals from the business directory. The list included business names, telephone numbers, and addresses. The researcher used the initial list to call and identify entrepreneurs in the area who had an interest in participating in the study and provided any interested participants with written invitations that included a brief overview of the study. The criteria for participation were as follows: The entrepreneurs must have had legitimate registered businesses, must have operated the business for at least 1 year, and must have believed that they were experiencing difficulty obtaining financial capital. Consistent with phenomenology, the study included interviews with 20 entrepreneurs throughout New York State.

3.3 Research Design

The study involved investigating the lived experiences of small and new entrepreneurs in New York State as a social and economic phenomenon in terms of entrepreneurs' personal interest and the impact technology has on entrepreneurial businesses and the communities within which they operate. In many communities, leaders of entrepreneurial organizations are the only employers to provide opportunity for the residents. Therefore, understanding the impact warranted an investigation.

3.4 Instrumentation

The main data collection instrument was face-to-face interviews guided by prepared questionnaires. The process also included audio recordings and written notes. Properly executed face-to-face interviews are more effective as a data-gathering instrument than are self-administered questionnaires [28]. The researcher developed the questionnaires based upon the research questions in an effort to gather data that would specifically address the entrepreneurs' issues. The prepared interview questions facilitated descriptions of the core issues and provided an understanding of the entrepreneurs' lived experiences in obtaining initial and working capital [7, 8].

3.5 Epoché

The researcher applied epoché while conducting the research. Epoché involves intentionally suspending personal biases and experiences to view a phenomenon from a fresh perspective [8]. The foundation of the concept is in transcendental phenomenology, which focuses on the participants' lived experiences rather than on the researcher's interpretation.

3.6 Sampling Procedure

This phenomenological research involved investigating the experiences of entre-preneurs in New York to learn how web-based systems, computer networks, and mobile technology affected their experiences. The research involved comparing and contrasting the experiences of 20 entrepreneurs to identify patterns and similarities among the participants [29]. Patterns and similarities help researchers to gain insight into participants' lived experiences. The study included a combined sam-pling strategy to select the participants who would provide a rich source of credible information.

3.7 Population

The entrepreneurs who participated in the study operated in New York. A combination of snowball and purposive strategy was suitable due to the reluc-tance by members of the targeted group to publicize their experiences. Because of its unique referral characteristic, snowball sampling allowed the researcher to identify individuals who appropriately fit the criteria and who would provide rich entrepreneurial experiences. The purposive sampling method allowed the researcher to select participants who were typical of the entrepreneurial population by exer-cising professional judgment [28]. Data were organized by frequency and per-centage for easy calculation.

The study began with a list of 100 potential participants selected randomly from the local telephone directory in New York and contact was made by telephone. The researcher secured interest by making brief phone calls to potential participants from the initial list of names. The phone calls involved providing potential par-ticipants an introduction to the study, and 20 individuals showed initial interest. Interested participants were processed and selected in accordance with the research methodology.

Eight of 20 participants (40%) were female and the remaining 12 (60%) were male. Both male and female participants engaged in a wide variety of business activities such as restaurants, supermarkets, podiatry-foot care centers, hair and beauty centers, business technologies, event planners, eye care centers, special education services, dry cleaning services, real estate services, retail stores, impor-tation, and financial services. Educational attainment included high school diplo-mas, associate of applied science, bachelor of arts, master of science, medical doctor, doctor of education, and doctor of philosophy degrees. The ages of the participants who engaged in the study ranged between 36 and 72 years.

3.8   Data Collection and Analysis

The essence of a good study exists in the integrity of the data collected. The larger the pool of participants in a scientific study the greater the chance of producing a substantial theory that reflects the lived experiences of the participants [29]. Twenty small and new entrepreneurs in New York participated in interviews. Each interview lasted for 45–60 min.

Data collection took place in New York. New York has a business community comprised of a large number of small and new businesses; these businesses have tremendous data sources to facilitate empirically designed research. The population included Caucasians, African Americans, Jews, Hispanics, Asians, Caribbeans, and other nationalities.

NVivo 10 software helped to classify the data and establish patterns, themes, and similarities among the participants' responses from the unstructured interviews collected using electronic media and written notes. By using NVivo, I was able to identify trends, patterns, and similarities in the data that were common in the experiences of the participants. The personal interviews of the participants served an essential role in this qualitative phenomenological research. Interviews are important elements in phenomenological studies because they help researchers to collect experiential stories that develop a richer and deeper understanding about human lived experiences [7].

4   Results

A brief discussion with the participants took place before the interviews to reiterate the procedures, protocols, and purpose of the study. The intent of the preliminary discussion was to allow the participants to share or clarify any concern they had regarding their role in the study. The research questions solicited answers based on the lived experiences of the phenomenon through the lens of a phenomenological approach.

4.1   Analysis of the Relevant Research Data

Data analysis is a dynamic process in which researchers collect and organize texts, transcripts, electronic data, and images and reduce them into statements, themes, meaning units, and descriptions [8, 30]. NVivo software served to organize and analyze the vast volume of unstructured data in media and written forms, to classify the data, and to examine relationships between the participants. By using NVivo, the researcher was able to identify similarities in the data that might be common in entrepreneurs' experiences.

To engage in the analysis process, the researcher created files for the interviews and organized them in alphabetical order for efficient processing. The researcher read margin notes and interview transcripts to identify trends in the research results; used the data collected to write a description of the essence of entrepreneurs' lived experiences; and organized, transcribed, and cross-examined the data for evidence that supported the authenticity of the research findings [7, 8, 29].

Reliability and validity are integral to qualitative studies because reliability emphasizes the consistency and dependability of the data collected, and validity is the most accurate estimate of truth. Addressing reliability and validity served to ensure the integrity of the research. The study also involved a process of establishing external and internal validity. External validity is important because it is the means by which the conclusion holds true for participants in other studies, and internal validity is the measure of approximate truth regarding inferences and causal relationships [27]. The objective of this research was to present a phenomenological qualitative study that was dependable, credible, and reliable.

4.2 Significant Themes

Table 1 contains the themes that answered the questions based on the identification of significant categories from more than 30% of participants' responses.

4.3 Credibility and Validity

Qualitative research is credible if the results are satisfactory to the participants [27, 29]. The participants were the only ones capable of judging the correctness of the results because their lived experiences served as the basis of the results. The purposively selected sample was from a diverse group of entrepreneurs who produced thick and rich data. This study was internally valid in terms of research design, operational definition, instrumentation, and conclusions [30]. The major categories that emerged were fear of approaching lending institutions, fear of closing down, fear of becoming an employee, the refusal of banks to provide loans to entrepreneurs, the use of own savings to start and fund businesses, the acquisition of

Table 1 Significant themes that answer the research questions

Themes	n	%
1. Difficult to raise financial capital	19	95
2. Likely to close business soon	6	30
3. Experienced loan denial	13	65
4. The impact of business closure	14	70
5. One's savings as a source of capital	17	85

business funds from friends and family, the lack of cooperation among local entrepreneurs, business closures, and the lack of personal plans for the future. The experiences shared by the research participants in New York were similar to the experiences of other entrepreneurs in the United States, which served as an indication of external validity.

4.4 Discrepant Findings

Discrepant cases are contradictions and variations from the general experiences of the studied phenomenon. The difficulty-raising-capital theme varied markedly between two participants. Participant 20 reported the bank was helpful and supportive, and she had no difficulty getting the bank to finance her multi-million-dollar business operation.

Participant 3 had some challenges with the bank during the early phase of his business. However, the bank eventually provided financial assistance that changed his financial trajectory. Variation is a significant component of iterative qualitative research [8, 30]. Variations reflect the integrity and the independent collection of the data. Although the intent of a phenomenological study is to find commonality among the lived experiences of the participants, a small variation does not alter the results significantly. The variation of this research was relatively small; nevertheless, it offered authenticity to the research process and content.

5 Discussion

Entrepreneurs who are unable to acquire adequate business technology for their business have experienced operations deficiencies that have resulted in slow sales and unsustainable profitability. Entrepreneurs who are unable to acquire modern technology experienced operations inefficiencies and challenges, such as improper inventory control, poor cash management accountability, inaccurate accounts receivable, and ineffective customer service.

The research revealed that 95% of entrepreneurs found it difficult to adopt advanced technology due to the high cost of these technological systems. Thirty percent feared they might have to close their businesses soon due to financial challenges that resulted from outdated systems, and 65% of the participants interviewed had their funding applications denied due to inadequate economic resources. Seventy percent indicated that business closures have a negative social and economic impact on the community, and 85% financed their businesses with their own savings due to the inaccessibility.

5.1 Recommendations

The need for technological resources was the central concern for entrepreneurs in New York City. All the participants (100%) reported that they would support an institution established solely to assist entrepreneurs with business operations technology. Numerous agencies and organizations provide training, mentoring, and consulting services to entrepreneurs; however, these entities are unable to meet the primary need, which is the need for appropriate operations technology.

Thus, a future study could include the practicality of the SBA offering technology funding and education instead of generic business consulting. Entrepreneurs enlisted in the SBA protégé–mentor program have maintained strong and stable businesses [6]. Their stability is the result of the close supervision of their mentors and technology funding. Future studies could involve comparing mentored businesses with businesses that did not receive mentoring as a means to measure their success. Leaders of venture capitalist firms also engage in the supervision and mentoring of selected businesses. Venture capitalist firms provide operations management, advice, and technology funding [5]. Therefore, future research could involve examining the viability of establishing venture capitalist firms that would focus on helping small businesses as their core business strategy.

5.2 Implications for Social Change

Entrepreneurs are individuals who want to make a difference in their community and the world. The risk of losing one's life savings and in many cases the family income is not a small matter. Entrepreneurs are determined individuals who do not become discouraged easily [20]. Thus, entrepreneurs have the ability to bypass barriers to financial capital by using credit cards, family savings, and informal borrowing to take advantage of business opportunities.

6 Conclusion

The lack of adequate business operations technology has presented tremendous difficulties for many entrepreneurs. However, inadequate technology did not prevent entrepreneurs from seizing business opportunities and pursuing their ambition to become business owners. Through their resilience and creative efforts, many entrepreneurs were able to implement some forms of technological systems.

The participating entrepreneurs in New York City experienced various hardships, including the use of outdated technological systems, the inability to compete effectively in the marketplace and to meet recurring businesses expenses, an uncertain business future, the threat of losing their life savings, the abuse of predatory lenders, the pain of terminating key employees, and the experience of rejection during due to inefficient service. Eight-five percent of the entrepreneurs who participated in the study could not obtain adequate technology for their businesses. Hence, they operated with limited business technology and they had technological limitations that stifled business growth and limited their abilities to advance in new market opportunities. Despite the technological challenges, many entrepreneurs in the City of New York have been able to maintain stable and successful businesses.

References

1. Mitter, C.: Business angel: issues, evidence, and implications for emerging markets. J. Int. Bus. Econ. **12**(3), 1–11 (2012). Retrieved from http://www.iabe.org/domains/iabex/journal.aspx?journalid=9
2. Winrow, B.: Entrepreneur beware. Entrep. Exec. **15**, 39–46 (2010). Retrieved from http://www.alliedacademies.org/public/journals/JournalDetails.aspx?jid=9
3. National Economic Council: Moving America's small businesses & entrepreneurs forward: Creating an economy built to last (2012). Retrieved from http://whitehouse.gov/administration/eop/nec
4. Shane, A.S.: The Illusions of Entrepreneurship: The Costly Myths That Entrepreneurs, Investors, and Policy Makers Live By. Yale University Press, New Haven, CT (2008)
5. Bengtsson, O., Wang, F.: What matters in venture capital? Evidence from entrepreneurs' states preferences. Financ. Manage. **1**, 1367–1401 (2010). https://doi.org/10.1111/j.1755-053X.2010.01116.x
6. Small Business Administration: Mentor-protégé program (2012). Retrieved from http://www.sba.gov/content/mentor-prot
7. Van Manen, M.: Researching Lived Experience: Human Science for Action Sensitive Pedagogy. State University of New York Press, Albany (1990)
8. Moustakas, C.: Phenomenological Research Methods. Sage, Thousand Oaks, CA (1994)
9. Small Business Administration: Small business loans are rejected by banks (2012). Retrieved from http://www.sba.gov/community/discussion-boards/discuss-populartopics/loans-grants/small
10. Federal Reserve Bank of New York: FRBNY small business borrower's poll (2012). Retrieved from http://www.newyorkfed.org/smallbusiness/2012/
11. Su, Z., Xie, E., Li, Y.: Entrepreneurial orientation and firm performance in new ventures and established firms. J. Small Bus. Manage. **49**, 558–577 (2011). https://doi.org/10.1111/j.1540-627X.2011.00336.x
12. Sullivan, D., Marvel, M.: How entrepreneur's knowledge and network ties relate to the number of employees in new SMEs. J. Small Bus. Manage. **49**(2), 185–206 (2011). https://doi.org/10.1111/j.1540-627X.2011.00321
13. De Bettignies, J.: Financing the entrepreneurial venture. Manage. Sci. **54**, 155–168 (2008). https://doi.org/10.1287/mnsc.1070.0759
14. Kaplan, J.M., Warren, A.C.: Patterns of Entrepreneurships Management. Wiley, Hoboken, NJ (2013)
15. Markova, S., Petkovska-Mircevska, T.: Entrepreneurial finance: angel investing as a source of funding high-growth start-up firms. Ann. Univ. Petrosani Econ. **10**, 217–224 (2010). Retrieved from http://upet.ro/annals/economics/

16. Dyer, L.M., Ross, A.C.: Seeking advice in a dynamic and complex business environment: impact on the success of small firms. J. Dev. Entrep. **13**, 133–149 (2008). https://doi.org/10.1142/S1084946708000892
17. Clarke, J., Holt, R.: The mature entrepreneur: a narrative approach to entrepreneurial goals. J. Manage. Enq. **19**, 69–83 (2010). https://doi.org/10.1177/1056492609343030
18. Sardana, S., Scott-Kemmis, D.: Who learns what? A study based on entrepreneurs from biotechnology new ventures. J. Small Bus. Manage. **48**, 441–468 (2010). https://doi.org/10.1111/j.1540-627X.2010.00302.x
19. Dunn, P., Liang, K.: A comparison of entrepreneurs/small business and finance professors' reaction to selected entrepreneurial and small business financial planning and management issues. J. Entrep. Educ. **14**, 93–103 (2011). Retrieved from http://www.alliedacademies.org/public/journals/JournalDetails.aspx?jid=8
20. Elston, J.A., Audretsch, D.B.: Financing the entrepreneurial decision: an empirical approach using experimental data on risk attitudes. Small Bus. Econ. **36**, 209–222 (2011). https://doi.org/10.1007/s11187-009-9210-x
21. Naughton, M., Cornwall, J.R.: Culture as the basis of the good entrepreneur. J. Relig. Bus. Ethics **1**, 1–13 (2009). Retrieved from http://via.library.depaul.edu/jrbe/
22. Fuster, A., Willen, S.P.: $1.25 trillion is still real money: some facts about the effects of the Federal Reserve's mortgage market investments (Public Policy Discussion Paper 10–4). Federal Reserve Bank of Boston, Boston, MA (2010)
23. Lahm, R.J., Stowe, C.R.B., Carton, R.B., Buck, L.E.: Small businesses and credit cards: new rules for plastic in an economic recession. J. Mark. Dev. Competiveness **5**(5), 101–109 (2012). Retrieved from http://www.na-businesspress.com/jmdcopen.html
24. Federal Reserve Bank of New York: New York Fed's new small business poll shows evidence of credit demand; cash flow for small businesses key to credit approval (2010). Retrieved from http://www.newyorkfed.org/newsevents/news/regionaloutreach/2010/an101018.html
25. Samuels, L.B., Joshi, M.P., Demory, Y.: Entrepreneurial failure and discrimination: lessons for small service firms. Serv. Ind. J. **28**, 883–897 (2008). https://doi.org/10.1080/02642060701882098
26. Fourie, W., De, L.: Establishing a culture of entrepreneurship as a contributor to sustainable economic growth. J. Global Bus. Technol. **4**(2), 34–40 (2008). Retrieved from http://gbata.org/journal-of-global-business-and-technology-jgbat/
27. Trochim, W.M.K., Donnelly, J.P.: The Research Methods Knowledge Base. Cengage Learning, Mason, OH (2008)
28. Singleton Jr., R., Straits, B.C.: Approaches to Social Research. Oxford University Press, New York, NY (2010)
29. Creswell, J.W.: Qualitative Inquiry & Research Design. Sage, Thousand Oaks, CA (2007)
30. Corbin, J., Strauss, A.: Basics of Qualitative Research. Sage, Thousand Oaks, CA (2008)

How Communities Affect the Technology Acceptance Model in the Retail Sector

Daniele Pederzoli

Abstract The technology acceptance model has greatly evolved since its first appearance in the literature around 30 years ago. One of the most important changes has been the increasing influence of social activities on the adoption of technology in everyday life. Technologies allow customer to create communities that can exert a strong influence in the process of technology acceptance, especially in retailing where the relations between companies and consumers are a fundamental part of the everyday activity. In our study, we have analyzed how groups of consumers create value during the shopping process and help one other to manage relations with technologies and overcome the perceived threats of the shopping and user experience.

Keywords Technology acceptance model · Community · Retail · Co-creation

1 Introduction

The Technology Acceptance Model (TAM) has attracted huge attention from scholars since it appeared in the literature concerning the relations between users and technology [1, 2].

At the end of the 1980s the world was at the dawn of a technological revolution, after the first industrial revolution in the mid-19th century, with the introduction of steam in the textile industry and for long-distance transport; and the second revolution, with the introduction of electrical power in both industry and consumer markets in developed countries. The third revolution was based on the rapid spread of Information and Communication Technologies, and on their continuous improvement, with increasing functionality and rapidly decreasing costs. Since then, these technologies have quickly expanded throughout developed countries and into developing countries.

D. Pederzoli (✉)
NEOMA Business School, 1 rue du Maréchal Juin, 76630 Mont-Saint-Aignan, France
e-mail: daniele.pederzoli@neoma-bs.fr

© Springer Nature Switzerland AG 2019
Y. Baghdadi and A. Harfouche (eds.), *ICT for a Better Life and a Better World*,
Lecture Notes in Information Systems and Organisation 30,
https://doi.org/10.1007/978-3-030-10737-6_26

395

TAM has been widely used since 1989 to analyze user acceptance of technologies because it is linear, simple (based on just three variables), and reliable as it has been tested in different context and cultures.

Many researchers have tried to enrich basic TAM and to explain user acceptance of technologies using other, more detailed variables [3–5]; others have applied TAM to specific technological fields like e-shopping [6] or m-commerce [7] and have proposed other components for the user acceptance model.

However, none of these scholars have challenged the original TAM paradigm. Rather, they have in general tried to improve the model's content to explain consumer acceptance of or resistance to technology.

In 2007, Bagozzi [8] challenged TAM and proposed a "paradigm shift" suggesting some limits into the TAM paradigm. One of these limits, according to Bagozzi, is that it considers only individual users when assessing technology acceptance, so under valuating the social component of technology acceptance and in particular "social influence", "virtual communities", "open source software user communities" and "recreational chatter and collaborative browsing in online environment" [8, p. 248].

Our article concentrates on communities as a way to influence users' acceptance of technologies. One of the main, and perhaps unexpected, results of the ICT third revolution is the development of virtual communities that come into being, develop and end without their members ever meeting in person; these communities spread all over the world and bring together millions of individuals with a shared interest, favorite brand, or cause. They create and share knowledge for social reasons, as in the case of Wikipedia, or work together with a specific brand to develop products or improve customer service.

In this article we mainly analyze how retail companies encourage technology acceptance among their customers through their strategy. We chose retail companies because they interact every day with hundreds of thousands of consumers and have to adapt very quickly to consumers' attitudes, behaviors and expectations. But we also selected the retail sector because it is certainly one of those most disrupted by the new technologies that have emerged since the end of the 1980s; many major retail companies were slow to respond to this disruption, as the emergence of relatively young companies like Amazon clearly shows, and they need to be very aware of future technological challenges if they want to maintain and consolidate their market share and profitability.

This paper is organized as follow: in the first part we review the literature concerning the evolution of TAM; in the second section we present our research questions and the methodology adopted to answer these questions; in the third section, we present the main results of our study; the last section contains the discussion, managerial and theoretical contributions, limitations of the research and perspectives for future research.

2 Literature Review

2.1 Evolution of TAM

The Technology Acceptance Model [1] is elegant in its parsimony because three factors affect users' technology acceptance: perceived usefulness (PU) and perceived ease of use (PeU) determine Intention to use the technology (Behavioral Intention). PeU represents the user's belief that using a particular technology will require no effort; PU represents the utility value of a specific technology, namely the user's belief that the use of the technology will improve his/her performance. The higher the PeU and PU, the higher will be the user's intention to adopt the new technology.

Since its presentation, different scholars have enriched this "pure" model. As early as 1989, Davis et al. [2] introduced attitude as the mediator between PU, PeU and BI. Attitude represents the user's assessment of the technology and in the new "TAM with attitude model", attitude influences BI, the degree to which the user is willing to perform a certain behavior [3].

Svendsen et al. [4] made another very interesting contribution to TAM, introducing the Big Five Personality dimensions which influence users' assessments of the core TAM construct.

These authors demonstrate that one of the Big Five dimensions, extraversion, is positively related to PU and PeU, and hence to BI. Three out of the other four dimensions also influence BI, directly or through the mediation of TAM beliefs: Conscientiousness and Openness to experience influence BI positively, while Emotional stability is negatively related to BI and is not mediated by PU and PeU. Agreeableness was removed from the model because of low reliability. Another interesting facet of the model proposed by Svendsen et al. is the introduction of Subjective Norms (SN) as a belief in TAM that directly influences the other beliefs and BI. Subjective norms can be described as social pressure; the way users' acceptance of new technology appears to be influenced by others' opinions. The concept of SN was introduced in TAM literature in 2003 by Venkatesh et al. [9], well before the research of Svendsen et al. [4], but these authors show that Conscientiousness positively influences SN and that Subjective Norms positively influence BI.

2.2 TAM and E-Commerce

One of the most interesting research fields for both academics and practitioners in the field of technology acceptance is e-commerce, because of the steady increase in on-line shopping turnover in many different sectors, and also because new technologies have been developed to encourage e-commerce, including mobile applications, social network "buy" buttons, digital displays in high pedestrian traffic hubs, connected stores that offer giant interactive windows, and in-store screens to allow customers to browse the brand's entire product range. E-commerce is a fundamental innovation from both academic and managerial points of view. Researchers have demonstrated that multichannel consumers are more profitable for retail companies than single channel consumers [10], have defined what conditions can help multichannel firms to increase sales [11] and have showed the effect of social networks in increasing store frequentation and purchases [12]. The spread of the smartphone has created a new type of online purchase, so-called m-commerce, and researchers have studied the specific value that this new channel can offer consumers [13] and have applied TAM to explain consumers' intentions to use this technology in their purchasing process [7].

Many efforts have been made to try to understand multi-channel shoppers. McGoldrick and Collins [14] studied shopper behavior in three different channels, stores, catalogues and the internet and found four major components in channel choice, namely risk reduction, product value, ease of shopping and experience.

Konus et al. [15] identified three segments of multichannel shoppers, namely multichannel enthusiasts, uninvolved shoppers and store-focused consumers. The consistency of the three categories varies across different product categories, with the concepts of "consumer implication towards products" and "need to feel and touch the goods" being the main determinants.

More recent research shows that multichannel customers that buy multiple categories are most valuable [16]. However, when we distinguish between utilitarian and hedonic products, the findings are more complex: for hedonic products, multichannel shoppers provide the highest monetary value, while for low risk/ utilitarian products, traditional channel shoppers are the most valuable.

The development of online shopping has generated a strong research stream to explain technology acceptance by consumers and to identify variables that should be included in TAM in this context.

2.3   TAM and the Hedonic Dimension of Retailing

One of the most important contributions to TAM was the introduction of the hedonic dimension of shopping.

The importance of store atmospherics as a fundamental component of the consumer purchasing process and of consumer behavior motivation has been analyzed by many scholars, starting with the seminal article by Kotler [17].

The importance of consumer feelings and mood for the purchasing process was greatly developed later on with the introduction of the concept of experiential consumption [18]. Experiential consumption does not mean that the "classic" model of consumer behavior as a rationale choice is completely outdated, but it implies that new components have to be taken into account, namely the role of the product esthetic, multisensory aspects of product enjoyment, product related fantasies and imageries, and the role of play in providing enjoyment and fun [18, p. 139].

In the fierce battle for market share and profitability, retailers try to attract more customers, but also to retain existing ones and to increase their share of wallet, as a way of improving turnover and revenues. In this strategy, in-store atmospherics and consumer experience have become more and more important tools to differentiate a retail brand from its competitors and create consumer loyalty. In an extension of the Donovan and Rossiter study [19], Donovan et al. [20] demonstrated that experienced pleasantness generated by the shopping environment and measured during the shopping experience is a good predictor of customer willingness to spend time into the store and of the intention to spend more than planned before the shopping trip.

In another study conducted some years later, Babin and Attaway demonstrate that the positive effect of store atmosphere strongly influences hedonic shopping value and to a lesser extent utilitarian value and this, in turn, will affect customer share [21]. Interestingly, hedonic shopping value and utilitarian shopping value are very similar in terms of influence on customer share, and this implies that retailers should invest in both traditional retention systems based on utilitarian value (purchase incentives for accumulating purchases) and experiential and hedonic ambient elements to increase customer loyalty and share of wallet.

However, other research suggests that retailers should consider consumer's motivational orientation when proposing a stimulating shopping environment [22].

Motivational orientation moderates the effect of the excitement produced by a store environment on the pleasure consumers feel toward this environment. Excitement created by store environment influences pleasantness positively when consumer motivational orientation is recreational, but the effect is reversed when consumer motivational orientation is more utilitarian and task-oriented. Moreover, high arousal increases the intention of recreationally oriented consumers to visit and make purchase in the store, while this impact is negative for task-oriented consumers.

Technology can greatly help retailers improve store atmosphere and create consumer experience, and to learn more about their consumers [23]. But results should not be overestimated and can be disappointing; a study conducted by Backström and Johansson [24] demonstrates that in-store experience as described by consumers comprises mainly traditional elements such as personnel behavior, a satisfactory assortment and a facilitating store lay-out rather than technologically improved components. Perhaps these results were influenced by the fact that in-store technologies were at an early stage of development at the time of the study, because more recent research conducted in a flagship toy store shows that the use of new technologies has a significant, positive effect on holistic perceptions of store atmosphere, shopping value and positive emotions [25]. According to these authors, perceived store atmosphere is positively influenced by two in-store technologies, but particularly by one of them, the magic mirror. Store atmosphere positively influences the perceived value of shopping, and this creates positive emotions.

As demonstrated by these different studies, consumer experience cannot be analyzed only with regard to technologies with which shoppers interact directly, because in many stores consumers also interact with sales employees. Human relations can significantly influence shopper perceptions of store atmosphere, and in-store technologies can replace sales assistants or help them to interact better with customers and improve customer service. Very little previous research has addressed the issue of technology acceptance by sales assistants and the implication of such adoption or rejection on retailer-employee-consumer relations. One of the first attempts to study these relations has concluded that sales staff can mediate between the technologies introduced by a retailer and the consumers frequenting the store. Another very interesting finding is that the best results in terms of innovation process efficiency and profitability are obtained by companies that support the coexistence of virtual and real salespeople in their stores [26].

2.4   TAM and On-Line Retailing

TAM has been greatly enriched by researchers studying e-retailing technology acceptance.

Analyzing the literature in different domains, including computer science, innovation, human-computer interaction and technology management, Pantano and Di Pietro [3] added ten different variables to the TAM with attitude model; they divide these variables into four main groups: Consumer perception of technology safety and cost; Consumer personality traits; Social pressure; and Hedonic values. According to these authors, social pressure is similar to the subjective norms described in previous research into technology acceptance, but they improve these concepts, defining two components of SN: external influence and interpersonal influence. While external influence includes traditional mass-media and expert influence, interpersonal influence appears more relevant in the age of social networking and peer-to-peer communication, because it is determined by word-of-mouth and reference groups; consumers usually choose to belong to reference groups, so their influence over attitudes and behaviors in the field of technology acceptance is greater than the role of more traditional, impersonal influencers, who were the only ones available before the development of social networking.

In another meta-analytical review of TAM and e-shopping, Ingham et al. [5] note that four variables have frequently been added to the original TAM with attitude model in the e-shopping context: trust, perceived risk, enjoyment and social influence. Most of the research we have reviewed explains social influence through subjective norms, but two authors introduce the concepts of Peer-group norms [27] and of peer influence [28]. The latter concept is broader that the first, because Peer influence includes "friends, classmates, people who influence me think that I should use online shopping". Some of the results of this meta-analysis of the TAM literature published over the last 12 years are unexpected:

- Trust, supposedly one of the most significant variables in the field of e-shopping, influences intention strongly only when considered alone, but its influence is greatly reduced when other variables, such as usefulness, perceived risk, and enjoyment, are also taken into account;
- The social influence influences online purchase intentions to a modest degree, but the impact on attitude toward purchasing products and services online is more significant

In the specific field of mobile shopping, Agrebi and Jallais [7], add perceived enjoyment and satisfaction to TAM to investigate how these two components influence purchase intentions for French trains tickets. Interestingly, perceived enjoyment and satisfaction only influence intentions to use a mobile phone for purchasing amongst purchasers. For non-purchasers, the only component of the extended TAM that influences the intention to purchase using a mobile is perceived usefulness.

In the e-shopping field, TAM has been studied and applied mainly in developed countries, where technologies usually appear and spread due to consumers' cultural openness and purchasing power. We may assume that cultural features influence technology acceptance in the e-shopping field, as this influence has been demonstrated in many other cross-cultural consumer studies. One of the few studies to cover developing countries shows that TAM integrating trust and perceived behavioral control can be applied outside the USA, and not only in very developed countries such as Canada, but also in a transition economy, such as Pakistan [29]. It is true, however, that the study reveals some significant differences between Canada and Pakistan: PU only has an indirect effect on people's online shopping intentions in Pakistan, which is still at an early stage of e-commerce adoption; whilst the influence of PU is stronger and direct in Canada. Perceived Ease of Use, on the contrary, plays a critical role in early adoption stages and decreases when the e-commerce market is more mature. So, PeU strongly influences the e-shopping intentions of Pakistani consumers, whilst it is non-significant for Canadian consumers. The results concerning trust are somewhat different from those in the meta-analysis conducted by Ingham et al. [5], because trust plays a critical role in e-commerce adoption in both these countries. However, trust appears far more important for Canadian than for Pakistani consumers. The authors try to explain this difference in terms of a single cultural dimension, individualism vs. collectivism. Finally, contrary to expectations, Perceived Behavioral Control (PBC) strongly influences purchasing intentions in Pakistan, while it is insignificant for Canadian consumers.

2.5 Towards a New Paradigm of Technology Acceptance

Despite all the improvements made since it first appeared, TAM presents some shortcomings that have been illustrated by one of the most important authors in the creation and successive consolidation of the model, Bagozzi [8].

In this seminal article, the author proposes a paradigm shift to overcome the limitations of TAM. The main components of the new proposal are:

- Goal striving, to fill the gap between intention and behavior, and between behavior and goal attainment;
- Action-desire, as an essential mediator between the many reasons for acting and the decision or intention to act;
- Goal-setting, as a precursor of goal striving but also as a way to consider context and the specific circumstances of decision making, as opposed to general approaches;
- The role of the group not only in influencing individual intentions and behaviors, but also as an essential component of decision making and technology use;
- The need to use social identity, as defined by Tajfel, as a totally unique kind of social behavior, different from intra- and inter-personal modes of behavior, because this construct influences decision making in "network and small group based virtual communities" but also in "recreational chatters and collaborative browsing in online environments" (p. 248);
- Emotions and their effects on technology acceptance through decisions to act and attitudes;
- Self-regulation, to reduce the deterministic approach of TAM and to introduce will and the reasoning process into technology adoption. Self-regulation can also help reduce peer-pressure and group pressure.

3   Main Trends in Relations Between Retail Companies and Consumer Communities

As illustrated by previous research, technology acceptance has become a social as well as an individual process, since the social environment, both institutional and peer-based, can strongly affect individual attitudes and behavior towards technologies.

In this third section we will analyze how retailers are trying to exploit technology to improve customer retention and loyalty through social influence.

To respond to this question, we conducted qualitative research to analyze the main activities of retail companies around the world with regard to relations with customers and consumer communities. For this research we used different sources, including:

- the website of Planet Retail, a major retail research consultancy firms;
- the French and international marketing and retailing press, including LSA, Point de Vente, Linéaires, Retail Week, and Stores;
- international websites specializing in technology and consumption, including Wired, and Tech crunch;

- Company websites for detailed accounts of experimental activities, or to observe the behavior of on-line brand communities (ethnography).

The data was mainly collected by students on a Master level program in a leading French Business School; the students collected information about and conducted in-depth analyses of the community experiences of major retailers for an advanced retail and e-commerce course. The collection and analysis was supervised by two professors responsible for the course.

The data reveal three main ways retailers engage with consumers using technology and social influence:

- Crowdsourcing, both for products and services
- Crowdfunding
- Crowd-sharing: for information and competences.

3.1 Crowdsourcing

Crowdsourcing is perhaps the most common way retail brands engage with consumers. We present two main possibilities in this study: co-creation of new products for the retailer, and co-creation of services related to the retail main activity that can be sold or exchanged between customers.

These activities illustrate very well the concept of value co-creation that scholars consider as one of the main innovative components of a new marketing paradigm [30–33]. The concept of value co-creation has also been applied to retail companies [34, 35] to explain how actors and processes can create experiential value and the role of social influence.

In our study, we found some interesting examples of co-production, where the company involves customers in the creation of new products, new varieties or new specifications to respond to a social expectation.

One example of new product or new variety creation is the CVOUS website owned by the French Group Casino, a platform giving customers the opportunity to propose new ideas that will be shared and assessed by the community. Another example is the British company Made.com, from which consumers can order for home delivery furniture and accessories that are manufactured individually for each order. The company was initially a pure play e-retailer, but is currently developing a multi-channel strategy by opening showrooms in capital cities.

The French retail giant Carrefour has recently begun experimenting a very innovative co-creation process; in collaboration with a community called "La marque du consommateur" (The consumer brand), the company has produced and is now selling a milk whose specifications and final sale price have been decided by the community's online vote. The product is sold under the brand "C'est qui le patron?!" (Who is the boss?!), and the co-creation also aimed to respond to a social issue that occupied newspaper front pages throughout 2015 and 2016: what is "fair" compensation for farmers and milk producers in France. During the survey period, customers gave their opinion on expected milk quality, sale price, animal feed, place of production, minimum price guaranteed to farmers, and packaging.

In this case, value co-creation involved not only customers and a specific retailer, but also the retailer and suppliers.

Apart from product co-creation, a very rich field of retail co-creation is service co-production. Many examples have been studied and we can group them into two main categories: professional services and peer-to-peer services. Some services are provided by specialist companies in a specific field, and can provide service providers with most or all of their revenue. One example is Instacart, a platform that provides a personal shopper who purchases the products and delivers them to the end customer. Similarly, Ubereat delivers a meal purchased in an agreed restaurant using an Uber Cab to customers at home or at the office. The Internet giants are showing great interest in this type of collaborative economy project, as demonstrated by the launch of Google Shopping Express in different US cities. This kind of service can be very attractive not only to consumers who do not want to spend time doing their supermarket shopping but also to retailers who thus greatly reduce the cost of "the last mile" of home or office delivery.

In other cases, the activity is not the main source of revenue for workers, but rather a way of sharing costs and providing a service. One interesting example is the Walmart PtoP delivery service, by which customers can deliver shopping to other customers on their way home. Amazon has also experimented with the idea, through its "On my way" program. In France, a platform has been set up to send parcels anywhere in the country or abroad using people who plan to make a trip and that have space available in their car (Colis Voiturage). The concept is based on the success of vehicle sharing platforms, but applies to parcels rather than people.

3.2 Crowdfunding

Crowdfunding involves funding new products or services with the support of hundreds or thousands of individual lenders rather than using the usual methods of funding new ventures.

There are different crowdfunding models with different objectives:

- Lending-based crowdfunding, where money is collected and lent, but the recipient has to return the funds by a predefined date; leading French firms organizations include Prêt d'Union and Babyloan.
- Reward-based crowdfunding, when lenders do not expect any monetary return; examples are Ulule and KissKissBankBank.
- Co-creation crowdfunding, when lenders pre-purchase a product or service and the project can proceed only if a minimum amount is reached; the best-known company in this field is Kickstarter.

- Equity-participation crowdfunding, where lenders buy shares in a firm and become shareholders once the company is launched; some brands well known in France are Wiseed and Smart Angels.

The best-known crowdfunding platforms, such as Kickstarter and Indiegogo, mainly fund new products, but they have also funded retail initiatives such as The Herbivorous Butcher, a vegetarian butchery that opened in Minneapolis (USA) in 2014.

Other retail projects are funded by lending-based crowdfunding companies like Babyloan, mainly in developing countries. This type of funding is also known as microcredit, a funding system with at least one social goal, to help poor people in developing countries improve their living conditions through economic activities linked to local culture.

3.3 Crowd-Sharing

Crowd-sharing is at the heart of both the value co-creation process and technology acceptance. The process involves exchange platforms provided by retail companies, but which are very often organized and led by customers who share their experience and skills with the platform's other users.

All the main brands develop forums for sharing experience, skills and tips for using their products and services; new technologies have enabled the creation of communities where expert consumers are available to help other less expert customers or, in some cases, to help the company improve the functions of specific products. Below, we present two examples, FNAC, the leading French entertainment retailer, and Leroy Merlin, the leading French and European DIY retail chain.

FNAC introduces customers to different "experts" certified by the company in a specific sector (books, computers, music, videos and so on) but with different backgrounds: they can be FNAC employees working in a specific store, bloggers, or journalists. The aim of this expert section on the FNAC website is to improve the company's legitimacy and reputation as the best qualified cultural and entertainment retailer in France, and to increase company employees' sense of belonging, as they enjoy national recognition on the company website.

The Leroy Merlin, "Communauté Leroy Merlin" has four different sections:

- A section to share skills and tips for home improvement and other DIY activities; the company announces that it will answer every request within 75 min, but most of those responding are other members of the community, especially "super experts."
- A section called "Le wiki" that contains a DIY encyclopedia.
- A section to propose new products or services, or ideas for using products; ideas endorsed by the company are then proposed for assessment by the entire community.

- A section where the company or other participants can propose a competition for the community; the idea is to give a prize to the member who comes up with the best idea for a product or service to use in the home decoration or home improvement domain.

4 Conclusion and Limitations

The technology acceptance model has greatly evolved since it first appeared in the literature around 30 years ago. One of the most important changes has been the increasing influence of social activities on the adoption of technology in everyday life. Social activity is particularly significant in the retail sector, where the retail environment provides consumers with ways of interacting with companies and other customers. Shopping is itself often a very social activity and technology can help consumers to overcome the feeling of isolation that virtual channels tend to develop because they offer a strictly individual relationship between the retailer and its products, and the customer.

In our study, we have analyzed how groups of consumers create value during the shopping process and help one other to manage relations with technologies and overcome the perceived threats of the shopping and user experience.

According to the paradigm shift proposed by Bagozzi [8]:

- When a group of consumers/users have a specific goal, this can influence behavior towards technology, as demonstrated by crowdsourcing activities and especially co-creation of new products and services.
- Customer community help can greatly improve the technology acceptance of less expert consumers reducing their feeling of isolation with regard to a given technology and allowing them to test their ability to manage it in a specific context.
- The role of the group can strongly influence the decision-making process in crowdfunding activities, where the use of a technology platform to lend money can be a significant obstacle for customers unfamiliar with electronic payment processes.
- Social identity as expressed in crowd-sharing communities strongly influences collaborative behaviors among consumers and towards retail brands.

Another very interesting point revealed by our study is that technology makes it possible to improve the value co-creation process through better retailer/consumer relationships. Retailers have been trying to involve consumers in the decision-making process for many years using different means (focus groups, suggestions boxes, customer surveys, etc.) but current technologies allow them to interact with consumers in greater depth and more frequently to create value by developing new products or services, or by improving the use of current products and services.

One of the main contributions of this study to the literature is its application of the TAM model to the retail sector and especially to the role of customer communities in technology evaluation and acceptance.

Another contribution is the link we make between the value co-creation process and technology acceptance: our examples show that community activities can help retailers and consumers co-create value using encounters organized by the company. This point confirms the need for retail companies to create places for structured exchanges between the firm and its consumers, and between consumers. Companies cannot completely control the information flow during these encounters, but they can help establish them and build trust within the community and between the community and the brand.

The main limitations of this study are its qualitative nature and the use of mainly secondary sources. Future studies should study consumer perceptions of these "crowd" activities, and the kind of activities perceived as most favorable for technology acceptance in the specific context of retail.

It would also be interesting to measure which co-creation activities are perceived as most appropriate for value co-creation. Value co-creation can be an extremely effective way to create consumer engagement and loyalty, but detailed analysis is required to understand which factors are fundamental to improving this engagement and, on the other hand, what factors are secondary and not worthy of significant investment.

References

1. Davis, F.: Perceived usefulness, perceived ease of use, and user acceptance of information technology. MIS Q. **13**, 319–340 (1989)
2. Davis, F., Bagozzi, R., Warshaw, P.: User acceptance of computer technology: a comparison of two theoretica models. Manage. Sci. **35**, 982–1003 (1989)
3. Pantano, E., Di Pietro, L.: Understanding consumer" acceptance of technology-based innovations in retailing. J. Technol. Manage. Innov. **7**(4), 1–19 (2012)
4. Svendsen, G.B., Johnsen, J.-A.K., Almas-Sorensen, L., Vitterso, J.: Personality and technology acceptance: the influence of personality factors on the core constructs of the technology acceptance model. Behav. Inf. Technol. **32**(4), 323–334 (2013)
5. Ingham, J., Cadieux, J., Abdelouahab, M.B.: e-Shopping acceptance: a qualitative and meta-analytical review. Inf. Manage. **52**, 44–60 (2015)
6. Ha, S., Stoel, L.: Consumer e-shopping acceptance: antecedents in a technology acceptance model. J. Bus. Res. **62**, 565–571 (2009)
7. Agrebi, S., Jallais, J.: Explain the intention to use smartphones for mobile shopping. J. Retail. Consum. Serv. **22**, 16–23 (2015)
8. Bagozzi, R.P.: The legacy of the technology acceptance model and a proposal for a paradigm shift. J. Assoc. Inf. Syst. **8**(4), 243–254 (2007)
9. Venkatesh, V., Morris, M.G., Davis, G.B., Davis, F.D.: User acceptance of information technology: toward a unifying theory. MIS Q. **23**(3), 425–478 (2003)
10. Venkatesan, R., Kumar, V., Ravishanker, N.: Multichannel shopping: causes and consequences. J. Mark. **71**, 114–123 (2007)

11. Cao, L., Li, L.: The impact of cross-channel integration on retailers' sales growth. J. Retail. **91**, 198–216 (2015)
12. Sevitt, D., Samuel, A.: How pinterest puts people in stores. Harv. Bus. Rev. 26–27 (2013)
13. Ström, R., Vendel, M., Bredican, J.: Mobile marketing: a literature review of its value for consumers and retailers. J. Retail. Consum. Serv. **21**, 1001–1012 (2014)
14. McGoldrick, P.J., Collins, N.: Multichannel retailing: profiling the multichannel shopper international review of retail. Distrib. Consum. Res. **17**(2), 139–158 (2007)
15. Konus, U., Verhoef, P.C., Neslin, S.A.: Multichannel shopper segments and their covariates. J. Retail. **84**(4), 398–413 (2008)
16. Kushwaha, T., Shankar, V.: Are multichannel customers really more valuable? The moderating role of product category characteristics. J. Mark. **77**, 67–85 (2013)
17. Kotler, P.: Atmospherics as marketing tool. J. Retail. **49**, 48–64 (1973/74)
18. Holbrook, M.B., Hirschman, E.C.: The experiential aspects of consumption: consumer fantasies, feelings, and fun. J. Consum. Res. **9**, 132–140 (1982)
19. Donovan, R.J., Rossiter, J.R.: Store atmosphere: an environmental psychology approach. J. Retail. **58**, 34–57 (1982)
20. Donovan, R.J., Rossiter, J.R., Marcoolyn, G., Nesdale, A.: Store atmosphere and purchasing behavior. J. Retail. **70**, 283–294 (1994)
21. Babin, B.J., Attaway, J.S.: Atmospheric affect as a tool for creating value and gaining share of customer. J. Bus. Res. **49**, 91–99 (2000)
22. Kaltcheva, V.D., Weitz, B.A.: When should a retailer create an exciting store environment? J. Market. **70**, 107–118 (2006)
23. Pantano, E., Naccarato, G.: Entertainment in retailing: the influence of advanced technologies. J. Retail. Consum. Serv. **17**, 200–204 (2010)
24. Bäckström, K., Johansson, U.: Creating and consuming experiences in retail store environments: comparing retailer and consumer perspectives. J. Retail. Consum. Serv. **13**, 417–430 (2006)
25. Poncin, I., Ben Mimoun, M.S.: The impact of "e-atmospherics"on physical stores. J. Retail. Consum. Serv. **21**, 851–859 (2014)
26. Pantano, E., Migliarese, P.: Exploiting consumer-employee-retailer interactions in technology-enriched retail environments through a relational lens. J. Retail. Consum. Serv. **21**, 958–965 (2014)
27. Henderson, R., Rickwood, D., Roberts, P.: The beta test of an electronic supermarket. Interact. Comput. **10**(4), 385–399 (1998)
28. Barkhi, R., Wallace, L.: The impact of personality type on purchasing decisions in virtual stores. Inf. Technol. Manage. **8/4**, 313–330 (2007)
29. Ashraf, A.R., Thongpapanl, N., Auh, S.: The application of the technology acceptance model under different cultural contexts: the case of online shopping adoption. J. Int. Market. **22**(3), 68–93 (2014)
30. Prahalad, C., Ramaswamy, V.: Co-creation experiences: the next practice in value creation. J. Interact. Mark. **18**(3), 5–14 (2004)
31. Grönroos, C.: Service logic revisited: who create value? And who co-create? Eur. Bus. Rev. **20**(4), 298–314 (2008)
32. Payne, A., Storbacka, K., Frow, P.: Managing the co-creation of value. J. Acad. Mark. Sci. **36**, 83–96 (2008)
33. Ranjan, K.R., Read, S.: Value co-creation: concept and measurement. J. Acad. Mark. Sci. **44**, 290–315 (2016)
34. Shamim, A., Ghazali, Z.: A conceptual model for developing customer value co-creation behaviour in retailing. Glob. Bus. Manage. Res.: Int. J. **6**(3), 185–196 (2014)
35. Andreu, L., Sanchez, I., Mele, C.: Value co-creation among retailers and consumers: new insights into the furniture market. J. Retail. Consum. Serv. **17**, 241–250 (2010)

Printed in the United States
By Bookmasters